Deciphering the Rising Sun

Deciphering the Rising Sun

Navy and Marine Corps Codebreakers, Translators, and Interpreters in the Pacific War

ROGER DINGMAN

NAVAL INSTITUTE PRESS
Annapolis, Maryland

This book has been brought to publication with the generous assistance of Edward S. and Joyce I. Miller.

Naval Institute Press
291 Wood Road
Annapolis, MD 21402

Library of Congress Cataloging-in-Publication Data
Dingman, Roger.
Deciphering the rising sun : Navy and Marine Corps codebreakers, translators, and interpretors in the Pacific war / Roger Dingman.
p. cm.
Includes bibliographical references and index.
ISBN 978-1-59114-211-9 (acid-free paper) 1. World War, 1939-1945—Military intelligence—United States. 2. United States. Navy. Japanese Language School—Biography. 3. World War, 1939-1945—Cryptography. 4. Cryptographers—United States—History—20th century. 5. Translating and interpreting—United States—History—20th century. 6. Military intelligence—United States—History—20th century. 7. World War, 1939-1945—Pacific Area. I. Title.
D810.S7D57 2009
940.54'8673—dc22

2009009083

Printed in the United States of America on acid-free paper

14 13 12 11 10 09 9 8 7 6 5 4 3 2
First printing

For the Japanese-language officers

They rose to the challenge

Contents

Preface

Saturday, 8 June 2002, was a glorious early summer evening in Boulder, Colorado. The sun had barely dropped behind the granite, pine-covered slopes of the Front Range, and the sky stilled glowed in an incandescent mix of orange and blue. I parked my car and joined a trickle of white-haired men and women walking into the stone-clad University of Colorado Memorial Center. We took the elevator to its second floor and entered a large dining room, where more than a hundred guests awaited us. They were alumni of the World War II Navy Japanese Language School, and the culminating event of their sixtieth reunion was about to begin.

When I sat down at one of the tables, the place settings immediately caught my eye. Photographs on the placemats made it clear that this was not just another class reunion. They showed the men and women around me now as they were at Boulder sixty years earlier—young, dark-haired and bright-eyed students, smiling alongside their Japanese-American teachers, playing football, and standing with their skis in the snow. They also showed these same young people at war—WAVES in their dark blue dress uniforms posing outside a Washington office building; khaki-clad ensigns clustered around a paper-strewn desk in Hawaii; and helmeted, disheveled, and sweaty Marines looking down on a prisoner on some Pacific island.

This was a gathering of old men and women who in their youth had gone off to play a special role in the greatest war of their century. They learned the language of the enemy. They used it to help speed his defeat. And, as those placemat photos revealed, they put their new language skills to work moving

Japan in the aftermath of war into decades of peace and friendship with America. The people surrounding me were very special indeed.

As the evening wore on, it became clear that this was a magic moment for them. They spoke about defining events and places in their lives—Pearl Harbor, the trumpet that summoned them to war; their first days at the Navy Japanese Language School at Boulder; and distant Pacific islands and Japan itself, where they had seen the face of the enemy. They also talked about the challenges they had met: learning Japanese, one of the world's most difficult languages; giving up the happy days of their twenties for the dangers and drudgeries of duty as naval and marine junior officers; leaving the familiar for the exotic, the safe for the risky, a continent for islands in the world's greatest ocean. They had gone off to become warriors, peacemakers, and, over the course of the ensuing decades, bridge builders to lasting friendship with Japan, the enemy that sixty-one years earlier had attacked their country and changed their lives.

By the time the banquet ended, I realized that the evening had been a magic moment for me too. I had done—much later, in peacetime, and under circumstances far less trying than theirs—some of the same things these men and women had: joined the Navy, learned Japanese, and gone on to an academic career devoted to trying to understand the relationship between America and Japan. My life experience had triggered an interest in these men and women and enkindled an empathy with them that I hoped would give me deeper insight into their experience. Now I felt that these sometime naval and marine Japanese-language officers were challenging me to tell their story to the world. I left the banquet room that night knowing, as never before, that I must use whatever talents I had to do so.

What follows is that tale. I have tried to tell it as a good historian should, drawing upon documents and books to complement what former language officers told me. Weaving together their individual accounts, I have tried to draw a picture of their collective experience and place it in broader context. Inevitably, my words highlight what some have said and leave in the shadows the deeds, words, and memories of others. For whatever distortions or errors have resulted, I alone am responsible.

This book also tells another story of how two previously distant sectors of American public life, the military and academia, came together in an effort to defeat a daunting foe. World War II revolutionized the relationship between brainpower and government power, especially in the fields of intelligence and diplomacy. It demanded that language—the knowledge of "exotic" tongues—be mobilized to listen to the enemy to more readily learn his intentions and defeat his designs. It required systematic cooperation in pursuit of victory. What follows will show how naval and marine Japanese-language officers, their teachers, and their academic and naval superiors struggled to achieve that cooperation.

This book tells one more tale, the story of how war transformed two distant enemies, the United States and Japan, into intimate partners in postwar peace and friendship. The Japanese-language officers were important agents of that change. Transformed themselves by what they saw and did in the great Pacific conflict, they struggled to understand as well as defeat an alien "other." After the war, they strove to deepen Americans' knowledge of and appreciation for Japan, its people, and its culture. In so doing, they became builders of a bridge to the rising sun.

A book is a journey, and in traveling the road that led to the appearance of this one, I have made many choices and incurred many debts. The key decision was to follow the paths of the graduates of only one of the fourteen wartime military Japanese-language programs. That trail clearly diverged from the others. The overwhelming majority of Boulder naval students, unlike army Japanese-American enlistees, had to learn the language from scratch. They did so sooner, in less time, and in greater numbers than army Caucasian officer linguists. The students had to learn more and bear greater responsibility than marine-enlisted Japanese speakers. Narrowing my focus has allowed me to tell the story of the naval and marine officer linguists in greater depth and detail than would otherwise have been possible. That, I hope, will make their experience come alive and their significance clearer for those who read this book.

My debts in telling the navy and marine language officers' tale are numerous. The first and greatest debt is to them themselves. From the coasts of Maine to the islands of Washington State, from the leafy greenery of Washington, D.C., to the fire-ringed valleys of exurban San Diego, and in so many other places in between, they have welcomed me into their homes. I have sat at their tables, broken bread with them, and shared in their marvelous recollections. In so doing, I gained not just information but also their trust and friendship. For all of that I am deeply grateful.

My second debt is to Dr. Pedro Loureiro, creator of the larger project of which this book is but one part. He and the late Frank Gibney, a wartime naval language officer, sparked the idea of bringing graduates of the Boulder school together for a conference at Pomona College's Pacific Basin Institute in April 2000. Dr. Loureiro pressed the Navy into honoring their Japanese and Japanese-American teachers at a second gathering there five years later. He provided the equipment and technological expertise needed to video record many of the interviews upon which this book relies. Dr. Loureiro is producing a documentary film about the Boulder Navy Japanese Language School. Without his assistance, this book could not have become what it is.

I am also indebted to three other groups of people who helped in the book's production. Archivists are the indispensable guides for historians in their search for knowledge. I could never have found my way through the treasures at the University of Colorado, Stanford, Yale, the University of California, Berkeley, Rutgers, the National Archives, the Naval Historical Center, and the Marine Corps Historical Center without their generous assistance. One among them, David Hays at Boulder, deserves special mention not just for helping me but also for his assiduous collecting of language officers' letters and memoirs, for organizing their June 2002 reunion, and for creating *The Interpreter* newsletter that has helped Navy Japanese Language School graduates reconnect with one another.

Financial support for my research and travels in search of those whose story this book tells came from the Naval Historical Foundation; from then-dean Josef Aoun of the College of Letters, Arts, and Sciences at the University of Southern California; and from the late Frank Gibney, president of the Pacific Basin Institute. Edward S. Miller generously provided additional funding for the publication of my work. I am deeply grateful to them all.

I also want to thank those at the Naval Institute Press who have helped move my text to print. Paul Wilderson, former executive editor of the Naval Institute Press, recognized the importance of this story and was the first to commit to its publication. He and his successor, Rick Russell, have been extraordinarily patient during its research, writing, and transformation into this book. Elizabeth Bauman, Patricia Bower, and Susan Corrado skillfully piloted its pages from manuscript to print. Chris Robinson transformed my vision of the maps into reality.

Last, but not least, I want to thank my wife, Linda. On the journey to this book and on so many other travels over more than forty years, she has stood by me on good days and bad, endured my tales and travails, and comforted me in so many ways.

Note on Orthography

Individual Japanese names are given in the normal Japanese order, that is, surname followed by personal name. I have used the normal American order for the names of Japanese Americans.

With the exception of the capital cities Tokyo and Beijing, I have romanized place names and personal names in the manner used during World War II. For the Japanese I have used the Hepburn system; for the Chinese I have used the Wade-Giles method. Pacific island names are rendered as they were in the war.

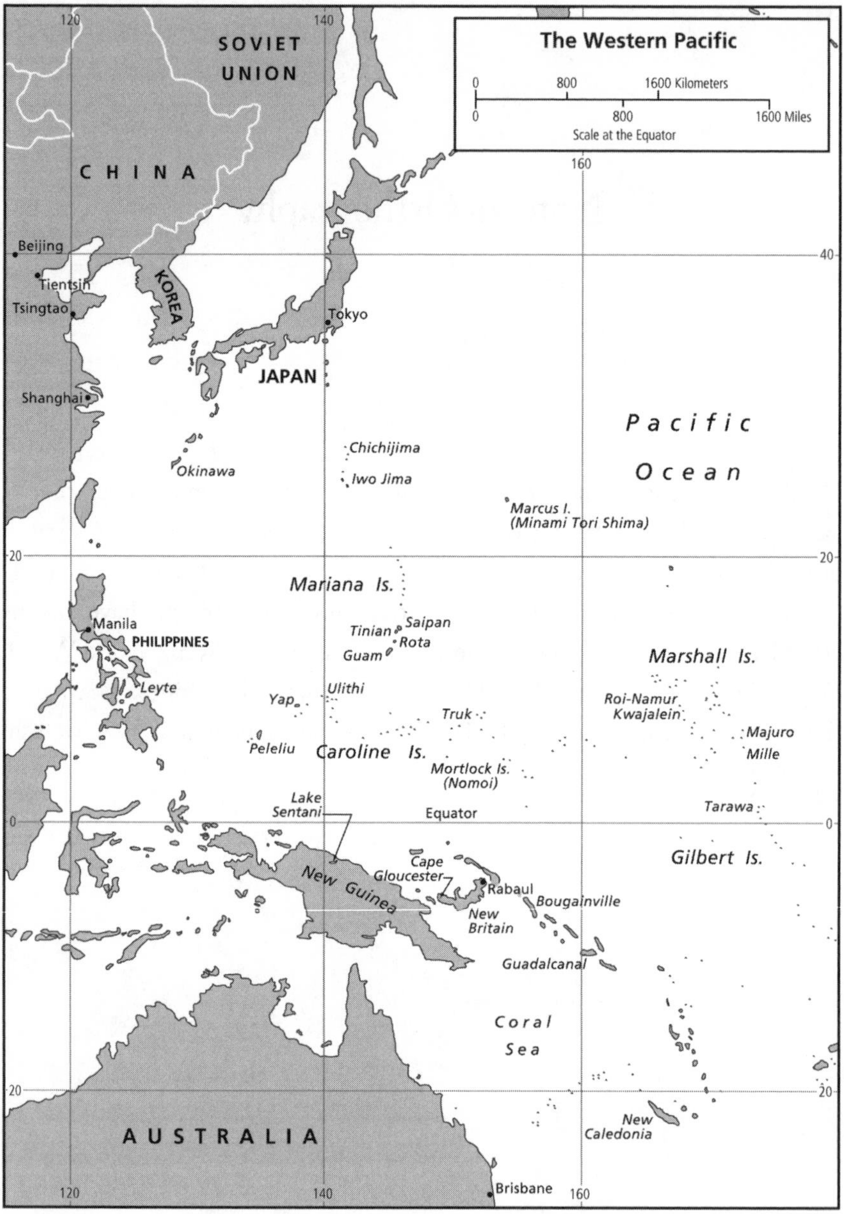
The Western Pacific
0
800
1600 Kilometers
0
800
1600 Miles
Scale at the Equator
SOVIET UNION
CHINA
KOREA
JAPAN
Beijing
Tientsin
Tsingtao
Tokyo
Shanghai
Okinawa
Chichijima
Iwo Jima
Marcus I. (Minami Tori Shima)
Pacific Ocean
Mariana Is.
Saipan
Tinian
Rota
Guam
Manila
PHILIPPINES
Leyte
Marshall Is.
Yap
Ulithi
Truk
Roi-Namur
Kwajalein
Majuro
Mille
Peleliu
Caroline Is.
Mortlock Is. (Nomoi)
Lake Sentani
Equator
Tarawa
Gilbert Is.
Cape Gloucester
Rabaul
New Guinea
Bougainville
New Britain
Guadalcanal
Coral Sea
New Caledonia
AUSTRALIA
Brisbane
120
140
160
40
20
0
20

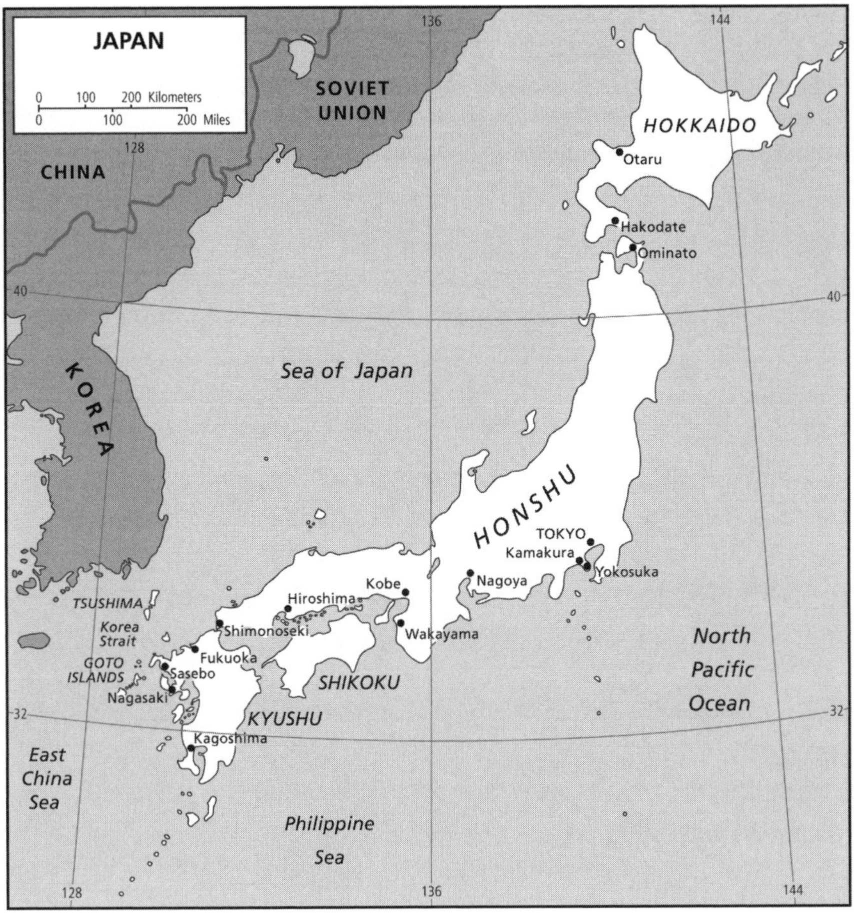
JAPAN
0 100 200 Kilometers
0 100 200 Miles
SOVIET UNION
CHINA
KOREA
HOKKAIDO
Otaru
Hakodate
Ominato
Sea of Japan
HONSHU
TOKYO
Kamakura
Yokosuka
Nagoya
Kobe
Hiroshima
Wakayama
Shimonoseki
TSUSHIMA
Korea Strait
GOTO ISLANDS
Fukuoka
Sasebo
Nagasaki
SHIKOKU
KYUSHU
Kagoshima
North Pacific Ocean
East China Sea
Philippine Sea
128
136
144
40
32

Prologue: Chaff before the Wind

It began as an ordinary Sunday. In New England, it was cold. Reporter John Rich planned to stay inside at home in Portland, Maine. Robert Schwantes, a Harvard student, hung around his dorm room in the morning, enjoyed midday dinner, and then went off to the library to study. In New Haven, Yale students got up a little late and spent the day in much the same way. Arthur Dornheim studied in his room, and Hart Spiegel went off to meet a collaborator at the *Law Review* office. A bit farther south, in New York City, it was warm enough for Columbia student Donald Keene and a Japanese friend to go for a hike on Staten Island. Still farther south, outside Baltimore, engineer Bill Gorham painted the exterior of his house.[1]

In the heart of the Midwest, in Northfield, Minnesota, Chuck Cross relaxed for a while and then went off around noon to his job as a waiter in the Carlton College Tearoom. In the Pacific Northwest, Seattle high school student Pat O'Sullivan took advantage of a rare sunny December day to wash her family's car. Not far away, Al Weissberg, a Naval Supply Depot worker, chatted with his prospective best man before going to meet his fiancée to talk over plans for a January wedding.[2]

In California, it was a pleasant day, perfect for leisure activities. At Berkeley, the hills beckoned Wayne Suttles and his girlfriend out for a picnic and hike. Down in Orange County, marine private Elmer Stone lolled late in bed at a friend's house, recovering from the excitement of the preceding day's USC–UCLA football game.[3]

But this was not to be an ordinary Sunday. At 7:50 in the morning in Hawaii, the first wave of more than 350 aircraft took off from six Imperial

Japanese Navy aircraft carriers bound for Pearl Harbor. Two hours later, when the attackers departed, five battleships and two cruisers had been sunk, and three battleships, three destroyers, and several other ships were damaged. Most of the planes on the ground there and at Kaneohe Naval Air Station had been turned into smoking ruins. More than 2,400 Americans lay dead and nearly twelve hundred more were wounded. The Japanese air strike was the most devastating surprise attack in American history up to that point.[4]

News of the attack crackled across the United States like lightening portends a coming storm. In Seattle, Pat O'Sullivan heard about it on the car radio and rushed inside to tell her parents. In Berkeley, the news interrupted music wafting out the windows of houses that Wayne Suttles and his girlfriend passed on their hike. At Stanford, law student Robert Newell thought the first word of the attack was just another trick like the one Orson Welles had played on radio listeners by announcing that Martians had landed. In Southern California, news of the Pearl Harbor disaster jolted Elmer Stone out of his reveries over late morning coffee into the realization that he must get back to his San Diego marine base. When marine lieutenants Gene Gregg and Bill Shaw heard the news there, they scrambled to find a car and then raced to defend La Jolla beach against possible Japanese invaders.[5]

As news of the attack traveled eastward, it evoked various responses. Youthful defiance was one. At Texas A&M, students rushed out into the streets shouting "Beat the hell out of the Japs!" as if the attackers were just another football rival. At Chapel Hill, Tarheels shrieked the rebel yell. Concern for the safety of family and friends was another reaction. At Tuscaloosa, University of Alabama graduate student Dan S. Williams was filled with fear for his missionary father, who had stayed on in Japanese-occupied China to help his flock of converts. Lieutenant Shaw's sister, Daphne, who had been born and raised in Japan, shuddered in horror. Her "beloved place" Japan, home to so many childhood friends and memories, had suddenly become an enemy land. Anger was yet a third response. Up in Minnesota, Chuck Cross was stunned by the ignorance of a fellow student who did not even know where Pearl Harbor was. He himself felt certain that the Japanese were going to really "get it" from enraged Americans.[6]

In the Northeast, news of the attack evoked disbelief and fear, belligerence, and enlightenment, and even general confusion. When Donald Keene and his friend returned from their Staten Island hike, they saw headlines blaring out the news in a tabloid newspaper. Keene laughed, thinking it just another hoax, then fell into stunned silence when he learned it was true. His Japanese friend ran away and hid in an all-night movie theater. Yale students responded in confusion. Some vowed to join up and fight while others quietly determined to keep on with their studies. At Harvard similar emotions warred with one another. A drumroll of bad news from across the Atlantic had steeled students and the American people as a whole to the possibility of war with Germany. Very few had paid any attention to Japan. Now that war in the Pacific was real, they did not know quite what to think. Robert Schwantes was so troubled that he did not sleep much that night.[7]

Up in Maine, reporter John Rich rushed to his newspaper's office, where the editor sent him to the town square to interview sailors on leave. They were "all steamed up" about what had happened in Hawaii and full of bluster. One boasted, "Ah, the Japanese. They can't fight. It'll all be over in a couple of months. They have all these battleships with top-heavy superstructures. They can't fight. Their mothers carry them around on their backs, and their heads waggle around. They can't do anything!" But an old chief sobered up the crowd by asking, "Where were our patrol planes off Pearl Harbor?" He rightly sensed that a tough war loomed ahead.[8]

The next day President Franklin D. Roosevelt proclaimed "December 7, 1941, [is] a date which will live in infamy!" His words seared the significance of the Pearl Harbor attack into the consciousness of the nation forever and sent its sons and daughters off to war. They were chaff before the wind, scattered to fight and work, die and triumph in places they had never heard of or imagined they would ever see. Little more than a month after Pearl Harbor, Elmer Stone sweated in American Samoa, struggling to prepare that island for a possible Japanese attack. A year later, Hart Spiegel, the sometime Yale Law student, was leading Marines on patrol in Bougainville, an island he could not have found on the map in December 1941. Reporter John Rich met his first Japanese a little more than two years later, in a bomb crater on Kwajalein, a place no Maine man knew of when Pearl Harbor was attacked. Robert Schwantes spent most of the war that followed at Indooroopilly, Queensland, Australia, which he, a brilliant Harvard graduate, found difficult to spell. Daphne Shaw and Pat O'Sullivan left home and college for work in Washington, D.C., a capital as distant for most young American women of their day as the Emerald City of Oz.[9]

These young people did things they never in their wildest dreams would have imagined before 7 December 1941 they would do. Hart Spiegel scavenged Japanese corpses in search of maps and diaries. Gene Gregg interrogated Japanese prisoners in New Guinea; Bill Gorham quizzed them on Oahu. Chuck Cross pulled cowering children out of holes on Saipan, and Al Weissberg and Donald Keene flushed enemy soldiers and civilians out of caves and tombs on Okinawa. Wayne Suttles went to occupied Japan and fathered a child there. And the skeptical Stanford law student, Robert Newell, interpreted for Genda Minoru, the master operational planner of the Pearl Harbor attack.[10]

These young men and women, the nation for which they fought, and the empire that attacked it were forever changed by the war that began on Sunday 7 December 1941. They, their country, and their world were transformed. Over the next forty-four months, America became the master of the Pacific. The Japanese Empire vanished, crushed in defeat. But the life-and-death struggle between America and Japan set the young men and women who fought it on course toward permanent peace and friendship with their onetime enemy.

This book is about a very special group of young Americans who experienced, and helped bring about, these sweeping changes. They were graduates of the Navy Japanese Language School at the University of Colorado, located at Boulder, and its satellite at Oklahoma A&M College at Stillwater. All were white—and very bright. These nearly twelve hundred men and women learned one of the most difficult languages on Earth in record time. They became codebreakers and translators, interpreters and interrogators. What they did in combat and far behind the front lines gleaned valuable information from the enemy that saved American—and Japanese—lives. And when the fighting stopped, they became instruments of surrender and agents of occupation in a Japan whose defeat they thought inevitable but whose cost none could have imagined on 7 December 1941. When their wartime duties ended, many of these men and women went on to help lay the foundations for lasting peace and friendship between the United States and Japan.

Theirs is an extraordinary and little-known tale. This book will tell their story, first by examining their recruitment and training, then by analyzing their contributions in and out of combat to victory, and finally by showing how they helped transform enmity into friendship between America and Japan.

Chapter One

PARTNERS

Nearly fourteen months before Pearl Harbor, on a late October day in 1940, Maj. Harold D. "Bucky" Harris strode up the steps of Harvard's Boylston Hall. His superiors at Marine Headquarters in Washington sent this veteran of service at Tientsin in China and the École Supérieure de Guerre in Paris to Cambridge to try to remedy an important deficiency in the Navy and Marine Corps' readiness for war. Although the two services had been sending young officers to Japan to study its language and culture for thirty years, the number of those on active duty who were truly fluent in Japanese was pitifully small. In the event of war, which in the wake of the just-signed Axis Alliance between Tokyo, Rome, and Berlin suddenly seemed much more likely, the sea services would be fighting blind. Not knowing the enemy's language or understanding his culture, they would be unable to decipher clues about weapons, tactics, or future strategy that the enemy might unwittingly provide.[1]

Harris hoped to enlist expert help from three professors who taught Japanese. The situation, he told them, was serious; their assistance was needed. His superiors were "absolutely certain" that war with Japan would come in "a very short time." Could the two of them who were American citizens join the only other one of their kind, a Columbia University professor, and come to Washington to train fifty men in Japanese? The academics expressed interest in that proposition but sputtered doubts about leaving their families and university positions. That prompted the major to get a bit testy. If worse came to worst, they might be drafted, he snapped. Then, after asking their help in developing a list of college students anywhere in America who had "even an elementary knowledge of Japanese," he got up and left.[2]

That brief encounter prompted the youngest of the academics, thirty-year-old Edwin O. Reischauer, then a new instructor in Far Eastern languages at Harvard, to pen a memorandum that incisively analyzed America's Japanese-language problem and proposed an elegant solution to it. Japanese was one of the most difficult languages to learn. The relatively few Americans who had been exposed to it, whether persons who had lived in Japan or second- or third-generation Japanese Americans "whose loyalty cannot be questioned," had, at best, an imperfect knowledge of it. Very few of either group knew military Japanese, and "practically none" could read the language when written "rapidly by brush or pen."

To remedy these deficiencies, Reischauer proposed a single "cooperative enterprise" that would create a cadre of capable translators and interpreters for the armed services. He recognized that there were questions about locating, staffing, and funding such a Japanese-language school. But the young instructor was confident that such problems could be solved. "An efficient [Japanese-language] training center" that brought together the best available faculty with the students who needed them most could be established "if and when there is a call for it."[3]

Doctor Reischauer and Major Harris were equally naïve in October 1940. Neither realized how long and difficult the struggle would be to forge a partnership between the Navy and academia that could find solutions to the United States' Japanese-language problem. It took nine months for the Marines to institute their Japanese-language training program. A year passed before the Army and Navy each started their own courses. And twenty months slipped away before Washington concluded that a single program for Navy and Marine Corps officer candidates was the best way to remedy the nation's ignorance of the Japanese and their language. Neither Reischauer nor Harris—nor anyone else—would have predicted, fourteen months before Pearl Harbor, that the school would end up at the University of Colorado, at Boulder, nearly a thousand miles from the sea.

Why did it prove so hard to marry the Navy and the academy in the service of national interest? Who was responsible for bringing the two parties together? And how did their union produce what became the Navy Japanese Language School, an institution very different from what the major and the young professor thought it might be?

MATCHMAKERS

Thirty years before Major Harris went to Cambridge, the Navy sent three young officers—two ensigns and a marine first lieutenant—to Japan. Their assignment was twofold: to learn the language and to discover all they could about the burgeoning Imperial Japanese Navy and its builders. Of the three, only one—Ens. Fred Fremont Rogers, a 1906 graduate of the Naval Academy—ever paid much of a dividend on the time and money invested in his education in Japan. He worked in Office of Naval Intelligence (ONI) in 1919–20, a time of rising tensions and intense competition between the American and Japanese navies. In 1933, as Captain Rogers, he returned to Tokyo for three years' duty as naval attaché. While there he witnessed the abortive coup of 2 February 1936, one of the key turning points that set Japan on course toward war, first with China, then with the United States and Britain. Stunned by what he had experienced, Rogers returned home in its wake, never again to serve in a capacity that demanded use of his Japanese-language skills. He retired twenty-two months before Pearl Harbor.[4]

Fred Rogers' career epitomized the U.S. Navy and Marine Corps' intelligence relationship with Japan during the first third of the twentieth century. Although the two services (then administratively one within the Navy Department) sent sixty-five young men as language students to Japan over the thirty years prior to Pearl Harbor, on the eve of the Pacific War the number of competent Japanese-language officers in naval and marine corps uniforms was tiny. All but one of the first wave of seven trainees had retired by 1941, and four of them had followed career paths unrelated to intelligence within their respective services so as to advance more rapidly in rank.[5]

The succeeding wave of thirty-one men, sent during the sixteen years between 1922 and 1936, when the Washington naval treaties limited competitive expansion of the American and Japanese fleets, became the skeleton crew of ONI's Japanese establishment. They were scattered from Washington to China. By the summer of 1940, when Japan's invasion of northern Vietnam pushed Washington and Tokyo to the brink of war, a third wave of thirteen young naval and marine officers was midway in their three-year course of study in Japan. But as tensions increased, ONI grew worried lest, in the event of war, these partially trained intelligence officer students who lacked diplomatic immunity be scooped up and interned by the Japanese authorities. They were ordered home in the summer of 1941.[6]

These prewar Japanese-language students returned to a Navy and Marine Corps that was painfully aware of the inadequacy of its Japanese-language intelligence capabilities. Over the preceding decade, the two services' technological intelligence-gathering capacity had outstripped their human resources. The number of radio intercept stations locked on to Japanese military and naval frequencies had increased, and progress was being made in breaking more Japanese naval and diplomatic codes. Shrewd and intrepid marine officers were sending back good field intelligence about Japanese weapons and equipment from the war in China. But the flow of information was overwhelming the very few Japanese linguists the Navy and Marine Corps had at their disposal. They simply could not translate quickly enough the quantity of material ONI needed to substantiate its assessments of what Japanese armed forces were likely to do next.[7]

No one in the Navy was more aware of the seriousness of that problem than Lt. Cdr. Arthur McCollum, head of the Far East Section of ONI. Born forty-two years earlier in Nagasaki to Baptist missionary parents, he had grown up in Alabama. After graduating from the Naval Academy in 1921 and completing a year of sea duty to gain his commission, he had returned to Japan for three years' language training. During that time the fun-loving young officer married a missionary's daughter, taught then–Crown Prince Hirohito the Charleston, and helped provide relief to victims of the great Kantō earthquake of 1923. After serving as assistant naval attaché in Tokyo during the peace and prosperity of the late 1920s, he had returned to Washington to work in ONI's Far Eastern Section.[8]

At that time the Japanese-language capabilities of the Far Eastern Section were pitiful. Only an eighty-year-old civilian and his wife, who volunteered to help on occasion, could translate technical data or handwritten material forwarded from Tokyo. Thanks to the efforts of McCollum's predecessor, Cdr. Ellis M. Zacharias, perhaps the most talented of all of the Navy's language students sent to Japan between the two world wars, that cadre of Japanese-language translators had grown to half a dozen by 1940.[9] But this small staff could barely keep up with the increasing flow of Japanese naval and diplomatic messages that were picked up by radio monitoring stations in Shanghai and the Philippines and then decoded by American cryptographers.

The situation took a turn for the better, however, in the summer of 1940, just when tensions between Tokyo and Washington heated up with the Japanese army's occupation of northern Vietnam. Two individuals who proved vital to the creation and sustenance of the Navy's future Japanese-language training program in the war that loomed ahead came to work for Arthur McCollum. The first, a trim man in his late thirties whose rimless glasses made him look every bit the academic that he was, simply showed up at the lieutenant commander's door. "I'm a naval reserve officer and I want to go to work," he volunteered. When he added that he was an associate professor of government at Harvard, McCollum protested that he was overqualified for the kind of work his office did. The visitor shot right back, saying that he could type, take shorthand, and "talk Japanese." When McCollum skeptically asked him what he based that claim on, the man replied that he had been a visiting professor at Tokyo Imperial University. That was enough to persuade the head of ONI's Far Eastern Section to arrange for his visitor to be put on active duty to work in his office.

Shortly thereafter Albert E. Hindmarsh moved with his wife and two children to Washington, D.C.[10] He was an unlikely matchmaker for the coming marriage between the military and academia. Hindmarsh was a naturalized, and very patriotic, citizen. Born in 1902 in British Columbia, he crossed the border to attend high school in Seattle and study at the University of Washington. Up to that point, he had no interest in Japan, and his graduate study at Harvard over the next half decade focused on the role of force in supporting international law. But Japan's invasion of Manchuria in September 1931 prompted him to turn away from what had been a focus on European affairs. As a beginning assistant professor at Harvard, he taught a summer course in 1934 on Far Eastern international politics, befriended Japanese students, and engaged a Japanese man to teach him the rudiments of the language.[11]

The following winter he published "The Realistic Foreign Policy of Japan" in the prestigious journal *Foreign Affairs*. His argument, which prefigured that of his second book, *The Basis of Japanese Foreign Policy*, published in 1936, was that Japan's aggressive and expansionist behavior had a rational explanation. Challenging the popular notion that "mere military madness" explained Japan's intrusion into north China, Hindmarsh insisted that Tokyo's attempt to gain economic and strategic predominance on the East Asian mainland was a rational response to overpopulation that could not be resolved by birth control, emigration, or increased agricultural productivity. Having opted for rapid industrialization, Japan's leaders needed resources and markets overseas—both of which were to be found in China. But pursuit of commercial gain and strategic security there inevitably pitted Japan against the interests of already entrenched great powers such as Britain and the United States.[12]

As he elaborated these ideas in book form, Hindmarsh sympathized with Japan and criticized American policy. On the one hand, he called for a deeper and more reasoned understanding of what Japan was doing. On the other, he argued that simply to insist upon respect of the shopworn Open Door policy toward China enunciated at the beginning of the century or to refuse to recognize the changes Japan had brought about there, as outgoing Republican secretary of state Henry Stimson had persuaded incoming president Franklin D. Roosevelt to do, was useless. Hindmarsh condemned both the means Japan was using to "solve" its domestically driven foreign policy problems and the emotionalism of Americans' debates over events in East Asia. He advocated hardheaded realism and careful analysis of Japan's position as the basis for "designing and erecting peace-preserving machinery."[13]

Barely ninety days after his book appeared, Hindmarsh took on a second role. He traveled to The Hague and delivered a series of lectures (in French) on "Japan and Peace in Asia" at a prestigious international institute. But he also volunteered and was accepted for special service as naval reserve officer for intelligence duties. He carried that split identity with him to Japan as an exchange professor at Tokyo Imperial University in the fall of 1937. His connection with American naval intelligence could not be revealed, of course, but his journey to Japan was facilitated and possibly partially funded by ONI.[14]

By the time Albert Hindmarsh got to Tokyo in September 1937, Japan and China had been fighting a "real" war for two months. That new and troubling reality may explain his actions during a ninety-day sojourn in Japan. He spent the first month in intensive and costly language tutoring by an associate of Naganuma Naoe, long the teacher of American diplomats and naval Japanese-language students in Japan. Hindmarsh emerged from that experience convinced that Naganuma's reputation as the best teacher and author of the best texts for adults trying to learn Japanese was well deserved. As a visiting scholar, he also met Professor Takagi Yasaka, Tokyo University's expert on American law, history, and politics. The professor sponsored Hindmarsh's speaking before a prestigious group of Japanese intellectuals and diplomats.[15]

But the diligence with which he queried Japanese officials about Tokyo's defense and foreign policies suggests that Hindmarsh was very much the covert

—or perhaps to the Japanese, obvious—naval intelligence operative. He pressed Prime Minister Konoe Fumimaro for clarification of Japan's military and political intentions in China. He asked foreign ministry officials, including Minister Hirota Kōki, why Tokyo had joined Germany and Italy in the Anti-Comintern Pact of 1936. He questioned finance ministry officials and found them convinced that Japanese would bear the financial burdens of war in China just like Britons, Frenchmen, and Germans had endured those of World War I. In a long and disturbing interview with vice minister of the navy Adm. Yamamoto Isoroku, "the most belligerent of the navy men I met" and the mastermind behind the Pearl Harbor attack, he learned that the Imperial Navy was confident that it could simultaneously pursue a "southward policy" aimed at economic penetration and acquisition of raw materials from Southeast Asia and fight a war in China.[16]

Hindmarsh left Japan chastened in his earlier belief that reasoned discourse could prevent international conflict. Unlike American ambassador Joseph E. Grew, who at this point placed great faith in Japan's liberal politicians and intellectuals as a counterbalance to the so-called militarists, Hindmarsh found them to be dissembling or impotent in their courteous expressions of opposition to Japan's actions in China. He was in Shanghai when Japanese pilots bombed the USS *Panay* on the Yangtze upriver from Japanese-occupied Nanking. While he believed the Japanese were genuinely concerned about American reactions to this "accident," he was decidedly skeptical of Tokyo's carefully orchestrated apologies. And what he heard and saw on a long journey through Soviet Russia on the trans-Siberian railroad convinced him that Japanese army and navy officials were correct in believing that they faced no immediate threat from the north.[17]

Chief of Naval Operations (CNO) Adm. William D. Leahy commended Hindmarsh for the report on his Japanese journey that he filed upon his return. That praise may have been one force that pulled him closer to the Navy over the next two years. Hindmarsh did not, as a rising young political scientist might have, plunge into the intensifying debate over American East Asian policy that engaged other academics, missionaries, businessmen, journalists, and politicians. No more articles on Japan flowed from his pen. Instead he spent six months in 1939 attached to the First Naval District Intelligence Office in Boston. He was assigned in November of that year to the office of the CNO in the event of national mobilization. But long before Pearl Harbor, the professor with a penchant for naval intelligence work volunteered for active duty.[18]

Just why he did so then remains unclear. He may have been convinced by Hitler's rapid conquest of the Low Countries and invasion of France that war was coming sooner rather than later. He may have felt somewhat estranged from his more traditionally academic colleagues at Harvard or tired of teaching part time at the Fletcher School of Law and Diplomacy at nearby Tufts University. In any event, he threw himself into his new job with a "can-do" spirit that delighted Arthur McCollum. The lieutenant commander quickly discovered that the man he first thought of as a stuffy Harvard international law professor was "a tower of strength." Hindmarsh, who for a time had been secretary of the faculty of Harvard College, quickly showed himself to be an administrative jack-of-all-trades, a "whiz-bang" who could, as McCollum put it, "run the office, . . . do anything . . . and he would."[19]

Hindmarsh, with equal dispatch, learned that his Japanese was not adequate for the specialized translation work of the Japan subsection in ONI. McCollum, not knowing just how the professor's talents could best be used, put him to work on a study of the Japanese economy and sent him off to lecture at the Naval War College. But he also acknowledged that Hindmarsh had "a feel for" the Japanese language, a sense that would help him assess the prospective value to the Navy of persons who claimed knowledge of it, of academic programs at the handful of universities where the language was taught, and of prospective students for a navy Japanese-language school.[20]

Hindmarsh could not have even begun such a task without the help of a second man, Glenn W. Shaw, who came to Arthur McCollum's attention quite by accident. The naval officer was surprised to see him, one day, on the steps of the Interior Department cafeteria. He remembered him from the summer of 1923, when they had met at Lake Nojiri, a resort in northern Japan favored by missionaries and other non-Japanese. Shaw somewhat dejectedly told McCollum that after fleeing Japan, his home for nearly a quarter century, he had just been turned down for a job at the State Department. The ONI official enthusiastically invited Shaw to his office and offered him a civil service position as research analyst. The offer was quickly accepted.[21]

In Shaw McCollum got a "Japan hand" who was everything Albert Hindmarsh was not. He was not an academic, but he spoke and read Japanese fluently. He knew the country and its people firsthand, having taught English since 1916 at what is now the Osaka University of Foreign Languages and at high schools in nearby Kobe and more distant and nationalistic Yamaguchi. He was a self-made man in Japan, having written a column in the *Osaka Asahi* for years and broadcast over the radio in Japan's second-largest city. He had published two books about everyday life in Japan. Shaw had also produced five volumes of translations of plays, short stories, and novels by the some of the most innovative Japanese writers of the early twentieth century. In hiring Shaw, McCollum netted the first great American translator of modern Japanese literature. That translator, it turned out, had also been friend and neighbor to the parents of those young men, born or raised in Japan, who would be among the very first students in a naval Japanese-language program.[22]

With Hindmarsh and Shaw at his side, McCollum was well positioned to deal, rationally and methodically, with the question of how best to remedy the Navy's Japanese problem. In December 1940, Hindmarsh proposed a solution to it for him. The Navy should survey all "available Japanese linguists, in and out of the armed services," as the first step in establishing "a practical course in the Japanese language" that would produce junior Naval Reserve officers "thoroughly competent in reading, writing, and speaking" the language. They would be trained "in quantity and quality sufficient to anticipate the demands" that might be made upon the Navy for their services, "particularly in the event of war between Japan and the United States."[23]

Arthur McCollum agreed with that idea, but it took more than a month to convince the Director of Naval Intelligence (DNI), the CNO, and the Bureau of Navigation (then responsible for personnel matters) to agree to it. Not until February 1941, when newly appointed ambassador Nomura Kichisaburō came to Washington for talks with Secretary of State Cordell Hull aimed at resolving differences between the United States and Japan, was Hindmarsh authorized to take action to remedy the Navy's Japanese-language deficiencies. He was instructed to begin a survey of candidates, to organize a training course or courses "in Japanese for naval officers," and to prepare to administer such instruction as might be subsequently offered.[24]

MARRIAGE

By the beginning of 1941 stiff competition among the armed services for the services of potential Japanese linguists had arisen. As one keen-eyed academic put it, "the usual foolish departmentalization" had reared its head among the armed services, "each of which is going its own way." That was true even within the Navy Department itself, where the Marines became the first to break from the pack. In January 1941, Major Harris traveled to Columbia University in New York City. There he succeeded in persuading John R. Shively, a graduate student who had been born in Kyoto and raised by his missionary parents in Japan, to leave school and accept a commission in the Corps. Shively would travel the country for the next five months in search of recruits like himself—men with some knowledge of Japanese. By May 1941 he had found twelve men who by virtue of birth, long residence in Japan, or significant study of its language and culture at the university level looked like promising Marine Corps Japanese-language students.[25]

Shively persuaded Major Harris and his superiors to set aside whatever qualms they may have had about noncitizens teaching officers Japanese. He was convinced that the University of Hawaii, where he had studied and native Japanese speakers were plentiful, was the best place to establish a "refresher course" for these young men. The Corps then moved quickly to get them there. It waived physical standards, dropped the requirement that language students be bachelors, and minimized their military training. In June 1941 eleven of these twelve pioneer American officer students of Japanese sailed from San Francisco on the SS *Matsonia* bound for Honolulu, where their classes were set to begin on 1 July.[26]

Well before that date the Army, too, had begun devising its own solution to the Japanese-language problem. Two veterans of the Army's language student program in Japan, Lt. Col. John W. Weckerling and Capt. Kai E. Rasmussen, began canvassing for persons who might become army translators and interpreters. Their efforts, quite logically, focused on a group that was rapidly coming under the Army's control: Japanese-American draftees. By the time of the Pearl Harbor attack, the Army had interviewed thirteen hundred nisei. But only fifty-eight of them were deemed suitable for the Japanese-language school it would open at the Presidio of San Francisco in November 1941.[27] Just as Edwin Reischauer had surmised, Japanese-American young men were not well versed enough in their ancestors' tongue to serve immediately as interpreters or translators.

The other services' actions in starting these programs alerted Arthur McCollum, Albert Hindmarsh, and Glenn Shaw to the fact that there was, and would continue to be, competition for the services of a very limited pool of young men with some familiarity with the Japanese language. But academic frictions, far more than interservice rivalries, shaped what emerged as the Navy's Japanese Language School. They surfaced only a few days after Major Harris left Cambridge late in October 1940, when graduate student Florence Walne was asked by her Harvard-Yenching Institute professors to comment on a proposal they intended to send to Washington. It would place the institute's resources at the government's disposal. Senior professor Serge Eliseef would direct a Japanese-language training course there that would be staffed by instructors brought from other universities and paid by the government. Such a program, it was suggested, could quickly turn out 250 Japanese linguists.

Miss Walne, a forty-five-year-old missionary daughter, reacted to the proposal cautiously but with barely concealed alarm. She said she would have to get advice from her home institution, the University of California, Berkeley. Indeed, she suggested, it might be necessary to establish two Japanese-language training centers, one on each coast. That idea elicited "a great outburst" from the Harvard professors, both because they did not think there were enough qualified instructors to staff two schools and because they assumed, to her irritation, that "Harvard is THE CENTER for all intellectual and cultural endeavors."[28]

Her guarded yet provocative reply suggested that Florence Walne, nominally a Harvard graduate student but actually an assistant professor of Japanese at Berkeley, was a shrewd academic poker player. Over the next nine months she became an untiring advocate for a naval Japanese-language program at the University of California, Berkeley. She stirred its senior administrators' competitive instincts, and they sent one of their number to query Major Harris about what might be up. When he indicated that any center was likely to be at Harvard, she defused that myth by sending Berkeley president Robert Gordon Sproul word that Arthur McCollum had rejected that idea "in the strongest terms."[29] After going to Washington, where she probably met with her old friend and fellow Baptist, McCollum, and perhaps with Hindmarsh and Shaw as well, she returned to Berkeley and presented President Sproul with three alternative courses of action.

Only one, the one she preferred, made any sense. The university should set up a small language school for service members, with reasonable tuition and a curriculum practical enough to meet military requirements. It would be a "separate enterprise" from the Department of Oriental Languages and be supervised by a military officer. Its program would try to reproduce "as nearly as possible" the conditions of earlier language training in Japan. That meant up to eight hours a day of intensive reading, writing, speaking, and translating, with additional tutoring for those who needed it. The Naganuma texts that Albert Hindmarsh had praised would be used. To be sufficiently flexible to meet the armed services' needs, the school should be set up "independently of everything else," responsible solely to President Sproul himself. Although she did not say so, Florence Walne was the obvious candidate to direct it.[30]

Her proposal intrigued Berkeley administrators, and over the next sixty days they refined it to enhance its appeal to the government. The university would offer through its Extension Division an intensive Japanese-language course for a minimum of forty students, for either one ten- or two twelve-month periods. Its cost, depending on the length of the term, would be between four and six hundred dollars per student, considerably less than the "extremely excessive" seven hundred dollars per student per term that Harvard had proposed. In mid-April 1941, President Sproul sent the plan to Major Harris, Lieutenant Commander McCollum, their counterparts at the War Department and Federal Communications Commission, and FBI Director J. Edgar Hoover.[31]

Only the Navy responded with a glimmer of hope that this proposal might be accepted. McCollum told Sproul that his office was then preoccupied with identifying possible students and instructors of Japanese. But it was "highly probable" that "something concrete" would develop within the next two to three months. He was more specific with his old friend, Florence Walne: by July or August the Navy would have "a line on enough prospective students" to make establishment of a Japanese-language school "worthwhile." He revealed that he was currently thinking of backing such establishments at three centers: one somewhere "on the east coast," one at Berkeley, and "probably" a third in Hawaii.[32]

Over the next two months the pace of preparations for some kind of Japanese-language training program accelerated as relations between Washington and Tokyo deteriorated. In the capital, Hindmarsh and Shaw culled three hundred civilian personnel files in search of prospective students. They were to be white men "and a few young women" between the ages of twenty and thirty who had college degrees and who had lived or studied in Japan or China.

In Philadelphia, the American Council of Learned Societies created a committee that planned a conference at Cornell University on the teaching of the Japanese language. Representatives of government agencies that might need Japanese-language expertise as well as professors from the half dozen universities where it was taught were invited. By the time they gathered late in July, Washington had raised the level of tensions with Tokyo by embargoing the sale of oil and aviation gasoline to Japan.[33]

Lieutenant Commander McCollum, his counterpart in the Army's Military Intelligence Division, Maj. Wallace Moore, and Albert Hindmarsh drove up to Ithaca for the meeting. The two naval representatives remembered it as a disturbing but decisive encounter. The academics could not seem to be able to get their act together. They complained about lack of appropriate teaching materials, inadequate support from their home institutions, and the government's inability to guarantee their students jobs if they revamped their curricula to meet current military, naval, and diplomatic needs. McCollum said "none of them . . . at our big eastern universities . . . had anything that we would find useful" because they regarded language instruction as a tool for gaining historical and cultural insights. Major Moore brought the encounter between the military and the academics to a sour end. "Well, gentlemen," he said, "you haven't got a thing that's any damned use to the government at all!" Thus, Hindmarsh recalled, he and McCollum left Ithaca convinced that the Navy must organize its own Japanese-language training program because "the teachers had developed no practical methods, had no adequate teaching materials, no practical standards, were primarily interested in Japanese as a philological subject." On top of that, the academics were "unduly skeptical as to the feasibility of doing a job which we were certain had to be done."[34]

In fact, the Cornell conference simply sealed what was to be a wartime marriage between the Navy and Japanese-language instructors. While neither had a clear definition of just what "competent" linguists for military purposes might be, both were willing to work with each other. Prior to the meeting, McCollum and Hindmarsh had affirmed the need to train "special students" soon to be identified at "at least two centers, one on the Atlantic, the other on the Pacific coast." They expected to complete student selection in mid-July and open contract relations with the universities involved to have instruction begin in the fall term. Moreover, they went to Cornell having already seen Berkeley's plan to teach the kind of course they wanted. They left it urging Florence Walne to produce a "carefully devised schedule of instruction" that would produce "fully qualified translators and interpreters" after no more than eight months' intensive instruction. She accepted that challenge in a "can-do" spirit: while the task would be "exceedingly difficult," careful planning and selection of students who already had some Japanese-language training might make it doable.[35]

Spurred by the knowledge that the Army was going to start a school for enlisted nisei linguists at the Presidio in San Francisco, ONI moved quickly thereafter to finalize agreements that would allow naval Japanese-language schools to open by 1 October 1941 at Harvard and the University of California. Hindmarsh and Shaw refined the essentials of what their courses must do: Produce individuals who could, at a minimum, read the first five Naganuma texts that demanded command of sixteen hundred "commonly used" Japanese characters; read and translate Japanese newspaper articles "on general subjects"; and transliterate and translate the two forms of "simple" handwritten Japanese, *gyōsho* and *sōsho.* In addition, the course would enable students to converse with a vocabulary of "at least eight thousand words" in common usage, including "frequently used military and naval terms." With that command of the spoken language, they should be able to interpret and summarize lectures and speeches on general topics. Depending upon their abilities, students would concentrate on either translation or interpretation, and they would complete the course within an eight- to eighteen-month period. Those who could not meet these tough standards would be weeded out in an "elimination" exam given at the end of the second month of the course.[36]

Lieutenant Commander McCollum then hammered out an agreement with the Bureau of Navigation on the military status of prospective students. They would be enrolled as active duty yeomen, second class, in the Naval Reserve. The roughly fifty dollars monthly pay they received would cover basic needs while they were students. Placing them under the administrative jurisdiction of the professor of Naval Science at each school would ensure proper naval discipline and would free faculty from administrative duties. Upon completing the course the students would be commissioned as intelligence officers in the Naval Reserve. The toughest part of this, McCollum recalled, was persuading the Bureau of Navigation to designate anyone who had not gone through basic training as a second class petty officer.[37]

With all of these details specified, the remaining tasks to be completed before instruction could begin were relatively easy. Late in August, Hindmarsh and Shaw set out on a cross-country tour to interview prospective students and complete contracts with Harvard and the University of California. They interviewed fifty-three students and thirteen teachers in nine cities from Philadelphia, New York, and Boston on the East Coast through Cleveland, Chicago, and Denver in the Heartland to Seattle, San Francisco, and Los Angeles on the Pacific Coast. With great dispatch, Albert Hindmarsh, now a lieutenant commander, initialed contracts with Harvard and the University of California on behalf of the Navy during the first weeks of September. The first forty-eight students selected for the Navy's Japanese-language courses were ordered to report to their respective schools by 1 October 1941.[38]

The students appeared on the Harvard and Berkeley campuses ninety days after their marine counterparts began classes at the University of Hawaii and a month before army nisei started receiving language training at the Presidio in San Francisco. That product of Major Harris' meeting with professors Reischauer and Eliseef and with Florence Walne at Cambridge a year earlier reflected the conflicting pressures, both military and academic, that produced the Navy's Japanese-language program. Those in uniform and those who wore caps and gowns agreed to collaborate, albeit with considerable give and take on both sides. The Navy showed itself willing to let academics perform a much-needed function in the interest of national defense. And the professors yielded their treasured academic autonomy to get naval support for a virtually undeveloped portion of their universities' curricula. All that remained, in the waning months before Pearl Harbor, was for the program they had designed to start producing the Japanese linguists that were so desperately needed.

DIVORCE

Things did not, however, go as smoothly as lieutenant commanders Hindmarsh and McCollum hoped. Almost immediately, problems surfaced at Harvard. There the marriage between the university and the Navy was fragile from the very beginning. Hindmarsh had negotiated a contract with his former employer through the dean of Harvard College without the sort of direct faculty input that Florence Walne provided at Berkeley. The contract provided that the instructors would use the Naganuma texts and follow a strict schedule to assess student progress in conversation as well as reading and translation.[39]

Professors Eliseef and Reischauer, although not trained as language teachers, had just completed—and naturally wanted to use—their own text, at least in the opening weeks of the course. Both taught on the assumption that students, normally scholars-in-the-making who wanted to learn the language for research in their particular fields, would "pick up" conversational skills when they went to Japan, just as they themselves had. Thus their text introduced literary rather than practical written characters and vocabulary. *Elementary Japanese for University Students* taught the proverb, "An ogress at eighteen—second grade tea in its first infusion" which meant "Even an ugly woman isn't too bad at a tender age." That prompted smiles from the lusty young students, at least one of whom was smitten by the beautiful half-Japanese teaching assistant in the Harvard course.[40] But the proverb alarmed Hindmarsh and Shaw.

When they came to Cambridge in November 1941 to check on students' progress, they found that several had failed their written and oral exams. The two men were reluctant to blame the young men whom they had personally selected for that result. After all, the Harvard class included students whose backgrounds suggested they should be quick learners: several missionary sons born in Japan, the part-Japanese grandson of a pioneering Yokohama editor, a former Lutheran missionary to China, a lawyer, a museum curator, and a would-be China scholar who had already studied Russian and Chinese. Instead, Hindmarsh forwarded to the dean of the college a list of remedial measures that must be taken, starting with the exclusive use of the Naganuma textbook.[41]

That rankled Professor Eliseef, who tossed off a letter to the Navy Department that, in effect, blamed Hindmarsh and Shaw for what had gone wrong. He defended the worth of his text and criticized the visiting examiners' emphasis on spoken, rather than written, Japanese. He attributed the failure of nearly one in five of the students to their backgrounds, lack of ability, or other personal factors. He regarded the Navy's suggestions for change as expressions of a lack of confidence in the course instructors and brusquely insisted that any future complaints be sent directly to him.[42] Such a self-defensive missive did not sit well with naval officials in Washington.

Thus, even before Hindmarsh and Shaw paid a second visit to Harvard in February 1942, they had decided against sending any more language officer candidates there. They found the students "confused," their instructors' morale low, and other financial and administrative problems lurking beneath the surface. Professors Reischauer and Eliseef, for their part, came to the conclusion that a divorce between Harvard and the Navy would suit them just fine. The older professor was "furious . . . and completely contemptuous" of Hindmarsh.

Reischauer found the ONI representative "incredibly disagreeable, offensive" and prone to take "a drill corporal's attitude toward others." He resented the fact that Hindmarsh, who "knew nothing" about Japanese, came to Harvard seeking experts but then treated them like "his lackeys." Barely sixty days after the naval representatives left Cambridge, the embittered Reischauer warned army officials that the Navy was likely to monopolize the best Japanese-language students and suggested establishing a special ROTC program to lure them into the Army.[43]

Feelings of that sort portended an end to the Harvard–Navy relationship. It came in September 1942. Nevertheless, the program in Cambridge produced some pioneering naval language officers. Although six of the original students failed or were dismissed from the program, six others completed the course by May 1942. The remaining fourteen "worked like stink" to finish, be commissioned, and begin working for the Navy in earnest in September 1942.[44]

HONEYMOON

Berkeley, by contrast, was, at least in Commander Hindmarsh's eyes, an unblemished success. There Florence Walne's attitude, experience, and innate shrewdness made all the difference in the world. After little more than a moment's hesitation, she took to the task of creating an intensive Japanese-language program for the Navy like a duck to water. Perhaps doing so made her feel that she had finally found her mettle. As a forty-five-year-old female Harvard graduate student, she probably sensed that she would never become the carefully sculpted and handsomely funded Japan scholar that Edwin Reischauer, nearly fifteen years her junior, already was. She may have known, too, from awkward moments when writing Japanese characters on the blackboard, that she was unlikely to become a star in the classroom. Directing an intensive language program for the Navy thus freed her from old constraints and gave her "the chance of a lifetime."[45]

Florence Walne knew what the Navy wanted, and her university superiors stood ready to help her produce it. Berkeley officials had long since purchased, with indirect help from the State Department, copies of the Naganuma textbooks. An early draft of her course proposal emphasized precisely the kind of "immersion" in everyday use of the language that the Navy wanted its students to experience. She suggested teaching the class in San Francisco's Japan town, where their eyes and ears would be trained by seeing and hearing

Japanese on the streets. That would parallel what Albert Hindmarsh himself had experienced in Japan four years earlier. Believing that "possession of a language" meant nothing unless accompanied by knowledge of the civilization it expressed, she wanted her students to "command" its vocabulary and understand the social context in which words were used.[46]

Miss Walne also demonstrated real skill, or enjoyed good luck, in choosing a varied group of instructors to staff her program. Susumu Nakamura, a hefty, gregarious, thirty-three-year-old Japanese-American teaching assistant who loved mahjong and good food, was the principal teacher. Scholarly and shy Ashikaga Ensho, the scion of a long line of priests and an expert on Tibetan Buddhism, had only recently come to Berkeley from Japan. A calligrapher, he introduced students to the rules for writing Japanese characters. Missionaries Willard Topping and James McAlpine added cross-cultural insights drawn from their years of residence in Japan. Miss Walne also persuaded Chitoshi Yanaga, a Hawaii native destined to become a distinguished analyst of Japanese politics and business, to join the group. Drawing from Nakamura's circle of acquaintances among Bay Area Japanese and her own experience as assistant director of Berkeley's International House where many Japanese Americans had lived as students, she added Stanford graduates Yūji Imai and Ariake "Larry" Inouye to the teaching staff.[47] Although few in the group had classroom experience, Florence Walne's teaching team was much more thoroughly bilingual and bicultural than its Harvard counterpart.

The twenty-three students at Berkeley resembled their East Coast counterparts because Hindmarsh and Shaw had used the same criteria in selecting them. At least three had been born in Japan, and two were offspring of China missionary families. Two were in their forties; only one had not reached his twenty-first birthday. They differed in that more came from West Coast universities, and at least one had gained some familiarity with Japanese language and culture through friendship with Japanese-American neighbors. But these students were also a feistier, more assertive lot. They protested early on when the Navy decreed that failure in the course doomed one to continued service as an enlisted man. Novices complained when they were thrown into conversation class with pupils who had been born in Japan. And one student chafed at Miss Walne's "old-fashioned" missionary mentality when she reported another who had moved in with his girlfriend to the NROTC unit commander.[48]

But overall, the Berkeley students took readily to what their instructors had to offer. Their teachers, in turn, devoted many hours outside the classroom to drilling and coaching them. That built bonds of friendship and admiration between students and faculty, guaranteed good test results, and yielded a high retention rate. Only four students left the program.[49] Perhaps the easy informality of the Berkeley campus was more conducive than Harvard's overpowering sense of tradition to the progress of would-be language officers.

FORCED REMOVAL

Whatever the alchemy, the Berkeley program worked. Shortly after the first of the New Year 1942, a pleased Albert Hindmarsh decided that all of the next batch of language officer candidates should go there. But long before their arrival late in February, larger events began casting shadows over the future of the naval Japanese-language program at Berkeley. Forced removal of "persons of Japanese ancestry," including the nine who taught for the Navy at the University of California, became more and more likely with each passing day.[50]

On 7 December 1941, people simply started disappearing. Mikio Fujimoto, a naval Japanese-language school instructor to be, left his San Francisco home that morning with a visitor from Japan. When the two men failed to return by evening, Mrs. Fujimoto called the police and learned that the FBI had seized them and thrown them in jail. She pleaded for, and got, her husband's release to house arrest. By New Year's Eve, nearly thirteen hundred Bay Area Japanese and Japanese Americans had been taken into custody.[51]

Thereafter ominous signs of probable forced removal of Japanese and Japanese Americans from the three West Coast states appeared with increasingly frequency. On 6 January 1942 the government began registering "enemy aliens." Three weeks later Attorney General Francis Biddle named twenty-nine West Coast areas that would have to be evacuated—including the San Francisco waterfront. Three weeks after that, despite having received a report that concluded that persons of Japanese ancestry posed no threat, President Franklin D. Roosevelt signed Executive Order 9066, which authorized the U.S. Army to designate areas to which people could be denied access. Before February ended, first-generation Japanese immigrants living in El Cerrito and Richmond, communities just north of Berkeley, were ordered to leave because they supposedly might pose a threat to a nearby Standard Oil refinery. On 2 March 1942 amidst growing public fears generated by a Japanese submarine's shelling of the coast north of Santa Barbara, Gen. John L. DeWitt, commander of the Western Defense Command, issued a proclamation that divided the three Pacific Coast states and Arizona into military areas and prohibited zones, a step that made it clear that the forced removal of Japanese Americans and Japanese was only a matter of time.[52]

These troubling events did not immediately disrupt naval Japanese-language classes at Berkeley, and until late February, despite the obvious reasons for concern, everyone there tried to carry on normally. Miss Walne prepared for the arrival of a second group of students that would more than double the size of her school. Faculty members worked late into the night grading papers. Berkeley's plum trees burst into bloom, and two of the teachers decided to marry. But everyone was nervous about the future—so much so that the Buddhist priest who came to marry Ashikaga Ensho and his Japanese-American bride at Berkeley's International House forgot the image of Buddha needed for the ceremony. By mid-March, James McAlpine, the Presbyterian missionary teacher who doubled as preacher for the Oakland Japanese Church found his congregation "all up in the air" over the evacuation proclamation that people had been "warned would come soon."[53]

No one who had been involved in creating the Japanese-language program at Berkeley wanted to let anything of that sort disrupt it. President Sproul cabled "urgent pleas" to Navy Secretary Frank Knox and Adm. Chester Nimitz of the Bureau of Navigation opposing the evacuation of its instructors. The chief of Naval Operations directed Rear Adm. John W. Greenslade, commandant of the 12th Naval District in which Berkeley was located, to make "every effort consistent with real security" to keep the program there. And Albert Hindmarsh told Florence Walne that his office preferred "above everything else, to have the course stay where it is with the present staff."[54]

That prompted actions that temporarily stayed the army evacuators' hands. Admiral Greenslade first begged for time to do background checks on the teachers, then asked for and received permits that exempted them from the curfew that restricted the movements of other Japanese and Japanese Americans and allowed their immediate families to stay in their homes. But the admiral felt the strength of anti-Japanese passions flowing through the body politic and doubted that anything other than delay was likely. His subordinates could foresee what was to happen. One noted that General DeWitt had already decided that the Army's Japanese-language school at the Presidio would move to the Midwest. Another doubted he could certify that "Japanese race instructors" were "loyal to the United States" and predicted that the Navy would suffer "much adverse criticism" from a public opposed to any persons of Japanese ancestry remaining in the San Francisco Bay Area if the Berkeley instructors were allowed to stay very long.[55]

Thus on 10 April 1942, at Admiral Greenslade's instruction, the district intelligence officer told the army assistant provost marshal overseeing evacuation that the admiral was "interested only in maintaining . . . [the] language school," not in its continuance at Berkeley. That led to local interservice agreement that it "would be better for all concerned if the school . . . moved inland, *in toto*," beyond the so-called restricted area.[56]

Arthur McCollum tried but failed to undo that accord. When he visited Twelfth Naval District headquarters in San Francisco en route from Pearl Harbor back to Washington, Rear Admiral Greenslade quickly told him there was no hope of changing General DeWitt's position on evacuation. When McCollum asked why, Greenslade replied that the Army was "publicly committed." The commander went to see the general, and just as the admiral had predicted, "got exactly nowhere." Then he had to perform "one of the hardest jobs I ever had to do." McCollum went to Berkeley and told university officials and Florence Walne that the Navy was going to have to move the school.[57]

That touched off a flurry of activity that sent the Berkeley students and their teachers to a most unlikely site: the University of Colorado in Boulder, more than a thousand miles from the sea. That was not Florence Walne's preferred location. When she heard that it and the University of New Mexico were being considered, she quickly opted for Albuquerque, as did General DeWitt. Rear Admiral Greenslade preferred Boulder, partly because that would keep the school in his naval district, partly because he had already dealt with University of Colorado officials.[58]

That factor appears to have prompted Arthur McCollum to choose Boulder. As he recalled it, the choice was made when he went to the education section of the Bureau of Navigation to look for some existing naval property that could be used for the school. There was none, but the official with whom he spoke introduced him to "a very nice man" who turned out to be the president of the University of Colorado. Robert P. Stearns was in Washington making "a sales pitch" to navy officials about what his campus had to offer as a training site. He had already convinced them to establish a school for enlisted radiomen there. What he said impressed McCollum, who ordered Commander Hindmarsh, then at Ann Arbor recruiting University of Michigan students for the language program, to go to Colorado immediately. He did so, and on 31 May 1942 President Stearns and Commander Hindmarsh initialed a contract establishing the school that was virtually identical to those previously concluded with Harvard and the University of California. The sole difference was a proviso that gave the Navy the right to continue Miss Walne and the teaching staff as director and faculty of the program.[59]

That hastily drawn agreement set the stage for many long treks eastward. Florence Walne and her mother, some sixty-two students, two Caucasian teachers and their families, and eight Japanese instructors and their spouses and children went by car, bus, train, or—in the case of supposedly "dangerous" Japanese and Japanese American—in shuttered Pullman cars from Berkeley to Boulder. By 23 June 1942, barely two weeks after the U.S. Navy inflicted the first great defeat upon the Imperial Japanese Navy at Midway, the Navy Japanese Language School was ready to begin anew.[60]

REFLECTIONS

Nearly two years earlier, when marine major Harris met Florence Walne and professors Eliseef and Reischauer in Cambridge, none of them could have imagined such a result. That what turned out to be the Navy Japanese Language School ended up in Boulder rather than Berkeley or Cambridge revealed how contested the process of mobilizing for war was. In this instance, it depended as much upon individual personalities and chance as upon design. To be sure, there was a master template for the school: the Navy's prewar program in Japan. But that design had to be revised to meet the changed circumstances of first spiraling tensions, then war, between the United States and Japan.

The partners who shaped that design turned out to be naval officers and a maverick missionary daughter turned academic because they had a clearer and stronger sense of immediate purpose than the few professors who taught Japanese at a handful of American universities. In 1940–42, university programs for the study of Japan and its language were in their infancy, so commanders McCollum and Hindmarsh had to step in on the Navy's behalf. Doing so was not easy because, as has been shown, those who wore uniforms and those who wore academic gowns lived in worlds apart. Thus it took unconventional but determined people—Arthur McCollum, Albert Hindmarsh, and Florence Walne—to bring about a marriage between the two.

In creating the naval Japanese-language program they drew upon old lines of connection to and within Japan that were straining to near the breaking point in 1941. Missionaries, especially American Baptists, and naval officers, who had never before been allies, now joined in common cause. Japanese and Japanese Americans who had crossed the Pacific repeatedly, stepped out of their isolation and, indeed, from their place of immediate peril in a society unwilling to recognize them as equals, into partnership with the Navy and the nation's universities. But could that partnership produce the kind of linguists the Navy and Marine Corps so desperately needed?

Chapter Two

STUDENTS ON AN ISLAND OF UNDERSTANDING

The success of the partnership between the Navy and academia would be evident over the next twelve months at Boulder, Colorado. There Florence Walne struggled to administer a school that mushroomed from sixty to nearly four hundred students. She recruited a faculty that blossomed from a handful to a staff of nearly ninety.[1] They shaped a still inchoate language course into what became arguably the best program for teaching Japanese to persons not of Japanese ancestry. The students wrestled with the intricacies of a devilishly complex language while university and community leaders worked to protect their instructors from rampantly anti-Japanese feelings among the wider public. And from Washington, the long hand of Albert Hindmarsh reached out to deflect attempts by more traditional naval officers to militarize or terminate the program. Together, academics, community leaders, naval administrators, and students made Boulder an island of understanding not just of a language but also of the people who spoke it.

What transpired there turned inexperienced young men into fledgling naval and marine officers of a very special sort. How that happened can best be seen by following the first class to complete all of its studies at Boulder through its year of language study. The pioneering "summer class" of 1942 set the pattern for the nearly twelve hundred men and women who eventually graduated from the Navy's Japanese-language school. Probing their experiences on the island of understanding at Boulder is thus an essential first step toward comprehending what naval and marine language officers would do in, and beyond, war.

FIRST ENCOUNTERS

Early in July 1942 the fourth class of language officer candidates Albert Hindmarsh had chosen, 152 strong, arrived in Boulder. "The most polyglot army ever assembled in one spot," they came from all over the country.[2] They arrived alone from small church-related schools such as Ohio Wesleyan and liberal arts colleges such as Bowdoin; in pairs from Carleton College in Minnesota and Duke University in North Carolina; in groups of three and four from Stanford and the University of Washington; and in larger but clubby clusters from Columbia, Harvard, and Yale. Some even came from places as far away as Shanghai and American Samoa.

The youngest among them—midwesterners Larry Vincent, Roger Hackett, and Chuck Cross—were plucked from their colleges at twenty. The oldest, Harry M. Cary, had been a businessman in Japan. Two were budding professors of romance languages and classics, respectively, already teaching at New York University and Northwestern. About one in ten had come into the world in Japan, and more than a third were born or raised there or in Korea and China. Only Tad VanBrunt, a handsome, street-smart fledgling actor from Pasadena, California, neither had nor was pursuing higher education. He said his degree in Japanese came from "the University of Yoshiwara," Tokyo's red-light district. Seventy percent of the new arrivals were in their early twenties—old enough to have sampled graduate or professional training but young enough not to have settled in a place or profession. All were white. Family background or merit scholarships had gotten these men into, or through, college. That guaranteed that virtually all would become members of the upper middle class.[3]

These young men began their journey to Boulder with an unforgettable encounter with Albert Hindmarsh, Glenn Shaw, or both. Their meetings with the language school recruiters were deceptively brief. Roger Marshall and Robert Murphy came up to Washington from Duke at their own expense. They expected to hear an explanation of the language program and then return to their college to consider whether it was for them. Instead, when they got up to leave, Commander Hindmarsh surprised them by asking them to sign up. They did so on the spot. In San Francisco, Stanford Law School student Frank Mallory politely asked a uniformed man in the elevator of an office building if he might be Commander Hindmarsh. The man snapped, "Oh, yes, dammit!" When they got off, he ushered Mallory into an office, thrust a contract under his nose, and said, "Sign it. You can read it later."[4]

Such brevity belied the fact that Albert Hindmarsh knew his criteria for selection and usually had some prior information about the interviewee. He peppered Robert Newell, Mallory's law school classmate, with sharp questions: "Know any Japanese?" Answer, "No." "Born in China or any knowledge of Chinese?" Reply, "No." "Any college course work related to Japan?" Answer, "No." "Well, then, are you a member of Phi Beta Kappa [the national liberal arts honor society]?" Answer, "Yes, sir." Reply: "You're accepted into the program."[5]

For those who claimed knowledge of an East Asian language, the interview became something of a dog and pony show. Hindmarsh spoke briefly about the Navy's program, then probed with a few questions to see if the interviewee was tough enough to withstand its rigors. Then the prospective student was shuffled off to Glenn Shaw. In nine cases out of ten, he knew the young man's parents. Shaw asked the interviewee to speak or translate a little Chinese or Japanese. If the young man got through the Chinese, Shaw took that as a sign of future success in Japanese. If he was doing reasonably well in a beginning Japanese-language class, even making such egregious mistakes in conversation as proclaiming oneself a barbershop did not disqualify him.[6]

Instead, as Ed Seidensticker realized years later, Hindmarsh and Shaw sized up prospective students much as a Japanese person might have done. Nothing terribly relevant was said, but the interviewers came away from the encounter with "a certain feeling for things" about the man before them. The interviewee left the encounter feeling that he had experienced if not a miracle, then at least a great stroke of luck. John Rich remembered Commander Hindmarsh glancing over his Bowdoin record, pronouncing it "not that bad, not that good," and then telling him "go out [to Boulder] and give it a try!" Rich went straight from the interview to Fenway Park, where he saw Boston Red Sox slugger Ted Williams hit a home run. Having struck out earlier with a Marine Corps recruiter due to his poor eyesight, Rich returned home that evening feeling like *he* had just hit a home run.[7]

Rich, like most students who came to Boulder in July 1942, had never visited Colorado, let alone the small town that lay thirty-two miles north of Denver. When the students stepped out of the bus or taxi that deposited them there, they were struck first by the sheer beauty of the place. The four out of ten of them who came from the densely populated Northeast had never seen anything like it. Their eyes blinked in amazement at the wide open and vividly colored landscape that unfolded before them—clear deep blue sky, white windswept clouds, charcoal-colored mountains clothed with evergreens, the red-orange Flatirons, and, of course, the lush greenery of the university campus. "I thought I had died and gone to heaven," Larry Vincent recalled.[8]

These newest students knew they were facing something quite different from their past educational experience. The University of Colorado did not look like the schools they had attended. Its red tile–roofed, sandstone buildings did not resemble those at Berkeley or Oberlin, let alone structures at Duke or Yale. Beautiful young women, creatures entirely absent from the all-male institutions that many had attended, strolled across the campus. Then there was the Navy. Barely visible before Pearl Harbor as the reserve officer training command (ROTC) on a few campuses, here the Navy would be the directing force in what they did.[9] Life in Boulder was going to be different.

If the new students felt uneasy about what might lie ahead, that emotion was overwhelmed by a shared sense of good fortune that bordered on deliverance. Unlike draftees, these young men came to the Navy by their own volition. They had chosen the sea service and felt luckier still to have been selected for its exclusive language-training program. That decision, as Yale Law School student Hart Spiegel put it, was a "wise choice that I'll not regret making." It brought them to this delightful place.[10]

The new arrivals' first full day at Boulder began with a general assembly on campus and ended with a "swell picnic" in the nearby mountains. Miss Walne explained their program of instruction and introduced their teachers-to-be in the formal gathering. At the picnic, they had a chance to interact informally with their predecessors, the nearly seventy Berkeley students who had trekked east to complete their training at Boulder. They were not happy campers. Finishing their studies looking out across a bay to the Golden Gate Bridge was much more appealing than doing so in a small, dry "worn out flea bag" of a Colorado town.[11]

Few, if any, of the new students spoke to their instructors to be. If they had, they might have gotten a much better sense of the emotional baggage that *they* brought to Boulder. Miss Walne had been forced to uproot her aged mother, who lived with her. Former missionary Jim McAlpine had to leave his wife and children behind. The core Berkeley faculty had avoided internment yet suffered forced departure from their homes just like other Japanese and Japanese Americans sent to internment camps. Five of the six new native speakers who joined the Boulder faculty had experienced great anguish at "temporary relocation centers." Nobutaka Ike had to beg for his fiancée's release so she could come to Boulder and marry him. Stanford graduate Joe Sano had at first refused to leave the internment camp at Tanforan Racetrack, just south of San Francisco, pleading the need to care for his aged parents. His words were ignored. And Takeo Okamoto, a young businessman, had to leave behind his wife, who had given birth to their third child in a horse stall at Tanforan without warm water to lessen her pain or bathe the baby. Only Henry Tatsumi had come east in relative ease. Perhaps his prior service as U.S. Army private in World War I or Albert Hindmarsh's high praise for his teaching at the University of Washington shielded him from the indignities that the others endured.[12]

Despite differences in their emotional states, students and faculty shared a common concern on the eve of their first classes: Could they work together to achieve the goals the Navy had set before them? The students brimmed with confidence tempered by uncertainty. Young men in their early twenties tend to be "full of piss and vinegar," that is, sure that they can do whatever they put their minds, hearts, and muscles to. Those who had a little knowledge of spoken Japanese or a semester's introduction to its basics, and the very few who had advanced degrees in Western European languages mistakenly believed that conferred an advantage upon them and were still more confident. But even they suffered the twinges of uncertainty common to all of the new students about their teachers and their peers. John Rich was not alone in realizing that he was about to meet a Japanese and hear the Japanese language spoken for the first time. And how would the newest arrivals deal with the handful of fellow students who sat around the table in class? The "best and brightest" of their generation were likely to prove stiff competitors in a program in which failure was not an option. No wonder that unease and confidence warred within the student body on the eve of first classes at Boulder.[13]

Those first meetings eased the anxieties that students and their teachers felt just a bit. Twenty-five-year-old instructor Noboru Arase left the classroom with confidence in his ability to get the job done. If he had learned English as an adult after fifteen years education in Japan, then he could teach these students Japanese. The Naganuma text, which looked to him like a Japanese third grade reader, could not be all that difficult. Takeo Okamoto, older, perhaps a little wiser, and scarred by racial prejudice, worried about attitudes rather than his incapacities as an instructor or his students' capabilities. Would his white, bright, monocultural students accept him—a Japanese American educated in Japan but without teaching experience—as their sensei, or teacher? When—much to his surprise—the students stood to attention when he entered the classroom, his fears faded away.[14]

The new students left the classrooms with much more mixed feelings, however. They really did not know quite what to make of their instructors or the strange language they spoke and wrote. One sensei began the first conversation class by saying, "'Ohayo' means 'Good Morning.' Say 'Ohayo.'" When his pupils hesitantly did so, he replied, "Very good. Japanese very easy to speak. 'Ohayo' is same as name of state; except you pronounce it [the state's name] 'Oheeyo.'" The students found it hard to suppress snickers and easy to racially stereotype or caricaturize their teachers. They nicknamed one "Tommy the Sandpiper" because the man was so short that when he tried to write on the blackboard he had to jump up, and "every time he sneezed he blew sand in his shoes."[15]

For more than one student, the first reading class turned out to be "a complete bust." Not knowing that the pages of a Japanese book turn from left to right, let alone that words on a page are read from top to bottom, right to left, they opened to the index rather than the first chapter. Once that mistake was corrected, the students came upon the first two sentences they were expected to learn: "*Kore wa hako desu. Kore wa akai hako desu.* [This is a box. This is a red box.]" Those words were so laughable as to be unforgettable.

But their homework assignment was something else. Memorize a smattering of vocabulary. No problem. Come to class tomorrow able to recognize 102 symbols—in two of the three scripts used to write Japanese. Big problem. As they picked up their books and left the last class on that first day, these new students may have felt what another Boulder neophyte said about his first Japanese-language class: "Oh, my God! What have I gotten myself into?"[16]

TRIMESTER ONE: SURVIVING JAPANESE

The new students began a forced march into the complexities of the language of the enemy. It would be tough. Japanese, unlike most Western European languages or even Greek, Russian, Arabic, and Hebrew, is not written with a limited number of symbols. It uses three different scripts. Two are syllabic: fifty-one angular katakana for telegrams and words of foreign origin, and fifty-one more flowing hiragana used for grammatical and pronunciation purposes. The third script is ideographic: thousands and thousands of Chinese characters, or kanji. Words are written by combining kana and kanji or by compounding two Chinese characters. To the untrained eye, these scripts seemed very strange indeed. One student's wife who taught elementary school said they looked like "little houses and places that the kids draw in kindergarten." Hart Spiegel compared them to "something off the wall of a public telephone booth."[17] Each of the ideographs can be read in two ways: multisyllabic like spoken Japanese or as a single syllable close to the sound of its Chinese original. Worse still, there are multiple readings of characters in both their Chinese and Japanese pronunciations. That means that a student must memorize the sound as well as the meaning of every word depending on the context in which it appears.

The new Boulder students started doing "sheer memory work" right away.[18] But very quickly they ran up against another problem: Japanese has a huge number of homonyms, that is words that sound the same but are "spelled" differently. But in Japanese one "spells" with kanji. Used alone, their meaning is clear. When combined with another, as they usually are, they produce homonyms that can have several, very different, meanings. Thus, for example, *gunki* can mean weapons, a battle flag, troop morale, a military secret, or a war history. A combat interpreter interrogating a prisoner of war probably could figure out the correct meaning from the context of the conversation. The poor Boulder student, however, simply had to memorize meanings for each of the five two-kanji compounds, all of which sounded alike.

Writing Japanese posed still more problems for the students. A kanji has two parts: a radical, which puts it in a broad category, and supplementary strokes of the calligrapher's brush or ordinary person's pen, which give it specificity. There are 214 radicals. The number of strokes in kanji, as commonly written before postwar reforms simplified them, ranged from 1 to 26. The Boulder students had to follow strict rules for writing kanji. The radical, if at the left or on top, had to be done first, and all strokes moved from left to right, top to bottom. One had to know that to have any chance of finding words in a Japanese dictionary, which arranged them by radicals.

Once the poor student figured out how to write a character or two-kanji compound, he had to get its pronunciation absolutely right. Jagged shards—long *o*'s and *u*'s—stud the seas of Japanese, and short *o*'s and *u*'s lurk just beneath their surface. Many a foreign mariner has repeatedly run afoul of both. Getting the pronunciation wrong could easily lead to verbal shipwreck. Students in a hurry might meet disaster if they misplaced or omitted the long *o* sound in a word. The syllables "*jo*" and "*ro*," for example, when combined in that naked form, meant "watering can." When joined in long form—*jōrō*—they signified "court lady." The Boulder men were not too likely to run into either during the war. But before their naval service was done, many of them would see, speak with, search for, or shut down the shops of *jorō*—prostitutes. Speaking Japanese properly was still more difficult because the enemy used variant combinations of hiragana to indicate how long sounds should be pronounced. Thus the students simply had to learn the meaning of a word and know exactly how it was written and pronounced.[19]

In 1942, linguistic experts disagreed on how best to teach all of this. Philologists at Harvard, Chicago, or Duke taught Japanese like classics professors taught Latin and Greek: students learned vocabulary and grammar—and then they read. At the University of Washington, Henry Tatsumi had devised his own approach: systematizing sounds and compounds, creating categories of verbs, and then teaching students both.[20] At Berkeley, Florence Walne and her staff taught as they themselves had learned, emphasizing the spoken language first and then teaching its written forms. She took the Navy's mandate to create Japanese linguists in a hurry as license to immerse students in the language. At Boulder, students plunged into the murky waters of Japanese without the life jackets of formal grammar and rules.

That approach had pluses and minuses. It frustrated those students who had learned other languages in more traditional ways. It made teaching more natural for Japanese and Japanese-American instructors who had no classroom experience. It introduced variations that left students in one class puzzled when they compared notes with those in another. But those variations bred a "just do it" approach to learning that inculcated the flexibility and practicality that fledgling linguists would need once they went off to war. It also opened the door to introducing elements of Japanese culture into the curriculum. Learning the sequence of katakana and hiragana did that. Henry Tatsumi probably taught it systematically, in the repetitive syllabic order—*a, i, u, e, o, ka, ki, ku, ke, ko, sa, shi, su, se, so,* and so on—that became common practice after the war. But the older Japanese teachers and younger Japanese-American instructors, some of whom had been sent back to Japan by their immigrant parents to learn the language, probably used a more traditional order. Taking a poem as a mnemonic device, they taught an *I, ro, ha, ni, ho, he, to,* and so on, sequence that expressed a Buddhist teaching: "Colors are fragrant, but they fade away. In this world of ours none lasts forever. Cross the high mountain of life's illusions today, and there will be no more shallow dreaming, no more drunkenness."[21]

Albert Hindmarsh and the Navy he served were not about to tolerate dreaming or drunkenness. He and Glenn Shaw devised a formidable regimen for the Boulder school. Students would work fourteen hours—faculty twelve—six days a week for fifty weeks out of the year. Three hours of class would be followed by nine of study, five days a week. After the first two weeks, no English would be spoken in the classroom. Students would use word and kanji lists to eliminate time-consuming searches in dictionaries, and all would have phonograph recordings to be able to hear spoken Japanese at any time. No time would be wasted on "useless playthings" such as kanji cards or vocabulary crib sheets. Every Saturday, students would be given "stiff and comprehensive" examinations to test their ability to read and write kana and kanji, take dictation, speak, and comprehend what they heard on transcriptions of Japanese radio broadcasts. That added up to 250 exams in a year of study. Three more extensive tests would mark the end of each term, and a final comprehensive examination would bring the year's instruction to a close. Albert Hindmarsh wanted this tough regimen to "challenge the intellectual capacity" of the students so they could get the most out of them.[22]

His vision translated into a tough schedule for everyone at the Boulder language school. The students got up at six, awakened either by "Anchors Away!" blasting at neighboring naval radio trainees doing morning calisthenics or by the bellowing of a Marine "whose father must have been a bull moose." After a quick shower and shave, they breakfasted and went off to small classes of five or six persons. Over the next four hours, several sensei appeared before them: first to query them on vocabulary and instruct them in the writing of kanji, then to ask them to read from a chapter in the Naganuma text, take dictation based on it, or write single characters or phrases on the blackboard.

The last could be both excruciating—and funny. These highly competitive students were embarrassed, to say the least, when a sudden failure of memory left one unable to write a kanji properly. Everyone saw what you did not know. Instructors watching students struggle to write characters correctly, something that they themselves did almost effortlessly, needed a great deal of patience and forbearance. Sometimes the only way to get through the ordeal was to mix humor and passive resistance. One tiny teacher taunted a particularly tall student by calling him a mammoth who belonged in the Tokyo zoo. The young man retaliated by writing his kanji at the top of the blackboard so that the sensei could not reach and correct them.[23]

Morning classroom tensions disappeared at lunch time. Several teachers followed Susumu Nakamura's example at Berkeley and walked toward the noon meal with their students. They exchanged simple comments in Japanese about the weather or food or other people. That bolstered confidence in a way that broke down the barrier between the classroom and the "real" world outside it. Mealtime conversations were not entirely in Japanese, as Commander Hindmarsh intended. But "Japanese boys and girls" waited on table just as university president Stearns had promised. One "quite classy-looking" waitress, the daughter of a Japanese-American economist, attracted students like bees to honey. She helped them discover that casual conversation in simple Japanese could be fun.[24]

After the noon meal, students and sensei parted. The teachers went off to prepare lists of vocabulary and kanji to supplement what students would be reading in the Naganuma text later on. The students retreated to preferred hideaways—library cubby holes or unused basement classrooms—to tackle the chapter or chapters assigned for the next day. By late afternoon students' heads were swimming in a sea of kanji and unfamiliar words. "Studied out," they needed, and took, a break. On some days, they had to do *undo*, or organized exercise, usually from five to six o'clock. On other days, they unwound in ways of their own choosing. Some joined in a rough and tumble football scrimmage, and by early fall they organized intramural games. Others who had lived overseas and who knew the game played soccer. In time, the struggling Japanese speakers challenged Spanish-speaking Latin Americans from the nearby Colorado School of Mines to a match. Still others relaxed by going up to a room high in the library to listen to phonograph recordings of classical music. Some during those declining days of summer just stepped outside and sat down or leaned back on the grass and looked up at the beauty of the world around them. Dinner—and more study—followed in the evening.[25]

As the week continued, however, the pace of work picked up for everyone at the school. Teachers had to agree on what should be on the Saturday morning exams. The students tried to absorb more and more while worrying about exactly what they might be asked. A malady dubbed "the kanji jitters" hit them late on Thursdays, spreading and growing more virulent as the "sledgehammer blow" of Saturday morning's exams drew near. The only remedies for it were cigarettes, beer (even if only the watery 3.2 stuff readily available in Boulder), black coffee, and ever more intense study. A group of Yale men tried to cope by cramming the whole night before the exam, just as they had done in New Haven. They liked to drink and sing "The Range of the Buffalo," a ditty that caricatured the language school's teaching methods and celebrated the university's mascot. It went:

> With kanji cards and *tokuhon* [reader] our troubles they began
> With muttered curse and swear word, our fevers highly ran.
> Monday, Tuesday, Wednesday, it doesn't pay to know
> It's what you learn on Friday
> On the range of the buffalo.[26]

No matter how much or how little one prepared for them, the Saturday examinations proved grueling. One student got so nervous in his oral test that he turned "white as a ghost." His teacher took pity and sent him out to get some water—and then continued the exam. Even if they did not suffer that obviously, students left the tests feeling totally drained. Some had strength enough to go for a walk or play a little baseball before lunch. Those who had stayed up all night Friday simply ate the noon meal and then napped until near sundown. Then they awoke to twenty-four hours or so of freedom before they had to start preparing for Monday's class.[27]

The sensei faced a less carefree weekend. Besides preparing for the coming week's first classes, they had to grade stacks of examination papers. Doing so demanded careful individual and collective scrutiny. Simply marking a badly drawn kanji or mistranslated word would not do. One had to provide the correct answer. And to be sure that no individual idiosyncrasies or grading errors crept in, a second team of readers had to double-check both the exam as given and the corrections written. This labor-intensive procedure was meant to minimize protests the following Wednesday, when graded papers were returned and test scores and class ranking were posted for all to see.[28]

Surviving so tough a regimen demanded three things: minimizing distractions, developing esprit, and forging bonds between students and teachers.

In the late summer of 1942 the school treated the Navy almost as if it were a distraction. Only once, in August, did demands of the service disrupt the normal weekly routine at Boulder. Students who came to the school that summer as civilian naval agents needed protection from suspicious or ignorant draft boards back home. Bused to the Naval Training Center at Denver, they took their first naval physical exam. For many in this group that had been selected for brains rather than brawn, standing naked alongside husky Colorado farmhands and cowboys who were also taking their induction exam was positively embarrassing. Examining naval doctors and corpsmen may have been appalled to see so many prospective inductees with eye or ear or foot problems, but they knew the students had been promised physical waivers and passed them. Then, raising their hands, the students were sworn into the Navy as yeoman, second class.

Nevertheless, they never put on enlisted men's uniforms. Their contact with the "real" Navy was strictly limited. They might see Capt. Leo Welch, who commanded the NROTC unit at the university, on paydays when they received their magnificent ninety-six-dollar monthly paychecks. His staff led them through a couple of hours of physical exercise each week. But apart from that, they had almost no contact with anyone wearing naval blue. That was just what Albert Hindmarsh and Florence Walne intended.[29]

Hindmarsh and Walne also wanted the students to develop a group esprit that would help them surmount any obstacles to learning Japanese rapidly. For a time old school ties threatened achievement of that goal. The first all-Boulder class was more heterogeneous than its Harvard and Berkeley predecessors. From the moment they first met, graduates of western public universities and alumni of eastern elite schools eyed each other warily. Each was shocked by the way the other dressed for their first dinner at Boulder. The Westerners could not believe the Easterners were wearing coats and ties; and the Easterners thought the Westerners' blue jeans were completely inappropriate. Disdain for Ivy League graduates was rampant. One western cartoonist lampooned the Easterners with a drawing captioned "No, I didn't come from Harvard or Columbia. I'm just naturally repulsive." Some Yale alums reciprocated by sticking together so closely that others who had been mere graduate students at New Haven declined to join their clique.[30]

Florence Walne took three steps to combat such divisions among the students. First she commissioned a school song for use on ceremonial occasions, just as Commander Hindmarsh wanted. Henry Tatsumi quickly penned its words, but Miss Walne scotched the irreverent suggestion that they be sung to the tune of "Onward Christian Soldiers." Susumu Nakamura promised a case of beer to the student section that came up with a more appropriate tune, and James C. Kremer claimed that prize for his classmates. Before long all of the students were singing—in Japanese—a song that urged them to "march on, march on . . . [alongside] the knights who soar into the blue skies, the warriors who cross the mountain paths, [and the] the seamen who sail the vast seas." They were to become "comrades who bravely seek the way of the pen" [and fighters] . . . for the increasing prosperity of the people under democracy."[31]

Miss Walne also approved publication of a student newspaper, *Sono hi no uwasa* [*The Day's News*], that appeared barely a month after the Boulder school opened. It was to be a means of forging group unity, a clearinghouse for news that would "dispel some of the misleading rumors" that circulated daily, and a bulletin board for extracurricular activities. It had a serious page in Japanese that gave students extra practice in reading the language. And it provided laughs with jokes written out in Romanized Japanese or cartoons with bilingual captions. During their first trimester, language school students also read news of faculty and administrators' comings and goings, simple stories in Japanese penned by their teachers, lists of recent books about Japan to be found in the university library, and mnemonic devices to help them remember radicals in stroke order. The newspaper went on to encourage them to donate blood and turn out for school dances.[32]

Miss Walne also co-opted the Fujin kai—the student wives' club—to serve the school's purpose. The women originally banded together to defeat their loneliness, help their husbands, and enlighten spouses-to-be about what lay ahead of them. But their organization soon became a tool for promoting group identity. The wives produced a guide to living in Boulder with a naval spouse. It forewarned readers that the Navy Japanese Language School was not just another college program where one could get along just by going along. Husbands had to strive constantly to finish in barely a year a course that normally took three to complete. New wives should not expect weekends to be "a time of complete freedom" anymore. Moreover, husbands would "probably be difficult to live with" before exams, and especially before the comprehensive tests on each of the Naganuma volumes.[33]

The Fujin kai also promoted esprit and group identity by sponsoring three school dances during the first trimester at Boulder. They brought everyone together for a good time, not just married students and their spouses. Single men were encouraged to find dates with campus co-eds. Sensei—married and bachelor alike—came. At these dances, barriers of age, rank, and ethnicity fell away. One student gallantly danced with Captain Welch's wife when the NROTC commander declined to come out onto the dance floor. Everyone—even Miss Walne, the more conservative of the missionary teachers, and the shiest of sensei wives who hovered on the sidelines—enjoyed themselves.[34]

Social events such as school dances helped students deal with what might have become a major distraction from their studies—sex. Commander Hindmarsh persuaded the Navy to reverse its prewar policy of requiring naval language students in Japan to remain single. That and the supportive Fujin kai helped lessen sexual distractions for married students. But bachelors, especially those who had come from predominantly or exclusively male institutions, were surrounded by sexual temptations. Early in the fall, throngs of attractive young women students returned to a university stripped by war of their male peers. For a time, that created a social situation that seemed almost too good to be true for the bachelor students. Frank Mallory could hardly believe his good fortune in going from Stanford, where the ratio of men to women was nearly four to one, to Boulder, where the reverse was true. Within days of his arrival there, Hart Spiegel was playing tennis with the university president's daughter and enjoying her company far more than he had expected he would.[35]

The presence of so many beautiful and intelligent young women forced language students to make choices about priorities. Some made the Japanese language their mistress. One composed a ditty that humorously explained his behavior. It ran:

> One day upon the campus, I met a CU gal,
> She slapped me on the back with a hearty "Hiya, pal!"
> Into my fair white body she tried to sink her hooks;
> But I shot her full of *kanji*
> And returned to the goddamn books."[36]

But nearly one in ten of the class that came to Boulder in the summer of 1942 fell fast, head over heels, in love. Two of them realized they could not go on without the girl they left back home and brought her to Boulder to marry before the first trimester ended. Larry Thompson met a Wyoming rancher's pretty daughter on campus. He found it hard to focus on kanji and sentences for conversation class when her face kept popping up in his mind. But he and nearly a dozen other students decided to postpone their weddings until their first trimester at Boulder had ended.[37]

The vast majority found they could enjoy a rich but not permanently entangling social life and make progress in their language study at the same time. Some went drinking and sang with their friends at local watering holes. They mourned the fire that destroyed the Grotto, a bar that served real beer on the edge of town; found a replacement at Bill's Place; or went to the Anchorage, where only 3.2 brews were sold. Once they discovered Ashikaga sensei's fondness for real beer, they brought bottles of that precious commodity to him. Others preferred the attractions of the great outdoors. Horseback enthusiasts found it fun to take teachers—especially pretty half-Japanese Betty McKinnon, who had been pirated away from Harvard—on their rides. Arthur Dornheim and another student climber included two of their teachers in their attempt to "bag" a Colorado "fourteener." They camped on a Saturday night before topping Long's Peak, just a few miles north of Boulder, the next morning. All of the students found diversions in Denver, ranging from the art gallery to movie theaters and dancing venues during their brief weekend breaks from study.[38]

The students were insulated, for the most part, from developments in the war they were preparing to fight. They knew of the forced evacuation of Japanese Americans but did not yet, as they would much later, condemn that injustice. War news was like a passing cloud that only occasionally darkened their days. It came in bits and pieces by word of mouth or in letters rather than through major media reports. Sensei Willard Topping's aged father was first thought to be doing well in Japan, then died suddenly at Karuizawa, the summer resort where missionaries and other American civilians were interned. Parents and siblings who had stayed on in Japanese-occupied China were reported to be aboard a ship that would exchange internees. Wendell Furnas, who came to Boulder as a new student in October, told them about his capture and escape from the Japanese in Shanghai. From Guadalcanal, the father of one of the Harvard-trained students wrote of his experiences as a marine interpreter. But these hints of what was going on in the wider world seemed to have left few, if any, traces on the minds of the language students in the late summer and early fall of 1942.[39]

Instead, they focused on problems nearer at hand, especially the comprehensive examinations set for the end of their first trimester at Boulder.

They were certain to be more difficult than the weekly tests the students had endured. Anxiety levels rose, but so too did the language officer candidates' determination to succeed. Chuck Cross, for example, had despaired of ever learning Japanese, lamented his weak performances on earlier tests, and insisted that it was impossible to keep up with his fellow students. But by the eve of the comprehensive examination, his mental attitude had changed. He recognized the justice of removing poor performers from the program, struck his own balance between study and leisure time, and simply pushed ahead doing the best he could. Indeed, he came to share the outlook of some of the best students: The problem was not that they were being asked to learn too much Japanese too quickly but rather that they would leave knowing too little to succeed in their future duties as language officers.[40]

That mix of strengthened self-confidence, humility, and determination to succeed helped Cross and most of his classmates pass the fall comprehensive examinations. Only nine of them failed and were dismissed from the Boulder school. Indeed, even before the test results were known, the students determined to make the most of their first leave. Single men traveled as far as New York City or San Francisco while the married stayed in Boulder to enjoy free time with their spouses. And nine students were confident enough about the future to celebrate their weddings and enjoy brief honeymoons during the first real break in their language studies.[41]

TRIMESTER TWO: TURBULENCE

Students returned from leave early in November 1942 to a school on the cusp of dramatic changes. Over the next four months their numbers grew exponentially. More—and different—instructors came to teach them. The institutional Navy intruded on their lives, briefly heightening tensions between military and academic objectives. Their attitudes and those of the surrounding community toward the sensei shifted in ways that set them and their school even more apart from the passions of war that swept over the rest of American society.

Albert Hindmarsh—and the U.S. Army—were responsible for the rapid growth of the Boulder language school. By November 1942, Hindmarsh had persuaded his superiors in Washington that five hundred Japanese-language officers, in addition to those already training at Boulder, were needed. They would serve in what looked to be a long war with more and bigger operations.

He knew that the pool of qualified language students was limited, and competition for their talents intensified with every passing day. Only two students not of Japanese ancestry graduated from the Army's first school at the Presidio in San Francisco, and it relied primarily upon enlisted nisei for language work throughout the war. But in the fall of 1942, believing that Caucasian language officers were needed to keep enlisted Japanese Americans from mistranslating or deceiving their superiors, the Army began implementing plans to set up its own Japanese-language school for officer candidates at the University of Michigan. Albert Hindmarsh knew he faced stiffer competition for students when army officers started querying him about the instructional program at Boulder.[42]

Hindmarsh's second grand recruiting tour was thus a much more intense journey than the first. Wherever he and Glen Shaw went, they were besieged by applicants. Hindmarsh had scheduled 50 appointments at Yale, for example, but ended up talking with more than 250 young men eager to get into the Navy's Japanese-language program. Before the trip ended, Hindmarsh met dozens of deans and language teachers and nearly 1,600 applicants. When he and Shaw reached the University of Michigan, they got a double shock. First, it was evident that an army intensive Japanese-language school would soon become a reality there. Second, a telephone call from Washington informed him that he could no longer sign on new students as naval agents. Recent presidential proclamations on selective service would require incoming students to report to local recruiting stations for preinduction physicals and designation as yeoman, second class before going to Boulder.

Hindmarsh panicked at the possibility of uninformed naval corpsmen rejecting his recruits who did not need the perfect eyesight of a pilot or the physical strength of a Marine to become valuable linguists. Justifiably confused, new prospective students bombarded him with questions about the validity of the contracts they had just signed. All he could do was continue as before, and by the time he returned to Washington just before Christmas, he had chosen 302 new students. But Hindmarsh also lost 110 selectees, young men put off by doubts about the validity of the contracts they had just signed, to the Army. Chagrined but undaunted by that setback, he fought for and got administrative changes that allowed him to sign up prospective students as naval agents for a short term. Once at Boulder, they would be given conditional commissions as officers, valid only so long as their academic performance was satisfactory. Relieved at resolving that administrative difficulty, Albert Hindmarsh assured his superiors that there would be 500 new students at Boulder before Easter 1943.[43]

That prospect intensified Florence Walne's already serious concern about recruiting and retaining enough faculty to maintain the quality of the Boulder language program. Adding more than 150 language officer candidates in July 1942 had already changed the student–teacher ratio for the worse. At Berkeley, a dozen instructors had comfortably handled 41 students each. By the late summer at Boulder, two dozen were supposed to teach more than 200, and childless faculty wives were mobilized as part-time teaching aides. If, as Miss Walne confidently told students in September, the student numbers would more than double "until there is at least one [Japanese-speaking intelligence officer] . . . on board every ship in the Pacific Ocean," the faculty would have to grow correspondingly. That was essential if the key feature that sustained the program's quality—personalized learning in small classes taught by competent instructors—was to be maintained.[44]

Miss Walne knew that finding those teachers would be difficult. The very few Japanese-language instructors at major universities were swamped by students eager to learn a skill that might help them avoid the draft. Just as Edwin Reischauer had predicted in 1940, they were not willing to leave their permanent academic positions. Susumu Nakamura's hope of finding at least a dozen more faculty among the thirty-two hundred Japanese and Japanese Americans living in Colorado had yielded only three—that despite the fact that his advertisement for the positions said "no qualifications are necessary and educational history would not be considered."[45]

Walne herself had not fared much better back in August, when she recrossed the burning deserts of Utah and Nevada to the Manzanar and Tule Lake "relocation centers" in California. Only three sensei were chosen from among twenty interviewees at the ten-thousand-person camp on the dry eastern side of the Sierra Nevada, and it took months to pry them loose from the War Relocation Authority's clutches. A scant six more came from the even larger relocation center on a dry lakebed near the California–Oregon border.[46]

Thus when Miss Walne set off early in October 1942 for Amache, the better part of a day's drive distant from Boulder, her hopes were tinged with anxiety. More than seventy-five hundred stunned, embittered, and exhausted evacuees from southern and central California dwelt there in barracks planted on a square mile of "desolate prairie" ringed by barbed wire. Armed with tips from Susumu Nakamura and other faculty members and preceded by a recruitment ad in the camp newspaper, Florence Walne knew that these people were her best hope for new instructors. She identified twenty-eight of them in or near Amache and left hoping they would soon come to Boulder. But it was nearly Christmas before the first of them—less than 60 percent of the candidates she had selected—arrived. The rest had not survived the required FBI vetting required for persons on "indefinite leave" from relocation centers. Indeed, the second trimester had ended before Miss Walne had a full complement of eighty-eight instructors—enough to meet the Navy's mandate for a six to one student to faculty ratio at the language school.[47]

Who were the new arrivals? Why did they heed the call to become sensei at the Boulder school? And what difference would their presence there make? The new instructors differed in several ways from the original Berkeley sensei and from those who had joined them at Boulder. Out of seventy-one men and seventeen women, only a dozen, mostly missionaries or their wives plus a single Korean, were not of Japanese ancestry. They constituted barely an eighth, not a fourth, as at Berkeley, of the faculty. While a quarter of the California teachers had been born in Japan, the overwhelming majority of those who taught at Boulder during the first half of 1943 were native born Americans. They represented a much broader cross section of the mainland Japanese-American population because many came from Southern California, where Los Angeles County alone had been home to more than a quarter of all Japanese and Japanese Americans living in the continental United States.

The new faculty certainly included some of the "best and the brightest" of their generation. Several had college degrees. But unlike the Berkeley sensei, few had teaching experience or aspired to a career in higher education. Most came from the world of business and the professions. One was the first nisei to be hired by a major Japanese trading company. Another was a dentist, and three were doctors, including one of the first Japanese-born graduates of the Stanford Medical School. Two were journalists. The new faculty also included an architect, an attorney, a musician, and a doctor of divinity.

The newcomers were also more bicultural than the existing faculty. Many were *kibei*, or persons born in America who had gone to Japan for extended periods of education and then returned to the United States. Some *kibei* had even earned degrees from Japanese universities. They disliked that label, for the term took on pro-Japanese connotations immediately before and during the war. But their bicultural experience in Japan made them especially effective guides to its society as well as its language.[48]

Why were these people, who had suffered evacuation, incarceration, and dispossession at the hands of the U.S. government, willing to teach at a naval school? The newer faculty's motives for answering the call to Boulder varied wildly. Some had very immediate, personal reasons for doing so. They wanted to join friends or relatives on the core faculty. Others, such as Dr. Lee Watanabe who had fled California for the Midwest in vain hope of being able to continue his medical practice, needed a sensei's salary of a little more than two hundred dollars monthly to feed their families. Widower Suzuki Koshi, the father of three teenaged children, one of whom was nearing the age for college, knew that teaching at Boulder would be more profitable than make-work in a Utah desert relocation center. Some just wanted to escape the boredom of the camps. Lilian Inana thought life in Boulder would certainly be more interesting than the routine at the Minidoka relocation camp in Idaho. James Tsugio Ota longed to leave Poston, Arizona, to be with his girlfriend, Kay. Her family had established itself at Rocky Ford, Colorado, not far from Amache, and offered him the guaranteed employment needed for temporary release. Once there, he saved a little money, eloped with Kay, and then drove to Boulder where he convinced Susumu Nakamura to hire him.[49]

Others had more complex, political reasons for going to Boulder to teach. Japan-born Takekoshi Takeo was an enterprising community leader who wanted to demonstrate his Americanism. A graduate of New York University, he had headed the Southern California [Japanese] Businessman's Association and Exchange before evacuation and developed a thriving business supplying foodstuffs to internees thereafter. But he turned the business over to his wife, started teaching, and recruited other community leaders like himself to join the faculty. John Yumoto, who had left parents and relatives behind in Japan, felt he must cast his lot with the United States, regardless of the acts of its government. Fred M. Tayama went to Boulder to escape the wrath of other internees and to demonstrate his patriotism. Already a leader of the strongly pro-American Japanese American Citizens League, he called for Japanese Americans to be allowed to serve in the military and was nearly beaten to death by pro-Japanese men at Manzanar. After soldiers killed two inmates in the ensuing riot, he and his family had to be removed to a camp in Death Valley. For Tayama, teaching at Boulder was deliverance as well as a demonstration of patriotism.[50]

In other cases, a combination of motives convinced individuals that becoming sensei for the naval school was the best thing to do. Rayer Toki, a thirty-year-old son of Sacramento, California, was a case in point. His widowed mother had taken him to Yokohama, where he finished high school. But he yearned to return to the United States, where he worked his way through junior college and then earned a business degree at Berkeley. In March 1942 he was snatched from a promising job in international trade and thrown into converted stables and ramshackle barracks of the Santa Anita racetrack just east of Los Angeles. There he became a facilitator who helped others adjust to "assembly center" life. In the fall of 1942 he was cast into the harsh Utah desert at Topaz—a huge mountain-ringed camp about a hundred miles south and west of Salt Lake City. Even though the camp newspaper (and later historians) sarcastically proclaimed it "the jewel of the desert," Toki concluded that life there was "not as bad as I had expected." Rather than sullenly protesting, he thought Japanese Americans should "make the best of the situation" while hoping that "the whole insane nightmare" of war and internment would soon be "put forever behind us."[51]

But Toki was not willing to just wait passively for what the future might bring. Ignoring the possibility that American acts of war might harm his mother back in Japan, he wanted to demonstrate his patriotism. He tried and failed, according to family legend, to join the then racially exclusive Navy. He did not want to be drafted into the Army. Teaching at Boulder gave him a chance to serve his country and yield to the first stirrings of love. He had met beautiful young Akiko Nishioka at Santa Anita, but she won release from internment there to attend the University of Northern Colorado. Teaching at Boulder would put Rayer Toki much closer to his heart's desire.[52]

He and the other new instructors arrived at a critical moment in the school's history. Its creators and students, each in their own way, fended off an effort to make it more like the "regular" Navy. When the students' status shifted from naval agents to yeomen, second class, and soon to be intelligence officers, the senior naval officer at Boulder, Capt. Leo Welch, Annapolis class of 1906, decided that they should no longer be "taking it easy." From November 1942 on, they must follow a strict naval regimen, rising at 6:30 in the morning, drilling every weekday afternoon, putting lights out by 10:00 PM, and returning to campus by 6:00 on Sunday evenings. Captain Welch bawled out some students for dawdling over breakfast and instituted inspections of their dorm rooms. His chief "got snotty" about those that were not shipshape. Welch made matters worse by insisting that students get short haircuts so they would look like real naval men.

These changes contradicted Albert Hindmarsh's orders that "no distractions—no parades, no drills, [and] no extraneous military or naval subjects" be allowed to disturb the intensive teaching and learning of Japanese at Boulder. Miss Walne disliked the changes but wisely and temporarily acquiesced in them. Hard-pressed students like Chuck Cross complained that the new rules cut into study time and predicted that they would force teachers to slow down the course or students to go without sleep and get lower grades.[53]

Three dozen lucky students who lived in a former fraternity house barely felt the sting of Captain Welch's lash. They ruled their own lives beyond the classroom, confining a housemother to her room and the kitchen; playing pool in the basement; and stocking a larger refrigerator with *real* beer and hard liquor to enliven their weekend parties. But other students resisted. One particularly obstreperous young man who got extra garbage and head (lavatory) cleaning punishments was dismissed from the program. The more subtle objectors practiced passive resistance. Two students arose early, got fully dressed, turned off the lights, and sat down at their desks to await the morning inspection. They did not respond to a knock on their door, and when a chief burst in shouting, "Hit the deck!" expecting to find slug a beds, they jumped to attention. Truly savvy students eventually learned that even U.S. Navy chiefs were unlikely to enforce Sunday evening curfews.[54]

The controversy ended in mid-January 1943, when someone in Washington—probably Commander Hindmarsh armed with confidential reports from Florence Walne—engineered Captain Welch's departure. He was replaced by a more understanding former NROTC unit commander from the University of Southern California. His subordinate, Lt. G. K. Conover, irked the students with his martinet-like ways, but they refused to let him or the watered down remnants of traditional naval discipline seriously interfere with their academic or personal lives. Thus the Boulder school remained "the oddest naval organization anywhere."[55]

The arrival of so many new non-Caucasian instructors triggered a second, less easily resolved controversy. Their numbers threatened to disrupt the delicate balance between naval needs and popular anti-Japanese feelings that local and state leaders had struck. Back in the spring of 1942, Gov. Ralph L. Carr stood alone among noncoastal Western state governors in welcoming evacuees; he reminded his fellow Coloradans that it was their patriotic duty to do so. That summer University of Colorado president Robert Stearns worked hard to smooth the way for the arrival of Berkeley sensei and out-of-state Japanese-American students in Boulder. The city council welcomed the students but unanimously passed a resolution limiting the number of Japanese-American residents to no more than seventy-five individuals or twenty-five families, all of whom would have to be approved by the commandant of the Twelfth Naval District in San Francisco. But local officials did not rigidly enforce that rule, and they simply overlooked the fact that three teachers at the naval school were "enemy aliens," born in Japan.[56]

During the fall of 1942 and winter of 1943, community leaders and university officials kept trying to dampen anti-Japanese feeling. Governor Carr spoke out in defense of racial tolerance, an act that probably shattered his hopes of becoming a U.S. senator. The Colorado Council of Churches published *The Japanese in Our Midst*, a pamphlet that explained the ejection from the West Coast of Japanese and Japanese Americans and proclaimed their loyalty to America. President Stearns' administrative assistant persuaded the Boulder city council not to take any action even though the new sensei would include "enemy aliens" and would swell the town's Japanese-American population beyond the previous limits. Favorable articles about the Navy Japanese Language School that appeared in the local newspaper and in the *Christian Science Monitor* as well as an appeal by civic leaders for more housing for additional sensei may have influenced the council's decision.[57]

But then latent racial hatred reared its ugly head. The *Rocky Mountain News* headlined an article about Amache: "Japs Feast as Yanks Fast," and the *Denver Post* followed with articles that portrayed camp inmates as coddled and lazy. In Boulder, hostility toward Japanese and those associated with them surfaced in surprising places. Some members of the faculty wives' club objected when the university president's wife proposed inviting spouses of language school instructors to join the group; she just overruled them. When one of the missionary sensei brought some of the naval school's Japanese teachers to the local Presbyterian church, people got up and moved when the visitors sat down next to them, even though the pastor had said they would be welcome.[58]

The teachers, new and old, tried to deal with such anti-Japanese feelings as best they could. Only one dared speak out in defense of Japan's actions before the war. Several never lost the sense that they must be "very careful [and] always guarded" in and beyond the classroom. Many heeded President Stearns' advice to work in the local community to demonstrate their patriotism, even though a hospital patient screamed in terror at the very sight of a faculty wife volunteer. Most just suffered in silence the hostility that some local citizens showed them, picking up the garbage that hooligans hurled at their rented homes and counseling their children to ignore racial taunts at school.[59]

Ironically, prejudice outside the school enhanced cross-cultural understanding within it. Students found it easier to relate to the newest instructors because more of them were single, younger than the existing faculty, and only a few years older than they were. Seven were unmarried young women, one of whom—Grace Nakasone—was so attractive that students wanted to date her then and remembered her striking beauty decades later. One student even claimed his nisei teachers were more likeable than his fellow students. They also saw much more of the new instructors because anti-Japanese prejudice in town turned them into neighbors. Some married students lived in the same house as their teachers, and other new arrivals had to move into dorms with bachelor students. Such proximity created opportunities for informal student–teacher interaction that even Albert Hindmarsh had not imagined would be possible.[60]

That closeness prompted a reexamination of attitudes. When they first came to Boulder, students, like most Americans, were inclined to look upon ethnic Japanese as "Orientals," a people truly alien and inscrutable. Stereotypical remarks about their teachers' small stature punctuated their letters home. Even the highly intelligent Hart Spiegel described his instructors as "stranger every time you meet them, . . . polite to the point of sycophancy, [and] yet adamant as can be." Students did not look upon their teachers as victims of forced and unjust evacuation. But by the end of the second trimester, regular contact with their teachers in and beyond the classroom wiped away "any race theories" the students may have had. Their teachers became friends who bore little resemblance to the racial stereotypes of Japanese so prevalent in wartime American society. Thus Roger Marshall, who came from still-segregated North Carolina, became such fast friends with Johnny Satō that he took him home on leave. Marshall had his sensei sit on the couch while he proposed to his wife-to-be and made him a groomsman at his wedding back in Boulder.[61]

Actions such as that suggested that the naval language school had become, by the end of the second trimester, truly an island of understanding. Its denizens were not just learning the language and mores of the enemy. They were learning to look beyond the barriers of race and prejudice to see persons of Japanese ancestry as individual human beings not so very different from themselves.

TRIMESTER THREE: TRIUMPH

By the beginning of the third trimester in April 1943, that island of understanding had grown larger and life within it became extraordinarily intense. The number of students and teachers was now more than ten times the size of that of the first naval Japanese-language classes at Harvard and Berkeley.[62] Faculty and students were more determined than ever to meet and surmount the challenges that the Navy had put before them. Both had to work harder and harder toward their common goal: graduation for the largest group of language students yet.

For the faculty, especially the newest arrivals, that meant learning to teach more effectively. As Rayer Toki explained to his beloved Akiko, that was anything but easy. After completing a short training course by one of the missionary teachers, he and the other newcomers had to scramble to make sense of a syllabus that now included supplements to the Naganuma text prepared by the senior faculty. Toki spent so much time preparing for class and grading students' work that more often than not it was well after midnight when he wrote to Akiko. In a typical week, he taught for five hours and attended the evening Japanese movie on Mondays; spent three hours in the classroom on Tuesdays and then corrected exams until 11:00 PM; Wednesdays got up, taught another five hours, and studied until 1:00 AM on Thursday mornings. On Thursdays he taught for three hours and then worked into the night making up quiz questions. Fridays looked like Mondays but without the evening movie. And on Saturdays he had to proctor the morning-long weekly exams. Little wonder, then, that Toki felt that "we instructors are working so hard [that] everybody . . . is just about on the verge of nervous breakdown." Under "ordinary circumstances" he might have gone "insane" under such a heavy workload. But because "we're now in this total war and people are suffering all over the world, my work is nothing," he wrote.[63]

For the students, success still meant acquiring within a year competence in Japanese that their predecessors had acquired in three. They had to ignore everything that might keep them from doing so and work harder at an ever more torrid pace. They stopped griping, as they had in the depths of winter, about their new instructors' ineptitudes. They ceased complaining about changes in their individual schedules made necessary by the school's rapid but uneven growth. But Washington protested that their progress was too slow. Florence Walne called in those who appeared not to be working hard enough and warned them that their commissioning as language officers was not a foregone conclusion. The sensei demanded that those nearing graduation master a thousand characters in their next exam—and then concocted a test that was simply too difficult to finish in the allotted time. That left the students "nearly sick from exhaustion" but more determined than ever to succeed in becoming Japanese-language officers. They just gritted their teeth and pushed ahead.[64]

The intense and demanding schedule inevitably increased frictions within the school. Although most students got along with the others in their six-man groups, some "fairly hate[d] each other." One faculty member described his colleagues as "a very strange assortment of Japanese" and admitted that "some of them I just cannot stand." The students grew more and more competitive in and even beyond the classroom. One small group jousted with another for the privilege of lunchtime conversation—in Japanese—with one of the loveliest of the single female sensei. Pejorative terms—"sacker" for someone who studied in the sack (bed), and "throat-cutter," for someone who studied when you didn't—came to be bandied about. In May 1943 nerves got so frayed and tempers so short that virtually all of the students did poorly on a weekly exam. Their teachers even experienced "a little dissension of opinion" over how to grade it. One student got so mad that he "corner[ed a group of] sensei in the hall and berated them."[65]

Fortunately, such behavior proved the exception rather than the norm. Laughter in and beyond the classroom became a tool for defusing the tensions that arose. In class, joking was the preferred way of doing so. In preparation for the rough-and-tumble of military life, the students learned the word *konchikushō!* which meant "sonofabitch!" When one forgot it, another whispered to him that it meant "bombadier." The second student then asked another "*Anata wa konchikushō desu ka*," believing that he was asking if the young man was a bombardier. The savvier students burst into laughter, and the teacher, despite the fact that all of this came in the midst of a discussion of a simulated bombing of Tokyo, the capital of his family's homeland, "almost split a gut." Outside class, on one of the university stages, a group of student thespians put on a revised version of *The Mikado* that satirized the school. Everyone—students and teachers alike—left the performance smiling.[66]

When spring unfolded in all its glory, both found additional release beyond the campus. The older male teachers played and gambled at mahjongg. The mountains beckoned hikers and fishermen anew. Shōzō Fujii got soaked in an icy stream—but brought back six trout for his family's dinner table. The students started playing baseball again, and in April their younger teachers formed a team to challenge them. Even a very structured event—mass calisthenics in the university stadium that were part of the "CU Days" celebration—turned out to be fun. When the chief calling the cadence got nervous, counted wrong, and disrupted the would-be language officers' performance, they howled at themselves. For the single, movies and dates—beyond the compulsory Monday night Japanese film—provided much-needed relief. In May, Rayer Toki became engaged to Akiko Nishioka, occasioning a round of parties not unlike those that students who had found their mates-to-be in Boulder put on.[67]

By late June 1943 triumph for students and teachers alike was near. The would-be linguists who had come to Boulder in July 1942 sensed the end of their struggle. Suddenly they started studying and hearing about navies. The last of the Naganuma readers conquered, they struggled slowly through the *Kaigun tokuhon*, or Navy Reader, which senior sensei had devised to introduce them to the language of war at sea. Despite Albert Hindmarsh's previous prohibition, they attended lectures on naval and international history by visiting professors—one of whom was destined to become *the* expert on the Spanish Armada.[68]

The class that had entered the school in July 1942 was bused to Denver for precommissioning physical examinations that were both encouraging and worrisome. This second encounter with the "real" Navy put to rest lingering fears that some last-minute bureaucratic snafu might keep them from becoming officers. But some had worked so hard and felt so worn out that they were afraid they might not pass the physical. To quiet their fears, they joked that their collective physical attributes would not have added up to those of a single naval pilot. But Commander Hindmarsh's promised physical waivers, tricks, and panache got them through the ordeal. Short and skinny Chuck Cross stuffed himself with bananas and milk to pass. A skeptical naval corpsman thought Hart Spiegel was blind in one eye, but he retorted that he had a perfectly good other one. The examiner shot back, "I'm going to give you a waiver, and you can join the Marine Corps. But if a sea gull shits in your eye, don't you come back and blame me!" Not long after their physical "ordeal," commissions for all but nine of those who began the Japanese course the preceding July were issued from Washington.[69]

The completion of the physical exams set the stage for the last rites of passage through the Navy Japanese Language School at Boulder. The first was a semiformal dance on 3 July honoring the graduates-to-be. Everyone—students and their dates or wives, teachers and their spouses, Rayer Toki and his fiancée—turned out for it. Before the evening was out, all were jitterbugging to a jazzy tune. A student provided its words, which parodied those in the last lesson of the Naganuma reader titled "The Racetrack of Human Life." They proclaimed:

> Everybody's doin' the *kei-ba-jō* [racetrack]
> Now that we've finished with the *kokubō* [national defense]
> *Ichi, ni, san, shi* [One, two, three, four] here we go
> With a *jinsei no* [human life] and a *kei ba jō* [race track]

Sunday July 4th provided a day for recovery from the Saturday night revels as well as time to celebrate America's independence.[70]

Then students and teachers went to the last class, which they all longed for. Just like the first, it proved tough for all concerned. Takeo Okamoto had his class spend what seemed like an interminable four hours plowing through the last pages of the *Kaigun tokuhon* (Navy Reader). Jim McAlpine tried to ease the pain of getting through what was arguably the most difficult reading in the course by providing coffee for his students.[71]

Roger Pineau experienced an even more sobering final hour of instruction. His teacher had promised to give the students a sample of what to expect when they left school and went to war. He read from a Japanese newspaper for fifty-five minutes. The students "sat transfixed . . . , concentrating on every lightning syllable" their teacher spoke. Realizing they understood barely 10 to 15 percent of his words, their "concentration turned to perspiration . . . [and] growing apprehension." The instructor then "folded the paper, . . . wished us *gokigenyo* [good luck, and], said *sayonara*" as he walked out the door. The students sat there for some time, then rose and marched in silence like zombies out into the "fresh Colorado breeze."[72]

At that "sobering" moment, fellow student Hyman Kublin turned to Pineau and said, "Rog, I know just what I'd do if I was on a flagship and the admiral called for me to translate an enemy broadcast which sounded like that." "What would that be," Pineau asked. "I'd sit down before the radio speaker, listen intently for about 30 seconds, stand up, look the admiral square in the eye, and say, 'I'm sorry, sir, but the SOB has switched to Korean.'"[73]

That gutsy attitude probably helped some of the weaker students through the last ordeal of every academic course: the final examination. Its written portion focused on the battleship and the philosophy of life embraced by Mr. Watanabe. He was the character Naganuma Naoe had created to take users of his text from "This is a box" to far more sophisticated ideas. In his final remarks to the students, Watanabe offered counsel that they, at that moment in their lives, were only half prepared to accept: Life was a journey, not a destination, in which happiness was to be found along the way. For these bright, eager, highly competitive, and goal-oriented young men about to go off to war, that proposition probably did not seem entirely true. But when they passed their last exam at Boulder, they—and their teachers—were ready to savor the moment as Mr. Watanabe advised.[74]

Commencement came on Saturday morning 10 July 1943, when the whole school assembled in Mackey Auditorium for a "very solemn and colorful" ceremony. It opened, as most graduation ceremonies do, with a musical prelude, the singing of a patriotic song, and an invocation by the university chaplain. Miss Walne then introduced the graduates. But then the program diverged from the ordinary to demonstrate what the 142 graduates were about to become: Japanese linguists and naval officers. The program seesawed back and forth between Japanese and English in a manner that put one student's wife to sleep. The valedictorian, Lionel "Jim" Casson, amazed his peers with his fluency in the language of the enemy; Commander Hindmarsh provided relief for those who understood only some of what he said by speaking in English. Then Capt. Ellis M. Zacharias, the deputy director of the Office of Naval Intelligence (ONI) who had studied under Naganuma in prewar Japan, confounded many with a rapid-fire speech in Japanese that he then translated for the broader audience. The graduates and the rest of the student body mustered up enough courage to sing the far simpler Japanese words of the school song. The new senior naval officer at Boulder, Capt. F. H. Roberts, then charged the graduates to become good officers, and each came up on the stage to receive his certificate of completion from university president Robert L. Stearns.[75]

Captain Roberts then departed from the program to read to the crowd a certificate that recognized the faculty's contribution to the school's success: "American citizens of Japanese descent . . . [had] labored with outstanding faithfulness and diligence, despite conditions of racial unrest" so that the graduating students could complete a three-year course in twelve months. That made it possible to send to the fleet language officers who were "as important to the United States Navy and Marine Corps as guns, bombs, and torpedoes." Those words triggered a burst of applause. Henry Tatsumi then presented Captain Roberts and President Stearns with a resolution signed by all of the sensei. It thanked them for their efforts to eliminate "any and all incidents that might be directed against" the teachers and their families. The teachers vowed to "carry on to the utmost of our ability" to "hasten the day of complete victory for the United Nations." That brought the audience, cheering and clapping, to its feet.[76]

After that, things returned to normal. The chaplain gave a benediction, and all present sang "Star Spangled Banner." The graduates, now ensigns I-V(S) USNR or second lieutenants, USMCR, stood up, reached into their pockets for *kanji* cards used to cram for exams over the preceding year, tore them up, and tossed them into the air. For a moment they looked just like Naval Academy midshipmen who traditionally threw their covers into the air at graduation. Then the class of July 1943, 143 strong, filed out of the auditorium and walked through its great oak doors out into the brilliant sunshine of a Boulder summer's day.[77]

Those young men had met the challenge that Albert Hindmarsh, on the Navy's behalf, had put before them. They and their teachers had proven that Japanese could be taught and learned at a pace previously thought impossible. Together, students, faculty, and administrators during the Boulder language school's first twelve months had shown the way for all who would follow them over the next three years.

TRANSFORMATIONS

Over the next two years, hundreds more students completed their language training at Boulder, and nine graduation ceremonies followed. For the next year, those occasions resembled the July 1943 festivities. Although the first two were small, with no more than thirty graduates each, each of the three that followed sent more than one hundred new Japanese-language officers off to war. All of these later graduates were white males, mostly in their twenties, who had come to Boulder with college or postgraduate degrees. More than 40 percent came from the Northeast, one-third hailed from the West Coast, and only a handful came from the South. Commander Hindmarsh and the teachers took great pride in the fact that nearly 90 percent of the young men who came to Boulder in these classes left as commissioned language officers.[78]

From the fall of 1944 onward, however, graduating classes included women and foreigners as well as white males. In July 1943 the first of three groups of women, eighty-nine in all, came to the language school. Albert Hindmarsh persuaded his superiors—and Capt. Mildred McAfee, commander of the newly created WAVES (women accepted for volunteer emergency service)—that they could be trained for duty in the continental United States to free up more male Boulder graduates for service overseas. He recruited the women much as he had their male predecessors. He placed a call for female volunteers in the newsletter of the national liberal arts honor society Phi Beta Kappa. He made a whirlwind national recruiting tour early in July 1943 and accepted only one out of every six interviewees for the Boulder program. Nearly a third of them came from West Coast states, more than one-quarter were Phi Beta Kappas, and 75 percent were in their early twenties. Hindmarsh chose well, for despite more health problems (and two pregnancies) than men, 90 percent of the women he selected graduated from the Navy Japanese Language School.[79]

The women brought new energy, fresh brainpower, and determination to equal or best any man in the Boulder program. But in keeping with the social mores at America's most elite colleges and universities in those days, they were taught in separate classes and lived under closer supervision than male students. They resided in three former fraternity houses where two WAVES, one a former chairman of the English department at Texas Christian University and the other a onetime Houston elementary schoolteacher, functioned as house mothers. Lt. (jg) Rebecca Smith, the WAVE officer-in-charge of the women students, apparently thought it her duty to protect them from members of the opposite sex. She blamed fraternity boys' eating habits for the plethora of rodents that the women found in their bedrooms. She let them keep "Heidi," a huge Saint Bernard that came with one of the houses. The dog accompanied them wherever they went. A collie named "Nami" ("wave" in Japanese) was also acquired to shuttle back and forth between the two other houses as pet and protector. Lieutenant Smith relented just a bit and let photos of handsome Byron "Whizzer" White, then a University of Colorado football star and later a Supreme Court justice, stay on the walls of the former Phi Delta house.[80]

The women also lived under more direct naval discipline than the men. Lieutenant Smith and (eventually) three other WAVE officers saw to it that they kept their rooms "shipshape." They were commissioned (in a series of low-key ceremonies in a dingy dormitory basement) only two months after arriving in Boulder, and they wore uniforms to class. They endured having a male ensign supervise their required physical exercise. His zeal to save them from drowning when their ships went down in enemy waters, a highly unlikely event since they were limited to shore duty in the continental United States, resulted in life-saving drills and mock fights in the water that sometimes got out of hand. The women students had to march in parade on ceremonial occasions far more frequently than their male counterparts—presumably to show that they were fully a part of the war effort. They did not particularly like drill but accepted it as part of their duty. Eventually they acknowledged that it "made us feel like we were really part of the Navy."[81]

The WAVEs developed positive relationships with their teachers more quickly than male students did. To some degree, that was only natural. At least one sensei admitted that the women were much more fun to be with than the men. They seemed brighter, were more eager to speak in Japanese, and—for the bachelor male sensei—looked much prettier. Sometimes the teachers took the initiative in starting a friendship. Paul Aiso, "a nervous little man who was obviously . . . worried about doing a good job" went so far as to go to the Phi Delta house one night to "clarify a grammar point" that Mary Jane Konnold had struggled with in class. When she met him at the door with Heidi, the teacher tipped his hat and said "How do you do, madam" to the dog. That act and his willingness to let Heidi come to class endeared him to Ensign Konnold.[82]

At other times, adversity brought the WAVE students and faculty closer together. After a week of classes, Irene Slaninka informed Miss Walne that she could not understand her instructor's limited English and was going to leave the school. The director kindly told her, "You'll regret it for the rest of your life if you quit" and assigned her a tutor who spoke better English. Miss Slaninka stayed on and befriended the tutor. On another occasion, some of the very best women students "went to pieces" and did poorly when Ashikaga sensei challenged them with a conversation exam twice the normal length. One of the female examiners later burst into tears over the incident and told Susumu Nakamura what had happened. He in turn invited the WAVEs to his home and reassured them that they could succeed.[83]

Before long the women and their teachers came to really enjoy one another's company. The students became dinner guests and participants in their teachers' family celebrations. They reciprocated by inviting sensei to a "Hell" party in which roles were reversed. They donned caps and gowns and asked the teachers funny or unanswerable questions. One instructor feigned nervousness and confusion and stuttered when he answered. Another made puns on the Japanese words the students used. All howled at a mock interrogation skit in which the pretend Boulder graduate spoke only "a jumble of sentences" and reported to her superior using words that completely changed what the prisoner she had interrogated really said. Such good-natured interaction blossomed into better understanding and genuine friendship between female students and their instructors. By graduation time, one of the teachers was giving poems in his calligrapher's hand to the departing WAVEs.[84]

The women, just as the men before them, found they needed diversions without which life at Boulder "would have been intolerable." One young woman vented her frustration with kanji and *kaiwa* (conversation in Japanese) by shouting that she was going to join the kamikaze corps. Another tried to relieve tensions from a hard week of language study by prancing around shaking her long tresses in imitation of the famous Lion Dance performed in Kabuki. Ruth Sigerson transformed herself from a "pale bookworm" into a "lover of the great outdoors" by going hiking, horseback riding, and ice-skating. And, of course, with five times as many men than women in the school, the WAVES dated. Men could visit the women's residences for only one hour nightly during the week, but the women were free to go out. On one triple date, two of the three WAVES met their future husbands. Eventually ten "Boulder girls"—more than one of every eight female graduates—married "Boulder boys." Little wonder, then, that the women students looked back on their time at the Navy Japanese Language School as "hard, good, bad, and unforgettable."[85]

In October 1943, five officers, the first of an eventual fifteen who served the British king, arrived in Boulder. With their different accents and uniforms, they added a note of the exotic to the language school. They also brought a whiff of the war to the island of understanding. All of the Britons were Royal Naval Volunteer (Reserve) officers who were required to serve afloat as enlisted men before going to officer candidate school. They had experienced war at sea directly. William Beasley, for example, after serving on a destroyer that escorted the cruiser carrying Winston Churchill to the first summit meeting with Franklin D. Roosevelt in August 1941, participated in the sinking of the *Bismarck.* Another destroyer man turned student had barely escaped death when the Japanese sunk HMS *Prince of Wales* off the coast of Malaya two days after the Pearl Harbor attack.[86]

These foreign students treasured their time at Boulder and readily fit in with the other students. For them it was "a moment of . . . life taken out of context" in which they were unworried by the demanding pace and different norms of the language school. Although they studied in separate small classes, the Britons—and a single Canadian—quickly adjusted to the patterns of life at Boulder. They studied hard, ate and drank with their sensei, and formed lasting friendships with their fellow students. One of them eventually took a Boulder WAVE as his bride.[87]

In April 1944, however, one of these exotics provoked another crisis in the never-ending struggle between the naval and the academic at Boulder. The much-maligned Lt. G. K. Conover favored the clean-shaven look then prevalent in the U.S. Navy and ordered Lt. John Catt to shave off his beard. Catt's whiskers supposedly made him too conspicuous—and a security risk—in a town in which everyone knew naval officers studying Japanese were present. Catt refused to remove the offending facial hair. Conover hinted he might refer the issue to Washington, but the senior British student officer quickly contacted his superiors there, and they, after consulting with the Navy Department, approved his plan to silence Conover. The senior Briton at Boulder told him that a Royal Navy officer had to get permission to change the image that appeared on his identity papers. Such a change simply could not be made in Boulder. That bureaucratic argument laid the matter to rest. Lieutenant Catt smiled behind a full beard on his graduation day at Boulder.[88]

That resolution of the Catt's whiskers affair reflected Albert Hindmarsh's determination not to let anything or anyone at Boulder or in Washington interfere with the school and his students. As the years passed, he became their evermore resilient and resourceful manager and protector. In the spring of 1943 he was tough, but that fall he yielded to faculty complaints that a year was not enough time to produce practical linguistic competence and extended the course to fourteen months for future graduates. That provided time for more specialized naval readings, an introduction to Japan's geography, and a week of naval indoctrination just before graduation.[89]

When three students cheated on exams in the fall of 1943, Hindmarsh had Miss Walne call an assembly to discuss the problem and then threw them out of the school. There was no school Christmas party that year because students took exams on Christmas Eve. He infiltrated ONI agents into the school to see that students' sexual behavior and political opinions did not get out of line. In April 1944 he reinstated the rule that all language students live on campus. That imposed a particular hardship on married students, but it guaranteed that all of the students could hear Japanese radio programs rebroadcast there. And when participation in amateur theatricals appeared to lower test scores, he banished students from the stage.[90]

That mix of toughness and understanding helped Commander Hindmarsh steer the school through crises in 1944 toward triumph in 1945. At first he suffered apparent defeat. The Bureau of Naval Personnel tried for a second time to cut the number of commissions for specialized officers such as the Japanese linguists. That temporarily suspended recruitment of new students and, worse still, required Hindmarsh to order Florence Walne to cut the size of her faculty. She did so with tact, compassion, and a very heavy heart. But such action, coming on the heels of renaming the program the Navy School of Oriental Languages and adding sixty-eight instructors in Russian, Chinese, and Malay sent waves of anxiety through the Japanese faculty.[91]

Then Florence Walne left Boulder. In June 1944 she sought and got ninety days' leave—much needed after five years of uninterrupted work for the Navy. By September she knew she must step down as the school's director and return to Berkeley. Precisely why she did so remains shrouded in mystery. Maybe the altitude at Boulder strained her heart. Perhaps the shots of whiskey she was known to down frequently—despite her Baptist missionary heritage—got the best of her. Maybe she felt overwhelmed by the difficulties of caring for her aged mother or was herself weakened by what was then euphemistically termed "the change of life." Or perhaps she just did not feel she could effectively manage a multilingual faculty after having dismissed some of the Japanese instructors she had worked so hard to get.[92]

Whatever the reason, Walne departed Boulder in a blaze of glory. She had been promoted to full professor at the University of Colorado. On 15 September 1944 she delivered her farewell speech to assembled students and faculty, challenging them to do their best under a new director: Albert Hindmarsh's longtime assistant and Colorado College graduate, Glenn Shaw. University officials lamented her departure and heaped praise upon her. She had risen to the challenge the Navy put before her, managing a program that produced linguistically competent officers in unprecedented time. Then, amidst a standing ovation from the audience, Florence Walne left the school she had done so much to create and sustain.[93]

Barely ninety days later, Commander Hindmarsh scored his triumph, bringing about a change in the language school no one would have imagined when it came to Boulder nearly three years earlier. In December 1944 he visited naval military government, communications, and intelligence officers in Washington, eliciting their estimates of future Japanese-language officer needs. In January and February 1945 he did the same at Pearl Harbor, getting confirmation and expansion of those projections from the fleet. That enabled him to launch a new student recruitment effort from within the Navy and, even more importantly, to secure authorization to establish a second unit of the language school on the campus of Oklahoma A&M College in Stillwater, Oklahoma.[94]

Planting the new language school in a dry college town whose citizens' anti-Japanese prejudices were even stronger than those in Colorado demanded leadership of the highest order. Hindmarsh found it in the Boulder faculty. Glenn Shaw stayed at the main campus but served as adviser to the satellite school. A naval war hero who had previously served on a college campus became its senior officer-in-charge. Shaw dispatched former missionary James McAlpine to direct the new school and disabuse the Oklahomans of their fear and distaste for the Japanese-American staff. Susumu Nakamura named John Yumoto and Rayer Toki as head teachers, and they in turn convinced reluctant colleagues to leave Boulder for a "cow town" that welcomed visitors with a sign proclaiming "Alcohol is the end-all of humanity."[95]

The new school flourished in Stillwater's barren soil. In June 1945 its faculty set out across the high plains for Oklahoma with 116 grumbling pioneer students in tow. By the time they arrived, Albert Hindmarsh had received authorization to recruit an additional 800 navy Japanese-language students; 7 out of every 8 of them were destined for Stillwater. The satellite school there became an islet of linguistic and racial understanding that replicated Boulder's successes. Despite teetotaling locals who chased students and disposed of whatever booze they might have, the would-be linguists and their teachers were so devoted to their respective duties that the school continued to produce graduates until nine months after Japan surrendered. Nearly 500 men enrolled there, and 112 of the migrants from Boulder completed the program at Stillwater. That achievement attested to the soundness of the program that Albert Hindmarsh, Florence Walne, and their devoted faculty had created in—and beyond—Boulder.[96]

ACHIEVEMENT

Why, in the end, did the builders of Boulder and their students achieve that success? Individual determination, patriotism, and shared devotion to duty combined to produce that result. But something else was needed to bring about the unprecedented marriage of the Navy and academia, the emergence of an exemplary language instruction program, and the creation of an island—and then an islet—of cross-cultural understanding at Boulder and Stillwater. Something else was needed to make students and faculty feel that the time they spent there was a magic moment in their lives—"hard, good, bad, and unforgettable," as one WAVE had put it. Rayer Toki put his finger on it when he said, "Learning the language of one's enemy is not merely an immediate military necessity, but it's the best media by which one can understand the mental state of his enemy—and build a better world later."Without such idealism, the island of understanding at Boulder, and at its Stillwater islet, would have vanished into the sea of wartime passions and prejudices.[97]

The young men and women who departed from it had been transformed into fledgling naval and marine officers of a very special sort. They left Boulder proud of their success in learning the language of the enemy but humble in their awareness of what they did not know about it. They departed with more maturity, an enhanced sense of self-confidence, and undiminished determination to succeed. But most importantly, they carried away a warm feeling for their instructors as fellow human beings that set them apart from those who saw only an inhuman alien enemy in a Japanese face. That nascent cross-cultural understanding, no less than the linguistic skills they had gained, would serve them well in meeting the challenges of war that lay ahead.

Chapter Three

MARINE COMBAT INTERPRETERS

On 10 July 1943 as they stepped out of Mackey Auditorium into the brilliance of a Colorado summer's day, the language school graduates began their journey from Boulder to war. At that moment, their chests swelled with pride, filling out their unadorned new uniforms. In the eyes of their teachers, their sweethearts, and their relatives, they were academic heroes who had every reason to march jauntily and confidently into the future.

But in the eyes of their graduation speaker, ONI Deputy Director Cdr. Ellis Zacharias, who along with Arthur McCollum and Albert Hindmarsh was responsible for their having come to Boulder, the uniforms hung loose on these young men. They were, at best, half full, half empty vessels. Yes, the "Boulder boys" as they would come to be called, had crammed an incredible amount of Japanese into their skulls in an unprecedentedly short period. Yes, they were men of good character who should make fine officers. But, as Arthur McCollum could attest, they knew Japanese in general and would have to rely on a stack of dictionaries to help them in their new duty stations. They had no military experience and only a tiny military and naval vocabulary. "Naval intelligence" for them—unlike professionals who had devoted their careers to it—was just a phrase. Would they in fact prove successful as linguists and intelligence officers?

Twenty-five months later, on 15 August 1945, these young men would be scattered from Washington, D.C., to Pearl Harbor, and to Australia and the islands of the Pacific. The uniforms they wore that day would no longer be pristine but stained by sweat and ink. The Boulder boys would have matured into competent, innovative, and well-respected specialist officers who made important contributions to the winning of the war. No one would doubt that the pride and joy that swelled their chests on that day were well deserved.

How did that transformation in these young men and in the eyes of those who beheld them occur? There is, of course, no single answer that will fit every individual, but certain commonalities and patterns in their wartime experience emerge. Marine and naval Japanese-language officers both sought to do valuable language and intelligence work that would hasten the end of the war. But they pursued that goal in varied ways that were rooted in the mission, particular experiences, and specific subcultures of their respective services. Those who wore marine khaki confronted, captured, and quizzed Japanese soldiers amid the horrors of combat. They saw the enemy face to face and learned directly from him. Those who wore navy blue learned about the foe indirectly—intercepting and recovering information from his radio messages, translating documents he left behind on the battlefield, and only rarely prying tidbits out of those unfortunates who became prisoners of war. The obstacles they encountered in pursuit of their common goal, the environments in which they confronted those challenges, and the means by which they tried to overcome them were quite distinct.

Thus their paths from school to war must be examined separately. Although the Marines were a decided minority among naval Japanese-language school graduates, their story must be told first. They were the first to see significant numbers of the enemy face to face. They encountered him in battle, which made all the difference in the world in the way in which they themselves grew into and shaped the role of the combat language officer.

SPECIAL MARINES

On 10 July 1943, forty-three of the naval Japanese-language school graduates—nearly a third of this class, and the largest number of any in the nine classes that followed—wore marine khaki rather than navy blue. They were about to enter a new and still more difficult course than that they had just completed. They faced the daunting task of turning their textbook knowledge of Japanese into practical communication skills. They were going to become combat linguists—men who fought to capture and interrogate prisoners of war, scavenge the enemy dead, and find and translate documents the fleeing foe left behind. They were pioneers, men whose experiences encapsulated those of the other 101 language school graduates who later joined the Corps.[1] These men were going to become a new kind of Marine—one that fought alongside the Old Breed of the Marine Corps from the islands of the South Pacific to the insular approaches of Japan itself.

How did Boulder Marines help change the way marine intelligence operated in combat? What difference did they make in the way Marines fought and in the outcomes of the battles they survived? And how were these young men themselves transformed by becoming combat linguists? Any answer to those questions must begin by recognizing how very special these young men were. Like all Marines who joined the Corps before December 1943, they were volunteers. Indeed, they were a special, self-selected group of volunteers. But why did these language students choose to join the armed service most likely to put them in close, kill-or-be-killed combat with Japanese?

While no single answer to that question is valid for all of these Boulder marine volunteers, three common themes recur in their responses to it. First, they had a preexisting positive image of the Corps. Those who had lived in China remembered the glamorous "horse Marines" who protected foreigners and their properties and paraded in resplendent uniforms. Those who had grown up in America had seen marine heroes worthy of emulation in the movies and on recruiting posters. Still others wanted to join the heroic, single-minded fighting organization depicted in the best-seller that became the movie *Guadalcanal Diary*.[2]

Second, these young men shared individual character traits. Most of them were, by their own accounts, "macho jocks." More than others at the Boulder school, they liked the rough-and-tumble of sports and delighted in "playing the field" of plentiful co-eds. They were also risk-takers, young men who wanted to experience the war firsthand rather than command an LMD (large mahogany desk) as a translator or codebreaker in Washington, D.C., or Pearl Harbor.[3]

Finally, these young men had bonded through shared living experiences at Boulder in ways that pulled them collectively into the Corps. Thirty-five of them took over a vacated fraternity house where, in their hours together outside the classroom, they sized up one another's characters, saw each other's strengths and foibles, and pinned nicknames on everyone. These young men took charge of their collective lives by firmly, if not politely, relegating the fraternity housemother to her own room and the kitchen. They repeatedly tested each other's reactions to risk—in preparing (or not) for exams; in countless practical jokes; on the playing field; and in late-night escapades that pushed the limits of the acceptable. Thus, by the time graduation approached, they knew one another so well that they were willing to do what every Marine in combat must: entrust his life to his fellow Marines. These young men were so confident of their ability to detect that character trait in others that they recruited eight other students who did not live with them to volunteer for the Corps.[4]

The first Boulder Marines also represented a significant shift in the Corps' approach to getting competent Japanese linguists in adequate numbers. Before dispatching an officer from Washington in the spring of 1943 to recruit them, the marine leadership tried to acquire Japanese speakers in two self-reliant ways, neither of which had proven entirely satisfactory. The first was to commission directly the extremely few men who had, or who could be expected to develop quickly, Japanese-language competence. In January 1941, John R. Shively, a Columbia University graduate student who had been born and raised by his missionary parents in Japan, accepted a commission in the Corps. For the next five months he traveled around the country in search of young men who, by virtue of birth or long residence in Japan or significant study of its language and culture at the university level, seemed to be promising marine Japanese-language officer candidates. By July 1941, when Washington set the clock ticking toward war by embargoing oil and gasoline sales to Japan, he had found a dozen. Anxious to obtain their talents, the Corps took them in—waiving physical requirements, dropping the requirement that language students be bachelors, and minimizing their military training.[5]

These young men then sailed to Honolulu, where they began a six-month "refresher" Japanese-language course at the University of Hawaii. Shively had chosen that institution, where he himself had previously studied, because Japanese speakers were plentiful there. The students attended classes Monday through Friday and were taught by two professors and a Buddhist priest. Two of their instructors were *kibei.* In the classroom, the students concentrated on learning as much military Japanese as quickly as possible, using Japanese army field manuals as texts. Outside it, they honed their conversational skills by attending Japanese-language movies that included newsreels of the ongoing war in China. Hoping to become truly fluent, one student moved into a Japanese-run hotel that was later discovered to have been a nest of spies.[6]

Even before the attack on Pearl Harbor cut this program short, however, it was plagued by problems. Some students found the instruction disorganized and ad hoc. Others were alienated by the transfer of their born-in-Japan colleagues, whose reading and translation skills lagged far behind their conversational abilities, to Florence Walne's program at Berkeley. Still others were deeply suspicious of their Japanese-American instructors, so much so that they contacted the local naval intelligence office about one of them. The man turned up on the Navy's suspects list—and the register of FBI informants. By December 1941 only eight students remained in this program, and when the Japanese attacked, they scattered to various emergency military duties in Honolulu before their training was completed. "We were," one of them recalled, "the guinea pigs in a hopelessly confused experiment."[7]

The Marines' second approach was to teach Japanese themselves in field schools. The first of these was established within the newly formed 2nd Marine Regiment, which in January 1942 rushed from San Diego to defend American Samoa against possible Japanese attack. Maj. Ferdinand W. Bishop, a forty-ish scholarly veteran of two years' language study in prewar Japan, headed the school and was its only teacher. His students, enlisted and officer alike, were a mixed lot with only some prior foreign language study or occasional contact with Japanese Americans. They studied day and night, huddled in palm-thatched huts while the sun shone or gathered around campfires under the moon. Theirs was a marine field school par excellence.

Bishop struggled with indifferent success to give this eclectic group of students the intensive language training they needed. He got them separated from their regular units so they were better able to study. He had them use the same Naganuma text that he brought back from Japan and that Boulder students struggled through. Bishop had the men work with military dictionaries to learn the language of war. He gave them vocabulary tests every day. And in an effort to improve their conversational skills, he sought out and pressed the Japanese owner of a small store on the island to speak to the class. Unfortunately, the old man, who had left Japan thirty years earlier, had forgotten most of his native tongue. Only half of the students at this rough-and-ready six months' introduction to the Japanese language completed the course before the demands of war took them off to combat duties.[8]

Two graduates of the Hawaii marine Japanese-language program, Paul Dull and John Merrill, joined University of Oregon professor Harold J. Noble, the son of missionaries to Korea, as founding fathers of the Corps' second field language school. It was established in July 1942 at Camp Elliott, near San Diego. Dull taught reading and Merrill taught conversation in a "rush" course originally intended to last for three months that was subsequently extended to six. Their aim was to give enlisted men, who had been chosen on the basis of high IQ scores, basic knowledge of Japanese. The students were expected to master five hundred kanji and both of the kana scripts used to write Japanese. They were taught how to use a Japanese dictionary and expected to build a basic vocabulary of fifteen hundred spoken words. This foundation was supposed to enable the graduates to read Japanese field orders and maps and to serve as competent combat prisoner of war interrogators.[9]

A plague of difficulties beset this program, however. Combat duty called Merrill and the school's senior officer away. Dull suffered from recurrent illnesses that hindered his effectiveness. The texts used were improvisations. Dull scrambled to get copies of a handbook of Japanese field orders and supplementary materials development at the Army's Military Intelligence Service Language School at Camp Savage, Minnesota. No native Japanese speakers served as instructors, and frictions developed within the small teaching staff when untrained marine regulars took on instructional duties. The teachers had to beg from unsympathetic unit commanders for their students to be freed from regular marine duties so they would have study time.[10]

This field school did survive in modified form and at another location (Camp LeJeune, North Carolina). Indeed, Robert S. Kinsman, one of the July 1943 Boulder Marines, served as an instructor there when the war ended. But from the very beginning, the mission and competency of the field school were limited. It taught only the rudiments of Japanese to enlisted men who were thought to need only limited linguistic skills for a very particular function. The students were to be the first point of contact with enemy prisoners whom they would screen and pass on to more thoroughly trained officers for "real" interrogation.[11] By the spring of 1943, marine leaders in Washington apparently decided that this school, despite its staff and students' hard work, simply could not produce the more comprehensive Japanese-language competence that the Corps required. Men who had that kind of linguistic capability would have to come from the naval school at Boulder.

But the graduates of the Boulder school presented a problem. Every man who came into the Corps was expected to be a Marine, capable of fighting alongside the men of the unit to which he was assigned. Marines were soldiers who could fight as infantrymen first, specialists second. Normally they first proved themselves in basic training and then went on to a specialized school. But the young men who left Boulder as marine second lieutenants in July 1943 reversed that pattern. They had plenty of Japanese-language study but only minimal exposure to the vocabulary of their prospective foes, the Imperial Japanese Army and Navy. Worse still, they had none of the military training, infantryman's skills, or leadership indoctrination that a freshly minted marine second lieutenant was expected to possess.

In an effort to remedy the first and, from a marine perspective, more serious of these deficiencies, Washington ordered all of these inexperienced new officers to a shortened basic training program at Green's Farm, located within what was to become Camp Pendleton, just north of San Diego, California. There, mercifully shielded from the eyes of their peers-to-be, ordinary marine second lieutenants, they hurried through basic training in a rugged, hot, and hilly terrain shared with men in scout and sniper training. The contrast to life at Boulder was startling. They had to get up early and do physical exercise before breakfast, which appeared as "a strange series of contradictions" in which potatoes came first, coffee last. They heard slurs against women and African Americans that not even the rowdiest of their college classmates would have uttered. They had to clean their quarters—in a barn—and then go to classes in basics such as map reading, sanitation, and military life that struck them as necessary but boring. In the afternoon they went off to the drill field to learn how give and carry out commands as well as how to relate to gunnery sergeants "as tough as the back end of an over-all tractor." Over time, they toughened up on ten-mile hikes carrying packs and guns that they learned to fire and care for properly. Eventually they practiced small infantry tactics in ways that taught them to distinguish between their own and Japanese machine-gun fire.[12]

The Boulder Marines also learned, formally and informally, how to be officers. They were introduced to the traditions and organization of the Corps and picked up such pithy leadership maxims as "Marines are like a string of spaghetti; they cannot be pushed from behind, but can always be led from in front." They learned the fine points of making the military postal system work to their advantage. One officer wrote his parents detailed instructions on how to mail a vital item, a jockstrap, never in stock at base exchanges, so it would reach him right at Green's Farm rather than the distant Camp Elliott post office. And, of course, these young officers, flush with more cash that many had ever had before, quickly developed the skill of making the most of weekend liberty, finding the prettiest girls and taking them to the beach at La Jolla or dances in San Diego hotels.[13]

They also got a last chance to learn some military Japanese before joining the units in which they would fight. For some, that opportunity was nothing more than a few sessions at the Camp Elliott Japanese school that did not prove very helpful. After the skilled and stimulating instruction he had received at Boulder, one new second lieutenant complained that the teaching there was as uninspiring as the instructor's name, Capt. Paul Dull. A lucky dozen, those who would go to the still-forming 4th Marine Division, were shipped off to Camp Savage, Minnesota, for a "cram course" in Japanese military documents taught at the Army Military Intelligence Language School. John Rich looked back on that as the very best, most useful language training he got. Chuck Cross remembered his sojourn there more for what it taught about the limits of rank. A fledgling second lieutenant should overlook slight offenses, such as nisei enlisted men from Hawaii and California occasionally missing roll call because they were out scrounging wood to keep their National Guard huts warm. And he had to acknowledge that his charges were "infinitely superior to us in Japanese."[14]

By the hundredth day after their graduation from Boulder, all of the marine officers in the class of July 1943 were at sea, headed for units and places as yet unknown to them. They may not have been truly ready for combat, but the box of books and dictionaries they had carried away from Boulder and stored in their gear and the marine training they had just completed made them feel that they could cope with whatever lay ahead. Their self-confidence had grown, and their spirits were high. As one of these green second lieutenants crowed to his parents, "I'm too valuable for the Marine Corps to risk—and I feel very lucky."[15] He, and indeed all of the Boulder Marines heading west across the Pacific, would need that luck to survive and succeed as officers and combat linguists.

ON-THE-JOB TRAINING

The freshly minted Boulder Japanese-language officers joined their respective units at a critical moment in the development of Marine Corps intelligence.

Marine Corps Headquarters knew that they were desperately needed. The best of the very few prewar marine Japanese-language officers had put their talents to work in radio intercept and cryptographic work for the Navy. Only three of them are known to have seen combat in the first year of the war. Planners had devised a general scheme for distribution of the young and inexperienced Boulder language officers. As the Corps expanded from a collection of regiments in January 1942 to four full divisions by late 1943, the notion had taken root that two language officers each should be assigned to a division headquarters staff and two to each of three regimental staffs. The Marines had also developed, based on their experience in the "banana wars" in the Caribbean earlier in the century, operational guidelines for the incarceration and interrogation of prisoners of war. Language officer interrogators were supposed to bombard captives with rapid-fire questions to cause the foe to inadvertently spit out the particular information desired.[16] But in the wake of the Marines' first sustained encounter with the Japanese, particularly the series of struggles in and around the island of Guadalcanal in the Solomon Islands, these notions as to how and where language officers should be used and what they should do appeared outdated and inadequate.

That was the conclusion that one of the first and most remarkable marine combat interpreters drew from his experiences during the Guadalcanal campaign. Sherwood F. Moran, whose son was a student at the Boulder language school, was a fifty-six-year-old missionary who had first gone to Japan in 1916. He had volunteered for the Corps in the belief that his linguistic talents should be used to help defeat the Japanese thereby purging them of any faith in extreme nationalism and militarism.[17] On 12 August 1942, less than a week after the Marines landed on Guadalcanal, Moran and the Marines learned a bitter lesson: the tip of the spear was not necessarily the best place to put interpreters. On that evening, Moran's fellow interpreter, Lt. Ralph Cory, a forty-five-year-old State Department Japan hand and sometime codebreaker who had volunteered to serve in the Marines, set out on patrol with twenty-three other men under the division intelligence chief, Lt. Col. Frank B. Goettge. During their night landing they were instantly ambushed by the Japanese. Lieutenant Cory was not among the three survivors of this operation.[18]

Cory's death along with the subsequent departures of a Korean Marine thought to be untrustworthy and another Marine who was deemed incompetent—the son of an American businessman in Japan—left Moran as the only

Japanese speaker on the staff of the Marines' commanding general, Alexander A. Vandegrift. Moran's sunny disposition and ability to endure without complaint the everyday miseries and dangers of life on rain-soaked Guadalcanal endeared Moran to his fellow Marines, who dubbed him "Pappy." But he soon discovered that his fellow Marines could be a problem. His superiors expected him to be a linguistic jack-of-all-trades who not only translated documents and questioned prisoners but also went out on demand to crawl around and identify machinery and equipment that the fleeing enemy left behind. Ordinary Marines, men of the "Old Breed" whose tattooed torsos fascinated Moran, were loath to take prisoners; he persuaded General Vandegrift to offer them three days away from the fighting front with all the ice cream and hot food they could eat as an incentive to bring in live captives. The men also scooped up as souvenirs documents and other material of intelligence value before he could stop them. Moran first tried exhortation to check this "souvenir mania" but eventually turned to trickery of sorts, setting up a "store" where inconsequential items were traded for those of potential intelligence value.[19]

Moran also realized rather quickly that standard marine interrogation procedures were not of much use. The Japanese were tough and at times fanatic. On one occasion while he was questioning one man, the man's superior officer committed suicide on the spot. "Tough guy" interrogation tactics would not work. Instead, humane treatment, kindness, or even "wooing" a captive by evoking memories of home or praising his physical strength prompted enemy prisoners to talk. Missionary that he was, Moran would lie down next to a wounded Japanese to talk with him or spend hours with some captive discussing philosophical matters in the belief that a conversion ranging from devotion to radical emperor-centered nationalism would follow.[20]

By the time Moran left Guadalcanal in December 1942, army units that included Japanese-speaking Japanese Americans; Eugene Boardman, one of the Hawaii program graduates previously stationed on nearby Tulagi; and two enlisted Marines trained in Japanese had come to the island. Moran realized that a division of labor was now possible. The newcomers could do translations at division headquarters while he focused on interrogation. Moran wrote a long and reflective letter from Australia, where the 1st Marine Division had gone to recover from the battles on Guadalcanal, detailing who the marine interpreter is and what he must do. The interpreter as interrogator must first present himself as a humane person who understands the feelings of a prisoner and pities, rather than hates, him. The interpreter must be "a man of culture, insight, resourcefulness, and with real conversational ability." He must be tough, yet alive and warm and, "above all" possessed of evident integrity and sympathy. To succeed, the interrogator needs to know technical terms, but it is much more important for him to possess "freedom in the real idiomatic language of the Japanese." That is essential if he was to worm his way into the confidence of the captive by talking first with the man about himself and his experiences and then moving on in "a business-like, systematic and ruthlessly persistent approach." Moran also condemned formality as poisonous to the success of an interview. Even if, as was often the case on Guadalcanal, one's superior officer were present, the interpreter/interrogator had to be in command of the situation, verbally parrying with a captive in the way he thought would be most effective rather than simply translating questions and answers.[21]

Moran had advantages of rank, age, and affability that enabled him to persuade his superiors to let him do things as he saw fit. His more junior colleagues, the four Japanese-language officers and enlisted men who served with the 2nd Division on Tulagi before coming over to Guadalcanal, did not enjoy that latitude and drew rather different conclusions from their first taste of combat. Lacking Moran's long experience of residence in Japan and command of the language, they found themselves struggling to develop conversational skills and were only indifferently successful in translating the handwritten documents picked up on the battlefield. They felt they knew too little about the Marines' operational and intelligence procedures and even less about the composition of the Japanese forces they were fighting. As juniors unable to resist the demands of superior officers, they had all too frequently been sent into prisoner of war compounds without knowing "with sufficient clarity" what to ask. They had also not felt free to point out that there might be points in a document where the translation was uncertain.

However, these younger officers did propose what eventually became standard operating procedure in battlefield interrogations. Enlisted men with some training in Japanese should be used at the battalion level to perform such limited tasks as reading dog tags, pay books, and maps and asking simple tactical questions. Prisoners, who were likely to be in "much too straitened physical condition immediately upon capture," should then be sent on to the regimental level for brief but limited questioning before going to divisional headquarters. That was where the real interrogation and the most thorough scanning and translation of documents should occur.[22]

The incoming Boulder marine language officers learned these first lessons born of combat experience only slowly and imperfectly. Those who were assigned to the 1st Division had the advantage of getting "Pappy" Moran's counsel firsthand during the months before its next operation at Cape Gloucester late in 1943. Eugene Gregg, one of the first Boulder graduates to join the division, was ecstatic in his praise of "Pappy" Moran. When the 2nd Division left Guadalcanal for its base near Wellington, New Zealand, its enlisted interpreters under the command of Major Bishop, their sometime Japanese instructor from Samoa, escorted captives into Allied prison camps. Arriving just after a prisoner uprising had been put down, they spoke with officials still trying to figure out how to prevent a recurrence of such trouble. But no one seems to have debriefed them on what they learned. Lt. Eugene Boardman got the chance to go north to Auckland, where he lectured men of the 3rd Division assembled there on his experiences.[23] But what he said was a mere drop in the bucket.

Instead, the new language officers learned their craft in this early phase of the war from that most cruel of teachers—combat. Over the next year, they fought in jungle-clad islands in the south and dry coral atolls at the center of the Pacific. What they experienced in those first clashes with the enemy and what they accomplished were shaped by a combination of factors: the terrain on which they fought; the behavior of their Japanese foe; and the particular characteristics of the unit to which they were attached.

1ST DIVISION, FIRST BLOOD

The young language officers who joined the 1st Marine Division made perhaps the smoothest adjustment to life as a combat interpreter. After stopping briefly at Nouméa, New Caledonia, to sample naval translation and interrogation procedures at Adm. "Bull" Halsey's headquarters, they joined a battle-hardened but rested and improved division. "Pappy" Moran had observed army interrogation techniques and knew his own more informal approach was better. He also gained a very valuable assistant, Capt. Eugene Gregg, one of the "hybrids" who had started his naval language training at Berkeley and finished up at Boulder. Gregg had studied in Japan for a year before the war and took away from that sojourn some knowledge of the rough colloquial language frowned upon by his Boulder teachers that ordinary Japanese soldiers used. In addition, the 1st Marine Division borrowed ten enlisted nisei graduates of the Army's language school at Camp Savage, Minnesota, who had had specialized training in reading and translating Japanese army documents. Capping all of this, Moran enjoyed such fame from his exploits on Guadalcanal and such good relations with a succession of commanding officers that the division interpreters were his to command without interference from anyone.[24]

The six Boulder men were received with open arms when they reached the division in Australia early in December 1943, only a few days before it embarked for a forward base to prepare for its next operation. They were a mixed lot: Roger Hackett was a missionary's son who "greeted 'Uncle Sherwood' like a long-lost friend." Harry "Bare" Foote was a Maine man who had spent part of his youth in Japan. John Baptiste Hasbrouck was a one-of-a-kind Yale graduate: a devout Catholic who found time to pray daily while in the combat zone and eventually became a Trappist monk. Dick Greenwood, "a mild, soft-spoken blue-eyed boy," was a former University of Washington football player with the arms of a blacksmith.

Recognizing that the newcomers were "pretty green," Moran and Gregg did all they could to prepare them for what lay ahead. "Pappy" Moran treated them as if they were his own sons, lecturing them every morning for six days straight. He gave them as vivid and factual an account as he could about the duties and responsibilities of Japanese-language officers in combat. They loved that so much that one wondered aloud to another why they hadn't gotten such information instead of the dry, academic stuff offered in their earlier training. Moran also bolstered their collective esprit by urging them to ignore whatever criticism might come from outsiders and to remember that they alone could do the kind of work that lay ahead of them.[25]

Nothing he or anyone else said could have prepared them fully for what lay ahead. On the day after Christmas 1943, they landed with the first wave on the beach at Borgen Bay, near Cape Gloucester, on the western tip of New Britain. The invaders' mission was to seize outlying airfields to neutralize the massive Japanese fortress of Rabaul, nearly 250 miles away at the eastern tip of the island. No planners' map, however, could have revealed the miseries they would face in trying to do so. From time to time, retreating Japanese who had yielded the beaches virtually without a fight counterattacked. But climate and terrain were their real enemies. New Britain received 265 inches of rainfall a year. Mud was everywhere, and mud got everywhere. Sherwood Moran could not see the dial of his mud-spattered watch because mud clouded his glasses.

Mud coated his clothing, and shedding underwear in the heat only made matters worse. When one tried to rinse off in a stream, he only got more mud. Then there were insects—caterpillars that bit; "little black ants, little red ants, big red ants, and their cousins"; and, of course, malaria-bearing mosquitoes who demanded that a man take atabrine until his skin turned yellow.[26]

Despite such delights, the 1st Division Boulder Marines took to learning their job with zest and determination over the next four months. Hackett understudied Major Moran at the division command post most of the time, except when he went out on patrol with Lt. Col. "Chesty" Puller, got lost, and was mistakenly reported as killed in action. Two other men worked directly under Captain Gregg, and the rest went out to work in the regiments as the situation demanded. For the first six weeks there wasn't much call for their services as interrogators. Only twenty prisoners were taken, and another month passed before fifteen more fell into American hands. That was because this was a war of pursuit, in which the Japanese retreated ever farther into the mountains and jungle at the core of the huge island that was four times the size of Guadalcanal. Army nisei, in accordance with Major Moran's dictates, did virtually all of the translation of documents that were captured from the fleeing foe.[27]

The Boulder 1st Division Marines, thanks to Major Moran, did get systematic training in interrogation techniques. At first they sat in on sessions where another officer posed standard questions, and Gregg or one of the more fluent army nisei translated. They watched as prisoners reacted in disbelief to the presence of Japanese Americans on their side and silently applauded when one of them retorted "We're Americans and proud of it!" They learned by doing Moran's humane approach to interrogation that emphasized soliciting cooperation rather than confession from a captive. They made repeated visits to the stockade, improving their conversational skills and psychological insight from captives who knew they were being used as linguistic guinea pigs but enjoyed the conversations nonetheless. Their confidence grew to the point that they could handle interrogations on their own, especially during the "mopping up" phase of the campaign when hundreds of stragglers came before them. Some among them even screwed up the courage to protest gratuitous violence. Lt. Thomas Kaasa complained bitterly about the "careless shooting and killing" in a medical treatment area of one prisoner who was trying to escape. That resulted in the death of another wounded man who had already shown signs of being "particularly open" to providing tactically valuable information to the Marines.[28]

Indeed, by mid-March 1944, when Major Moran was called back to the United States, it was clear that the 1st Division Boulder Marines had contributed greatly to the development of a combat intelligence system that was working well. They brought a sufficiently broad command of the Japanese language to be able to absorb quickly the specialized vocabulary they needed. They had proven themselves versatile, both as marine officers on patrol and as supervisors of enlisted army nisei. The latter, Moran reported, were absolutely indispensable as document translators, and they had overcome whatever prejudices others may have had against them to work well within the division. Indeed, the combination of Boulder-trained linguists and army nisei rendered the much less thoroughly trained enlisted Marines useless and at times even dangerous due to their imperfect command of the language. By the time they gladly left New Britain in April 1944, this small group of language officers had proven the worth of the Boulder program, demonstrated their value in combat, and—most importantly—gained the respect of their fellow Marines.[29]

3RD DIVISION TRAVAILS

The Boulder men sent to the 3rd Division had a much more difficult time of defining their role, fulfilling assigned tasks, and finding acceptance among their fellow Marines. Their first taste of combat came on 1 November 1943, when they stormed ashore on a wide beach at Empress Augusta Bay on Bougainville, another large, wet, jungle-covered mountainous island. Lying some three hundred miles northwest of Guadalcanal, it, like western New Britain, had to be seized to flank the Japanese base at Rabaul. Bougainville presented the same sorts of physical challenges as Cape Gloucester and then some: endless rain and mud and an enemy who refused to engage in sustained fighting yet who remained capable of lobbing shells into supposedly secure areas.[30] Like their brothers in the 1st Division, the Boulder Marines here would have to demonstrate guts and grit no less than linguistic skill.

Their situation on Bougainville differed in important respects, however, from that of their former classmates at Cape Gloucester. They were attached to units cobbled together to form a 3rd Division that was making its first opposed landing. They fought in advance of, and without the loan of colloquially skilled Japanese-American enlisted men from the Army. There was neither a "Pappy" Moran nor a Captain Gregg on hand to teach them how to interrogate prisoners or to run interference for them against senior officers not particularly sensitive to the potential importance of their task. Their superiors and the enlisted Marines along whose side they fought regarded them as "something akin to combat dogs or Navajo code talkers—a novelty they didn't know what to do with." Ordinary Marines were at best indifferently supportive of the notion that prisoners needed to be taken. A young sergeant from Mississippi offered to get a prisoner for Larry Vincent—if the language officer nicknamed "the Jap lover" would let him kill the man when the interrogation was finished. Had second lieutenants Hart Spiegel, Larry Thompson, Robert Kinsman, and Glen Slaughter read the rhetorical question that "Pappy" Moran cut out of his report on intelligence in the Cape Gloucester operation, they might have shouted "Amen!": "What hope is there of our enlisted personnel catching the idea of the desirability of capturing prisoners for Intelligence purposes, when even a field officer in D-3 [Operations] exclaims, upon hearing that a prisoner has just been taken, 'Shoot the bastard; that's the way to treat them!'?"[31]

These Boulder officer-interpreters really had to fight to prove their worth. There was no single safe place where they could set up shop for translation and interrogation. Their trunks of reference books and dictionaries had to be hauled, much to the regimental commanders' and enlisted Marines' disgust, from place to place. Before long, rain, mud, and humidity rendered the books useless, and many were tossed away. The Boulder Marines themselves went out on patrols, probing up ravines on trails that were little more than scratches in the earth or outward along points of the compass from blocking points in search of an elusive enemy.[32]

When the shooting stopped and the enemy retreated, the language officers had to go out and get documents in a particularly dangerous and grisly way. Accompanied by eight or nine enlisted men, they scavenged the enemy dead, reaching down into pockets and packs of the foe to get bloodstained but tactically useful maps and diaries. They watched, but did not stop their men, who, gripped by "souvenir mania," looted corpses for knives, weapons, charms, and even gold in the dead men's teeth. Theirs was, as Lt. Hart Spiegel put it, "dismal, dirty, dark, [and] frightening work." But they did it.[33]

These young officer linguists had much less control than their 1st Division counterparts over what happened on the rare occasions when prisoners were taken. The very few captives they encountered did not surrender but simply collapsed, wounded, into American hands. Their jubilant captors then hauled them down from the mountains, threw them into a cage, and paraded them around in a truck on the beach to the jeers of the Marines there.[34] Such treatment was hardly likely to make them more cooperative when interrogated at regimental headquarters. Thus interrogation sessions were not very productive.

Lt. Laurence G. Thompson recalled, years later, everything that was wrong about his first—and only—prisoner of war interview on Bougainville. Marines pointed rifles at the terrified Japanese and pushed him into the regimental colonel's tent. The superannuated commanding officer ordered two chairs to be brought in, one for himself and one for the prisoner. Thompson, the interpreter, had to squat in a demeaning position between the two. Then the colonel began asking "appropriate" questions: What did the prisoner think of the emperor? What did his highness do every day? What was life like in Tokyo? The baffled and terrified captive mumbled some answers—any answers—which Thompson struggled to translate. The interview ended in about five minutes with nothing really useful gained because someone at division headquarters who had heard that a Japanese had been captured demanded that the man be sent there immediately.[35]

Encounters of this sort were terribly frustrating for marine language officers. One of them probably spoke for all when he described Bougainville as "two months of mud, dead Japanese, and no live Japanese to talk to." Miserable though it was, however, the fighting there did have positive effects on 3rd Division Boulder Marines. One of them boasted in a letter home, "I am now a campaign veteran. The Empress Augusta Bay, Bougainville, action." The inexperienced officer had learned to "go along, get along" with enlisted men who knew the craft of killing. The classroom Marine had become a "real" Marine. Clothed with that status and newfound self-confidence, he began trying, while aboard ship heading back to Guadalcanal, to convince his fellow Marines of a vital but counterintuitive truth: getting more prisoners and gleaning information from them would help save U.S. Marines' lives in future battles.[36]

4TH DIVISION MARINES IN THE MARSHALLS

The ten men who became 4th Division officer linguists were the best prepared of any of the Boulder Marines who graduated in July 1943. They received three months of intensive training from the U.S. Army on how to read Japanese military documents. Their commanding officer, a cigar-chomping colonel of the "old breed," did not look down on them as reserve officers, and his subordinates worked hard to teach them what a good marine officer should do on the sensible premise that no one would be safe in combat unless everyone knew his job. The ten officers also had the longest time between graduation and embarkation and made four practice landings before leaving Camp Pendleton. By mid-January1944, when they embarked for combat, their place in the general scheme of things—in a headquarters company that would go ashore between the last of the assault and the first of the reserve battalions—had been determined. They carried books and dictionaries—but also an SOP (standard operating procedure) that gave them guidance on what to ask Japanese prisoners. And they got an eye-opening taste of how the military worked during their long, unprecedented direct voyage from San Diego to Kwajalein in the Marshall Islands. When Marines started sleeping on the deck of their combat-loaded naval transport to escape hot compartments below, two men rolled overboard in the dark. The ship's captain refused to stop and search for them and ordered every Marine, officer and enlisted alike, to sleep below. That showed the Boulder Marines that mission and safety were more important than individual comfort.[37]

Four of the ten had some acquaintance with the Japanese military by virtue of having grown up in Japan or Japanese-occupied north China. Nevertheless, these especially well-prepared young officers felt a good deal of apprehension as they set out across the Pacific. John Rich recalled being struck by the thought that he had grown up on the shores of one ocean, the Atlantic, but never dreamed he would be crossing another. Bill Brown was so nervous that one night while smoking in his rack he set off a fire by stubbing his cigarette out in a nearby mattress rather than a butt can. Ray Luthy was "so full of piss and vinegar" that he could douse most of his fears. But Chuck Cross, at twenty-one the youngest officer in the group, was much more worried about proving himself a good officer than turning out to be a good combat interpreter. "No one else knew any Japanese," he thought, "so what the hell!"[38]

These Boulder men did not go ashore to the muddy hell that their counterparts in the 1st and 3rd divisions had faced. Their target, Roi-Namur, the northernmost of a string of islands that made up Kwajalein, the world's largest coral atoll, was dry and tiny, not soggy and rainy. Carrier-based aircraft had pounded it for days, disconcerting the Japanese defenders and making it possible for the ships of their convoy to sneak inside the ring of islets where the defenders' sea-based guns could not hit them. The Marines who waded ashore met relatively slight resistance; with the exception of one islet that took more than a day to secure, target islands were taken within fifteen to ninety minutes. Furthermore, because there was no interior into which to retreat, most of the Japanese positions were destroyed and their defenders killed.[39]

That presented problems for the Boulder Marines. They were supposed to get tactically useful information from prisoners and captured documents. But hardly any captives were taken, and those that they first encountered were in no position to tell them anything of immediate significance. Dan Williams' first interviewee, taken just before the landings, was a wounded Japanese whose small boat had been sunk when it tried to approach the American command ship. The conversation was about surgery, not enemy secrets. Ray Luthy's initial encounter was with a half-naked captive; when he walked up to him speaking rough, colloquial Japanese, the man drew a grenade out of his clothing and handed it to him. John Rich met his first prisoner under almost comic, and certainly unproductive, circumstances. He was called to a part of the beach where a huge Marine was carrying a naked Japanese hung over his shoulder like a big fish. The Marine threw the man into a bomb crater nearby, and Rich scrambled down it, not knowing what to say. With Marines with loaded rifles pointing at them both, Rich startled the poor prisoner with a cheery "*Konnichi wa*," which meant "Good day!"[40]

Instead of getting information of immediate tactical value, the Boulder Marines stumbled into other more or less useful tasks. They counted and scavenged reeking Japanese corpses, as 3rd Division Marines had done on Bougainville, hoping to find clues for the enemy's table of organization and force structure. Much like Sherwood Moran on Guadalcanal, Ray Luthy went out with naval demolition experts to defuse armed torpedoes stacked on racks at a forward submarine base on one of the islets. When he voiced worries about what might happen if they were wrong in figuring out which valves to turn, his companion nonchalantly replied not to worry; they wouldn't be around to see the results if they erred! The Boulder Marines, armed by new orders that required all battlefield souvenirs to be vetted by intelligence personnel, sifted through and retained many more enemy documents than in past operations. One of them revealed how the Japanese had taken nine Americans captive on Wake Island, cut them to death with sharpened pikes, and then hacked their remains to pieces. But David L. Anderson, a tall, dark third-generation Chinese hand nicknamed "big gook" by the 23rd Regiment Marines, scored an intelligence coup. Rummaging through the rubble of the Japanese command post, he found red-covered, metal-shielded codebooks that the enemy had been unable to destroy. This prize was rushed back to Pearl Harbor by a waiting seaplane.[41]

Ironically, these best-prepared Marines ended up doing most of their language work in not particularly productive ways after the fighting stopped. Only thirty-one prisoners, most of them civilians, were taken in the Roi-Namur phase of operations, and another sixty-four individuals were picked up in and around Eniwetok two weeks later. The Boulder Marines quizzed them as they were being taken back to captivity in Hawaii. John Rich, who interviewed a group of mainly Okinawan and Korean laborers, was able to draw some information—and not a few gripes about their Japanese military masters—out of several of them. But the details they gave were old and the information they volunteered suspect. Rich got the feeling that these battered survivors, some of whom had not eaten for days, would say just about anything they thought their captors wanted to hear. Aboard a different ship headed back to Hawaii, Ray Luthy found himself serving more as a cross-cultural interpreter than an interrogator. When Marines wanted him to taunt captives by having him tell the prisoners "Tojo eats shit," he foiled them by explaining that he couldn't do so because the Japanese would take the statement seriously and respond, "No, he eats rice!"[42]

That exchange pointed to what was perhaps the single, most important result of 4th Marine Division officer-interpreters' first combat experience. The men from Boulder had demonstrated that they were "real" Marines who bonded with their units in ways that enabled them to do whatever had to be done. With but one exception, these ten young officers stayed in exactly the same 4th Division positions they had in the Roi-Namur battle for the rest of the war. But they had also shown that they could act, when necessary, in ways that set them apart from their fellow Marines. When they persuaded their own men to take prisoners rather than slaughter all of the foe, the 4th Division Boulder Marines became cross-cultural interpreters as well as communicators who could speak to the enemy.

After their first fight in the Marshall Islands, the 4th Marine Division went to Maui where they established a camp on the slopes of Mt. Haleakala.

For the first month their interpreters, who—like so many others in the division—had contracted dysentery, stayed in camp. Their health recovered, some ventured out into nearby towns where they improved their conversational skills by dating lonesome Japanese-American girls and, on occasion, meeting their families. But then, in a move that reflected the Corps leadership's absorption of the message that more senior marine interpreters had been preaching, they were sent on temporary duty to the Joint Intelligence Center at Pearl Harbor to hone their linguistic skills. There they alternated weekly between translating documents and interrogating prisoners. They also reunited with their Boulder classmates, Marine and Navy alike, sampling the restaurants and bars that had sprung up in Honolulu to serve the hordes of men in uniform.[43]

What they discussed in those reunions with classmates, one suspects, blended pride with uncertainty. They had proven themselves as Marines, surviving battle with minds and bodies intact. They had made the transition from classroom to combat successfully. But they had yet to prove their worth as intelligence officers, and the results of their endeavors were uneven. Boulder Marines had identified enemy codebooks and translated valuable technical information on captured enemy equipment. But after four major amphibious assaults, they had, thanks to the foe's determination not to surrender and to their fellow Marines' reluctance to take risks to get prisoners, taken relatively few captives. By the spring of 1944 only seventeen hundred Japanese prisoners had been taken in the assaults in which the Boulder Marines fought; of these only a few were in naval or marine custody. Statistically that record suggested that every marine Japanese-language officer had captured and interrogated thirty-four prisoners.[44] Factually that was not so, and the overwhelming majority of those in American hands were ordinary laborers, Koreans, and civilians rather than Imperial Japanese Army and Navy combatants. The character and paltry numbers of the prisoners that the Boulder Marines interrogated during their postcombat sojourns in Hawaii left them, one suspects, unsatisfied. They knew they faced the challenge of producing more results of greater intelligence value in the battles that lay ahead.

PERSUADERS IN THE MARIANAS

While the Boulder Marines in Hawaii relaxed, honed their skills, and reflected on their combat experiences, admirals and generals in Washington were preparing a new, much more comprehensive assault on Japan's Pacific island empire.

Their plan was to mount a massive, Army–Navy–Marine Corps strike on the Mariana Islands to retake Guam and capture positions on neighboring Saipan and Tinian that could be transformed into bases from which B-29 bombers could attack Japan proper. These islands presented in prospect a battleground that would be different—and more formidable—than anything the Marines had experienced. The islands were larger than the coral atolls farther east in the Central Pacific and more temperate in climate than the islands south of the equator. Their terrain—encompassing beaches, cultivated plateaus, jungle-covered mountains, and even small urban areas—was much more complex than that of other islands the Marines had assaulted. Although their land area was only a tiny fraction of that of Guadalcanal or Bougainville, 52,000 Japanese troops—more than 12,000 more than on both of those islands together—were in place to defend them.[45]

The Marianas were also home to a large civilian population, a mix of native peoples and colonists sent out from Japan over the preceding 30 years to develop their sugar and other tropical products. More than 20,000 Japanese lived on Saipan, three-quarters of them in the city of Garapan. Another 18,000 had colonized tiny Tinian, only 3 miles away. Guam, 100 miles to the south, had a population of nearly 22,000 natives plus nearly 2,000 more Japanese. These civilians, in the eyes of one of the more senior marine language officers, loomed as "the big problem." Coping with civilians while fighting enemy soldiers would truly test the language skills and cross-cultural savvy of Boulder Marines.[46]

Those who came to the Marianas were part of a combined naval and two-corps amphibious force of more than 120,000 men—the biggest American assault force yet assembled in the Pacific. Although the individual divisions in which Boulder Marines served were an eighth smaller than those previously committed to battle, they were accompanied by one army division each on Saipan and Guam. The latter, rather than relieving frontline Marines or operating independently of them as they had earlier, formed a second arm of the American forces as they advanced from particular beachheads over the whole of these two islands. The assaults, the first against Saipan on 15 June 1944, only nine days after the D-day landings in Normandy, stretched over a five-week period.[47]

The Boulder Marines who took part in these battle were more numerous and better prepared than those who had fought in the Marshalls or the Solomon Islands. Those in the understrength 2nd Division, for example, added nearly one-quarter of the thirty Marines who graduated from Boulder between the summer of 1943 and May 1944 to their ranks. These newcomers "weren't very well oriented" when they hit the beach, but experienced veteran language officers helped speed up the on-the-job training.[48]

These men joined a fighting organization that, like all of the others that would land in the Marianas, had tasted Japanese blood. The 2nd Division had landed on Tarawa in the Gilbert Islands the preceding November to fight a battle of the "utmost savagery." American forces suffered as many losses there in 76 hours as had occurred on Guadalcanal in 6 months. The marine language officers did not go ashore there until the slaughter was well under way, and they spent much more time fighting, carrying ammunition, pulling wounded men back, and trying to get medical help than they did interrogating. Of the nearly 150 prisoners they took, only 17 proved to be Japanese. The documents they scooped up turned out, in large measure, to be "a lot of junk." But they came away from Tarawa with the conviction that "sheer guts plus a tremendous pride in . . . [one's] ability to carry out a difficult and dangerous mission" had enabled their division to turn what began as disaster into a triumph. Such confidence would serve them, and all who fought in the Marianas, well.[49]

Nevertheless, battles of annihilation like Tarawa and Kwajalein must have given Boulder Marines and their superiors in intelligence pause for thought. Did every fight have to be one in which virtually every enemy combatant was killed? What, if anything, could be done to increase the number of captives and speed up the flow of information to save American lives? How, indeed, could marine language officers make themselves more useful?

In the interval between their previous battles and the assault against the Marianas, Boulder Marines and their immediate superiors had ample opportunity to ponder those questions. Veteran combat linguists were detached from their 2nd and 4th Division units and sent to JICPOA, the Joint Intelligence Center, Pacific Ocean Area at Pearl Harbor, to improve their language skills by translating captured documents and talking with captives. They left Pearl Harbor having gotten "invaluable . . . practice" in both written and spoken Japanese, which made them feel "all set" for the next operation.[50]

Some among them used that opportunity to prepare better tools for taking more prisoners. New, more colloquial leaflets calling on the enemy to surrender were prepared. The Boulder Marines had pocket-sized cards printed up for men on patrol to use. Frontline Marines were admonished: "Every prisoner turned in means the saving of American lives, time, [and] materiel." These patrol cards also instructed men on how to ask questions—in English, Japanese, and Korean—in a manner likely to yield such valuable tactical information as the identity of an enemy unit, its location, and its size. The cards went on to provide guidance on how Marines might, with the help of one captive, approach and take alive members of the unit from which he came—without themselves getting killed.[51]

These new but still far from perfect tools helped marine language officers increase the number of prisoners taken and documents acquired in the Marianas. They enjoyed some notable successes. Japanese prisoners became "just easy marks" in interrogation because their superiors had not instructed them on what to do or say if captured. One Imperial Army officer even went up in a plane with his captors and provided accurate targeting information for bombing Japanese positions. Marines in the field scooped up numerous official diaries that the Imperial Army had provided its soldiers in which they scrawled valuable tactical information. Within forty-eight hours of the landings on Saipan and Tinian, 2nd Division headquarters had put together the basic Japanese order of battle from information provided by captives and enemy documents. By day four on Guam, enlisted Marines had found, and Boulder marine officers translated, enemy headquarters documents and maps that pinpointed the location of every Japanese unit on the island.[52]

The Boulder Marines in the Marianas also enjoyed more success because they accepted help from men in other services. One of those on Guam readily acknowledged the indispensability of army nisei who, with the exception of Marines born or raised in Japan, were "better than we were" in oral communication with the enemy. Men of the 23rd Regiment on Saipan dubbed 2nd Lt. Mike Moss a "doggie," just like they did every other army man. But they put the fluency of this "observer" who had been born and raised in Japan and trained at the Army's Language School to good use. Cooperation with naval Japanese-language officers sent out from JICPOA at Pearl Harbor also paid dividends. One of the latter, Griffith Way, found, translated, and recognized the significance of hydrographic charts that helped shape the decision to shift landings on Tinian to improbably small beaches. That bit of deception on 24 July 1944 resulted in much less loss of American lives than would have occurred at the originally planned site.[53]

Heartwarming though their greater success in the Marianas was, marine language officers recognized their limitations. Unprecedented numbers of the defending force—about 6 percent of that on Saipan and Tinian, and more than one out of every ten defenders on Guam—surrendered. But a huge problem remained once the initial landing phase of operations ended. What could be done to convince those who did not—combatants and civilians who crawled into caves or other remote places—to surrender? In the minds of some, the only alternative was to hunt down and kill them. On Guam alone, nearly five thousand men and women—nearly half the number of enemy killed in action—died during the first six weeks after the island was declared secure.[54] In the minds of others—the Boulder Marines' superiors—these soldier "stragglers" and civilians should be saved. The attempts to do so during the so-called mop-up phase of operations in the Marianas presented the Boulder Marines with their greatest challenges yet.

They approached the holdout enemies in operationally similar ways. After a beachhead and such key sites as harbors or existing or projected airfields were secured, American forces moved to establish a continuous line across each island. Then they advanced, driving all before them—soldiers and civilians alike—in much the same way that hunters flush game birds up and out of the stubble of fields or the underbrush of woodlands. The surviving enemy were then pushed toward cliffs overlooking the sea, to the north on Saipan and Guam, the south on Tinian. There, presumably, realizing that their only choice was suicide or surrender, at least some Japanese would opt to give themselves up.[55]

Just how the Boulder Marines functioned as part of the hunting force varied considerably depending on their unit's experience, the terrain, and the mix of civilians and soldiers they pursued. The hunt proceeded most quickly on Tinian. Marines from the 4th Division took barely a week to move from their narrow landing sites at the north of the island, through the sugarcane fields at its center, to its rugged southern end, where they joined up with the 2nd Division. Most of the frightened Japanese plantation workers and their families, their numbers reduced by nearly a quarter during the preinvasion bombing, scattered before the invaders like frightened quail. Japanese-speaking Marines, aided by some later naval products of the Boulder school, helped shoo them into makeshift internment camps.[56] The few civilians who stayed with Japanese troops as they scrambled to the southern tip of the island faced a more uncertain fate.

On Guam, 3rd Division and 1st Provisional Brigade marine language officers hunted live Japanese in much the same way as they had pursued dead and dying foes on Bougainville. They had survived the particularly ferocious fight to take the Orote Peninsula, which formed the southern arm of the island's principal harbor at Agana, its capital. The stench of death was still in their nostrils and those of their men. Hart Spiegel recalled seeing "more dead and dying Japanese and Marines in two days" of that fight than he had seen in the entire war up to that point. He led patrols of a dozen or so infantrymen who advanced slowly and cautiously, a thousand or fifteen hundred yards at a time, ahead of established lines that moved slowly toward the northern tip of the island. His husky Marines had gotten ample "proof" that Japanese were simply savages from recent events. Enemy soldiers had attacked them at night, shrieking insults in broken English. The foe also beheaded and threw into mass graves native islanders who got in their way. Not surprisingly, Spiegel had little luck in persuading his men not to kill Japanese on sight. When, for example, they came upon a group of three Japanese soldiers eating and sitting peacefully in the jungle, his men, spooked by past incidents in which the Japanese had hurled grenades while feigning surrender or had booby-trapped their dead, simply refused to take the risk of talking with the foe. They shot and killed the Japanese.[57]

On other occasions, when their bullets simply wounded a foe, the Marines would throw the man onto a poncho stretched between two poles and carry him back to Spiegel. Drenched in his own blood and too stunned or weak to say much, the victim was in no condition to provide any information of immediate intelligence value. The most that a Japanese-language officer could do was to offer him a cigarette and exchange a few words that might lower his anxiety level and increase the chance of his surviving and talking another day.[58]

On Saipan, however, marine Japanese-language officers of the 2nd and 4th divisions hunted down the foe—and Japanese civilians—in a more humane but extremely risky manner. They were not simply soft hearted. After all, the initial landings on the island had been marred by gross underestimation of enemy strength, punishing gunfire in the first wave, traffic jams of landing vehicles that stalled or went to the wrong place, and very heavy casualties. These Marines, like those on Guam, had every reason to kill Japanese at first sight.[59]

But something about the character of the Boulder Marines and the leadership that they demonstrated kept that from happening. Maybe Chuck Cross and David Anderson of the 23rd Regiment in the 4th Division had inherited just a bit of DNA from their missionary parents that made them believe common humanity required them to make every effort to capture rather than simply kill Japanese. Maybe it enabled them to preach that message with greater success to their fellow Marines. Perhaps intense curiosity and determination to get the job done right made Bob Sheeks, a chicken rancher's son who had gone to Harvard, more willing to take risks to save lives—Japanese lives. Maybe John Rich's earthy sense of humor supplemented his demonstrated courage in the attack on Saipan in a way that strengthened his ability to lead and control fellow Marines. When, in the midst of the hunt there, men of the 25th Regiment came upon an abandoned Japanese "comfort station," Rich gave everyone a laugh by translating the brand name of the condom packets they found scattered around. *Totsugeki,* he announced, meant "charge!" or "penetrating attack!"[60]

In any event, Boulder Marines on Saipan risked their own lives and those of their men to root out Japanese who fled before their advance. At first, interpreters crawled up to a place as close as possible to an enemy hiding spot; from behind as much cover as they could find, they tried to talk the foe into surrendering. They enjoyed some success. John Rich was summoned to the edge of the front one night to shout "stay still" and promise rescue the next morning to frightened civilians who were darting around 4th Division Marines' positions. Dan Williams, with the aid of "Father Noah" Cho, a Japanese-speaking Korean Episcopal priest from Honolulu, bagged his first captive, "George," a Hawaiian nisei impressed into the Japanese army who had managed the sex workers at one of Saipan's "comfort stations." Bob Sheeks achieved more success by trying a slightly more advanced technology. He put together a primitive bullhorn with speakers that amplified his calls to the enemy to surrender. Sometimes the bullhorn was handheld, and sometimes it was mounted on "sound jeeps" that gave him greater distance from the foe—but also pinpointed his position for enemy snipers.[61]

Chuck Cross got so good at prying Japanese out of caves and other hiding places that he earned the nickname "satchel," derived from the charge that he and his Marines used in the last instance, when the enemy refused to heed calls to come out and surrender. He and his men took on the particularly dangerous and often grisly task of combing through caves and bunkers, to make sure no more Japanese were hiding there, and then sealing them. On one occasion Cross came close enough to an underground bunker to shout to those inside; then he heard women's voices and the sound of a grenade exploding. He kept on calling but after hearing only shrieks and yells decided that it was too dangerous to try to enter the bunker. But when he and his men returned the next morning, they heard children sobbing and decided to look inside. What they saw was horrifying: a few children whose throats had been slashed by their parents before the adults committed suicide. As time passed, however, the marine interpreters got better at producing happier results. They would try to wait out civilians, who after they came out of their hiding places and received decent treatment, would urge soldiers still in hiding to surrender themselves.[62]

On all three islands, the hunt ended in the same sort of drama. Cornered Japanese survivors—civilians and soldiers alike—prepared to commit suicide at the order of senior officers. On Guam, American planes flying overhead broke up the attempt, but on Saipan and Tinian hundreds died. Some civilians jumped off a cliff into the shard-strewn sea below, pushing others who were sick before them. Others let themselves be encircled by soldiers and then blew them up with grenades. Japanese troops "shot each other [or] joined hands to jump into the sea." Marines, on land and in small boats at sea, surrounded them.[63]

Marine language officers armed with loudspeakers did what they could to save survivors and to try to stop those about to kill themselves. On Tinian, Chuck Cross persuaded some civilians and their children to give up. On Guam, Larry Thompson, in the 3rd Division, had little luck. He got into a landing craft and used a loudspeaker to broadcast appeals to surrender to Japanese who had jumped from the cliffs into the surf. Unfortunately, most of them chose drowning over boarding American boats. A few days later, that drama repeated itself in more brutal fashion. Four marine officers aboard LCI (G) 466 spotted a single naked Japanese soldier on a reef on Guam. They first tried shouts, then a few shots to try to get him to give up. He dashed toward a nearby cave, only to be killed by 20-mm gunfire from the ship. Bob Sheeks, who had persuaded his regimental operations officer, future marine commandant David Shoup, to take risks to save large numbers of civilians and capture the soldiers among them, enjoyed some success by broadcasting offers of drinking water to the drought-starved Japanese.[64]

What Boulder Marines did in the Marianas earned them praise, taught them lessons, and presented them with opportunities to change things in the future. Bob Sheeks, Ray Luthy, John Rich, and Chuck Cross all were awarded bronze stars for their innovative and courageous work in broadcasting surrender appeals and rescuing civilians. The 24th Regiment intelligence officer reported that "the value of Japanese linguists cannot be over estimated." He spoke of the "superlative job" they had done on Saipan and recommended that still more of them be assigned to each regiment. His 1st Provisional Brigade counterpart stressed their importance in warning ordinary Marines against document-destroying souvenir hunting and proposed using men who did not heed their words to bury enemy dead. Division and regimental intelligence officers downplayed the value of threatening propaganda leaflets and urged that every unit be equipped with the mobile loudspeakers that had proven so effective in getting individuals to surrender. Clearly, the Boulder Marines and their superiors learned a great deal about how to be tactically more effective in future operations from their experiences in the Marianas.[65]

Lt. Robert Sheeks, however, perceived an even greater opportunity in his experiences on Saipan—a chance to begin to change broader public attitudes toward the Japanese. Famed war correspondent Robert Sherrod published an article in *Time* magazine that suggested that the civilian suicides there might be harbingers of millions more in Japan itself. Hoping to dispel the notion that Japanese people in general were suicide-prone subhuman "others," Sheeks penned an article that described what happened to Japanese civilians on Saipan. Even after military censors removed words that bluntly challenged a war correspondent considered valuable and friendly to the Corps, the article made its key point: one should not conclude that all Japanese were suicidal fanatics. Far more civilians died as a consequence of fighting between the combatants than at their own hands.[66]

Sheeks' article was not published until nearly eleven months after the fighting in the Marianas began. But it showed how the marine combat interpreter's role was changing. He was a fighter, when fighting had to be done. He was an increasingly innovative and effective hunter: the number of prisoners taken on Saipan in one month was nearly double that acquired in all marine operations during the previous two years.[67] And he enjoyed some success as a persuader, convincing ordinary Marines not to kill every Japanese soldier or civilian who came in sight. The marine language officer had become a lifesaver as well as a life taker, a cross-cultural interpreter no less than a combat interrogator.

MATURITY: PELELIU AND IWO JIMA

Sheeks' message about Americans' shared humanity with the Japanese enemy was premature. During the six months that followed the conquest of the Marianas, Marines fought two battles that reinforced the very stereotypes of the "fanatical" Japanese he sought to dispel. At Peleliu, in the Caroline Islands east of the Philippines, and on Iwo Jima, some six hundred miles closer to the Japanese homeland than Tinian, the Japanese defenders were slaughtered in numbers that dwarfed the alarmingly high casualties suffered by their American attackers. Only 2 percent of those on Peleliu and 4 percent of Iwo Jima's defenders survived and were taken prisoner. The enemy fought tenaciously for a month on both islands. They killed or wounded more than 25,000 Marines—more casualties than Japan suffered on the islands. Indeed, nearly a third of all Marines who perished in World War II died on Iwo Jima. And the Japanese foe repeatedly appeared to be choosing death over surrender. All of the numbers—Japanese and American dead and killed and prisoners taken—strengthened the notion that the Japanese were, and would always be, a "fanatical" foe.[68]

Neither battle displayed significant American innovations in combat intelligence, but both demonstrated how the Marines, as an organization and as individuals, were maturing in its practice. By the autumn of 1944, the Marine Corps had a self-sustaining and well-supported system for transforming Boulder graduates into effective combat Japanese-language officers. Men like twenty-year-old Jim Brayshay, who fought in the first regiment of the 1st Marine Division on Peleliu, and Ed Seidensticker, who was attached to the headquarters company of the new 5th Division, had two more months' language training at Boulder than those who graduated in July 1943. They enjoyed a longer time between graduation and their first battles—time that was put to good use in more extensive training at Camp Lejeune in North Carolina and California's Camp Pendleton. Brayshay, a cotton broker's son who had grown up in Japan, could be counted on to speak colloquially to the enemy wherever he might be found. Non–Japanese speakers like Seidensticker, who knew only what his Boulder teachers had crammed into him, were sent to an old hotel, Byron Hot Springs in northern California, to practice interrogating prisoners.

There the captives gleefully mimicked their fledgling inquisitors' shaky spoken Japanese. Both men got time to improve their interrogation and translation skills at Pearl Harbor before their regiments went into battle.[69]

When Brayshay and Seidensticker reached their assigned intelligence sections, combat-seasoned elders took them in hand and instructed them in their craft. When Brayshay joined the 1st Division on Pavuvu, Maj. John Merrill, who had previously fought with the New Zealand Army and headed the 3rd Division's intelligence effort, was its Intelligence Section commander. Roger Hackett and the other five regimental language officers who had left Bolder in July 1943 and fought through the Cape Gloucester campaign were on hand to introduce him to the hands-on work of combat interpreting. In the new 5th Division, Seidensticker and J. Owen Zurhellen Jr. were welcomed by the redoubtable Maj. John C. "Tiger" Erskine, whose experience of rapid-fire document translation stretched back to Tulagi. He ran newcomers through mock interrogation sessions in which they had to play the roles of captive and questioner alike. New arrivals John K. McLean and Richard S. White in the 5th's 28th Regiment consulted and learned from Roger L. Marshall in the 26th, who had fought in the marine parachute regiment on Bougainville.[70]

These newest Boulder Marines went into battle with a much better sense of what to do and say than their predecessors had had. By late 1944, for example, they had a standard procedure for interrogations that listed twenty-one key questions to be asked of every new prisoner as soon as possible. By that year's end, some regimental language officers had personally tutored enough enlisted men in basic Japanese to make it possible to assign one to each battalion. Before they assaulted Iwo Jima, 5th Division enlisted Marines were bombarded by pamphlets and posters that warned against gratuitous killing of captives and emphasized their value as potential collaborators who might help save American lives. If they heeded them, the marine language officer's job would be a lot easier and much more productive. The 5th Division also took time to run through three practice landing exercises that revealed repairable problems before its assault against Iwo Jima. Armed with advice from an earlier Boulder marine graduate, a very green second lieutenant, Owen Zurhellen, called his superiors' attention to what was going wrong at the battalion level. Prisoners were not stripped and searched. A musician who knew not a word of Japanese escorted them from the fighting front to the stockade. And frictions between escorts and military police kept interpreters from quizzing captives quickly and thoroughly. Presumably Zurhellen's regimental intelligence officer did what he could to remedy the situation before the division embarked for Iwo Jima.[71]

Marine Japanese-language officers on Peleliu and Iwo Jima also demonstrated that they had learned from past assaults and could adapt quickly to new combat conditions. In September 1944 on Peleliu, they showed they could work effectively with army enlisted Japanese Americans. At first the nisei tried to show them up as incompetent with fake untranslatable documents. The newest Boulder men were not fooled and gained the respect of the enlisted linguists. The nisei, who previously had been confined to division headquarters work, now worked alongside the Boulder men on the front lines. They won commendations and high praise for their "invaluable" work there. Regimental language officers from the 1st Division also put into practice innovations that they learned about from their Boulder brothers in other divisions. They made their own propaganda leaflets, used loudspeakers to call out to the foe, and crawled into caves in hopes of getting enemy soldiers to give up. They concluded that only the last, highly dangerous method of seeking prisoners had a noticeable, if limited, effect on the enemy's behavior.[72]

On Iwo Jima, the battle-hardened 4th and inexperienced 5th divisions fought side by side, suffering greatly but also performing intelligence tasks in ways not seen before. A green Ed Seidensticker had been unable to sleep the night before the assault for fear of what might happen, and veteran Chuck Cross had learned from enlisted Marines how not to show the fear he felt. But both men did what they felt had to be done. Seidensticker, weighed down by a pack filled with dictionaries, slogged through the black volcanic sand that grabbed his ankles, found the 5th Division intelligence command post, and dug a foxhole—right next to a half-buried Japanese corpse whose hand stuck straight up out of the ground. Cross went ashore with the first waves of assault battalions and survived the hellacious Japanese artillery fire that pummeled them as they jammed up on the black terraced beach. Ray Luthy was not so lucky. An enemy shell hit him almost immediately after he got ashore, and he had to be evacuated to a hospital ship where his leg was amputated.[73]

Despite the dangers to themselves, 4th and 5th division Marines learned to manage risks and innovate. They pursued the Japanese foe—above- and underground. Richard White mounted a speaker on a jeep and drove it up the side of Mount Suribachi; he attached a very long cord to his bullhorn so he would be far away and safe when the Japanese, as he suspected they might, blew up the jeep from which the sound of his voice came. Undaunted, White got another jeep and repeated this more refined way of calling for surrender. When it became necessary to crawl into caves and bunkers to try to persuade Japanese to come out before engineers sealed their entrances, the Boulder linguists risked the disdain of their fellow Marines by making use of enemy captives. On one such patrol, Chuck Cross took along a Doberman dog and a prisoner whose perfectly accented words would appeal far more effectively than his own imperfect speech to any who might be hiding inside caves. Larry Vincent did the same thing with another captive and achieved success within the thirty-minute time limit his inexperienced commander set. On another such patrol, the same captive saved his life by pushing Vincent aside from an exploding grenade. Dan Williams dared to entrust a prisoner with a note calling upon the Japanese commander to surrender the entire enemy garrison.[74]

Indeed, by the early spring of 1945, the Boulder Marines on Iwo Jima had achieved a level of respect and cooperation from their fellow Marines that was unimaginable back in the dark days of Guadalcanal and Bougainville. Barely an hour after they went ashore, enlisted Marines called Chuck Cross over to their foxhole to talk with a wounded Japanese. Then they helped carry the man on a stretcher first to the nearest aid station and then to the line for evacuation to a hospital ship. That would not have happened on Saipan. The enemy gave riflemen in the 28th Regiment good reason to simply surround and kill every Japanese soldier they encountered. One of their own had been captured, taken into a cave, knifed, burned with cigarettes and acid, had his wrist broken, his left ear cut off, and his heels slashed by a saber or bayonet. But they and men in the 23rd Regiment waited and gave the language officers a chance to lure the living foe out of his hiding places. Indeed, some enlisted Marines volunteered to go into a cave to rescue a cooperating prisoner of war. When they subsequently heard a shot and the man ran out safely, they cheered. Their superiors saw to it that the Boulder Marines who engaged in such risky work were decorated for their bravery. There was nothing wrong about being ingenious in saving one's own skin while trying to take prisoners and save their lives.[75]

MARINE COMBAT INTERPRETERS TRANSFORMED

At 7:30 AM on Monday, 26 March 1945, lieutenants Richard White and John McLean and the officers and men of the 28th Marine Regiment prepared to depart Iwo Jima. They marched to the 5th Division cemetery that now held the remains of nearly a third of the men who had come ashore with them thirty-six days earlier. After pausing for a brief and tearful memorial service, they picked up their gear and began trudging back to the volcanic ash beaches on Iwo Jima's eastern shore. There they clambered aboard landing craft and headed out to sea to board the ship that would take them back to Hawaii. For them, the bloodiest battle in Marine Corps history had ended. For the 5th Division in which they served, the first and last battle of the Pacific War was over.[76]

That moment marked a turning point in the larger story of the Boulder Marines. While some in other divisions had yet to experience combat, the men who had graduated in July 1943 and most of those who followed them had completed their journey from school to war. They and the Corps in which they served had learned over the preceding thirty-two months what the combat interpreter must do and how he should be used. Everyone had come a long way since those first desperate days in the summer of 1942 on Guadalcanal. Then the marine Japanese-language officer had been pretty much of a one-man band—Sherwood F. Moran, who relied more on linguistic skill and psychological insight gained from years of residence in prewar Japan than on any standing operating procedure to squeeze tidbits of information out of the few prisoners brought to him. There and on New Britain in late 1943 he and other 1st Division interpreters worked almost exclusively with fellow marines. The few army Japanese-American enlisted men on hand were limited to reading documents at division headquarters.

By early 1944, there were enough Boulder Marines to staff each of four fully activated divisions. Their time in language and precombat training was longer than that of their predecessors. But combat—on New Britain, at Tarawa, and on Kwajalein—was their real teacher. They proved themselves capable Marines. They became hunters, scavenging the dead in the mud and rain of Bougainville and New Britain and querying the few living captives taken in the Marshalls for any information that might hasten the defeat of their enemy. They also gained sufficient stature with their fellow Marines so as to be able to function as policemen of sorts, preventing the private hoarding of "souvenirs" that might be of intelligence value and the harassment of prisoners of war. These men formed a cadre of battle-taught combat interpreters.

In the spring of 1944, the Boulder Marines began to play a much more active role. No longer mere students who imbibed what lessons they could from combat, they took a much more active part in determining what they would do in the next battles. They traded stories and tips and improved their language skills while on temporary duty at the Joint Intelligence Center in Pearl Harbor. Doing so helped prepare them for the assault that summer against the Marianas. There they fought as part of a multiservice team. Rejecting "Pappy" Moran's counsel, prior Marine Corps institutional prejudices, and doubts about Japanese Americans' viability in combat, they made these army soldiers—and Navajo code talkers and marine war dog handlers—vital partners on their patrols. On Saipan, Guam, and Tinian they used tools of their own making—patrol cards, propaganda leaflets, and, most importantly, the loudspeaker—to increase their catch of enemy prey, soldiers and civilians alike. There, too, they conducted more extensive interviews that helped determine which prisoners of high value should be evacuated to Hawaii.

In the Marianas, Boulder Marines became lifesavers as well as life takers. Americans took more prisoners not just because these islands had larger populations but also because combat interpreters made unprecedented efforts to acquire them. The Boulder men took on responsibility as well as risk when they crawled into caves to try to persuade enemies within—both soldiers and civilians—to surrender. They led in extremely dangerous situations and got their men to follow. And in extraordinary moments, like those on the cliffs of Tinian, they breached the prejudices of their own men and the fears of the enemy before them to save Japanese lives. In so doing, they helped keep alive that spark of human understanding that battles so often and so easily extinguish.

The bronze stars awarded to Boulder Marines by their commanders in the Marianas recognized something more than their individual accomplishments in battle. By the time they left those islands, they had become teachers, setting patterns of action and behavior that they and their counterparts in other divisions would follow in future battle. There were no tactical or organizational innovations in combat interpreting at Peleliu or Iwo Jima. But what was done there was done better. That result flowed in part from the increased experience of individuals in the 1st and 4th divisions. But it also grew out of the interdivisional sharing among Boulder Marines that prompted those in the 5th Division to codify and practice procedures for taking, querying, and transporting prisoners of war. On Iwo Jima, the men from Boulder took relatively few captives, but their roles and responsibilities as combat interpreters were perfectly clear. No one doubted their utility.

The uniforms that hung hollow on their frames when they left the Navy Japanese Language School were now filled with muscle and sinew. Heads once empty of real knowledge of the Corps—or war—now brimmed with battle-won wisdom about both. The marine combat Japanese-language officer had arrived. He stood ready to crush—and save—the enemy in the next battle, the biggest and bloodiest of them all.

Chapter Four

NAVY DISTANT LISTENERS

While the Boulder Marines traveled their rough roads toward maturity as combat interpreters, their naval classmates took very different paths to utility as intelligence officers. Eight among them—three new lieutenants, junior grade and five ensigns—reported to their very first duty station, an old hotel at Byron Hot Springs, California, on 22 July 1943. For the next five weeks they practiced their Japanese, listening to twenty-three "guests" at the facility, prisoners from the Imperial Japanese Army and Navy, whose cells were bugged. The men fresh from Boulder thought they would ship out quickly for the South Pacific. One, George Nace, did. The others took a slow train to New Orleans where they boarded four newly commissioned tank landing ships (LSTs). Seventy days later, after creeping across the Caribbean, through the Panama Canal, and then southwest across the Pacific, they finally reached their new duty station, Commander South Pacific, the headquarters of Admiral "Bull" Halsey, at Nouméa on New Caledonia.[1]

There they worked under pioneering marine and naval language officers, this time really interrogating Japanese prisoners. The captives were recalcitrant, responding "I don't know" to almost every question they were asked. When a dozen survivors from a sunken Japanese destroyer committed suicide barely a week after coming to the interrogation center, the Boulder men fished for all kinds of reasons for such action and then concluded, self-deprecatingly, that the prisoners had simply wanted to escape their atrocious spoken Japanese! Their written and spoken language abilities improved, but there were not very many prisoners to interrogate. Barely six months after their arrival, the command in which they served was broken up and most of the language officers were shipped back to Pearl Harbor.[2]

There they stood out as rare birds—naval Japanese-language officers who had actually queried the enemy face to face. The overwhelming majority of Boulder naval graduates neither saw nor spoke directly with the Japanese before 1945. Instead, they listened to them from a distance. They tried to pick up clues as to who the enemy was, how he thought, and what he was likely to do from bits and pieces of information—intercepted radio transmissions and encoded messages, captured documents, and even weaponry left behind on the battlefield. The naval language officers were simply small pieces in growing naval intelligence structures far from the battlefield.

Despite their distance from the enemy, the Boulder-trained men and women helped bring about a transformation in American naval intelligence. What had been a somewhat disjointed, occasionally failing, and sometimes extraordinarily successful intelligence endeavor in 1942 became, over the next two years, a systematic and ever more effective instrument for discerning the enemy's intentions and capabilities and using that information to speed his destruction. Just how the Boulder naval graduates contributed to this transformation of American naval intelligence—and were themselves changed by their experiences—is the tale that must now be told.

CHANGING EXPECTATIONS

When their orders arrived, not one of the Boulder naval graduates of July 1943 was sent to sea. They went east to Washington, D.C., west to Pearl Harbor, and beyond to Australia in the Southwest Pacific Theater. Those first duty assignments represented a big change in everyone's expectations. Commander Hindmarsh and Miss Walne had repeatedly said the goal of the Boulder program was to put a Japanese-language officer on every U.S. Navy combatant ship in the Pacific. That man would presumably monitor, translate, and, if necessary, decode intercepted enemy radio messages that provided real-time information for immediate use in battle.[3]

That vision never became reality for several reasons. First, the Pacific War neither unfolded as prewar planners had expected nor repeated the pattern of the first terrible six months of the fighting. There was no great fleet engagement between Midway in June of 1942 and the Battle of Leyte Gulf in October 1944. Instead, the Navy became the critical supporting element for the island battles Marines and army soldiers fought in the southern and central

Pacific. When in that capacity American ships got close enough to monitor enemy tactical communications, they found, as Commander McCollum put it, that the Japanese had "smartened up," tightening up their communications security in ways that precluded immediate decoding, translation, and use of intercepted messages about their intended actions.[4]

Second, with rare exceptions, newly minted naval language officers simply did not have the understanding of naval operations and the mastery of a naval technical Japanese vocabulary needed to function effectively as combat intelligence officers. Even if the Japanese had been more open in their radio communications, most of the new language officers lacked the skills needed to simultaneously monitor and translate them.

Third, the Boulder graduates' superiors realized that these new language officers could do more ashore—immediately—to repair a strained and rapidly expanding naval intelligence system than whatever they might do aboard ship. Indeed, they saw these newly produced naval Japanese-language officers as intellectual manpower—"brain" to be added to the "brawn" of an ever-growing fleet—that would enable naval intelligence to become an accurate, respected, and ever more lethal instrument for destroying the Japanese foe.[5]

The Boulder naval men contributed to that great achievement in clusters that ranged from tiny outposts in "free" China to huge intelligence bureaucracies in Washington and Pearl Harbor. They became "experts" of three sorts: codebreakers, translators, and on-the-spot "jacks-of-all-trades." The codebreakers clustered in Washington, D.C., Honolulu, and Melbourne, Australia. The translators helped transform what had been only a vision of a joint intelligence facility at Pearl Harbor when they graduated from Boulder into the largest and probably the most effective intelligence center for the war against Japan. The last group followed the fleet and American ground forces as they pushed northward from Australia to the Philippines and did things they could never have imagined at Boulder.

WASHINGTON, D.C.: BOULDER "BREAKERS"

When fresh Boulder graduates reported to ONI for duty late in the summer of 1943, they may have felt that going to the nation's capital rather than Pearl Harbor or the ships of the fleet was a "bitter blow." They did not realize that they were going to work on the cutting edge of naval communications intelligence, entering a super-secret, rapidly changing realm of war activity. They could not see this because they were preoccupied with mundane things: finding a place to live and coping with naval bureaucracy. Neither was easy. Washington was bursting at its seams with old residents, New Deal bureaucrats, and a horde of war workers, civilian and military, black and white. "How can a man live in this invented city, neither Rome nor home?" one of their Harvard predecessors lamented poetically. The new arrivals from Boulder had to scramble to find someplace—an apartment, hotel, a room in a family home, and even a yacht on the Potomac—to live.[6] Then they struggled to cope with the Navy, a huge organization whose arcane norms, customs, and vocabulary were a mystery to them. It made them wait, and wait, and wait while security checks on their backgrounds were completed. The delays prompted worries that their linguistic talents might slip away or, worse still, not be appreciated.[7]

When they finally went to work in Op-20-GZ, they found themselves, ironically, on another school campus.[8] The subunit of naval intelligence devoted to "breaking"—technically "recovering"—and translating intercepted Japanese radio traffic began the war as a "black hole."[9] It was buried within the sixth wing of the "temporary" World War I Navy Department buildings on Constitution Avenue, not far from where the Vietnam War Memorial now sits. Within a year more than a thousand men and women were working in radio intelligence, so the Navy spent a million dollars to buy and refit the Mount Vernon Seminary for Women. That site, near the intersection of Nebraska and Wisconsin avenues in what was then the outer fringe of Washington's northwest section, was where the Boulder men labored.[10]

Working in Op-20-GZ and its sister cryptological unit, Op-20-GY, was very big change from learning in Boulder's classrooms. The boss was tough and omnipresent in ways that Florence Walne and their teachers at Boulder had never been. They technically served under Cdr. Alwyn Kramer, but no one who worked in the two units doubted that Lt. Cdr. Redfield "Rosey" Mason was in charge. Thirty-eight years old, he had graduated from the Naval Academy in 1925, completed mandatory sea duty tours, and gone to Japan in 1930 to study under Naganuma Naoe. Mason knew his business—and war—firsthand. He learned to intercept, break, and translate Japanese radio messages as fleet intelligence officer for Commander Asiatic Fleet in 1940–41. When the enemy attacked the Philippines on 8 December 1941, Mason helped evacuate radiomen and cryptanalysts at Station CAST, the Navy's listening post there, to Corregidor near the mouth of Manila Bay. In March 1942, when the fall of Corregidor appeared imminent, he and three other men evacuated by submarine to Australia. There Mason coparented the establishment of a new listening post, Fleet Radio Unit, Melbourne (FRUMEL).[11]

In contemporary photographs, Mason appeared as a smiling, balding man with a glint of determination in his eye. But in his subordinates' eyes, he was an omnipresent, cigar-chomping bear—at least when he first took charge at Op-20-GZ. He startled the somnolent by shouting "coffee!" to compliant yeomen and pressed everyone to work more quickly by using profanity "to the point of . . . great pleasure." Mason made Op-20-GZ work twenty-four hours a day by splitting his crew into three eight-hour watches. He even slept on a cot in a nearby room to be immediately available if needed. Mason was the classic naval "hard-charger" who wanted, above all else, to become an admiral; he chafed at having to fight the war from behind a Washington desk rather than from the bridge of a ship at sea. But he understood and conveyed to his subordinates the value and importance of what they were doing. Whatever could be gleaned from some intercepted Japanese message might mean the difference between success and failure in battle for Americans. A highly competitive individual, Mason wanted his unit in Washington, not its rivals at Pearl Harbor and Melbourne, to decode and translate that vital message.[12]

By the time the July 1943 Boulder graduates arrived, Mason understood that the best way to achieve that result was to present himself as the tough coach rather than the salty sea dog. Mason recognized that these young officers had come straight from school to Washington with only the barest introduction to the Navy and its specialized vocabulary, procedures, and customs. He toughened them, insisting that they persevere despite difficulties. When, for example, Ens. Frank Mallory, a former Stanford Law School student, took it upon himself to move reference books from a sunny spot in an unair-conditioned workroom, Mason stopped him, shouting "Goddamit. It was hot in the Philippines. It was hot on Corregidor. You guys can stand the sun!" He might bark "Translate this!" to one of the new arrivals. But when the work was finished, he reviewed and evaluated it in a way that helped build up the newcomers' self-confidence. He got to know them well enough to nickname some. One baby-faced later arrival was dubbed "killer" precisely because he looked nothing like a murderer. In time, the Boulder men came to welcome Mason's presence, respecting him as a good language instructor and supervisor.[13]

Unlike Boulder, Op-20-GZ also had more senior workers who smoothed the way for new arrivals. Their Harvard counterparts had come a year earlier to a tiny eight-person office. They were so awed by Red Mason that they turned for help to his very unusual civilian staff. The staff included a half-Japanese offspring of a prewar American resident of Japan, a woman who had been certified to teach in Japanese schools, and an art historian and curator from Harvard's Fogg Museum and the Boston Museum of Fine Arts. These people reassured the new language officers, telling them that imagination—a quality that poets and scholars-to-be from Cambridge possessed in abundance—was as important as linguistic skill in uncovering what was buried in encoded messages. At Mason's direction, these more senior language officers compiled a "GZ handbook" that helped the newcomers from Boulder learn the vocabulary for Japanese naval organizations, ships' names, and standard terms and abbreviations.[14]

The newcomers discovered—to their delight—that working in Washington was more varied and intellectually challenging than studying kanji and practicing *kaiwa* (conversation) back in Boulder. By the late summer of 1943, ONI had refined its notion of what they should be doing. On the eve of the Pearl Harbor attack, Arthur McCollum had grumbled that codebreakers spent too much time on trying to read "the blatherings of . . . Japanese diplomats" while the Imperial navy's principal operational remained "a closed book to us." In its wake, every nerve and muscle in naval radio intelligence, an ever-growing team of three hundred radio intercept operators, cryptographers, code recovery men, and translators, strained to unscramble messages sent out in the Imperial Navy's general operational code, JN-25 (b), and its succeeding variants. But as the months rolled by, the Japanese made that task more difficult by changing keys to existing codes and developing additional, more specialized ones.[15]

That made transforming an intercepted message into a readable, usable bit of information a formidable task. The Boulder-trained men in Op-20-GZ and Op-20-GY tried to move backward from the enemy's finished product to the original text. The Japanese encoded their messages in five-figure groups drawn from a codebook that had more than 30,000 words or phrases used by the Imperial Navy. Those groups were then enciphered using a table of additives that were placed in a ten-by-ten matrix on each of several pages. Two figure numbers atop each column and alongside each row were added to each page so that the receiving party would know where to look for the beginning and end points of his additive table. The two five-number groups were then added together using a system in which numbers greater than ten were not carried over. The resulting number then became part of a larger numerical text that was then broadcast to its intended recipients.

The American language officers and cryptographers had first to reverse this process and then translate the resulting Japanese words that emerged from under doubly numerical shells. If one had both the codebook and its updated supplements that indicated what day the matrix table on a particular page was to be used, the task was relatively easy. But in 1943, no such aids were at hand. Consequently, "Rosey" Mason's men had to do three things: reconstruct the matrix used to encipher a Japanese message as originally coded, determine what the resulting five-number groups meant, and translate the resulting words.[16]

That was not easy. It demanded teamwork rather than the competitive individual effort required at Boulder. So the newest Boulder men often worked together with their older and more experienced Harvard counterparts. Their task in Washington was linguistically less taxing than memorizing kanji or reading the handwritten scrawl called *sōsho* at Boulder because virtually everything they tried to translate was Japanese written in the familiar Roman alphabet. But the intellectual challenge was constant, varied, and fascinating—especially for those who worked in cryptography. As Larry Myers, who had pumped gas for "Okies" driving into California's Central Valley and studied at Berkeley and Boulder before coming to Washington, put it, "I had never heard of cryptography. Got thrown into it by accident [and] . . . took to it like a duck to water. I loved doing it. [I] hated to quit in the morning, after a mid watch. I [felt like] I was onto something [and] I had to find the answer. It was a puzzle to solve."[17]

By the time Myers got to Op-20-GY, Boulder "breakers" had helped make work there much more systematic. Some had translated a urine-stained codebook recovered from a latrine where Japanese troops fleeing Guadalcanal had thrown it. That book gave them a "clear understanding" of how five-digit groups indicating the geographic position or makeup of convoys were put together before being encoded. They also kept previously broken archetypical communications, such as ships' daily position reports, to compare with incoming messages. Huge scrolls of papers contained fully or partially recovered matrices, which they compared with those they were trying to reconstruct. The men even developed categories for the reliability of their guesses about unbroken portions of a message. A "WAG" was a "wild-assed guess." D meant pretty certain; C, probable; and B signified something confirmed by analysis. An A message had been deciphered with the help of an enemy codebook. Such increased systemization meant that the Boulder-trained officers broke a growing percentage of the ever-increasing number of messages that crossed their desks.[18]

They became happy workers. Commander Mason increasingly let them work independently, sometimes even on "their own" codes. They enjoyed privileges denied to their peers elsewhere, such as living in a large and pleasant city with their spouses. They readily poured their emotions as well as their intellects into what they were doing. Sixty years later Frank Mallory recalled the thrill he felt when, with the aid of a captured codebook, he recovered and read flawlessly what the Japanese naval attaché in Berlin was reporting to Tokyo. Anxiety swept through Op-20-GY and -GZ men when they found out that Germans, thanks to a spy in Madrid who had loosened the tongue of the American naval attaché there, had told the Japanese that the Americans had broken their codes. But the Boulder men heaved a sigh of relief a few days later when they read Tokyo's haughty reply to Berlin: There was no way the Yankees could have performed such a feat.[19]

As the months rolled on, the Boulder men in Washington surged with pride and satisfaction at what they were doing. Knowing how vital their work was to the outcome of the war salved their frustration at not being able to tell anyone—not even their wives—what they were doing. That conviction bred an esprit that increased their productivity and sharpened their competitive edge. By the spring of 1944 the "paragraph troops," as some nicknamed themselves, worked hard, fast, and long in hopes of beating former classmates from Boulder at code-breaking facilities similar to theirs in Hawaii and Australia. By early 1945, the green Boulder ensigns had become so skillful that their superiors looked upon them as interchangeable parts in the Navy's giant intelligence machine. They could be sent wherever they might be needed. The language officers' talent, diligence, and increasingly sophisticated interaction with one another enabled the Navy to listen to the Japanese enemy as never before.[20]

HAWAII: TRANSLATORS AND COLLECTORS

The Boulder "breakers" who came to Washington in the late summer of 1943 rendered an existing intelligence organization more efficient and productive. Their twenty-five classmates who went west to Hawaii that same summer helped transform their duty station into the largest joint intelligence organization in the Pacific. In so doing, they developed new ways of listening to the enemy—from a distance.

Arthur McCollum and others like him in the other armed services gave these Boulder men the opportunity to play a more proactive role than their brothers in Washington. He recognized the need to broaden intelligence collection, processing, and distribution and place those activities as close as possible to major combat commanders—even before the Pearl Harbor attack. In the fall of 1941, he returned from England deeply impressed by the combat intelligence centers already at work there in the war against Germany. McCollum wanted to see something of that sort take shape under Adm. Ernest J. King, the chief of naval operations (CNO) and commander in chief U.S. Fleet in Washington. But he sensed that Pearl Harbor was where intelligence could most readily be made combat-useful. In March of 1942 the commandant of the Marine Corps, Lt. Gen. Thomas Holcomb, proposed creating a joint intelligence center in the Pacific to facilitate planning for future amphibious operations. Shortly thereafter McCollum traveled to Hawaii with senior army and army air corps intelligence officers to confer with 14th Naval District intelligence officers and those on the staff of Commander in Chief Pacific/Pacific Ocean Area (CINCPAC/CINCPOA). He wanted to persuade them and their boss, Adm. Chester W. Nimitz, to create a combat intelligence center that would combine and coordinate intelligence activities to make them more immediately effective.[21]

McCollum knew he had a "tough sell." He understood the naval officer culture in which intelligence was subordinate to, and far less valued than, operations. At Pearl Harbor he spoke first with the brilliant but idiosyncratic commander Joseph Rochefort, whose improvised intelligence operation would soon accurately predict the Japanese attack on Midway. Rochefort was open to McCollum's proposal, and Admiral Nimitz's chief of staff did not oppose it. CINCPAC, as expected, was skeptical of anything that smacked of a bigger staff and wondered how so many intelligence officers could be accommodated on his flagship when he went to sea. McCollum declined to reveal that the proposed intelligence center would be permanently shore-based and finessed Nimitz's doubts by saying that the admiral could select only a few of its officers to go to sea with him. Over the next two weeks he worked to get space and equipment for the proposed center and to weaken Nimitz's staff intelligence officer's initial coolness to it. By the time he paid the admiral a farewell call, CINCPAC promised "to give it [a combat intelligence center] a whirl," and said he hoped it would work.[22]

Thus, ICPOA, a purely naval Intelligence Center Pacific Ocean Area, was born in July 1942. Fifteen months would pass before it metamorphosed into JICPOA, the truly comprehensive, multiservice organization that McCollum had envisioned. Pioneering language officers—thirteen from Berkeley who arrived in the fall of 1942 and another twenty-six who started there and finished at Boulder in February 1943—suffered through its birth pangs. When the first of them arrived, ICPOA was just a small radio intelligence unit housed in the basement of the Pearl Harbor Navy Yard Administration Building with a photographic intelligence unit on Ford Island. The Berkeley men were shown around makeshift work spaces that were "hot and humid by day, surprisingly cold between midnight and morning, . . . [and] heavily infested with mosquitoes at all hours." Put in awe of the cryptographers who labored there, they were handed off to a lieutenant who had studied in prewar Japan; he was stunned and dismayed by their ignorance of the Navy. The "hybrid" linguists from Boulder did not lighten the first arrivals' workload much, for many of them were parceled out to other subunits of naval intelligence—some of which made absolutely no use of their Japanese-language skills. Barely one in four of this second group of linguists ended up working in what eventually became JICPOA's Translation and Interrogation Section.[23]

The ICPOA linguists suffered from a variety of problems. Leadership was one. Their nominal commanding officer longed to go to sea and stayed only for a few months. His deputy was a battle-hardened captain who had survived the loss of his ship in the Battle of the Java Sea; he was not an intelligence expert. He routinely berated their immediate superior, Cdr. Alwyn Kramer, who, much to "Rosey" Mason's delight, was reassigned from Op-20-GZ in Washington to ICPOA. "Kramer!" the captain would shout into the telephone, "if you had a few more brains, you'd be a moron!" Kramer and his assistant, sometime Berkeley professor Woodbridge Bingham, ruled over the language officers like Edwardian schoolmasters, sitting at desks facing their charges. The young officers labored in enforced silence, poring over dictionaries and documents. "So help me God," one remembered decades later, "if a man had to pee he had to get permission." The language officers pitied their uninspiring superior as a regular naval officer who struggled to manage reserve officers he knew were "brighter and abler than he was."[24]

The second problem that plagued ICPOA linguists was the lack of significant materials to work on. A few documents trickled in after the Guadalcanal operation ended in February 1943, but many of them were written in *sōsho*, a cursive script that the young officers found fiercely difficult to decipher. Much of what came before them was highly technical, yet they had no specialized dictionaries at hand to help with the translation. No one had yet done any research on Japanese ship or place names, order of battle, or military terminology. In the absence of anything better to do, some of the recent graduates were ordered to complete "stupid and tedious" tasks such as translating the Imperial Japanese Navy's bluejackets' manual for enlisted men. As Donald Keene, one of the best of these early translators put it, he and his colleagues spent all day working on material that "it was difficult to imagine . . . was of any conceivable use to anybody."[25]

Poor leadership and boring work bred low morale and the desire to escape ICPOA if possible. Young officers who only a short time earlier had been highly motivated and fiercely competitive students nicknamed their workplace "the Zoo," attesting to the fact that they felt like caged animals while at work in the Navy. Enlisted men accorded them little respect, dubbing them "Japoons" and their workplace the "language head" because the slatted swinging doors at its entrance were just like those to restrooms in naval shore facilities. One language officer committed suicide, and another developed such severe psychological problems that he was invalidated out of active duty. The translation section "was loping along at a snail's pace," not publishing very much; the information it produced was not of particularly high quality and thus commanded only slight attention in the fleet. Little wonder, then, that those who could escaped from translation work at ICPOA. William Burd went to sea as a junior Fleet Radio Intelligence Unit officer. John Harrison fled to the estimates section because he believed his Japanese-language skills would be put to better and more exciting uses there. In the fall of 1943, Otis Cary, Donald Keene, Ted de Bary, and four other linguists happily left to take part in operations in the Aleutians. To get away from the tedium of translation in Hawaii, Frank Turner, one of the best linguists in the February 1943 Boulder graduating class, volunteered to join the force mobilizing for an assault on the Gilbert Islands later that fall.[26]

The situation at ICPOA left neither the young officer-linguists nor Admiral Nimitz happy. When Washington, anticipating the need for many more language officers once offensive operations got under way in the Central Pacific, proposed doubling their numbers, CINCPAC balked. Nimitz also complained to Admiral King that the new linguists were not much good because they knew so little about the Navy. Their "general lack of qualifications" had to be remedied quickly. Washington responded by ordering the Boulder school to teach more Japanese military and naval terminology. It also created ANIS, an advanced naval intelligence school in New York City to which most Boulder graduates after July 1943 were sent before reporting to their first duty assignment as language officers. Gleeful attendees made puns based on the school's acronym, but they learned naval terminology, ship and aircraft recognition, and a bit about photographic intelligence. Their two weeks in Manhattan were not nearly as demanding as their year at Boulder. Off duty, they enjoyed Broadway shows, visits to the city's museums and concert halls, and, for the married men, second honeymoons with wives soon to be left behind. They left New York City for Pearl Harbor with a better, if still minimal, understanding of naval intelligence, customs, and terminology than their predecessors had.[27]

Those changes came too late to help the July Boulder graduates who reached Pearl Harbor in the fall of 1943. But the Joint Chiefs of Staff's decision to expand ICPOA into JICPOA—a bigger, more structured, truly multiservice organization—most certainly did. That choice followed operational logic more than Admiral Nimitz's preferences. Guadalcanal, the first land battle against the Japanese, had metastasized into a protracted struggle that demanded the services of the Army and Army Air Corps, the submarine service, and even the Coast Guard in addition to the sacrifices of sailors and Marines. Prospective operations in the Marshall Islands were certain to be joint. The new JICPOA, established in September 1943, was housed in a new radio intelligence building that perched on Makalapa Hill, the rim of the crater overlooking Pearl Harbor, right below Admiral Nimitz's and senior intelligence officers' quarters. There translation and distribution were separated from radio interception and cryptography. The codebreakers worked at FRUPAC—Fleet Radio Intelligence Unit Pacific—which Boulder graduates dubbed "fruit-pack." They formed the translation section of JICPOA, which—thanks to the nomination of an army brigadier general who had studied in Japan before the war as its commanding officer—enjoyed a measure of autonomy from the whims of Admiral Nimitz and his staff.[28]

During the year following the arrival of the July 1943 graduates, Boulder men took the lead in changing the way the translation section operated to increase its production of data readily usable to the fleet. New superiors who were exemplary and permissive leaders made that possible. Cdr. John "Jack" Steele replaced the hapless Alwyn Kramer. A Naval Academy graduate who had been forced by illness to resign his commission, he had been called back to active service at Pearl Harbor because he was self-taught in Japanese. Highly intelligent and normally rather shy, he would nevertheless growl "I'll have his ass with an apple in it!" when someone made a stupid mistake. He set a superb example of devotion to duty, never taking a day's leave from work until the war ended. That commanded the Boulder graduates' respect. Steele left hands-on supervision to army major Lauchlin Sinclair. This onetime typing teacher tried to impose strict military discipline but failed because he was "abysmally anxious" to be looked upon as a "good guy." Consequently, he welcomed initiatives for change that came from below.[29]

Sinclair let talent, not just seniority, determine who became supervisors in an ever-growing, increasingly specialized translation operation. Those who could quickly scan and get the gist of captured documents or find "top secret" marked on them became "sparrows," so called because, like birds in the barnyard who picked edible bits out of the muck, they could discern what should be translated immediately and what could be safely sent to "ORBA," the "over-the-river-burial association" in Washington, D.C. By the autumn of 1943, the more experienced JICPOA translators had already informally established specialized subsections devoted to place names, captured diaries, and the filing and dissemination of translations. The influx of new men from Boulder allowed them to create additional subsections that focused on air, ships, communications, geography and hydrography, Japanese land forces, and enemy order-of-battle. The Boulder men dubbed these subunits *han*, a term that referred to the domains of the daimyo, or feudal lords, who ruled Japan under the Tokugawa shoguns during the Edo Period [1603–1868]. Unlike that system of hereditary rule, however, one could rise quickly through demonstrated ability to supervisory positions at JICPOA. Tim Harrington, a July 1943 Boulder graduate, headed the aviation *han* within nine months of his arrival at Pearl Harbor. He and others like him acted like friendly daimyo, roving the work space and helping their younger and newer coworkers with translations.[30]

This sort of workplace resembled academia more than the seagoing Navy. That probably enhanced the linguists' productivity, and it certainly elevated their morale. A spirit of friendly competition and even wonder at what was being done pervaded the JICPOA translation section. Arthur Dornheim mastered a Japanese typewriter that had been "liberated" from the Honolulu Branch of the Yokohama Specie Bank. With it, he and others labored twenty-four hours a day over a four-month period creating a specialized dictionary of Japanese naval and military terms. Another seven-man team produced a gazetteer of Japanese place names. The *han* system allowed men with technical skills to transform novices into experts. Howard Boorman was delighted to find Al Karr—"a round peg in a round hole"—in the aviation section. Drawing on what he had learned from tinkering with things mechanical before he came into the Navy, Karr helped Boorman translate a manufacturing manual on magnetos and superchargers.[31]

Greater specialization, more interesting documents, more manpower to work on them, and newfound autonomy transformed officers once indifferent to their work into increasingly valuable, productive, and even happy experts. Tom Ainsworth did not particularly like working on enemy ground forces material that arrived in "soggy old sea bags . . . picked up from heaven knows where," but he came to enjoy the challenge of figuring out language that was never seen in the Naganuma textbooks. Donald Keene, bored by his early work, plunged into it with newfound curiosity and enthusiasm when he was given responsibility for translating captured Japanese soldiers' diaries. Supervising army nisei enlisted men who labored at the downtown Honolulu JICPOA annex—an old furniture store—he began to see the human side of both his men and the authors of what they struggled to translate. Back at the Zoo, laughter rippled across the room when someone found himself translating Japanese pornographic and morale-building magazines.[32]

Life outside the Zoo also helped make work there more pleasant and productive. The Boulder men readily adapted to and came to enjoy wartime Hawaii's exceptionally rich physical and social environment. As officers, they did not have to live on base, at least initially. Like their Washington counterparts, they scrambled to find housing in "America's First Strange Place" rather than a big city. What places they found! Some of the first arrivals took shelter in homes shared with the prewar language officers who had become their supervisors. That arrangement was doomed not to last for long. Arthur Dornheim and Hugh Mitchell rented a room from a deaf old Japan missionary who had become famous for his courageous stand against the 1924 immigration act that barred persons of Japanese ancestry from becoming American citizens. Two men bunked on a boat in the Ala Wai Canal, close to what was then relatively pristine Waikiki Beach. Others rented a house in Manoa Valley, using it as a base from which to take long hikes into the beautiful tropical forest nearby.[33]

Harry Muheim and his buddies rented rooms from one of Honolulu's most notorious characters, Jean O'Hara. This former madam of a Chicago brothel set up a booming sex business in wartime Honolulu, flaunting her success by driving a Lincoln Zephyr convertible around town and throwing raucous parties to which her Japanese-language officer tenants were invited. When she was tried for attempting to run down and kill a friend and coworker's husband, the young officers (along with everyone else who could squeeze into the courtroom) came to watch the show. But they missed its end—an easy acquittal for Madame O'Hara—because Admiral Nimitz's chief of staff, who found even the slightest public link between naval officers and such a woman unseemly, ordered them to stay away from the trial.[34]

Flexible work schedules that allowed them a great deal of freedom in their off-duty hours lifted the young linguists' morale and probably their productivity as well. Some used their free time to explore Oahu. John Robinson and Paul Boller hitchhiked to the island's beautiful and undeveloped North Shore. Future biologists Bill Amos and Arthur Kruckeberg went on walks in search of rare birds and plants. Others continued their intellectual pursuits. Wendell Furnas taught high school two days a week, and Donald Keene took courses at the University of Hawaii. Some who worked the 4:00 PM to midnight shift became, to their own surprise, serious poker players, continuing until the wee hours of the morning or the moment when they sensed that their excessive winning threatened to destroy friendships. Orville Lefko organized a country-western band that toured officers' and enlisted men's clubs all over Oahu. And Gordon McClendon, who inaugurated regional broadcasts of major league baseball games after the war, gained fame as a radio announcer in his off-duty hours—until the Navy silenced him.[35]

The language officers' social lives had one major defect, however: a severe "shortage of young [married and] unmarried white women" existed because Uncle Sam had evacuated most Caucasian women to the mainland. Wendell Furnas was the exception to the norm among married linguists. On his off-duty days, he bummed rides on aircraft bound for Maui, where he paid visits to his wife who taught school there under her maiden name. Bob Thornton was more typical. Every night after work he rolled into bed, lit up "one last Chesterfield," and gazed longingly through the smoke at a photograph on the nightstand of his wife in her wedding dress. Even the most exuberant bachelor linguists found their style crimped by local social norms. As officers, they could not simply join the lines of enlisted men who waited patiently outside Hotel Street's brothels for sexual services. Coming from a monocultural, predominately white society, they had serious doubts about dating across racial lines. The protagonist of John Ashmead's postwar novel about one of them who did so was a rare—and troubled—bird. Japanese, Chinese, and Polynesian-American parents did not want their daughters to socialize with "outsiders." On the relatively few occasions when they invited Boulder bachelors to their families' homes, the young men had to observe traditional proprieties. Indeed, the linguists were more shocked than entranced by life beyond Honolulu where outhouses and washhouses occupied by ducks were common.[36]

Nevertheless, the Boulder men did not let forced sexual restraint or orders to move on base to alleviate Honolulu's severe housing shortage daunt their spirits. They found ways to make living at the BOQ (bachelor officers' quarters) bearable. Attorneys and legal "wannabees" bunked together and sat up late into the night drinking wine, talking about books, and debating left-wing politics. Almost all of the rest gathered around the BOQ bar, where they discovered that Al Karr had piano talents that made even Admiral Nimitz smile. They sat around talking, drinking, and singing because, as some of them put it, "the prevailing Polynesian picture of men without women becomes definitely worse if we were to face drinking without singing." Their songs laid bare these young men's triumphs, complaints, and aspirations in and beyond the JICPOA translation section. "The Translator's Lament" spoofed the effects on their manly vigor of long hours working in the Zoo. Another ditty, sung to the tune of "White Christmas" captured their longings for a richer sexual life and mirrored the racial attitudes of the day. It began, "I'm dreaming of a white mistress . . ."[37]

JICPOA WARRIORS

Despite their successes at work and pleasures beyond it, the JICPOA linguists felt unfulfilled as naval intelligence officers. While a few may have entered the Navy hoping never to see combat, most dreamed of doing so once they got to

Pearl Harbor. As John S. Robinson explained to his family, "Everyone . . . who is not in Honolulu wants to be there; and everyone who is in Honolulu wants to get out." The JICPOA translators' lives seemed pallid compared with those of their classmates fighting the "real" war. "Everybody," or almost everyone, "was anxious to go on an operation," and no one complained when ordered to do so. Combat would be a great adventure in which the Boulder-trained man tested his language skills, discovered valuable intelligence information, and proved his courage. He would return from it "salty," knowing firsthand the daily routines, customs, and smells—that unforgettable mix of sea air, fuel oil, and sweat that stalks the passageways of naval ships—of life at sea. Mentally and physically reinvigorated, his self-confidence soaring, he would return to JICPOA more committed than ever to doing his best. He would be a *real* naval intelligence officer because he had seen the war—and the enemy—face to face.[38]

Unfortunately, such dreams—shared by the young linguists and their JICPOA superiors alike—materialized slowly, if at all. All of 1943 and much of 1944 slipped away before only some of them came close to realizing those hopes. No one anticipated how greatly unreasonable expectations, command problems, interservice rivalries, and the unpredictable demands of war would slow the Boulder men's progress toward becoming effective intelligence officer linguists in combat.

The seven Boulder-trained linguists who went to the Aleutians in the summer of 1943 were the first to run in to those obstacles. Trouble started even before they left Hawaii. Vice Adm. Thomas Kinkaid, Commander North Pacific, deserved "the best" in what was to be a joint Army–Navy operation; but the Boulder linguists' immediate superior was reluctant to let "the best" leave ICPOA to go north to Alaska. Lt. Forrest "Tex" Biard picked Otis Cary, a missionary's son who had grown up in Otaru, a remote town on the Japan Sea coast of southeastern Hokkaido, because he spoke street Japanese like a native. Cary was told he could select "the best" available reader-translator as his companion, but when he chose Wilvan Van Campen, from the original Berkeley class, Biard balked. Cary had to settle for Donald Keene, the valedictorian of the February 1943 graduating class. A few months later, when the need for additional naval linguists developed, Biard let go five more who were either born or raised in Japan or were superb translators.[39]

When Cary and Keene reported aboard the battleship *Pennsylvania* for duty on a marine intelligence staff, a second problem became apparent. They had no military training and no idea of where they might be going. Several days at sea passed before they realized they were heading toward the cold North Pacific rather than the tropical seas of the south where most of the fighting up to that point had taken place. As they approached the Aleutians, the two ensigns remained sublimely ignorant of what they might experience in combat. Given a pistol and cartridges for possible use in battle, Keene felt a strange mix of curiosity and apprehension about what might lie ahead. He boasted that he would not be frightened in confronting death for the first time—but hoped he would not be nauseated by what he saw. He was not.[40]

When, on 12 May 1943, Keene and Cary went ashore on fog-shrouded Attu, the westernmost of the Aleutians, they ran into a third problem: interservice rivalry. Attu was the U.S. Army's first amphibious operation, and the soldiers were keen to assert their primacy. The naval linguists' commanding officer, who had spent only six months at Camp Savage, Minnesota, the Army's Japanese-language training program for officers, provided a frightening example of what the Boulder men did not want to be. He was totally dependent upon his subordinates, and his subordinate enlisted nisei interpreters treated the two ensigns with frosty disdain. The army men made it clear that they thought the two naval Caucasian language officers were incompetent. That touched off an unproductive contest of one-upmanship in dealing with yet another problem: the paucity of enemy prisoners and documents. Only twenty-eight Japanese, out of more than two thousand defenders, had survived the American assault against Attu.[41]

When the two ensigns went to Vice Admiral Kinkaid's staff later in May 1943, their situation improved only marginally. Their immediate superior was a marine lieutenant colonel and scion of a pioneering missionary family in Japan. At first he was loath to let Cary talk with a prisoner from his hometown, fearing, perhaps, that the ensign would be too "soft" on the man. When he later relented, the colonel insisted on eavesdropping on the two men's conversation.[42]

Still more problems arose when five more Boulder linguists arrived in August 1943 to bolster intelligence resources for the recapture of Kiska. Completely untrained in weapons use, they were issued rifles but, oddly, "nobody said a word about giving . . . [them] any ammunition." None of the linguists was likely to win a Purple Heart, for by the time the Americans landed, the Japanese had slipped away. All that the enemy left behind was a dog, a lot of equipment, and some documents. The seven young linguists wandered around that barren, windswept island for a few days looking for materials to translate and then spent the rest of their time in Quonset huts working on documents of no apparent importance. Frictions with army nisei continued. Donald Keene inadvertently raised fears of germ warfare when he corrected a previously mistranslated enemy sign. It read: "Bubonic Plague Victims Gathering Point."[43]

The seven naval language officers left the Aleutians with dreams of glory far from fulfilled. Riding back to Pearl Harbor on the USS *Shasta,* a fully loaded ammunition ship, turned out to be their most dangerous experience. Lieutenant Biard was pleased with what they had done, and Keene and Cary got letters of commendation for their work on Attu. But they did not feel they had accomplished much on their Aleutian adventure. Otis Cary's study of the Kurile Islands was its only concrete intelligence product, and he and his companions thought it could just as well have been written in Hawaii.[44]

No one wrote a full after-action report on the language officers' Aleutians experience. But the marine officer-in-charge of JICPOA's enemy land section suggested that in the future they should be dispatched as part of a JICPOA team of technical experts rather than as individual linguists. Thus in November 1943, when the Marines landed on Tarawa and the Army on Makin, a hundred miles farther north in the Gilbert Islands, two JICPOA linguists went ashore with an officer from the enemy bases section, a photographer, and two enlisted men. They were so busy as translators in combat that they had little time to carry out their primary mission: expediting the recovery and return to JICPOA of captured enemy documents. American souvenir hunters collected more enemy material in the Gilberts than the linguists did. Worse still, a potentially valuable Japanese codebook found its way directly into a sailor's seabag and was not rediscovered back at Pearl Harbor until long after it had been superseded.[45]

That unhappy experience prompted senior JICPOA leaders to insist that language officers form their own teams in the next major operation, the assault against Kwajalein in the Marshall Islands in late January 1944. By that time, documents from Tarawa were running thin at JICPOA, so the linguists' primary mission was once again to be document recovery. The three naval men who went on this operation considered it a reward for previous good work. Two of them looked forward to visiting their wives in California, where they would join the 4th Marine Division and sail directly to Kwajalein. These linguists, all members of February 1943 graduating class, were only marginally better prepared than those who had gone to the Aleutians. They at least visited a firing range for .45-caliber pistol shooting practice and talked with a few Japanese prisoners before departing on this operation. They expected, quite mistakenly, to get help from Marshall Islanders and wasted a lot of time on the long voyage out trying to learn some of the local language from two captives taken in the Gilberts operation.[46]

Once ashore, however, plain, tough English was the language they needed the most. The only Japanese they saw were dead. Only one of the three language officers went out with native guides to scour the island for documents. The other two spent most of their time behind a table, vetting souvenirs, including documents, that enlisted Marines wanted to take home. This primitive triaging yielded a Japanese operations order; Wayne Suttles had to argue with an enlisted Marine to get him to give it up. He and his partner, Harry McMasters, had better luck prying codebooks out of Marines' hands when they solemnly told them that "men's lives"—American men's lives—"depend upon this!"

The JICPOA language officer team returned from Kwajalein feeling that it had achieved at best partial success. The naval linguists did bring back documents useful for future operations. Ens. Donald M. Allen found and translated one that showed Eniwetok, site of the next landing, to be more heavily defended than previously thought. Charts that pinpointed existing minefields in Japanese home waters and revealed Tokyo's plans to lay a mine barrier from Kyushu to Taiwan were also discovered. But the JICPOA linguists had real difficulty in getting what was wanted from ordinary Marines. Their experience in the Marshalls suggested that future "document police" would need more support from the marine superiors and greater authority to triage intelligence resources effectively. They had to have the power to decide, on the spot, which captured documents and which prisoners should be sent immediately back to JICPOA.[47]

They exercised that authority and had a great deal more success in the summer of 1944 in the Mariana Islands. The planners of this, the largest amphibious assault in the Pacific to date, apparently realized that greater numbers and more specific allocation of responsibilities would make naval language officers more effective. Barely a dozen Pearl Harbor linguists saw combat in 1943. Nearly twice as many—almost one of every five ordered to JICPOA and its predecessors—landed on Saipan, Guam, and Tinian in the summer of 1944. With the exception of last-minute arrivals from the Boulder graduating class of March 1944, these men were better prepared than their predecessors for what lay ahead of them. Veterans like Otis Cary, Frank Turner, and Wilvan Van Campen joined them; they had worked at least temporarily in the JICPOA Interrogation Section created in January 1944, talking with the handful of Japanese prisoners held on Oahu. Most were assigned to naval or marine units, which minimized the likelihood of interservice friction. They also had more opportunity to accustom themselves to the sailors and Marines at whose sides they would work simply because the voyage to these more distant Central Pacific islands took more time.[48]

In the Marianas operations, the linguists and their superiors at JICPOA and in the amphibious force had a much clearer understanding of what they were to do once ashore. Some were to be "catchers," translators, and sorters of documents in the intelligence sections of marine divisional staffs. Others would find and interrogate prisoners of war. Still others would work with the thousands of civilians likely to be found on Saipan, Tinian, and Guam. Another group of naval language officers would serve as escorts for what all hoped would be large numbers of prisoners put on transport vessels bound for Hawaii.

Despite better plans and more realistic expectations, the naval language officers' experiences in the Marianas were neither uniform nor predictable. They had no common position in the landing forces. Wendell Furnas and three others waded ashore on Guam, clutching a .45 revolver and carrying Japanese dictionaries, barely an hour after the first wave of Marines hit the beach. Off Saipan, Harris "Jish" Martin watched the fighting from his ship for five days before being allowed to go ashore. Arthur Dornheim spent weeks at sea getting to and from Guam without ever setting foot on the island.[49]

Those who went ashore early had more than their share of adventure. Furnas landed amidst exploding mortar shells and had to walk over the bodies of dead Americans on the beach to get to a marine artillery unit, where shells and flares were going off all the time. Wilvan Van Campen and Kermit Lansner dug their own foxholes then learned, as the fighting advanced, to move ahead "like a lazy gopher," occupying those abandoned by others. Not all naval linguists reached their assigned posts, and those who did found the going anything but easy. Wendell Furnas and Mike Foley piled onto the back of a truck, alongside the general's portable toilet. When the driver took a turn too fast, they fell off and found themselves "charging toward the Japanese line along with the general's head." Their duty station, a marine division headquarters that was nothing like the JICPOA Zoo, moved with the progress of the fighting. It was first in a tent near the fighting front during their first days ashore and then shifted later to a former Japanese brothel in Agana, the ruined capital of Guam. Van Campen and Lansner felt so uncomfortable (and possibly superfluous) at the army division headquarters to which they were assigned that they "informally detached" themselves and reported for duty at the nearest marine headquarters.[50]

Once at their duty stations, however, the naval linguists functioned more smoothly and efficiently than their predecessors on earlier amphibious operations. When the front line was near, they worked at a furious pace alongside army nisei interpreters and even, on one occasion, Navajo code talkers. When the front line was more distant, they translated and triaged documents in the relative quiet of a marine headquarters staff. By the time the Marianas and Guam were declared secure in mid-August 1944, they had processed tens of thousands of enemy documents for shipment back to JICPOA. Among them were the complete administrative orders of Japanese Central Pacific Area Fleet Headquarters, which listed ships by class, their complements and home ports, and their assignment to divisions as well as detailed information on the strength and location of naval land units. The document catchers on Saipan also snared the Japanese Digest of Naval Air Bases. It revealed valuable information about such facilities throughout the enemy's empire that could not be obtained by photoreconnaissance.[51]

Sometimes naval linguists were lucky to find documents of great value for ongoing or impending operations. Griffith Way, for example, discovered one that outlined the complete Japanese order of battle on Saipan, including the location of ammunition dumps, equipment stockpiles, and troop encampments. It was passed on immediately to marine artillerymen, who fired right on targets. That, for him, made studying so hard at Boulder, working at the JICPOA Zoo, and abandoning Hawaii's comforts for the mud, heat, and dangers of the Marianas worthwhile.

Way got an even greater boost to his sense of worth a bit later on, when he found " an absolutely priceless document"—a Japanese study of the hydrography of the beaches on neighboring Tinian. Having specialized on hydrographic charts back at JICPOA, he recognized its potential significance. After forwarding it to the headquarters of the 4th Marine Division, which was scheduled to land on the island soon, he got permission to go to the flagship of Adm. Richmond Kelley Turner, the Amphibious Force commander, to argue for its importance. The document, as it turned out, prompted a fierce debate between marine and naval commanders over whether two smaller, narrower, and more remote beaches should be used as the landing site rather than the broad sandy expanse before Tinian town. Navy reconnaissance teams reported that the smaller beaches were usable. Thus on 24 July 1944, 15,000 4th Division Marines landed on the beaches identified in the document Way had found while 2nd Division troops distracted the enemy with preparations for a feint against Tinian town. A week later the island was secured with far fewer American dead and wounded than what had been projected for the original landing site.[52]

Navy linguists who triaged and escorted prisoners of war back from the Marianas had the most innovative and perhaps the most rewarding operational experiences to date. The more senior among them fulfilled their predecessors' dreams of questioning many enemy captives and deciding on their disposition. They had a well-honed standard list of questions, but conversational fluency, human empathy, and a measure of cross-cultural understanding proved much more important in their work. Kenneth Lamott, who had left Boulder barely a hundred days earlier, began triaging the twenty prisoners he was responsible for on Tinian with techniques that would later be called "brainwashing." When he first spoke with an old naval warrant officer, the man answered only routine questions and refused to sit down or accept the gift of a cigarette. Then, pitching forward in exhaustion, the prisoner asked the question uppermost in *his* mind—"When are you going to kill me?"—and began to cry. When Lamott got personal and asked where and how he had been captured, the man's resistance softened. Almost without thinking he revealed the location of Japanese heavy weapons and troops that were still fighting. By the time the interrogation ended, Lamott knew that the captive, even though forced by circumstance to betray his comrades in arms, should be sent back to Pearl Harbor for further questioning.[53]

Most of the more than twenty-five hundred prisoners taken in the Marianas were ferried to transports waiting offshore and taken to Hawaii with Boulder-trained men as escorts. Theirs was not the combat role dreamed of back at Pearl Harbor, but it proved richly rewarding nonetheless. Arthur Dornheim watched as a dozen prisoners were hoisted aboard the USS *Ormsby* (APA 49), one by one, with a crowd of sailors looking on. Once on deck, the Japanese were treated like diseased animals. Dornheim followed the prescribed protocol and ordered them to strip, saying simply, "It is for your health." The prisoners, not knowing what might happen next, did so in fear and trembling. Then they were doused with DDT, taken below, and shoved into the ship's brig.[54]

Events aboard the *Ormsby* and other transports during the long voyage back to Pearl Harbor cast the linguists in unexpected roles and changed their perceptions of the Japanese. The escorts saw their charges less as sources of information about the enemy and more as fellow human beings caught up in events not of their own making. Sometimes shared misery triggered that change in perception. When the Pacific swell made everyone seasick, Horace Underwood ran up on deck every ten or fifteen minutes to recover. When he realized that the prisoners had to remain below, he felt genuinely sorry for them. Food also helped the linguists become more empathetic toward their charges. Prisoners passed through the chow line just like everyone else aboard the *Ormsby*. They gobbled up everything indiscriminately, prompting Arthur Dornheim to explain that desserts should be eaten last. But when he realized that the food was like manna from heaven for men who had eaten little in weeks of fighting, he forgave the prisoners' seemingly rude behavior.[55]

Quite unexpectedly, language officer escorts became facilitators of cross-cultural understanding on these long return voyages from combat. Curiosity surged among men who only recently had been enemies, and before long Americans and Japanese were staring at, and learning from, one another. The Japanese watched the mess men and crew banter back and forth and listened to the musically talented among them play the mandolin. Dornheim encouraged the sailors to ask the prisoners questions when they were allowed up on deck for fresh air. That helped the Americans see the Japanese as individuals not so very different from themselves rather than as a faceless foe. They learned that the prisoners had parents, friends, and hometowns as deeply missed as their own. Dornheim found that facilitating such encounters between captives and crew greatly improved his conversational skills and, even more importantly, enhanced his sense of worth as naval officer and a human being.[56]

Indeed, that greater sense of self-worth was perhaps the greatest benefit that naval linguists gained from their experiences in the Marianas operation.

They returned from it knowing more about the seagoing Navy and combat and eager to be more proactive in determining how their talents were used. Otis Cary wangled a plane ride back to Pearl Harbor to keep his superior at JICPOA's interrogation section from turning over newly taken prisoners to the Army. Thrilled to have found more than one "absolutely priceless document" on Saipan, Griffith Way returned to the Zoo "knowing what the possibilities were" and more determined than ever to uncover secrets the enemy thought would never fall into American hands.

Arthur Dornheim's experience emboldened him to write a blistering critique of what he considered misuse of naval language officers in the Marianas. The picture he painted was not pretty. There was too much fragmentation of linguistic talent and an appalling duplication of effort. Some Boulder men were sent to army units already rich with their own officer and nisei enlisted linguists. Others went to marine units that were suspicious of JICPOA men and excessively possessive of information gleaned from enemy documents and captives. Senior officers still had completely unrealistic expectations about what a single language officer could do. Dornheim complained that Rear Adm. Richard Connolly, on whose staff he served, thought that he could monitor Japanese radio broadcasts, go ashore to triage documents, and interrogate prisoners of war just to get information for his particular command's exclusive use. That, Dornheim insisted, would have been "a superhuman task."

The young linguist proposed remedies for the frustrations he and his peers had experienced in the Marianas. Some ideas were old: they should be assigned in teams, be better briefed before leaving Hawaii, and have more leeway in interrogating captives ashore. Other ideas were new: linguists with the operating forces should be able to communicate quickly and directly with their superiors at Pearl Harbor. That would make it possible for fewer linguists to be more effective and allow "more hands" to remain at JICPOA to process rapidly incoming intelligence materials. Still other ideas betrayed lingering desires for greater autonomy within the naval hierarchy. Dornheim wanted language officers in the field to have more control over the uses of the intelligence data that they gathered.[57]

No junior officer linguist's screed such as Dornheim's was likely to bring about fundamental changes in JICPOA warriors' experiences on operations later in 1944. What Woodbridge Bingham complained of as "confusion" continued to frustrate language officers' aspirations for great success in combat.

Each operation was unique, and all were surrounded by the uncertainties and "fog" of war that made it impossible for eager young naval linguists to be as empowered and efficient as Dornheim would have liked. David Osborn departed for an island in Palau in September 1944 attached to an army division and hoping to net many captives with his extraordinary conversational skills. He returned having won a Bronze Star for heroic actions in an assault that killed virtually every Japanese defender of that island. Frank Gibney went on that same operation at Peleliu and expected to escort prisoners back to JICPOA, but there were none. Harry Muheim, Donald Willis, and Horace Underwood were blindsided, in different ways, by interservice rivalries on Leyte in October 1944. Gen. Douglas MacArthur refused to let any of the five hundred captives Muheim was supposed to bring back leave army control. Willis became a courier rather than a combat interpreter. And Underwood slipped into lassitude as a prisoner "catcher" due to clashes between army and naval counterintelligence operatives in the Philippines.[58]

The JICPOA warriors' combat experience in 1943 and 1944 did not fulfill all of their dreams, and they proved powerless to right what they saw as wrongs. Nevertheless, their experiences transformed them as naval intelligence officers and as human beings in more ways than they could imagine. They got the taste of combat and the seagoing navy that they craved. They returned with an experiential feel for war that strengthened their intellectual grasp of the words and phrases they translated. They took pride in having shown their worth by capturing a horde of documents, some of which contributed directly to saving American lives. Most importantly, they took their first steps toward listening to the enemy from something other than a distance. Seeing the Japanese in combat and in its wake not just as a faceless, distant foe produced an invaluable spark within them. That glimmer of empathy for the enemy would make them better intelligence officer linguists in the battles of war—and peace—that still lay ahead.

MORE DISTANT LISTENERS

By the time the JICPOA language officers returned to Pearl Harbor from their combat assignments late in 1944, the network for listening to the enemy of which they were a part had spread still farther west and added a new element far to the east. To the west there were two relatively small components, one at sea, the other in China, and a much larger group of language officers working for Arthur McCollum scattered from Australia north to New Guinea and the Philippines. And in the east, Washington created a new naval intelligence subunit that became home to Boulder WAVES.

The handful of Berkley and Berkeley-Boulder graduates who rode major combatant vessels at sea as radio intelligence unit (RIU) officers came closest to turning into reality Albert Hindmarsh's early naïve visions of what most Japanese-language officers would do. Although they started out in the traffic intelligence section of what became FRUPAC in the fall of 1943, their experience soon diverged from that of the JICPOA linguists. From the very beginning, the RIU officers were part of a team comprising two or more enlisted radio interceptors. They worked directly for senior commanders, bunked in senior officers' cabins, ate in their wardrooms, and hand-carried immediately relevant information to them in flag plot during combat. Because their work was super-secret, they worked virtually independently and escaped routine officers' chores. Working closely with particular admirals, they tended to follow them from one major combatant vessel to another. That meant that, unlike the naval linguists assigned to particular amphibious operations, they spent very long stretches of time at sea.[59]

By late 1944 at least three of the dozen or so who served as fleet radio unit officers had become expert providers of immediately relevant combat information.[60] Back in May 1942 senior intelligence officers at Pearl Harbor had been reluctant to send Tex Biard, a prewar naval student in Japan, to the USS *Yorktown* as a pioneering RIU officer. During and immediately after the Battle of the Coral Sea, he got more information about the enemy from messages sent out from Pearl Harbor and from listening to Japanese civilian shortwave broadcasts than he did from intercepted radio traffic. But as the war at sea progressed in 1943 through the Aleutians operation and raids against Japanese-held islands in the Central Pacific, the RIU officers provided increasingly valuable information. First it was simply confirmation that enemy scouts had spotted American ships. Then it became data gained through radio traffic analysis and code recovery about the size and operational procedures of enemy forces. During the Battle of the Philippine Sea that destroyed the best of the Imperial Japanese Navy's airpower in June 1944 and guaranteed American command of the air and sea for operations in the Marianas, the RIU officers truly came into their own. Lt. (jg) Charles A. "Sandy" Sims provided instant translations of the enemy air attack coordinator's radio transmissions to the carrier task force commander off Saipan. Lt. (jg) Ernest Beath picked up messages from enemy scout planes that resulted in their destruction as well as attacks upon the bases from which they and other Japanese planes that might have attacked the task force sortied.[61]

Little wonder, then, that from mid-1943 onward RIU language officers were assigned to the staffs of every carrier division commander. The more experienced among them trained a small cadre of their juniors fresh from Boulder as replacements or assistants as the fleet continued to grow. And the best of this special group of linguists earned Bronze Stars for their contributions to victory at sea. Their morale soared, buoyed by compliments from the admirals they served. They had every reason to believe, as they said during and after the war, that theirs was "the best job in the entire United States Navy."[62]

The naval language officers who served in China had little reason to rate their duty assignment that highly. They were an eclectic group, some of whom were selected personally by Commander Hindmarsh because of their birth, education, or prior employment in China. At least one graduate from the first Harvard and Berkeley naval Japanese programs, plus one each from the February and July 1943 Boulder graduating classes followed by several others spent most of their active duty in China. Although they eventually served in what became known as U.S. Naval Group China, most were scattered far and wide across western and southern China, truly distant from the Japanese forces occupying its coastal region. They worked in a great variety of small facilities, ranging from the wartime embassy in Chungking to scattered naval radio intercept stations in Kunming, Foochow, and Sanpa. Unlike the RIU officers on flagships at sea, most labored independently, far from the control and perhaps even the knowledge of superiors of significant rank.

These men performed many tasks, some immediately useful, others whose relevance to possible combat and even the outcome of the war was rarely, if ever, clear. The first wartime-trained Japanese linguist to arrive, Berkeley graduate and the son of a missionary to China, Harned P. Hoose, bounced from Chungking to Kunming and eventually to Kweilin. An intercept from the last site helped locate the ineffective Second Japanese Strike Force in the October 1944 Battle of Surigao Strait. Houghton "Buck" Freeman, the son of a China teacher-turned–insurance executive, spent a year in Fukien Province reporting on the weather and the movements of Japanese ships and agents. Occasionally he provided information that helped rescue downed pilots. At the loftily titled Joint Intelligence Collection Agency's Japanese translation section in Chungking, first Stanley Townsend and then Howell Breece directed an office of two dozen Chinese who translated Japanese newspapers, magazines, and unencoded radio broadcasts. They and two other Boulder-trained linguists spent more time discarding useless messages and sending the rest to Washington than they did translating directly war-related Japanese materials. Royal J. Wald sat in Chungking sifting through materials of possible use to Chinese coast-watchers surveilling the Japanese foe, then retreated to Calcutta to work through data on potential landing sites for an American invasion of China that never occurred.[63]

Work of this sort, whether in the capital or at remote intercept sites, did not boost language officers' morale. Going to or from China over the dangerous and sometimes deadly "hump" route from India was exciting, but day-to-day work in China was mundane. "I cannot believe," Howell Breece later recalled, "that any of our intercepted messages provided a single bit of intelligence useful to anyone." Even in China's wartime capital, Chungking, only an occasional B-29 returning from bombing missions or the rare presence of a single Japanese prisoner of war gave the Boulder men working there any sense of closeness to the war. Sipping low-quality bourbon or vile faux gin brewed by an expatriate White Russian may have provided occasional temporary solace in such a situation. But except for a few, the naval Japanese linguists in China resolutely continued their daily drudgery without feeling the pride or graining the recognition that their brothers at sea or back at Pearl Harbor or Washington, D.C., achieved. They were truly distant listeners to the enemy.[64]

"JACKS-OF-ALL-TRADES:" NAVAL LANGUAGE OFFICERS "DOWN UNDER"

There were other Boulder-trained listeners who were still farther away from Japan and the fighting in the Pacific. The naval language officers who served down under, in Australia and the Southwest Pacific, had a much more meaningful—and exciting—war experience than their brothers in China. Bobby Curts was only nineteen years old when he stepped onto the tarmac at an airfield near Brisbane, Australia, in September 1943. He joined more than three dozen Boulder men who moved ever closer to the enemy over the next eighteen months. These men became "jacks-of-all-trades," working at sites that varied from the Allied Translator and Interpreter Service (ATIS), a kind of far western JICPOA, to Arthur McCollum's dream intelligence center, to army front lines, to staffs aboard the ships of the Seventh Fleet. While their experiences paralleled those of the JICPOA Boulder men in some respects, they differed in other ways that demand further explanation.[65]

ATIS had been set up in September 1942 at an old mansion at Indooroopilly, a suburb of Brisbane where Gen. Douglas MacArthur maintained his headquarters. Although it was essentially an army facility, the organization from its beginnings heavily depended on naval Japanese-language talent. Samuel Bartlett, one of two brothers from a missionary family who had an unmatched command of written and spoken Japanese, headed its examination [interrogation] section. By the end of 1943, nearly 150 army enlisted nisei whose spoken Japanese was good had come to ATIS. But they and the first graduates of the Army's Japanese-language program for Caucasian officers who arrived in April 1944 had trouble reading *sōsho* and *gyōsho*, the handwritten scripts in which most documents captured on Southwest Pacific battlefields were written. Six out of ten of the 1943 arrivals and nearly half of those who came early in 1944 simply could not decipher that hastily scrawled Japanese.[66]

That deficiency opened the door for the nearly forty naval language officers who served at ATIS in 1943 and 1944 to play roles disproportionate to their rank and numbers. Curts quickly became an expert on Japanese machine-gun tactics and soon was translating field manuals that army nisei sergeants could not. His knack for *sōsho* and *gyōsho* enabled him to read the diary of an uncooperative captive Japanese officer who had participated in the beheading of an Australian pilot. Frank Ikle used his German to interrogate recalcitrant crew members of a Nazi sub that had been sunk off Penang. S. Paul Kramer, who had worked in quasi-intelligence capacities with the British before entering the Boulder program, rated his own office, his own jeep, and a round-the-clock bodyguard as an assistant to the senior British naval officer at ATIS. Robert Ward, another July 1943 Boulder graduate, soon demonstrated the intellectual acumen and administrative skills that made him a major figure in the postwar development of Japanese studies in America. As second-in-command in ATIS's research section, he translated a captured version of Japan's November 1941 plans for the Pearl Harbor attack, used enemy diaries to show why the Japanese abandoned parachute bombing, and developed a comprehensive system for categorizing and utilizing captured documents. He earned the extremely prestigious Legion of Merit award.[67]

By the fall of 1944, the naval language officers scattered from ATIS in Brisbane in two quite different directions. Some men went to work for Arthur McCollum, now a captain and Commander Seventh Fleet's chief of staff for intelligence. After a long struggle with ATIS's commander, whom he belittled as "the Syrian rug merchant," and with a senior officer at FRUMEL who considered him "a nasty hunk of work . . . who wanted to run the whole goddam show," he succeeded in creating a comprehensive intelligence center close to the scene of fighting. At SEVIC, the Seventh Fleet Intelligence Center, McCollum corralled every scrap of information a fleet commander might want: prisoner-of-war interrogation reports, comments from naval radio intercept facilities, and eventually the full range of naval signals intelligence. To work on this treasure trove, he pirated away some of ATIS's best naval talent: a Harvard-trained lawyer, a linguistically gifted musician, and the precocious Curts. They and his other recruits quickly discovered that while McCollum was not an easy man to work for, he made those who were on his good side feel that they could do no wrong. That won their loyalty, boosted their morale, and fueled their eagerness to move ever closer to the front lines.[68]

For the next six months ATIS and SEVIC jockeyed for information and influence at Lake Sentani, some twenty miles from Hollandia, on the northwestern coast of New Guinea, where Gen. MacArthur and Adm. Thomas Kinkaid, now Seventh Fleet commander, established forward headquarters. The language officers labored in an exotic setting. Red-breasted cockatoos sang from their cages in working spaces. Scantily clad native women tantalized the young bachelor linguists, and army nurses helped them while away off-duty hours at a beautiful officers' club "perched on the summit of a high hill . . . [that overlooked] a lush valley." When not salving their loneliness in drink or floating lazily on the lake at night, the Boulder linguists either translated captured documents at headquarters or went out on temporary assignment as interpreters and document catchers with army units at the front lines. The SEVIC men did whatever Arthur McCollum wanted them to do in preparation for the impending Battle of Leyte Gulf and invasion of the Philippines.[69]

McCollum worked hard to get naval language officers as close as possible to the enemy in these struggles. John Ashmead landed on Leyte just a day after General MacArthur, having been "under torpedo attack, bombed, shelled, strafed, and sniped at." Attached to the Army's XXIV Corps, he set out in pursuit of the Japanese and soon became "quite expert" in the ways of soldiers—and biting insects. "I sleep with a knife in bed, rifle and helmet on the deck, [and am] ready to leap out at the slightest rustle," he boasted. Bobby Curts bummed a ride on a B-25 to army field headquarters on Leyte, taking Sam Bartlett and Jack Wiley, two of the best Brisbane linguists with him. They became the principal interrogators at MacArthur's Tacloban field headquarters where, without any army nisei help, they queried prisoners who were "literally wet."[70]

The SEVIC linguists sent to sea had wildly varying experiences. Arthur McCollum had a tough time persuading Admiral Kinkaid to take several of them aboard his Seventh Fleet flagship. Five Boulder men watched the Lingayen Gulf landings as helpless bystanders rather than useful interrogators because army intelligence officers refused to release captives for questioning aboard what was supposed to be a prisoner-of-war ship. The enemy cut short Frank Ryder's part in the reconquest of the Philippines. He was to have been put ashore to broadcast to the Japanese "as a diversionary tactic." But a kamikaze struck his ship, sending him to sick bay with multiple injuries including the loss of his right eye, for which he received a Purple Heart.[71]

Others had intelligence-gathering adventures whose excitement and value equaled, and at times even exceeded, those of the JICPOA warriors. In mid-April 1945, not long after SEVIC and ATIS shifted their advanced headquarters to the ruins of Manila, a group of SEVIC and Seventh Fleet staff intelligence officer linguists pulled off "the . . . intelligence coup . . . [that] dwarf[ed] perhaps any other . . . of the Pacific War." Bobby Curts, Dick Finn, Hammond Rolph, and four other Boulder men boarded the submarine tender USS *Chanticleer* (ARS-7) and headed out into Manila Bay to a spot near Corregidor Island where the cruiser *Nachi*, onetime flagship of the Imperial Japanese Navy's Fifth Fleet, had been sunk. They watched in amazement as divers brought up an unbelievable treasure trove of documents and equipment from the enemy ship. The linguists pored over materials that ranged from a November 1941 strategic war plan, to plans for the disastrous 1944 SHO (Victory) offensive, to charts of minefields, and the first examples of Japanese shipboard radar and infrared and ultraviolet signaling equipment. These Boulder men had every reason to believe that they had finally become *real* naval intelligence officers. What they achieved at that moment of triumph made their months of hard study at Boulder, the endless days spent waiting for transportation, and the hours and hours they had slaved in translating cryptic enemy documents worthwhile.[72]

LAST PIECES

Moments such as the recovery of materials from the *Nachi* rarely, if ever, happened for Boulder WAVES. They worked at the last major navy Japanese-language translation facility established during the war, eventually known as the Washington Documents Center. It combined the Far East subsection of ONI's Translation Section (Op-16-FE) and elements of Op-20-G and was housed in the Steuart Building, a former automobile dealership at 5th and K streets in the nation's capital. The Documents Center was the final resting place for captured materials that those in the Pacific considered too unimportant to bother with. There all sixty-nine of the Boulder women, together with a handful of older male language school graduates, labored to squeeze every drop of potentially useful information out of what crossed their desks.[73]

The women came to Washington fresh from their naval training at Smith College, in Northampton, Massachusetts. After the rigors of Boulder, their time at Smith seemed like a New England fall holiday. Their "crash course" was only half as long as that for other WAVES, and they left it with mixed feelings. Many of them had dreamed of going to Hawaii, as replacements for JICPOA men who would be freed for duty in the fleet or with the Marines. But a socially conservative senator who insisted that "the flower of young American womanhood" should not be sent overseas doomed them to duty in the nation's capital. That left many of these very bright and capable young women furious, but they accepted their fate.[74]

A few of them were lucky enough to land special assignments. Some transliterated interrogation reports of high-ranking prisoners of war written in *sōsho*. Nearly a quarter of those in Op-16-FE translated charts and hydrographic information needed for monographs on the Japanese ports that would be used in an invasion of the enemy's homeland. A handful among the fifteen who worked in Op-20-G's library section enjoyed the challenge of struggling with particularly difficult handwritten Japanese messages.[75]

Most WAVE language officers, however, performed more prosaic translation tasks in a huge room not unlike the JICPOA Zoo. Those who had grown up in Japan felt very much "at home" there because one of their two their immediate supervisors was Boulder Marine Roger W. Hackett's missionary father. They got along with their commanding officer, Edward S. Pearce, a handsome but alcoholic veteran of language study in Japan in the late 1920s. He could be violent, and once he kicked down the door to their work space. But he could also be charmed. When he was promoted to captain, the WAVE who pinned the eagles symbolizing his new rank onto his collar produced barely suppressed snickers by exclaiming, "I've never made a captain before!"[76]

The Boulder women rarely missed an opportunity to break the monotony of their daily routine. Some cast warm glances at a particularly handsome blond lieutenant working alongside a former classmate at the opposite end of the room. When movie idol Douglas Fairbanks Jr. paid a visit to the Steuart Building, work stopped. That was a pleasant diversion for women who felt their talents were underused in translating "everything," when "everything" included a treatise on the sex life of the lobster, reports of why socks wore out in one place and not another, and the musings of a Japanese soldier suffering from dysentery. Some of the women, bored and disgusted by the stench of bags fresh from Tinian, even took to racing the beetles that poured out of the bags alongside documents to be translated.[77]

Such light moments provided welcome relief from work the Boulder WAVES later remembered as boring, frustrating, and of no apparent use in the war effort. But at the time, even though they knew they labored at the bottom of the intelligence food chain, these young women worked long and hard nonetheless. Imbued by their teachers at Boulder with a sense of the larger importance of the language skills they had developed, they translated, translated, and translated some more—without openly questioning whether it many any sense for them to "translate everything." Their devotion to duty was every bit as strong as that of the Boulder men at ATIS and JICPOA, at sea, or with the Marines.

The WAVES in Washington were the last links in what by early 1945 had become a global naval network for listening to the enemy. What three years earlier had been a small, idiosyncratic, and underpowered effort to do so had become an enormous, sophisticated, and multifaceted endeavor to capture, translate, and use his every word against him. Albert Hindmarsh knew that Boulder men and women, regardless of the uniform they wore or where they served, contributed mightily to that result. He saw that in Washington, and that was what their superiors at JICPOA told him when he visited Hawaii in January and February 1945. Moved by that high praise and by concern that too much hard work in the same place for too long would devastate morale, especially that of married linguists who longed to live with their wives, he returned to the capital and engineered the first rotation of naval language officers between Washington, D.C., Pearl Harbor, and even Australia.[78]

The successful commencement of that exchange demonstrated how truly vital and useful the onetime Boulder students had become. True, most had never seen or spoken to a Japanese fighting man and only a few stayed at sea as Commander Hindmarsh and the other Boulder builders had imagined they would. But what they did as distant listeners had changed them as no teacher at Boulder, no "old salt" telling "sea stories" of *his* encounter with the enemy could have done. The naval language officers had matured. Strengthened and seasoned by experiences that sped their growth as individuals and enhanced their capabilities as intelligence professionals, they had become essential elements in the mighty machine that was hastening the day of Japan's defeat.

By the spring of 1945, the Boulder men, sailors and Marines alike, stood ready, at long last, to meet the Japanese—combatants and civilians, vigorous enemies and hapless victims—face to face in the last, bloodiest battles of the war.

Chapter Five

WARRIORS TRANSFORMED

On Easter Sunday, 1 April 1945, naval and marine language officers who had gone their separate ways since Boulder came together thousands of miles away on the beaches of Okinawa. They joined the largest armada America had ever assembled for an amphibious assault in the Pacific in what would be the last, the bloodiest, and the most decisive battle in the war against Japan. That contest would test the knowledge they had gained at Boulder, the skills they had honed in their various duties thereafter, and, most importantly, their character. It would put them face to face with more Japanese combatants than they had ever seen. On Okinawa, more than ever before, they would have to look beyond the immediate horrors of war to see their common humanity with the enemy. What they saw and did on that island prepared the Boulder men for their last wartime tasks: arranging the peaceful surrender of the enemy and preparing for the occupation of his homeland.

On that Sunday morning, two men who had walked next to one another across the stage of Mackey Auditorium at Boulder nearly two years earlier now waded ashore onto the soft white sands of Hagushi Beach. Marine first lieutenant Roger Hackett, who at twenty was one of the youngest of the July 1943 graduates, was now a seasoned combat interpreter—a veteran of tough fighting from Cape Gloucester to Peleliu. Navy lieutenant commander Willard A. Hanna, eight years Hackett's senior, came to Okinawa by a far different route. After serving at JICPOA at Pearl Harbor, he had gone to the Navy School of Military Government at Columbia University. The two men embodied what on that April morning seemed likely to be two very different roles: combat interpreter and keeper of the defeated. But in the weeks and months that lay ahead of Hackett, Hanna, and all of the other Boulder men who came to Okinawa, those two functions merged into a single, daunting task: fighting and saving the foe. In meeting that challenge, Boulder men of war would be transformed into point men for peace.[1]

UNEXPECTED ENCOUNTERS

On the morning of L-Day, 1 April 1945, such a change lay beyond the wildest imaginings of those who fought the battle of Okinawa. Both sides had known for months that it must occur. Each prepared for the fight determined to win. For the Japanese, that meant killing so many Americans that Washington would negotiate an end to the war. For the Americans, victory on Okinawa was the penultimate battle that would pre-position them for the final invasion and defeat of Japan. Both sides approached the battle expecting to see the very worst in the other.

Nearly a year before the Americans appeared off Okinawa's shore, Gen. Ushijima Mitsuru, who commanded its defenders, painted a grim picture of what lay ahead. An American landing would mean "death for you, death for me, death for all of us"—his 32nd Army and the more than 400,000 natives and Japanese immigrants who lived on Okinawa. To help prevent or delay that unhappy event, Ushijima and his naval counterpart, Rear Admiral Ōta Minoru, drafted nearly 40,000 young men to form a home guard and mobilized more than 2,000 teenagers. The boys joined Iron and Blood Volunteer units, and the girls formed an auxiliary nurse corps. They were no substitute for the division taken from Okinawa to help defend the Philippines, but they might help slow the enemy's advance once the Americans had landed.[2]

Hoping to achieve that result, Ushijima stealthily shifted his troops from the island's beaches and airfields to three fortified defensive lines thrown across the hills and ridges of the central and southern portions of the island. He also began pushing civilians from their homes in those areas to Okinawa's undeveloped north. That forced move only added to the psychological unease that everyone on the island felt as a consequence of American actions. In September 1944, a U.S. Navy submarine had torpedoed an evacuation ship with nearly fifteen hundred women and children aboard, sending all to their deaths. A month later, American planes flattened large portions of Naha, the island's capital city, with heavy loss of life. And in the last days before the invasion, guns from the American armada surrounding Okinawa rained down a hail of death and destruction that portended still worse to come. On 1 April General Ushijima urged "all people of Okinawa . . . [to] attack and annihilate the ugly Americans!" But terrified local residents simply fled from the beaches where the hated invaders were expected to land.[3]

The invaders were more numerous and better prepared than ever before. American planners amassed the biggest amphibious force of the Pacific War for Operation Iceberg, the assault on Okinawa. Some four hundred assault ships, accompanied by eight hundred other vessels, carried five army and three marine divisions (the 1st, 2nd, and 6th) to the island. In preparation for its invasion, occupation, and pacification of its inhabitants, American reconnaissance aircraft photographed nearly 90 percent of Okinawa. Civil affairs experts prepared a massive study of the island's terrain, climate, and people.[4]

Language officers were scattered throughout this invasion force. Two of the most senior among them—Bill Burd and Sandy Sims—intercepted, decoded, and translated Japanese messages aboard the ships of Task Force 51; one of the most junior, Neal Jensen, did the same as a member of the staff of Adm. Raymond A. Spruance, its commander. More than a dozen JICPOA men served on the staff at Tenth Army Headquarters, and three more were assigned to its marine counterpart, the III Amphibious Corps. Still more Boulder naval men served alongside seasoned marine combat linguists in divisions and regiments. In all, more than one hundred graduates of the Navy Japanese Language School joined in the battle for Okinawa. Some were old hands. Ted de Bary and Donald Keene had gone to the Aleutians in the fall of 1943, and Hart Spiegel had fought on Bougainville and Guam. Others, like ensigns Walt Bass and Abraham Cohen and marine second lieutenant James M. "Jim" Jefferson had completed their language studies barely a year earlier and were about to experience combat for the first time.[5]

By late March 1945, these invaders-to-be had few, if any, illusions about the toughness of their adversary they would face on Okinawa. They may not have swallowed whole the Army's portrayal of Japan as a "blood-drunk demon," whose people, soldiers and civilians alike, were brainwashed militaristic robots. But recent experience taught them that the enemy on Okinawa would fight ferociously in seemingly inhuman ways. In September 1944, Japanese defenders on Peleliu had killed themselves rather than surrender, and a month later the first kamikaze suicide bombers had appeared in the Battle of Leyte

Gulf. Intense, prolonged Japanese resistance on Iwo Jima had forced a postponement of the Okinawa invasion for two weeks. And the Japanese navy, despite its crippling losses in the Battle of the Philippine Sea, had sent *kaiten*, suicide submarine boats, and aircraft to attack the American fleet at Ulithi, the advanced base where it was preparing for the assault.[6]

Even the most empathetic of Boulder graduates approached Okinawa with trepidation. Those who had volunteered to leave the safety of Pearl Harbor to participate in the coming onslaught knew that the Japanese they would encounter in battle would not behave like the kindly Japanese and Japanese Americans they had known at Boulder. Nor would the enemy on Okinawa resemble the docile, playful, and only occasionally deceitful captives they had questioned at Pearl Harbor. The foe would be a fearsome "other," whose behavior in battle might be every bit as bad as that portrayed in the worst, most stereotypical propaganda. That truth struck Lt. (jg) Donald Keene with devastating force as he neared Okinawa. He saw "death headed in my direction" when a kamikaze approached his ship only to turn, hit the mast of another ship nearby, and plunge into the sea. The sudden, visceral rush of emotion that he felt at that moment made it perfectly clear that he was about encounter Japanese unlike any he had seen before.[7]

When he and 50,000 other Americans waded ashore on 1 April 1945, however, the ferocious "other" was scarcely to be seen. Only the 2nd Division marine decoy force met any serious resistance. On the five-mile-long beach where Roger Hackett, Willard Hanna, Donald Keene, Dan Karasik, and so many other Boulder men came ashore, only a horde of sand flies and an occasional civilian were on hand to greet them. Rather than killing or capturing Japanese soldiers, Lieutenant (junior grade) Keene ended up trying to get a terrified mother and child out of harm's way.[8]

That incident portended what naval and marine Japanese-language officers would experience during, and even beyond, the next eighty-two days of battle on Okinawa. They came to the island as warriors and aides to those who made war. But they ended up shepherding survivors toward peace. What they saw and did varied with their particular duties, but a common thread runs through their experience of war on Okinawa: the language officers met the enemy, combatants and civilians alike, more intimately and in greater numbers than ever before. When they came close to the foe, the mask of a ferocious, inhuman "other" fell away, and they saw simply another human being. In so doing, they and those whom they unmasked took the first steps toward peace.

LANGUAGE FOR VICTORY—AND LIFE

Boulder Marines met the enemy on Okinawa in ways that were unexpected, unimaginable, and ultimately inspiring and enlightening. Surprise characterized their encounters during the first phase of the fighting. Thanks to General Ushijima's changed strategy, what the Americans had expected would be "normal" fighting in the northern portions of the island turned out, with the exception of a tough five-day struggle on the Motobu peninsula, to be "pretty much . . . a hike to the top" of Okinawa. Only chance confidence-building but sobering encounters with civilians and a few irregular combatants ensued.[9]

Those first meetings, however, started to break down the barriers of fear and hatred between the American and Japanese "others." Some proved amusing as well as enlightening. Lt. James Brayshay, who led the first reconnaissance patrol to cross the island from west to east, approached a seawall convinced that "a slug of Japs" lay hidden behind it. When he called for them to surrender, only two old women appeared, and Brayshay heaved a sigh of relief. Lt. Hart Spiegel gained fresh confidence in his language skills in a funny way when he first encountered Okinawan Japanese. He had worried that he would be unable to understand the locals, who purportedly spoke an impenetrable dialect that bore little resemblance to the standard Japanese he had learned at Boulder. Sure enough, when he tried to question an approaching group of ragtag men, Spiegel could not understand a word they said. His sense of humiliation and incompetence vanished only when he learned that they had wandered out of a home for the mentally incompetent.[10]

Other first encounters literally terrified those on both sides. As Spiegel and his men pushed up the cove-strewn northeastern coast of Okinawa, they found farmers cowering in defense of their fields who could scarcely believe that the Marines were not about to kill them. When Lt. Jim Jefferson went out on patrol to find and remove local citizens likely to get in harm's way, he suddenly saw a Japanese soldier, helmeted, fully uniformed, and armed with a rifle and a grenade bag, step out of the brush onto the trail. The two foes stopped, looked at each other, but did not reach for their weapons. Both caught a glint of common humanity in each other's eyes that made them hold their fire and vanish from sight into the brush. Relieved that he had not been killed in his first encounter with the enemy, Jefferson and his civilian charges then "hightailed it" for 6th Division headquarters. He felt that the two "others" had best keep apart.[11]

That proved impossible in the second phase of the fighting. For five weeks General Ushijima and his men fought Marines and soldiers of the Army's 7th and 96th Infantry divisions along lines across the south central portion of Okinawa, just north of its capital, Naha. The struggle resembled World War I combat. But the opposing lines were much closer, the weapons more destructive, and the orders to go "over the top" constant. Hordes of civilians roamed the miniature no-man's-lands between the two sides. General Ushijima made devastating tactical use of them, pushing the helpless noncombatants ahead toward enemy lines. The Americans, fearing that combatant infiltrators were hidden among them, shot at them, betraying their own positions. That allowed the Japanese to bracket the soldiers and Marines with artillery fire. The result was slow, steady slaughter in which the combatants' humanity all but disappeared. No quarter was given. Few, if any, prisoners were taken. The Americans inched, rather than raced, forward. Yankee soldiers took three weeks to capture one ridge; and 6th Division Marines fought for eight days to take a hill they dubbed Sugar Loaf.[12]

In fighting of this sort, enemy civilians demanded the language officers' attention as much or more than combatants. Getting them out the killing grounds quickly required more linguists than the Marines had, so they sought help from naval language officers from III Amphibious Corps headquarters. Together they first tried to persuade teenaged enlisted Marines, who were grief-stricken at their buddies' deaths or just determined to push ahead of their army counterparts, to hold their fire. The men usually just shouted "*Dete koi!*" [Come out!] at civilians cowering in rough terrain between the two opposing forces and then shot them. Language officers such as Jim Brayshay, Dan Karasik, and Jim Jefferson found it "kind of tough" to get their own men to wait so that they could coax the locals out of hiding places with words, candy, or cigarettes.[13]

The language officers then had to deal with "jillions" of people who flooded across the battle lines. "Old men, old women, and hundreds of babies, [people] carrying stuff on their heads and backs came rolling in," Lt. (jg) Dan Karasik wrote. There were "missing babies [and] parents, [some with] no clothing, no food, no water." The situation was "just plain chaos," because these refugees "had a million problems," and because they spoke "this damn dialect." Karasik quickly realized that despite what he had thought his duty in battle would be, he first had to see that "this big mob was pretty well taken care of." Before he could coax enemy soldiers to surrender, he had to help care for Japanese civilians.[14]

Separating the hostile from the harmless among them proved challenging. Two of the best 1st Marine Division linguists, Roger Hackett and Jim Brayshay, did so by ignoring routine procedures. They simply stopped taking notes in interrogations and raced against one another to send more people to the rear for questioning. Jim Jefferson, one of the newest language officers, had honed his conversational skills by chatting, laughing, and even playing with prisoners back at Pearl Harbor. That enabled him to triage the enemy in a rough-and-ready way. After questioning someone found to be "safe," he scribbled "O.K." on a slip of paper and pressed it into the person's hand. Captives with such passes were then herded back to minimally guarded temporary stockades. Jefferson's regimental intelligence officer, another newcomer, thought this procedure far too risky and threatened to punish him. Fortunately, Jefferson's division intelligence officer took a different attitude. The lieutenant escaped censure and continued to put his considerable conversational skills to good use in battle.[15]

During the third and final phase of the fighting on Okinawa, marine and naval linguists worked more closely with local civilians than ever before, thanks to General Ushijima. In the third week of May, having lost 60,000 men, he ordered a general retreat to the southern hilly, cave-ridden third of the island that sloped to its southernmost shores. He intended to use his army and an expanded home guard that included young male teenagers and female nurses in training to make a last, determined stand against the invaders. But because he did not tell local civilian leaders of his plans, the battlefield brimmed with noncombatants. That recreated the tactical conditions that Americans had faced on Saipan and Tinian. But this time local people behaved like shepherds rather than lambs being led to the slaughter. They chose to help the invaders rather than their supposed defenders.[16]

The collaborators came from the nearly 32,000 men, women, and children who had fallen into American hands by the end of April 1945. Exhausted, disoriented, and frightened, these people were first herded into hastily constructed stockades where they were doused with DDT and given strange "C-rations" to eat. Men of military age were separated from their families and then all were marched to presumably safer but even more primitive living conditions further north on the island. Their "tents" had neither walls, floors, nor doors, and they provided little or no protection from wind and rain. People were crowded together in unsanitary, disease-causing conditions that appalled even their American captors.[17]

Nevertheless, local men stepped forward to help American Marines. At first the invaders "volunteered" their services as auxiliary linguists to call other civilians out of their hiding places. In the second phase of the fighting, men in "protective custody" genuinely volunteered to help Americans fight the Japanese. Some who did so may have been motivated simply by a desire to escape the camps. Others may have harbored genuine anger toward Japanese soldiers who had failed to protect them. Still others acted out of gratitude, like the wounded boy who stayed with Hart Spiegel and his men throughout the fighting after they gave him food and medicine. Feelings of that sort prompted some civilians to become document translators at 6th Marine Division Headquarters. But these emotions were not strong enough to survive the test of battle. Once they experienced its horrors, four out of five Okinawan volunteers decided to return to internment camps, despite the miseries and indignities they suffered there.[18]

What motivated the remaining local collaborators did not become clear until the third and final phase of the fighting. Glen Slaughter, the 29th Marine Regiment's language officer, realized what that reason was when he and his guide, Komesu Seiichi, found the ruins of the Okinawan's home in the rubble of Naha. The guide, nicknamed Tony, walked away from it stoically, determined, despite what the Americans had done, to help them end the fighting. Scarcely able to keep a dry eye, Slaughter realized that his companion could do that only if he saw the war in essentially the same way that he himself did. The conflict caught up every man regardless of individual feeling or state of life. The only way to escape it was to put aside one's strongest feelings about what had happened in the past and look to the future. That emotion kept Slaughter going, and it explained Tony Komesu's loyalty and determination to help him in whatever fighting lay ahead. The two men became inseparable companions for the rest of the battle of Okinawa.[19]

Together the language officers and their local collaborators helped speed the battle's end by saving as well as taking lives. They risked their lives to became lifesavers in three ways, some old, some new, and all very dangerous. Together they managed the negotiated surrender of Japanese defenders in open and still contested ground. One such place was just south of the Kokuba

River estuary behind the port of Naha. There the 4th, 22nd, and 29th Marine regiments converged to encircle a flat tidal area behind the seawall facing the estuary. In the first, dark hours of 12 June 1945, naval guns sent up star shells that drifted down on little white parachutes. Marine lieutenant Hart Spiegel used a big bullhorn to urge the Japanese defenders to surrender by putting up their hands with one of those parachutes. "It worked perfectly," he recalled. The unarmed among the Japanese followed his orders while American skirmishers covered by machine-gun fire advanced across the field. Japanese soldiers who continued to resist slithered along the ground to the sea wall, where most were killed.[20]

The tactic worked but not without one last risk. After the fighting stopped, when the Marines were starting to move out of the area, Glen Slaughter approached one of the Japanese who had supposedly surrendered. The man had apparently decided to kill himself and was holding a live grenade. Luckily, he hesitated for a moment or changed his mind. An enlisted Marine saw the grenade, reached past Slaughter to grab it, and then "tossed [it] . . . over the sea wall, where it exploded in midair."[21]

The linguists and their collaborators also perfected cave-crawling as a way of taking prisoners and saving civilians to the point that their exploits became the basis for a "how-to-do-it" publication circulated by JICPOA. Early in the fighting, Americans cave-crawled on their own by ferreting civilians and combatants out of Okinawan tombs. In its last weeks, such action became more difficult and dangerous because so many Japanese hid in concealed positions from which they could easily kill Americans. Marines responded by smothering or frying the enemy with hydrogen phosphorous or napalm as they had on Iwo Jima. If they were to take prisoners or save civilians, language officers and their local guides had to go into the caves before that happened.[22]

What they experienced was both horrifying and enlightening. Sometimes cave-crawling reinforced Americans' stereotypical views of the Japanese. Lt. (jg) Donald Keene's sometime empathy for the enemy melted away in the face of its dangers. He chided soldiers for building fires at the mouth of a cave to "smoke out" the enemy within. But he changed his tune when he himself crawled into one to try to persuade civilians to come out. When he ran smack into an armed Japanese soldier, he "leaped out of the way of his gun and never again attempted such heroics." Hart Spiegel and his men had cave-crawling encounters that suggested that the Japanese really were deceitful and inhuman. On one occasion a soldier they presumed dead reached for a grenade, and Spiegel shot him. On another, when they crawled into a U-shaped cave to try to roust out civilians, the Okinawans pointed them toward another entrance where they were hit by a big explosion from Japanese artillery. Spiegel's most harrowing crawl was in the cave that had been Rear Admiral Ōta's headquarters. He and his men came upon stacks of corpses crawling with maggots, then stumbled into a few men still alive who cried weakly for help. When they learned that the admiral had ordered his doctors to kill hundreds of wounded and then slit his own throat rather than surrender, they came away from the grisly scene more certain than ever that the Japanese enemy was an inhuman fanatic.[23]

In the end, however, cave-crawling helped to break down stereotypes and bring Americans and Japanese face to face with their common humanity. When Lt. (jg) William H. Allman went back to Admiral Ōta's cave to search for cryptological equipment and other information after Spiegel and his men left it, he discovered that his once-tough prisoner guides were afraid to go inside. At another site a Japanese who thought Marines were fiends silently chanted "Mother, please save me!" as three of them, tattooed and stripped to the waist, advanced with their automatic weapons pointed at him. But they did not kill him. Hart Spiegel especially pitied the "wrinkled old . . . women, some old men . . . , and quite a few children" who often shared a cave with Japanese soldiers. They risked being shot because they wore parts of Japanese uniforms while their supposed protectors wore their civilian clothes. Luckily their "haggard and bedraggled" appearance betrayed the civilians' status and stayed his Marines' trigger fingers.[24]

The third way in which the language officers and their local collaborators saved lives was brokering surrenders before fighting began. One of the most dramatic instances of that activity came only a few days before the fighting ended on 23 June 1945. By that time the 29th Marine regiment had trapped Japanese army troops on a high grassy bluff that overlooked a shard-strewn beach near Kiyotake. The marine regimental commander agreed to halt his advance for two days to "soften up the area by persuasion in order to save lives on both sides." That gave Glen Slaughter and Tony Komesu a chance to try to get people who had hidden in caves and on ledges on the bluff to give up. The two men boarded a landing craft (LCI), came as close to shore as the rocks permitted, and then slipped into a dory with some sailors to go ashore.

When they reached the site, they heard what sounded like a firefight on the bluff above. But that turned out to be people killing themselves with grenades. Eventually about forty Korean labor troops and Japanese soldiers came down to the beach, where a marine platoon leader escorted them away behind American lines to safety.

The next day Slaughter and his guide returned to the same spot. From the deck of the landing craft, Komesu broadcast another appeal to surrender. Only one man, Uchizono Yōzō, a medical officer attached to the Japanese 24th Division, heeded the call and started to swim out to the ship. Despite being raked by Japanese gunfire, he made it to the landing craft and clambered aboard safely. Then he grabbed a bullhorn and began calling upon the others to give up. Only some did so, but Uchizono had demonstrated extraordinary concern for his fellow Okinawans in a way that impressed Lieutenant Slaughter.

On the third day, Slaughter and Komesu returned to the same beach. They called out to those still ashore, telling them they were trapped between the sea and U.S. Marines above them. This time the call to surrender—and life—worked. The ensuing operation ended with the Marines taking several hundred prisoners and civilians with only nominal casualties to themselves. It had taken three tries, but the Japanese had shown themselves to be reasonable rather than fanatic; and Slaughter had accomplished his military—and humanitarian—mission.[25] He was just one of the many language officers on Okinawa who showed that they could kill when they must and save lives whenever possible.

THE ENEMY'S KEEPERS

Slaughter and Komesu's success in persuading trapped Japanese to give themselves up marked the beginning of a new trend in the last days of the fighting on Okinawa. The Japanese "other" started to behave more like the Americans. Although the enemy commanders, General Ushijima and Rear Admiral Ōta, committed ritual suicide, ordinary Japanese soldiers began surrendering as never before. Within three days the number who gave themselves up jumped from an average of 50 daily to nearly 1,000 in a single day. While some Japanese soldiers sought refuge in the wild, jungle-covered north of the island, many more streamed into open fields and roads in the south where American troops captured them. All told, nearly 7,500 Japanese combatants, three times as many in the Marshalls campaign, were taken prisoner on Okinawa. And during the last two weeks of the fighting, an estimated 80,000 civilians, a third to a half of whom were wounded, came out of their hiding places and turned themselves over to the Americans.[26]

By 23 June 1945, so many Japanese combatants had been killed or captured that marine major general Roy Geiger declared Okinawa "secured." But in fact the island was far from safe. It was 2 July before the new 10th Army commander, Gen. Joseph "Vinegar Joe" Stilwell, proclaimed an official end to the fighting. But even then, as a senior naval captain warned, that really just meant that there were "no more organized lines of resistance, . . . just fighting all over the damn place." His words aptly described the next seven weeks of "mop-up" operations on Okinawa. In the south, "an incalculable number of isolated individuals or small groups [were still] holding up in caves"; 6th Division Marines flushed out thirty-nine hundred Japanese soldiers and their supporting labor troops. In the north, men of the 1st Marine Division stalked Japanese stragglers, "shot them down with matter-of-fact efficiency," and took five hundred more prisoners of war.[27]

Boulder-trained language officers had more, not less, to do in this phase of operations on Okinawa. They helped enemy soldiers give themselves up and joined surrender-seeking and hunter-killer operations. They took on greater responsibility for more prisoners and squeezed more useful information out of them. They helped civilian survivors of the fight just ended begin their transition back to more normal life. The language officers became the enemy's keepers and thus became peacemakers of a sort.

The moment of surrender was a particularly dangerous time for everyone involved. It could produce savagery—by Americans. One group of Marines came upon a Japanese soldier beside two dead children and a woman. After learning that he had raped the woman and slit her throat, they used cigarettes to burn "USMC" on his chest then broke his leg by deliberately dropping the stretcher on which they were carrying him. Surrender also yielded enlightenment of a sort. Another group of Marines encountered four Japanese soldiers who showed signs of willingness to surrender. They were ordered to strip to their *fundoshi* (loincloths) and given food and cigarettes. But then nearly a hundred more Japanese soldiers appeared and surrounded the Marines. For a moment the Americans felt they were at a second Custer's last stand. But as one Marine put it, the Japanese "didn't seem to know what they were going to do, and we sure as hell didn't know. . . . [We knew] only that dying was their honorable thing and taking an American along was even better." After what seemed like an eternity, the Japanese "gave themselves up, the whole bunch." The Marines held their fire.[28]

Marine language officers were called upon to try to prevent incidents of excessive violence like the first sort and to facilitate more peaceful and humane surrenders like the latter. Particularly fluent conversationalists like Tad VanBrunt, Jim Brayshay, and Jack "Nabe" Pierce were as busy or busier in this "mop-up" period as they had been at the height of the fighting. Their naval counterparts brokered surrenders in which mutual restraint prevented indiscriminate and unnecessary deaths. Lt. (jg) David Osborn did so in a particularly brave way. He swam ashore from a small boat to a tiny offshore island and persuaded the Japanese major there to give up rather than fight to the death. A peaceful and orderly surrender ensued.[29]

Language officers in small units sent out to chase down armed Japanese who were still at large had risky but enlightening experiences. Sometimes failure proved their best teacher. Ens. Robert D. Thornton felt humiliated when the prisoner search he was on went awry. He and an army 7th Division reconnaissance patrol came upon a group of young men in farmers' clothes outside a large womblike Okinawan tomb. Their ramrod straight posture suggested they might be soldiers, and when one of them approached, ignoring Thornton's call to halt, the Americans became more suspicious. When the man turned and started to run away, they spotted a revolver sticking out of the back side of his *obi* (belt). The army captain quickly fired his own gun, but Thornton was so stunned that he forgot he had one. By the time the captain grabbed and fired it, the fleeing Japanese got away. Thornton later redeemed himself by persisting for more than a day—even when his army companions wanted to stop—in persuading other Japanese hidden in tombs to surrender.[30]

Al Weissberg and Dean Towner had a shocking but even more enlightening experience on patrol with Marines in northern Okinawa. What was to have been a life-saving expedition turned into a brutally efficient manhunt. The Marines surprised six Japanese soldiers nearby. A "sharp spatter of shots" crackled, and when the two language officers reached the saddle of a nearby hill, they spotted "only . . . [the] clothes and meaningless flesh" of a dead Japanese. Moving down into ravines clad with woods and thick grass, the two linguists came upon another body; and ten minutes there were four more splayed out at the bottom of the hill. Weissberg had mixed feelings about this kind of operation. He admired the marines—"a well-armed group which knew its business and did it—no hesitation, no slips." But he was shocked to "see life abruptly become meaningless death," and he pitied the dead Japanese. "Living like animals in filthy holes in the earth and being tracked down like animals is not a nice fate for a human being," he wrote his wife. But that was the essence of "the so-called 'mopping-up' period."[31]

The Boulder men who interrogated prisoners during this time saw their self-image and their understanding of the Japanese change. During the first weeks of the invasion, those at 10th Army Headquarters commanded little attention and enjoyed only slight success. Frank Gibney and Ken Lamott set up their own intelligence subsection but got more out of the sake stills they found than the few prisoners who fell into their hands. Even when, late in May, a general and a doctor, who as a Keio University student had played against a touring American baseball team that included Babe Ruth, came before them, they failed to get much valuable information. Gibney and other Boulder-trained staff members could not even tell whether prisoners were speaking the truth or feeding them lies. Their morale plummeted.[32]

But when, in the last days of the fighting, the trickle of captives became a torrent, the Boulder men's spirits rose. They became analysts, charged with finding out what prisoners knew and using that information to produce a history of the battle that was just ending that would clarify the enemy's organization and tactics. Such a work might also provide clues as to how the Japanese would defend their home islands. At first the language officers had little success in squeezing information out of freshly captured "close-mouthed, sullen, worried . . . farm boys." But when Okinawan civilian internees exposed more senior and better-informed Japanese hiding in their midst, they got what they needed. The Boulder men helped identify potentially valuable prisoners in the stockades and set up a special "bugged" interrogation center at 10th Army headquarters. Gibney and Lamott questioned two extremely knowledgeable captives—Colonel Yahara Hiromichi, senior operations planner for the 32nd Army, and Shimada Akira, private secretary to the 32nd's chief of staff—for three weeks in late July and early August 1945.

Their interrogations yielded just what the senior intelligence staff wanted: detailed information about the enemy's order of battle and decision making that would be useful in preparing the expected invasion of the Japanese home islands. But they also boosted the Boulder-trained interrogators' sense of worth and deepened their understanding of their more senior adversaries. Neither fanatics nor fools, these prisoners were tough, highly intelligent, competent professionals who were trying in the most reasonable way possible to prevent or at least delay the defeat of their empire. They deserved respect.[33]

Those who dealt with ordinary prisoners developed a very different view of the Japanese and a distinct understanding of their own role. They pitied their charges, who had surrendered in terrible physical and emotional condition. Many had been all but sealed up in caves for weeks, "blinded to light, but not to the knowledge that Japan was losing" the war. Covered with fleas, they were so starved for food that when given a tin of cheese and bacon they gulped it down—and then threw it right up. On top of that, fear consumed them. One man beseeched Bob Thornton, repeatedly crying "*Koroshimasu ka?*" (Will you kill us?). Ken Lamott found the prisoners he interviewed in a stockade convinced that they would be "staked out and run over by bulldozers, castrated, or—mercifully—shot summarily." Their fears and faces became so seared into his consciousness that years later Lamott wrote a thinly fictionalized novel about them.[34]

Recognizing that these prisoners must be helped before they could be questioned, the Boulder-trained language officers became protectors as much as captors. They tried to defuse the captives' fears and see that they got medical treatment. Bob Thornton did so during "three horrible weeks in June" 1945 that he spent inside a prisoner-of-war stockade. He worked so closely with Japanese that he had to shave his head to keep fleas from jumping from their scalps to his. He had to persuade a guard to let a Japanese army medic keep his scalpel and then ended up working alongside the enemy to save wounded prisoners' lives. That gave him valuable insights into the Japanese character. He marveled at badly burned patients' not asking for morphine to kill their pain but drew back in horror and then reprimanded the Japanese army medic who slapped a man who dared to flinch while he probed a bullet wound.[35]

Dan Karasik intervened on Japanese prisoner patients' behalf in a different setting—a U.S. Army field hospital, just the sort of multiservice staffed place that Gen. Vinegar Joe Stilwell termed a "bastard organization." Karasik functioned first as an administrator, working with two army nisei enlisted men in getting and filing basic information about the enemy men as they were brought in. Karasik interrogated those who were fishermen about the beaches of Kyushu that Americans were planning to invade. And he inadvertently became an advocate on the prisoners' behalf. U.S. Army nurses, their humanity shrunken by the horrible American battle casualties they had seen, at first refused to care for wounded Japanese. Karasik convinced them that they must do so. When he saw that enemy patients were recovering more slowly because they were not eating much, he scrounged rice and soy sauce for them. A colonel threatened to court-martial him for doing that, but he persisted, and the patients improved. Karasik's work with Japanese prisoners of war eventually earned him a letter of commendation.[36]

At least two other naval language officers came to know and protect prisoners of a very different sort—the feared and hated kamikaze. Ens. Henry F. May became a roving interrogator of kamikaze pilots who had failed in their mission. He went from ship to ship interviewing young Japanese who had tried to hit an American vessel, missed, and then plunged into the sea. Rescued by their intended victims, they awoke, amazed and ashamed to find themselves prisoners. May's job was to pry potentially valuable information out of them. But he realized he must first disarm them psychologically by refusing their requests to be killed and offering them cigarettes. Then, to quiet their fears and lessen their shame in failing to carry out their mission, he explained that they would be taken to Pearl Harbor and returned to Japan when the war ended.

May eventually received valuable information from these very special prisoners. When he asked, they told him what airfield they had departed from. Such data, when relayed back to Admiral Nimitz's headquarters, helped determine American bombers' targets on Kyushu. But May found that his conversations with the kamikaze distanced him from other Americans. On one dark and rainy night when he was approaching a ship that had picked up one of them, its sentries mistook his small boat as another suicide craft and fired warning shots that forced him to give up trying to come aboard. May heard officers and men speak of suicide attacks in the abstract as routine but then express real hatred toward a seemingly crazy pilot who had almost crashed into *their* vessels. He, on the other hand, came to see the kamikaze pilots whom he interviewed as just "scared and disoriented kid[s]."[37]

Lt. (jg) Edgar Whan picked up where May left off and eventually became an advocate and protector of sorts for failed kamikaze pilots and ordinary prisoners alike. He accompanied small groups of the would-be suicide bombers on a flight back to Guam, where they were to be interrogated more extensively. As they boarded the plane, the Japanese hung their heads in shame, but a sailor from Tennessee told them not to feel so bad, for he had been shot down at Guadalcanal and lived to see much better days. When the prisoners were not given any food on the flight, Whan shared his with them. Before the journey was over, the prisoners and their minder were trading names and peeks at photographs of their wives. That moment of shared humanity may have helped the prisoners endure American sailors' taunts once they landed on Guam, and it certainly enabled Whan to see them as people rather than hellish fiends.

His success in delivering these high-value captives in good spirits probably helped Whan do the same for a larger group of prisoners on a much longer voyage. He won a lottery among JICPOA linguists that made him the escort for fifteen hundred men back to prisoner-of-war camp at Pearl Harbor. The two-week voyage aboard the USS *Winged Arrow* (AP 170) tested his humanity and courage as well as his language skills. The captives came aboard virtually naked, and at first mess, mates were so hostile to them that their food was delivered in garbage pails. Whan helped put an end to that. He also dealt with life-and-death emergencies. One prisoner committed suicide by jumping overboard, and three others died of their wounds. But Whan helped save another captive by interpreting when the man told the ship's doctor his symptoms, which led to a successful appendectomy. He also helped lift the prisoners' spirits enough so that they worked hard at painting the ship. That considerably softened the crew's hostility, and by the time the *Winged Arrow* docked at Pearl Harbor, its sailors were noticeably more considerate of the prisoners than those who dealt with them ashore.[38]

Language officers who dealt primarily with civilians on Okinawa faced even greater challenges than those that Whan and others who worked with prisoners confronted. More than 320,000 men, women, and children had been uprooted from their homes on Okinawa and placed in "protective custody" by 15 August 1945. Nearly three dozen officer linguists interrogated and helped care for 7,500 captives, but barely a third as many were assigned to help civil affairs teams care for this population, which was more than 40 times as large. The prisoner language officers brought prior experience to their task and in many instances had proven their worth to skeptical superiors in battle. Those who dealt with civilians almost without exception confronted Japanese civilians for the first time. And they were not the same as the prisoners held in Hawaii that some of these officers had interrogated. The language officers working with civilians on Okinawa enjoyed little support from above. Unlike their counterparts on Guam, who looked forward to reestablishing control over what had been American territory, admirals who served as island commanders on Okinawa had no desire to rule an alien land. In their view, that was an army task not worth wasting naval energies on even temporarily. These circumstances boded ill for the language officers assigned to work with civilians on Okinawa.[39]

Their situation would have been much better had they known more about and built upon their predecessors' experience on Saipan and Tinian. Language officers' involvement with civilians there was a success story. Boulder men's encounters with noncombatants on Okinawa turned out to be a tale of woes rather than of triumphs. To understand why that was so, one must first consider what happened in the Marianas and then examine how military government training and command relationships limited what language officers could do in restoring civil order on Okinawa.

On Saipan and Tinian, naval language officers took part in an unprecedented endeavor: imposing alien rule over nearly 40,000 Japanese who had come to these islands as colonists. JICPOA dispatched only a handful of linguists—nine ensigns who worked under two lieutenants—to deal with enemy civilians in the postbattle phase of operations. They were expected to help a dozen 2nd and 4th Division marine civil affairs officers and plug the gap in the Army's 27th Division, which had none. They were few because planners expected a surviving Japanese colonial regime to control the local population. The tremendous death and destruction in the initial assault phase of operations on Saipan made that impossible.[40]

The exceptional linguistic talent and professional backgrounds of officers charged with managing civilians were supposed to compensate for their slim numbers. Those sent to Saipan included Harris I. "Jish" Martin, who had been born in Japan fewer than twenty-one years earlier; Russell Stevens, a lawyer-to-be who had started learning Japanese on his own in Hawaii before the war; and former Justice Department attorney P. R. Monahan. Another lawyer, Norman Meller, eventually joined them. The Tinian team worked under Lt. J. G. Reifsnider, son of a famed Japan missionary bishop, and it included N. G. Thorlaksson, a Japan businessman's son, and H. Telfer Mook, who held a Yale law degree. Four months after the Tinian landings, Lt. (jg) Warren R. Johnston, the first Boulder man to have attended the Navy School of Military Government at Columbia University, came to the island.[41]

The first naval language officers who went ashore on Saipan confronted "disaster conditions" for which neither they nor their superiors were mentally or physically prepared. Marines gathered civilians in temporary stockades on the beach; after minimal interrogation, the civilians were sent to what became Camp Susupe. Starting as just a bunch of tents, it expanded into a collection of wooden shanties twenty by forty feet each that were cobbled together from scrap lumber and tin roofing gleaned from the ruins of the island's one and only city. Siting it near a lake and using open-pit toilets guaranteed that flies and mosquitoes would abound. They fed on civilians who arrived in "horrible" physical and mental condition, "indescribably filthy, ill, and suffering from shrapnel wounds, shock, and malnutrition." For nearly nine months more than 17,000 of them lived cheek by jowl, four square feet per person, in what were supposed to have been short-term shelters.[42]

These people's needs—and the incompetence, bureaucratic infighting, and indifference of American senior officers to their condition—presented a tremendous challenge and great opportunity to the Boulder-trained language officers assigned to Camp Susupe. First they were simply overwhelmed by the magnitude of their tasks. Jish Martin found himself ferrying civilians from stockade to camp and scrounging food for them from Japanese bags of rice, many of which American troops had ruined by bayoneting. The mere 200 tons of food intended for civilians were not found and used until 90 days after the invaders landed. Russell Stevens was pressed into service as translator for the one and only American doctor, a man who, with the help of naval medical corpsmen treated 78,000 cases of sickness or wounds in the first 6 weeks of the camp's existence. Stevens had to really scramble to learn an entirely new vocabulary for that job.[43]

Fairly quickly, however, the Boulder-trained interpreters became administrators who, with the help of army nisei enlisted men, brought a semblance of order to Camp Susupe. Jish Martin worked for months to compile a register of who was there to identify inmates and ferret out Japanese soldiers who might be hiding among them. He, Stevens, and Monahan implemented a plan to separate the Japanese, most of whom were Okinawans, from Koreans and the local Chamorro people. Martin chose the camp's Japanese police chief; later on Norman Meller translated camp rules, and trial procedures for those who broke the rules, into proper Japanese. To prevent boredom from fomenting unrest, Boulder men started work programs. Internees earned a daily pittance by working on cooperative farms, fishing, and making handicraft items to sell as souvenirs to GIs.[44]

The Boulder men inevitably stumbled in fulfilling the administrative responsibilities thrust upon them. Lance LaBianca naively used known prostitutes as caretakers of the children in the camp orphanage. The language officers had to deal with some GIs who tried to break into the camp to get at the women there and with other Americans outside it who homosexually assaulted men sent out to work on cooperative farms. When they tried to explain such things to the camp police chief, he could not understand why the Americans didn't just bring in "comfort women," as the Imperial army had done, to meet soldiers' sexual needs. But the language officers also demonstrated imagination and initiative in trying to return life for camp inmates to something like normal. With half of their charges aged fifteen or younger, it was particularly important to restart schools. Although neither books nor desks were available, camp children started attending regular classes barely ninety days after Camp Susupe was established.[45]

In doing all of these things, the language officers gained as much as they gave. Working at close quarters with so many Japanese gave them cross-cultural empathy and insights that proved useful later in their naval and professional careers. Norman Meller feared the Japanese "other" enough to take a concealed .45 along on his first solo night duty at the camp. But after nothing remotely violent occurred, he set aside wartime stereotypes of the treacherous Japanese and never again went out armed. Russell Stevens first learned enough about Japanese psychology to work on propaganda pamphlets urging surrender and then went on a mission that got the entire garrison of a remote northern island to give up. Jish Martin came to understand and manipulate the psychology of defeat through his dealings with the camp police chief. The man thought he was going to be shot when Martin summoned him to an interview, and he remained fiercely patriotic. Rather than firing him or lecturing him on the inevitability of Japan's defeat, Martin handled the problem in an indirect, Japanese way. He simply drove the chief to a spot where the two men watched American B-29 bombers taking off for Japan.[46]

The language officers at Camp Churo on Tinian had an easier time of it than those on Saipan. The Marines learned quickly from what had gone wrong there, and relations between civil affairs and combat officers were good. Because the former were a regular section of the commanding general's staff, problems that arose got more attention and were quickly resolved. Military men helped build and police the civilian internee camp, and there were no transportation or food shortages. More naval language officers plus a Japanese-speaking army lieutenant and a dozen enlisted nisei were assigned to the camp, which was placed in a much more salubrious location. They had little difficulty in controlling and protecting their charges. Civilians only occasionally tried to escape into the countryside, and far fewer Japanese soldiers raided the camp than the camp on Saipan. When GIs broke into it for sexual or other mischievous purposes, the camp managers kept them under control.[47]

Boulder men thrived in this environment, in large measure because their boss, a marine colonel, recognized that he needed their brains and administrative abilities as well as their language skills. Their crowning achievement was the school at Camp Churo. Its founding father was Lt. (jg) H. Telfer Mook, a "bean-pole tall, pink-faced . . . earnest" Dartmouth graduate who had gone on to Trinity College, Cambridge, and then graduated from Yale Law School before going to Boulder. He recognized that getting the camp's more than three thousand children into school would help keep order and spark hopes for a better future. Mook first persuaded his colonel to let him and three Japanese teachers search the island for books and survey the number of potential students. Then he secured the island commander's approval for the school, unaccompanied, however, by any offer of help. Mook and his fellow language officers cadged surplus lumber from the beaches, traded liquor for "souvenirs" taken from defeated Japanese, and bartered them for the labor of otherwise unwilling Seabees. In three months they built five large school buildings with fifty classrooms—all on their off-duty time.

Aided by the senior surviving Japanese teacher on Tinian, Mook recruited a faculty that was reeducated and carefully managed. When it was decreed that English would be the medium of instruction, he got Hawaiian army nisei to teach the teachers. They used the same "immersion" method of teaching English that he and his colleagues had experienced in learning Japanese at Boulder. Mook dealt firmly but wisely with the teachers. He understood that these leaders in the preinvasion community harbored strong pro-Japanese feelings, feared being seen as collaborators, and hoped to propagate old loyalties. He worked with them to censor Japanese books that were used to create new texts in English, science, and mathematics. But when one teacher tried to keep old politically correct phrases in the new books, he banished him to crushing coral for a nearby runway under construction. And a physical education instructor who used exercise periods to have pupils bow reverently toward the emperor in Tokyo was told that such behavior must stop.

Mook believed the school represented a vision of future cooperation between Americans and Japanese. He and his fellow language officers made sure that the local community and the world knew about it. Mook started a parent–teacher association and instituted outdoor movies that drew all sorts of people to it. He recognized the public relations value of having such a school barely two miles from the runways from which B-29 bombers bound for Japan departed. In the school, the Japanese at Camp Churo saw the constructive, rather than the destructive, side of the American character. And Mook welcomed those who could present to others a positive image of Japanese teaching and learning rather than fighting and killing. Several war correspondents, a *Vogue* feature writer, and even Archbishop (soon to be Cardinal) Francis Spellman visited the school; all praised what was happening in it to Americans back home.[48]

Those responsible for postcombat civil affairs on Okinawa wanted to avoid the difficulties and repeat the successes of Saipan and Tinian on a much larger scale on *their* island. They might have done so had they consulted language officers such as Jish Martin or Telfer Mook or, better still, ordered them to Okinawa to work with newly trained military government officers. But that did not happen. Instead, planning for governance of the island and usage of language officers in controlling its civilians proceeded in an overly bureaucratic and academic way. The planners knew what had to be done: move a population roughly the size of Denver out of ruined homes to temporary camps; weed out the dangerous among them; and then plant the docile remainder in new villages in Okinawa's rugged undeveloped north. Thirty-four district civil affairs teams, supported by twenty-six dispensaries and field hospitals, would do that under the direction of a single military government officer responsible for the whole island. These agents of disaster control and reconstruction would be middle-aged experts in fields ranging from engineering and public health to agronomy and public administration. They were to have completed a year's training at the Naval School of Military Government at Columbia University or comparable army programs. And they would arrive having practiced what they had learned in joint mock operations in northern California.[49]

Language officers specifically trained for and helped plan this particular grand endeavor. Two Boulder men, Lt. (jg) Ward Hussey and Lt. Cdr. Willard

A. Hanna, spent a year at the Columbia military government school following their July 1943 graduation from the language school. Hussey went on to help produce a 394-page handbook that detailed "practically every aspect" of Okinawan society and history. Hanna worked on the overall scheme for civil affairs on the island. JICPOA linguists who joined them later, men such as budding anthropologist Wayne Suttles, got special civil affairs training before reporting to their new duty stations. Their boss, JICPOA commander Brig. Gen. Joseph Twitty, expected them to function primarily as supervisors of one hundred newly inducted Hawaiian nisei army enlisted interpreters. These "native speakers" would do the heavy lifting in communicating with civilians during Okinawa's transition from war to peace.[50]

This vision of how to reestablish civil order on the conquered island was clear, inspiring, and completely unrealistic. Snafus large and small dogged the operation from its inception. The experts turned out to be anything but. They went through the Columbia course believing they were planning for the occupation of Taiwan, not Okinawa. Their information about the island's civilians was old and distorted by Japanese mainlanders' prejudices against their charges-to-be. As Ward Hussey put it, "when we got to Okinawa, we found we didn't know beans!" Paunchy, middle-aged civil affairs technocrats were wrong for a job that demanded "young men, with general skills, common sense, and lots of energy"—precisely what the language officers on Saipan and Tinian were. The naval officer linguists had plenty of enlisted army helpers, but most were "illiterate in Japanese," and only a few were "reasonably proficient in the spoken language." To make matters still worse, senior commanders on Okinawa cared little about military government and provided little or no support for it. In the combat phase of operations, they simply wanted Japanese civilians out of the way. When the fighting stopped, the senior military government officer was a vainglorious buffoon who distrusted all Okinawan civilians and cared little about their fate.[51]

From the moment civil affairs teams landed on Okinawa, things went from bad to worse. The first naval civil administrators came ashore under "a cloud of gloom" having just learned of President Franklin D. Roosevelt's death. They arrived five weeks before their food, office supplies, and housing materials, which meant that they themselves had to live in tents awash in rain, mosquitoes, and mud while they tried to make life better for Okinawan civilians. Continued fighting, repeated displacement of these people, and scaling back medical facilities guaranteed that the civil administrators would fail in their "prime task" of organizing and controlling the civilians. They brought thousands to temporary camps, but up to 100,000 more roamed the hills. It was difficult to keep civilians from sneaking food out to Japanese soldiers and to stop troops from both sides from "molesting" people in the camps. Those responsible for temporary relocation facilities admitted that they could not fully control residents and acknowledged that they were "quite unprepared" to meet even the minimal needs of "hordes of [additional] civilians" expected to join them.[52]

Matters got still worse after the fighting officially stopped. What had been individual and group dislocation became massive, forced depopulation of outlying islands, peninsulas, and some of the best land at Okinawa's center. This happened because the Americans nearly doubled the number of bases to be built on the island. The 1st Marine Division alone evicted more than 20,000 people—in 72 hours. Civilians already in camps were shifted to new villages crammed into 10 percent of the island's total land area, half of which was "totally unsuitable for resettlement purposes." People whose spirits were already low were forced to live in very primitive conditions, and their woes increased when a food shortage cut their daily rations in half. While all of this was going on, generals and admirals bounced responsibility for civil affairs back and forth between themselves. Little wonder, then, that the senior naval captain responsible for civil affairs operations concluded that "the story of military government on Okinawa is one of mismanagement, stupidity, and injustice."[53]

The handful of language officers assigned to postcombat civil affairs duty could not fundamentally change this terrible situation. But they tried to ameliorate it and point Okinawans toward a better future. Tad VanBrunt did so simply by the force of his good looks, outgoing personality, and conversational skills. When it came time for him to leave, residents in the district to which he was assigned begged Gen. Lemuel Shepherd to let him stay on, but he left with other 6th Division Marines. Lt. (jg) Robert Scalapino served, for a short time, with one of the district military government teams. These units often lacked sufficient equipment, correct maps, and leaders with enough command presence to organize things properly. Nevertheless, even though lights could not be kept on at night, he started evening dialogues with teachers, a doctor, and a writer—people likely to lead in rebuilding their shattered communities.[54]

Two other naval language officers helped improve Okinawan civilians' morale by piecing back together parts of the island's shattered communications system. Husbands and wives, parents and children did not know where one another were because fighting had destroyed the formal communications infrastructure. Forced relocation, assignment to different work parties, and, in some cases, hospitalization shattered remaining informal communication networks. Lt. (jg) Ward Hussey tried to remedy the situation by using his position as chief censor on the senior civil affairs staff to restart mail deliveries among the resettlement camps and villages. Wayne Suttles helped revive the press on Okinawa. He went from camp to camp looking for printers and other newspaper workers to produce what was at first just a few pages of poorly translated mimeographed news from 10th Army Headquarters. Then he teamed up with a talented army nisei and the prewar editor of the Okinawan Social Masses party newspaper. They helped him find type and a printing press that had been hidden in General Ushijima's Shuri Castle headquarters. Suttles ended up running the island's only newspaper for six months; in time, it became *Ryūkyū Shimpo*, one of Okinawa's two leading newspapers.[55]

Working on the military government operations staff, Willard Hanna and Ward Hussey helped move Okinawan civilians toward a peaceful future in still other ways. Hanna, like Telfer Mook on Tinian, pushed to get schools started. Seventy-two had opened by September 1945, barely ninety days after the fighting formally stopped. He did everything he could to inform fellow occupiers about Okinawan culture, keep them from taking valuable art objects as souvenirs, and put local artists to work. His most important achievement was starting an advisory council that later became the foundation for a system of limited local government. Ward Hussey, working under Hanna, identified and brought together the cooperative Okinawa leaders who became members of these local councils.

In all of this, Hanna, Hussey, and other language officers working in civil affairs administration were driven by mixed motives. They felt as if they were not just witnesses but also parties to the destruction of a civilization and way of life on Okinawa. They could not undo the damage that had been done, nor did they have much power to remediate the lot of those who had survived it, so they felt guilt and remorse. But idealism spurred them on. Perhaps what Henry Tatsumi had written in the Boulder school song about promoting peace and democracy was true. On Okinawa they had the chance to do just that. Whether in fact they did so or fastened a colonial regime that its people despised and eventually destroyed remains a matter for debate. But that the language officers tried to ameliorate the evils that invasion and occupation visited on Okinawa cannot be disputed.[56]

WARRIORS TRANSFORMED

There can be little doubt that Boulder men themselves were changed by what they learned and experienced on Okinawa. Some of those changes were physical. JICPOA desk jockeys become "quite lean and tanned." They toughened up by digging foxholes, living in tents, sloshing through the island's rain and mud, and suffering the unwanted caresses of its insects. They found that they could get over the sleeplessness caused by air raids, endure "smelling like a dead goat" and even shunt aside fears that extended exposure to Okinawa's heat might render them sterile.[57]

Other changes that came over these young men were psychological. They became "can-do" people of the best sort. They took risks in brokering surrenders and crawling in caves to save lives. They suffered wounds but did not let that stop them. Hart Spiegel lost the sight in one eye for a time but came right back to fight as soon as partial vision in it would allow. They took on new and unexpected duties. Dan Karasik and Robert Thornton never imagined they would have to take on such grisly tasks such as preparing for surgery men burned by flamethrowers or eviscerated by shellfire. But they did so without complaint. The Boulder language officers innovated and improvised in "pure sink or swim" situations, managing, as Al Weissberg put it, "to dog-paddle my way through."[58] And they demonstrated finesse and courage in standing up to prejudiced superiors, as Jim Jefferson and Dan Karasik did, when circumstances demanded that they do so.

But the most important changes they experienced were attitudinal. They left Okinawa with a fresh understanding of war, a more realistic view of the enemy, and a keener sense of their own role in it. War was something real, deadly, and transforming. Marines like Jim Brayshay and Roger Hackett saw that truth in the mud and massive slaughter of the battles along the Shuri Line. Bob Thornton discovered it in the face of a beautiful young Okinawan woman who was brought into a prison camp writhing, biting, and kicking her captors. She was driven mad to the point of urinating in her food and wailing at the moon throughout the night. Al Weissberg told his wife how his thinking about war changed in these words: "You can go through battered towns and see a few long-dead corpses stretched out grotesquely in ditches or along roads and think you understand the horror of war. Actually you don't at all until you see men hurting other men with the same enthusiasm and efficiency with which they would greet arrivals on a fine Sunday afternoon; watch guns spat in earnest; and see life abruptly become meaningless death."[59]

Fortunately, the Boulder-trained language officers on Okinawa developed the capacity to look beyond the immediate horrors of war and see the enemy as something other than a fanatical, inhuman "other." Hart Spiegel and Henry May tore off the mask of that "other." The marine lieutenant did so by ripping the shoulder boards off the uniform on Admiral Ōta's blackened corpse. The naval officer did so by uncovering the fears and psychological vulnerabilities of failed kamikaze pilots. Others discovered the humanity of sometime adversaries who became collaborators. Jim Jefferson encountered it the very first day he came ashore, when an old man, a village elder and former college profession, came forward and offered to help the Marines. Sol Levine found it in a retired ship captain who helped correct navigational charts. And Glen Slaughter certainly recognized it in the loyal assistance that Tony Komesu provided throughout the last phase of the battle.[60]

What they saw in the faces of Japanese on Okinawa enabled the language officers to feel that the great battle in which they fought might be a gateway to a better future. Edgar Whan glimpsed that truth one moonlit night when he was walking down "a little silver road through the hills and neat fields." When he looked around and saw in his mind's eye "all kinds of Japanese prints in the bamboo against the sky" he wondered "if an Okinawan lover had ever sat out there on the hill and made love" as he and his wife had done in the past. Months later, after visiting and talking with people in one of the newly constructed villages, he felt it even more strongly. "They," he wrote, "are to be the new Okinawa . . . and will be the new Japan too." "I feel better now," he confided to his wife, "when I see all the carnage we have wrought and see the misery of these . . . people because I know they are really just starting to get a chance to be something more like man was intended to be."[61]

Finally, participation in the battle for Okinawa made the Boulder boys more sensitive to the dangers and responsibilities of their position. They must not allow themselves to become an American version of the Nazi gauleiter who ruled roughshod over occupied France. On the contrary, they must acknowledge responsibility for the death and destruction American invaders wrought and do their best to make up for it. That was painful, as Hart Spiegel learned when he tried to console the mother of a young boy that his Marines had killed in error. It was difficult, as Bob Thornton learned when working as a Japanese surgeon's assistant in a field hospital. But doing so could bring great rewards. "Seldom . . . have I . . . been prouder to be an American!" Thornton exulted about his work.[62]

That remark hinted at the most vital change that came over naval and marine language officers on Okinawa. They came knowing the Japanese in ways limited by their experience as students, combat interpreters, and distant listeners. On the island they got closer to more Japanese as well as different kinds of Japanese than ever before. They left knowing the Japanese not as abstract or dangerous enemies but simply as human beings. Their experiences on Okinawa strengthened their conviction that "peace is possible now!" Having survived and been transformed by the greatest battle of their war, they were poised to become point men for peace.

Chapter Six

INSTRUMENTS OF SURRENDER

On the morning of 6 August 1945, marine lieutenant Larry Vincent and a friend were sleeping soundly in soft beds at the beautiful new marine officers' recreation facility at Kailua, over the pali from Pearl Harbor on the windward side of Oahu. Suddenly they heard a steward pounding on the door. "Wake up gentlemen! Six o'clock and the war's over!" News of the atomic bombing of Hiroshima had just reached Hawaii.[1]

That apocalyptic event marked the beginning of the end of the war. Over the next eight days, Boulder men and women—and millions of people the world over—waited anxiously by their radios for more news that might signal Japan's surrender. It did not come as fast or as clearly as they hoped. At Camp Tarawa near Hilo on the big island of Hawaii, Ed Seidensticker and his fellow 5th Division Marines simply had a feeling that the war would end soon. But how soon? A statement from the Japanese news agency Dōmei on August 10 triggered hopes that the end might come any minute. When Al Weissberg heard "that marvelous, almost incredible announcement" in a hushed dining hall on Kwajalein, where he had stopped en route from Okinawa to Pearl Harbor, he jumped up from his table and rushed outside to tell fellow passengers the news.[2]

The news triggered pandemonium at 3:00 AM in the bachelor officers' quarters (BOQ) nearest JICPOA. "An unholy collection of screams, whistles, and shouts" awakened Paul J. Sherman, and before he knew it "scantily clad neighbors" were pouring into his room demanding "turn the goddamn radio on." News that Japan had accepted the provisions of the Potsdam Declaration—with qualifications—prompted "normally staid and scholarly" translators to break out whiskey stashed in closets and drink and douse one another with it. The talking got louder and wilder, turning from "reconversion" back to civilian life to unlimited gasoline to women. "The finest, the looniest, [and] the most enjoyable" partying Sherman had ever experienced went on for three hours. But when the sun came up that morning, the war was not over yet.[3]

In Washington, D.C., four days later, the final message confirming Japan's surrender came to Op-20-GZ "suddenly, without any forewarning, like a streak of lightning stabbing downward in a clear blue sky." It was rushed to the White House where President Truman read it and released the good news to the world. That touched off wild celebrations wherever Boulder men and women were. In Washington, the naval codebreakers and WAVES rushed out of their offices into the street, where people were hugging and kissing one another. Some sailors grabbed Daphne Shaw and tossed her about, adding a twinge of fear to her joy. Then those working at the 5th and K Street facility adjourned to the roof for a beer party.[4]

In Melbourne, Australia, five Boulder-trained naval Japanese-language officers stopped working, got drunk, and started planning a three-week trip to Tasmania. In Chungking, swarms of Chinese climbed onto naval lieutenant Howell Breece's jeep, hugged him, and shouted the good news that the war was over. On Guam, the 20th Air Force staff officers with whom naval lieutenant Ardath Burks worked at first simply refused to believe the report of Japan's surrender. But that news triggered "a tremendous explosion of shouts and cheers," tears, and then "epochal . . . revelry" that left the island's defenders so debilitated that "a small band of New Zealand Girl Guides could have captured the island without significant resistance." By contrast, Marines on Okinawa took the news soberly. For them, August 15 was "a moment of liberation" that brought "solid relief" and joy that "there would be a future."[5]

Back at Pearl Harbor, the partying went on for twenty-four hours. On the night of the thirteenth, searchlights, fireworks, and pyrotechnics of every sort glowed in the sky while ships sounded their horns. The spectacle brought Japanese prisoners of war to the fences of their compound, where they wept at the celebration of their country's defeat. The next morning Boulder Marines Chuck Cross and John Rich got a reconnaissance carrier from the marine replacement depot and drove through streets thronged with people into Honolulu, picking up friends, strangers, and women along the way. By the time they reached the Central Union Church for a service of thanksgiving, they presented a happy but most unmilitary sight. "Our caps [were gone] . . . , our faces and collars covered with lipstick, [and] our shirts [were] wet from spilled beer," Cross recalled, but the somewhat startled members of the congregation nonetheless greeted the victors "with friendly reserve." That night Honolulu became a madhouse with drunks staggering along the sidewalks and cars racing along the highways.[6]

For the naval and marine language officers, however, jubilation at the moment of victory was shattered by a stark realization: the war might be over for millions of others, but it was not about to end for them. The language skills they had gained in war must now be put to work in the immediate tasks of peace: carrying out the surrender and occupation of Japan; repatriating 6.5 million enemy soldiers and civilians scattered across a broken empire; and shepherding the Japanese people toward a peaceful future. That prospect triggered mixed emotions among the language officers. Nearly all lamented the prospect of a "tour of duty among the little men" that might keep them from an early return to wives and family, college study and professional careers back home. At least one—Al Weissberg—was overwhelmed by the weightiness of the moment: the war had gone on too long and there had been too much sadness and suffering for it all to dissolve easily into peace. Others looked forward to the chance to go to Japan with barely containable enthusiasm. Hart Spiegel, ever the Marine, put aside whatever apprehensions he may have had about what might await him in the enemy's homeland by proclaiming, "I'm not going to crawl into Tokyo—I'm going to storm the place with a real bang!" On the night of 15 August, Paul Kramer, who may have been more typical of hundreds of other Boulder men, simply "went to bed to dream of the Ginza and Geisha girls."[7]

RACING TO SURRENDER

Long before that night, naval and marine planners recognized that every available linguist must be mobilized and sent wherever Japanese forces remained to facilitate the enemy's surrender. Some would scatter to the bypassed island bastions of the central and southern Pacific. Others would go with the Marines to north China, which a virtually untouched Japanese army occupied. Still others would join an armada that would converge on the Japanese home islands to bring about their peaceful surrender and occupation. But just as it had been for island assaults during the war, so now in the first moments of peace what was supposed to go according to plan turned out to be chaotic and full of surprises.

Five days before Japan capitulated, a BOQ loudspeaker at Pearl Harbor blared orders for all JICPOA men to report immediately to their duty station. Lt. (jg) Paul J. Sherman threw on his clothes, jumped into a jeep, and drove to a meeting that was in "complete turmoil." When his coworkers quieted down, they heard a call for volunteers to leave that same night for "a little tour of Japan." Sherman "signed up . . . fast," and dashed back to the BOQ to pack. By nine that evening, after a farewell party at Commander Steele's house, he—armed with a ukulele—and nearly sixty other officers were on a bus bound for the airfield. They took off just before midnight. Four thousand miles later they touched down on Guam.

Sherman reported to Admiral Nimitz's advanced headquarters there. He and his fellow language officers sweated for nearly two days "in a state of excitement, confusion and such," uncertain of what was going on while their superiors determined who was going with which unit on what ships to Japan. Eventually twenty men each were assigned to the Third and Fifth fleets, respectively. But Sherman shrewdly volunteered to join the press censorship staff that would accompany the war correspondents who would cover the surrender ceremonies in Japan. The next morning he and the journalists boarded the USS *Meriwether* (APA 203), which had already loaded men of the 4th Marine Regiment. Six days later, they learned that they would be landing at the Imperial Japanese Navy Base at Yokosuka, just inside Tokyo Bay.[8]

Lieutenant (junior grade) Sherman did not know it then, but his confused and hurried journey to Japan was just one small part of a much larger Army–Navy struggle to get to the enemy's homeland first. By 10 August, when he departed Pearl Harbor, the Joint Chiefs of Staff had long since directed subordinates to draw up contingency plans for a peaceful occupation of Japan. President Truman had decided that Gen. Douglas MacArthur would be the Supreme Commander, Allied Powers (SCAP), and presurrender negotiations with an advanced party of Japanese officers and diplomats took place in Manila under his auspices. The defeated Japanese had no choice but to agree on the surrender procedures that the Americans proposed. But MacArthur and Adm. Chester Nimitz came up with quite different schemes for initial landings in Japan. The admiral wanted a small naval–

marine force to enter Tokyo Bay quickly, secure its naval facilities, and then rescue American and Allied prisoners of war known to be in the vicinity. The general, who feared that the Navy was trying to "horn in . . . and . . . keep him out of Tokyo," argued for a much larger, coordinated ground-air-sea investiture that he himself would command. The two men eventually agreed on a modified plan that projected the near-simultaneous arrival of army and naval forces in the Tokyo area. Their subordinates then defined priorities and responsibilities for surrenders elsewhere in accordance with a hastily drawn plan by State Department and Pentagon officials. The Navy would manage the surrenders on Pacific islands; the two services together would do the job in Korea; and the Marines would oversee the surrender of Japanese troops in China.[9]

But the immediate goal—for everyone from MacArthur and Nimitz down to Paul Sherman and the 4th Marines—was to get to Japan as quickly as possible. By the late afternoon of Monday 27 August, at least fifteen naval and marine language officers were aboard the armada of American and Allied ships in Sagami Bay, in the shadow of Mt. Fuji. They were there to facilitate the movement of nearly twenty ships carrying a task group of almost nine thousand American and British sailors and Marines into Tokyo Bay. Their mission was to seize the Imperial Japanese Navy base at Yokosuka, just inside the bay, and disarm the *Nagato*, Japan's sole surviving battleship. They approached that task in a mood that mixed trepidation and triumph. Because no one knew "whether the Japanese knew how to surrender or how they would behave," the Marines prepared to storm ashore from Higgins boats (LCVP) with their heavy gear and rifles at the ready. Admiral "Bull" Halsey, who commanded the armada, had loaded onto his flagship the saddle that the citizens of Reno, Nevada, had given him to use on Emperor Hirohito's white horse. But Rear Adm. Robert B. "Mick" Carney, his chief of staff, felt compelled to warn of "overt treachery" even after the Japanese base commander had come aboard the USS *San Diego* (CL 53) for instructions on how to prepare for the Americans' landing.[10]

The language officers harbored more positive, but still mixed, feelings about the impending landing. For Jish Martin, born and raised in Japan by missionary parents, the moment was magical. Being close enough to see ordinary Japanese walking up and down on the shore felt "like going home." Jim Durbin found the prospect of landing in Japan "really quite . . . thrilling" but felt that waiting to do so was "most tiresome." Hart Spiegel believed "the little

Japanese lieutenant commander" who piloted the ships through a minefield into the approaches to Tokyo Bay when he reassured Spiegel that the Marines would "have an easy time" and find everything on the base in order and the people of Yokosuka "stoical and resigned" to foreign occupation of their city. Even though this last amphibious landing of the war would be "quite a present" on his birthday, and quite a contrast from a year before when he lay sick with fever on Guam, Spiegel could not push aside feelings of regret. He was saddened that "so many of the fellows who were in the long fight [and who] got killed so late in the game [were] . . . not going to be able to see the show."[11]

The drama began to unfold just minutes before six on the morning of Thursday 30 August 1945, when Marines landed on a sand spit that jutted out into Tokyo Bay across from Yokosuka. The whole operation was pushed ahead by two hours so that they and naval underwater demolition team swimmers could beat the troops of the 11th Airborne Division who were scheduled to land moments later at Atsugi airfield in preparation for General MacArthur's arrival later in the day. At 8:45 that morning, just as the American flag was being raised over two forts that guarded the approach to Yokosuka, Paul Sherman, "wearing a pistol, battle helmet, life jacket and clutching a dictionary for dear life," stepped ashore with the newsmen who were going to film the landing. Where they landed was "absolutely deserted," its ghostly silence broken only by the approach of some Japanese policemen in a little red truck that looked like something out of the circus. They saluted, drove away without a word, and left the camera crews alone to film the great event.[12]

At 9:30 AM the Marines stormed ashore from their boats with fingers at the ready on their rifles' triggers. They had been ordered not to shoot unless fired upon and looked "bewildered and a trifle annoyed" at the absence of opposition and "complete silence" that greeted them. In a few moments, they met a column of Japanese English teachers mobilized from Tokyo schools headed by a few naval officers. The teachers wore white armbands to indicate that they were interpreters, but Jim Durbin and some of the other language officers discovered that their English skills were so shaky that it was better to talk with others who spoke only Japanese. Jim Jefferson, who interpreted for the regimental commander, had quite a different experience. The very first Japanese he met was Ensign Takemiya Takeji, who spoke first in Japanese and then asked if he could continue in English. Jefferson replied "gladly" in Japanese and then proceeded to discuss particulars of base occupation with the onetime student at San Pedro High School in Los Angeles.[13]

Once more senior American officers came ashore, however, things got much more hectic for the naval language officers. An uptight marine junior officer ordered Paul Sherman and another interpreter to tell "the little [Japanese] bastards to stand at attention" for Brig. Gen. William T. Clement, the landing force commander, because the Japanese had made Americans on Bataan stand until they dropped and "he was going to do the same goddamn thing" to them. When the general arrived he was furious not to find a Japanese admiral waiting to surrender his sword on the spot. He then drove off to a ceremonial raising of the first American flag on Japanese soil and "started howling" for the Japanese admiral. Followed by a horde of underlings and cameramen, he finally pulled up at the dock where the USS *San Diego* had tied up. Clement found Vice Admiral Totsuka Michitarō, "resplendent in white gloves [but with] black rings around his eyes" nervously awaiting the formal surrender ceremony. In a few moments it was over.[14]

But the language officers' duties had only begun. Paul Sherman stepped in to stop a Marine who was demanding from noncomprehending Japanese that they immediately deliver eight automobiles for the use of senior American officers. Then he drove around Yokosuka for hours scrounging up a fleet of battered alcohol- and charcoal-burning vehicles for the dignitaries. Glen Slaughter accompanied the marine regimental commander to survey housing on the base and cleverly managed things so that senior Marines got beautiful little Japanese-style houses atop a hill while naval officers were relegated to the dull officers' club. Bill Burd became the interpreter for admirals Nimitz and Halsey, when at 1:30 that afternoon—precisely a half hour before General MacArthur made his celebrated landing at Atsugi—Rear Adm. Oscar Badger, the task unit commander, showed them around the Yokosuka Base. He watched in horror as "Bull" Halsey spat upon the tatami floor mats of one of the Japanese officers' houses that his subordinates had appropriated and muttered "living like rats!"

That sour note could not spoil what was a day of triumph for the Americans even as it was a day of tragedy for their Japanese hosts. As 30 August 1945 drew to a close, the American language officers had every reason to consider themselves successful facilitators of surrender. They had risen to and met new linguistic—and military—challenges. Bill Burd, who had spent most of the war breaking codes rather than translating, made only a couple of nonfatal errors in interpreting for the Japanese pilot who guided the American ships into Tokyo Bay. Paul Sherman prepared a list of Japanese phrases for newsmen to help them cover the all-important ceremonies. And Glen Slaughter, more accustomed to coaxing trapped Japanese soldiers and civilians into giving themselves up in battle, found that he could speak properly to—and for—generals and admirals. That night, the Boulder men, whether Marines sleeping in dingy quarters on the base or naval officers in their ships' cabins, had every reason to feel proud. They were part of the Navy–Marine Corps team that had won the race to Japan, and they had performed ably in the first surrender ceremonies at Yokosuka.[15]

Ironically, none of the Boulder men played any significant part in the full, formal surrender ceremony aboard the USS *Missouri* (BB 63) forty-eight hours later. Five of them, including the valedictorian of the July 1943 graduating class, might have been there on Sunday morning 2 September 1945—if only they had packed more carefully. They were rushed from Pearl Harbor to the *Missouri* at sea and ushered into its captain's presence. He told them the Navy wanted to have its own interpreters present alongside those from State Department and the Imperial Navy at the upcoming surrender ceremony and asked if they understood "diplomatic Japanese." The men smiled and affirmed hesitantly that they did. The captain then told them to turn in their formal white uniforms for the ship's laundry to clean. The most senior Boulder man paled, looked knowingly at the others, and then begged the captain's pardon, confessing that none had brought white uniforms with them from Hawaii. The captain then glared at the five and ordered them to leave the ship immediately. Thus rejected, the Boulder men were transferred by breeches buoy, with a soaking along the way, to two other ships before going ashore with the Marines in the Yokosuka landing.[16]

They could still have been aboard the *Missouri* for the Sunday morning surrender ceremony for Admiral Nimitz had subsequently decreed that open-necked khakis like those the Boulder men wore would be the uniform of the day. As it turned out, the three naval language officers on the ship on 2 September—prewar linguist Cdr. Gil Slonim, Berkeley graduate Wilvan Van Campen, and Boulder-trained Donald K. Anderson—played no part in the historic ceremony. General MacArthur presided over Japan's formal surrender, and his chief of staff saw to it that a senior army language officer served as interpreter. The Japanese brought their own linguist, a diplomat who had mastered English while studying at Amherst and Harvard.[17]

BITTERSWEET ISLAND BUFFERS

The contrast between the Boulder men's passive position aboard the *Missouri* and their very active role in the occupation of Yokosuka prefigured a pattern that would repeat itself in the months ahead. Sometimes actors, sometimes mere observers, they time and again became cross-cultural as well as linguistic interpreters who eased Japanese and Americans alike through the difficult moments of surrender. But their actions and responses to the challenges they confronted in this last phase of their naval careers varied greatly depending on where they served. Overseas they became bittersweet buffers in the dismantling of Japan's empire. In the Japanese home islands, they proved eager but gentlemanly occupiers. Because their working environments and duties in each realm were so different, their paths of action in each area are best followed separately, in this and the following chapter.

The tasks that lay ahead of the language officers as dismantlers of Japan's maritime empire revealed themselves in microcosm in the events surrounding the first peacetime surrender. It took place on 22 August 1945, nearly a week before the occupation of Yokosuka, aboard the USS *Levy* (DE 162) off Mille, a tiny coral atoll that lay 350 miles southeast of Kwajalein in the Marshall Islands. The little destroyer escort carried Lt. E. Richard Harris (Boulder, July 1943) who was to serve as interpreter for "an old military lion," Capt. Harold Barley Grow (USNA, class of 1912) in a formal capitulation ceremony. Three days earlier Harris had interpreted in tense presurrender negotiations with Captain Shiga Masanori, IJN. The talks ran on for nearly three hours because the Japanese insisted on receiving confirmation from Tokyo that the emperor had in fact ordered them to give up. This time, having gotten that reassurance, a more compliant Shiga signed the instrument of surrender in proceedings that took less than an hour, while Harris, Grow, and the prospective commander of the U.S. Marine garrison for the island looked on. Once the deed was done, the *Levy*'s captain broadcast word of the surrender to his crew, and the men backslapped and congratulated one another. The war was over![18]

But the tasks of peace were just beginning. Six days later, the Marines went ashore on Mille, raised the Stars and Stripes, and started disarming some twenty-four hundred "half-naked, half-starving" Japanese, scooping up swords, pistols, and daggers as souvenirs. Then Captain Shiga and his officers were taken to Majuro, an atoll in the eastern Marshall Islands, where they became well-treated prisoners. When they came to lunch at the officers' mess there for the first time, Lieutenant Harris was pressed into service to break the awkward silence. He started chatting with Shiga's executive officer and then suddenly broke off the conversation. "My God!" Harris exclaimed, this man "says he personally beheaded the Corsair pilot [one of five] who crash-landed on Mille [in February 1944]. He says we owe him a debt of gratitude because he did it in one stroke."

That astonishing revelation set the stage for a still more shocking end to the drama of the Mille surrender. Captain Shiga took up residence in the base air operations officer's tent, forcing him to hastily gather his gear and get out. The next morning, the American could not find his toenail scissors and returned to the tent to get them. The marine guard standing outside it informed him that the prisoner "looks . . . uh . . . funny." When the two men went in, they found Shiga on the floor, "rigid, purple, [and] belly up." He had used the scissors to scratch his abdomen, hara-kiri style, and then taken cyanide to end his life. That, presumably, enabled him to take responsibility for torturing and executing American aviators but saved him from trial and punishment as a war criminal.[19]

What Lieutenant Harris experienced on Mille and Majuro prefigured what other Boulder men would see and do throughout Japan's empire of islands and conquered territories on the Asian mainland. They negotiated before, and functioned effectively in, formal surrender ceremonies. They helped American forces take over sometime enemy territory and foreign lands the Japanese had occupied. They served as go-betweens with defeated foes and as investigators of and interpreters for suspected war criminals. A few of them actually worked in war crimes trials. And in the year that followed this first surrender, the Boulder men assisted in the repatriation of nearly 700,000 Japanese, military and civilians alike, to their defeated homeland.[20] Overall, they helped ensure that the surrender of Japanese forces and transfer of the islands they occupied to American naval control would be peaceful.

The surrender process, however, was protracted, stretching out over weeks and months rather than days as on Mille. Although similar in form, it varied in substance from place to place, depending on physical location and the size of the Japanese forces involved. That presented the Boulder-trained naval linguists with particular challenges at each step of the surrender process. How they met those challenges and functioned as instruments of surrender can best be understood by looking at what they did, first on four widely scattered islands in Japan's maritime empire and then on the Asian mainland.

Most of the Boulder-trained men departed for island surrender duties from the Marianas, where Vice Adm. George D. Murray (USNA, class of 1911), who bore overall responsibility for dismantling Japan's maritime empire, had his command headquarters. Thus as August 1945 drew to a close, Bill Sigerson and Norman Meller found themselves racing from Saipan to miniscule Marcus aboard the USS *Mayrant* (DD 402). The Navy wanted to set up an air station on this islet, located roughly fifteen hundred miles south and east of Tokyo and about eight hundred miles east of Iwo Jima, before the Army Air Corps claimed it. The two linguists were unusual in that both had law degrees. They served on the staff of Commo. Vernon Francis Grant (USNA, class of 1917), a man already notorious for "barreling around Saipan" in a chrome-laden jeep. He wanted to make history by securing the capitulation of the Japanese garrison on Marcus before the surrender ceremonies in Tokyo Bay. To that end, he had insisted that the *Mayrant* get under way even before the B-29 that had been dispatched to drop surrender leaflets returned from Marcus.[21]

The cranky commodore put the two Boulder men through their paces. En route to Marcus he had them translate documents for surrender ceremonies that would vary, depending on whether his superior, Vice Adm. Francis E. Whiting (USNA, class of 1912), or he himself (as he fervently hoped) presided at the formal capitulation ceremony. He had them prepare questions and orders for the captain of a Japanese vessel reportedly on its way to take some of its garrison off Marcus Island. When the *Mayrant* reached that "flat piece of sand in the vast ocean" with nothing more than a couple of radio towers to suggest that it was inhabited, the Americans flashed a signal indicating that they had come to take the island's surrender. The Japanese simply flashed back that they were "consulting superiors." The commodore then put Bill Sigerson and army sergeant Nobuo Furuiye, a talented and experienced interpreter, into a small boat, and lowered them into rough seas with orders to go ashore and talk to the enemy. But after three false starts the two drenched men were called back to the *Mayrant* because a boat carrying four men was heading toward the ship.

The atmosphere once they came aboard was electric. The Japanese—a magnificently mustachioed lieutenant commander, a tough-looking army captain, an air corps lieutenant, and an interpreter who had lived in Hawaii as a youth—were docile. They listened dutifully while the Americans handed over documents and announced that *their* admiral would set the date for a formal surrender ceremony. A frightening exchange of small gifts brought this first presurrender encounter to an end. The Japanese gladly accepted a carton of Camel cigarettes. But when their senior officer reached down into his briefcase to take out two muskmelons to give to the Americans, nervous marine guards mistook the intended gifts for bombs, shouted a warning, and drew their guns. "For a tense moment," Norm Meller recalled, "time froze." Then everyone saw the gifts for what they were and relaxed.

The next day Bill Sigerson helped defuse what could have been an unpleasant incident when the commodore went ashore to inspect the island. American bombs had cratered its runways, but its tanks and coastal batteries were in good shape. The commodore was in a foul mood because he could not meet the island's purportedly ill commandant. When he got to the tatami-floored room where they were to lunch, he balked at taking off his shoes. Sigerson persuaded him it would be rude not to, and before long—their spirits warmed by Japanese whiskey and good but simple food—the commodore and his host, a mere lieutenant commander, were chatting about prewar geisha parties they had enjoyed in Shanghai. Then, "visibly moved and with shaking voice," the Japanese officer proffered his service pistol, to the commodore, saying that he had intended to kill himself rather than surrender the island. But after talking with the Americans the preceding day, he had decided it was his duty to return home "and build a new and better Japan."

That gesture made a big difference. Later that afternoon the Boulder men helped the *Mayrant*'s captain interrogate the "rugged, sinister-looking" and scarred captain of the Japanese relief ship that had just arrived. Convinced that the Japanese ship was a "die-hard," the American captain slipped his ship out of its anchorage and spent the night cruising in more distant, presumably safer, waters. The next day, however, the commodore went ashore bearing gifts for Lieutenant Commander Nakamura and the still indisposed Japanese admiral. After touring the island's hospital, he even ordered—to the dismay of some *Mayrant* sailors—that blood plasma be delivered to the Japanese. By the end of that day, even the *Mayrant*'s captain had calmed down, reassured that the seemingly dangerous Japanese relief ship captain would obey his orders to evacuate as many men as possible from the island.[22]

In these presurrender encounters, Sigerson and Meller helped defuse animosities that might otherwise have disrupted the formal surrender of Marcus Island. It began the next day aboard the USS *Bagley* (DD 386), commencing promptly at 9:00 AM Tokyo time to synchronize with the USS *Missouri* surrender ceremony. Vice Admiral Whiting presided, rather than Commodore Grant. Bill Sigerson, his legs "shaking and sore" from trying to keep his balance as the ship rolled in the offshore swells, looked on as Sergeant Furuiye did a "beautifully tactful job" of interpreting. But then the Boulder men's legal training suddenly became important. The Japanese admiral was not at all sure that he and his officers should have to hand over their swords. After considerable debate, it was agreed that he would do so, subject to confirmation from Imperial General Headquarters that they must be given up. If Tokyo did not so order, however, the Americans would return the weapons when their first landing party came ashore. With that, the Japanese handed three swords across the table to the Americans. One of them was Lieutenant Commander Nakamura's six-hundred-year-old family heirloom, beautifully wrapped in black silk with an orange tassel. Afterward, all that remained to be done that Sunday was for the victors to raise Old Glory ashore and the vanquished to burn the Rising Sun flag that they had taken down.[23]

The formal surrender of Marcus Island was over, but tensions between victor and vanquished remained high. Admiral Whiting had refused to return the Japanese officers' salute at the end of the surrender ceremony, and the next day he departed, taking Lieutenant Sigerson and Sergeant Furuiye with him aboard the *Bagley*. That left Norm Meller alone to deal with lingering animosities and prevent misunderstandings between the new and old occupiers of Marcus Island. On his first night ashore, he got quite a scare when he saw Japanese light tanks approaching the Americans' tents. It turned out that the Marines, who had been tipped off to a supposed plot to drive them into the sea, had commandeered them and were using them to form a perimeter, with guns pointed outward, to protect the encampment.[24] Later, a bulldozer from the Acorn Unit, a small group of naval men responsible for building, operating, and maintaining an advanced air base, hit an unexploded Japanese mine that wounded the driver. The Japanese deputy commander of the island used Meller to make apologies and provide explanations to the Acorn Unit commander.

Capt. Arthur H. McCollum, USN. (U.S. Naval Institute Photo Archive)

Capt. Albert E. Hindmarsh, USN. (Alan Hindmarsh)

Professor Florence Walne. (Roger Pineau papers)

Small class at Boulder, summer 1942, *left to right*: Instructor: Takeo Okamoto; students: Paul E. Farley, Robert S. Mandelstam, Roger Pineau, John B. Jago, Robert S. Kinsman, and David G. Parkes. (Roger Pineau papers)

Glenn Nelson burns the midnight oil. (Roger Pineau papers)

Boulder Halloween dance. (Roger Pineau papers)

Top teachers, *left to right*: Ashikaga Ensho, Susumu Nakamura, and Rayer Toki. (Roger Pineau papers)

Boulder wedding: Ensigns Solomon B. Levine and Betty Billett Levine. (Solomon and Elizabeth Levine)

Maj. Sherwood F. Moran, USMCR, interviews prisoner on Guadalcanal. (U.S. Marine Corps)

Marine linguists call on the enemy to surrender, Saipan, July 1944. (Pacific Basin Institute)

At work in the JICPOA "Zoo." (Courtesy James M. Wells)

Documents captured: JICPOA and 2nd Division language officers on Saipan, 1944, *left to right*: Otis Cary, USNR; Robert W. Speed; Harry P. Barrand, Erling J. Logan, and Reed Irvine, USMCR; unidentified; and John L. Decker, USNR. (Pacific Basin Institute)

1st Lt. James M. Jefferson interrogates a prisoner on Okinawa. (Record Group 127 GW-666, National Archives)

Okinawa collaborators, *left to right*: 1st Lt. Glen K. Slaughter, USMCR; "Tony" Komesu; and 1st Lt. Glenn W. Nelson, USMCR. (Roger Pineau papers)

Surrender interpreter, *far right*: Lt. (jg) Aloysius M. Soden, USNR, aboard USS *Portland,* at Truk, 2 September 1945. (Naval Historical Center)

Peacemaker: 1st Lt. James W. Brayshay, USMCR, in Tientsin. (Courtesy James W. Brayshay)

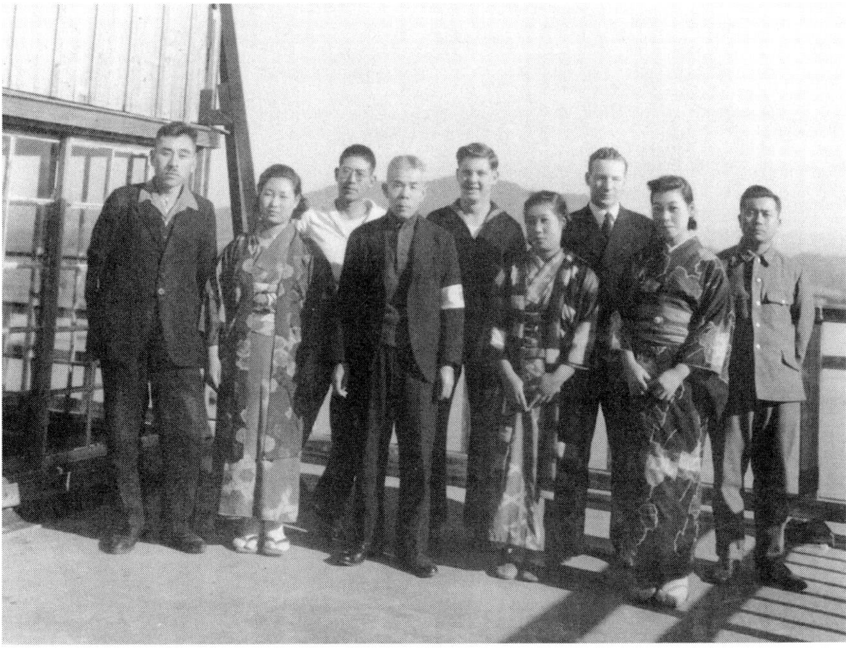

Working together: Lt. (jg) Daniel D. Karasik, USNR, officer-innkeeper, (*third from right*) and his staff, Wakayama, Japan. (Courtesy the Karasik family)

Yokosuka Christmas, 1945. Language officers, *front row*: unknown; Lt. W. G. Beasley, RNVR; Lt. (jg) Robert W. Christy; and Lt. (jg) James M. Wells, USNR. (Courtesy James M. Wells)

Tokyo explorers: Lt. (jg) Griffith Way, USNR (*left*); Lt. (jg) Donald C. Gorham, USNR. (Courtesy Griffith Way)

Reunion: Former Boulder students and teachers in Tokyo, 1946. (Roger Pineau papers)

Interrogators in war, bridge builders in peace: John Rich and Otis Cary. (Pacific Basin Institute)

Assistant naval attaché James M. Jefferson "goes native" on inspection tours of Japan (James M. Jefferson papers)

Master translator, Nobel Laureate novelist, and Journalist, *left to right*: Edward G. Seidensticker, Kawabata Yasunari, and Frank B. Gibney (Pacific Basin Institute)

Sixty years later: Language officers reunite at Boulder, Colorado, June 2002. (Author collection)

With the passage of time, Meller became even more of a mediator between victors and vanquished. A Japanized pronunciation of his name—"Meruru"—became the password that allowed Japanese entry into the American encampment at night. He translated when the Japanese admiral and his staff came to watch an American movie, and the skill he had picked up from the Boulder Monday night movies enabled him to do the same for the Marines and Seabees when the Japanese brought one of their films to be shown. Meller also helped bring the matter of the surrendered Japanese swords to a dramatic if not entirely amicable end. One day the island's second in command, an Imperial Japanese Army colonel, stormed into Meller's tent, angrily waving a paper. Shouting "Give back our swords!" he poked the stunned American on the chest with his index finger. Lieutenant Meller defiantly ordered the colonel never to yell at or touch him again. The colonel retorted by saying that the message he had from Tokyo said that General MacArthur had authorized Japanese military men to return home with their "household goods." That, he insisted, included swords. At this point, Meller the interpreter responded like the attorney he was. He said he thought the colonel was misconstruing the term "household goods" but promised to take the matter up with the Acorn Unit commander. The Japanese left in anger, and the senior American officer on the island, just to be safe, posted a twenty-four-hour marine guard around the boxed swords that were kept in a tent next to Meller's. A few days later a message from Saipan arrived. It confirmed the Boulder lawyer/linguist's interpretation of "household goods" and laid to rest the last and most deeply felt dispute over the surrender of Marcus Island. Peace would prevail until the more than two thousand Japanese troops were removed from the island.[25]

Two other Boulder graduates, lieutenants (junior grade) John G. Oliver and Paul F. Boller Jr., had a much easier time of it on Rota, where the surrender proceeded much more smoothly than it had on Marcus Island. Neither man commanded the extra professional skills of Bill Sigerson and Norman Meller, but both had toughened themselves as interpreters and interrogators by ferreting out and interviewing Japanese soldiers who had hidden in the jungle after hostilities ceased on Guam. On 26 August, Oliver came to Rota, which lay roughly halfway between Guam and Tinian, aboard the USS *Currier* (DE 700). He simply informed the island commander that the Marines would arrive on 2 September to take its surrender. Boller interpreted at the formal capitulation ceremony and helped it end with a moment of humor. He proclaimed in a loud voice that the United States was taking possession of the island. He translated all of the questions and answers that passed between the two sides as the Japanese handed over their swords. The marine commander of the occupying artillery battalion then ordered Boller, who had volunteered for the assignment, to inform the Japanese that they were "on good behavior." Momentarily unable to remember the specific Japanese military equivalent of that phrase, the flustered young officer just spoke a literal translation. Suddenly the senior Japanese officer present darkened his demeanor. He demanded to know why, after he and his men had been so compliant with American requests, they were being addressed in so insulting a manner. Quick-witted "Whiskeyhead" Boller shot back that he was only a junior officer obeying his commander's order to say what he did. That set off a wave of guffaws among the Japanese. When the puzzled marine commander demanded to know what was going on, Boller covered his error by saying that the Japanese were laughing because they were "nervous."

Paul Boller found little to laugh about during the remainder of his stay on Rota. He stretched his linguistic abilities and his emotions in the ensuing occupation, disarmament, and depopulation of the island. Working for days in blistering heat broken by tropical downpours, Boller helped Marines process three thousand Japanese troops who were going to be taken to Guam. He translated the compliments that the senior American and Japanese officers traded as they inspected the island. He went out on patrol with Marines searching the jungle for Japanese "die-hards" who had not yet given themselves up. And in a poignant episode that demonstrated what harm cross-cultural misunderstanding could do, he translated for a marine lieutenant who toured civilian villages demanding that every male, man and boy alike, surrender and burn his baseball-style cap simply because it resembled the headgear of Japanese army enlisted men. Boller left Rota unhappy about having unwillingly facilitated that extreme gesture of surrender but proud for helping the island be the very first to be completely depopulated of Japanese troops.[26]

The surrender of the Carolines further to the south took much longer and demanded the talents of many more Boulder-trained linguists than the handful who had gone to Rota, Marcus, and Mille. These instruments of surrender were a varied lot of naval officers. Very few of them had functioned as combat interpreters or encountered Japanese troops as prisoners of war. The youngest among them had begun language study at Boulder, graduated from its Stillwater satellite, and come straight from the continental United States to south central Pacific. Most had trained for duty as civil affairs officers, a duty that they did not perform. Their instruction at the Navy School of Military Government at Columbia University and minimal combat training at the Civil Affairs Staging Area (CASA) at Fort Ord, near Monterey, California, only marginally prepared them for what lay ahead. While instructors there correctly presumed that Japanese-ruled Pacific islands would "fall" to American control, the school prepared students for operations in the Pescadores, in the Taiwan Strait off the China coast, and on Japan's northernmost island, Hokkaido. Those locations bore little resemblance to the palm-dotted islands and coral atolls of the Carolines scattered across an enormous expanse of brilliant blue sea.[27]

Thus, much like their marine predecessors who went ashore in the first wartime island invasions, these men who served after Japan's formal surrender had to improvise and interpret the orders they had been given to deal with unexpected situations. Unlike the wartime invaders, however, they did not go ashore on isolated islands backed by overwhelming force. Yet their emotions as their surrender duties began echoed those of Boulder men who had gone before them early in the war. Lt. (jg) Oliver Benson, setting out for Truk in October 1945, felt just like Chuck Cross had when he approached Kwajalein in January 1944. He was "tremendously interested and excited" and "scared stiff" that his Japanese would prove "entirely inadequate."[28]

The U.S. Navy treated Truk as an object of surrender with justifiable apprehension. That atoll, which lay nearly 600 miles to the southeast of Guam, had been the Japanese naval, military, and civilian administrative headquarters for the central Carolines. Its lagoon embraced, depending on the eye of the beholder, between 70 and 250 islands and islets. American planes had bombed Truk, littering its lagoon with the hulks of more than 30 sunken ships and destroying 100 aircraft. But the atoll's inner islands and portions of its outer reef bristled with more than 4,000 mines, whose precise whereabouts were unknown to the Americans. At war's end, the Japanese vice admiral and lieutenant general on Truk commanded 40,000 armed and undefeated troops scattered throughout the Carolines. Their rank and those numbers demanded that the formal surrender ceremony at Truk for these islands take place at the same time and with just as much pomp as the proceedings aboard the USS *Missouri*.[29]

Three Boulder men aided by three army nisei plus two marine enlisted linguists helped that event unfold according to script. John G. Oliver reprised his role at Marcus Island, arriving off Truk aboard the USS *Stack* (DD 406) only four days after the smaller island was given up. He and the other interpreters spent about an hour with five Japanese officers in the *Stack*'s "intensely hot" wardroom, headed by a rear admiral. Their principal task was to minimize misunderstanding and tension on both sides. The senior Japanese army officer, who suffered from tuberculosis, shook uncontrollably and spoke softly while his chain-smoking colleagues looked on. The senior American officer, a marine brigadier general, mistook Japanese requests for clarification on what was being asked of them as objections and repeatedly declared quite forcefully that "he intended to make no concessions."

When the meeting broke into subgroups to study charts and other information about reef passages, minefields, and other hazards to navigation over an immense sea area, things went more a bit more smoothly. By that afternoon, having shed ties and other inhibitions, the Americans got the Japanese to reveal not only how very weak their forces in the Carolines were but also to acknowledge that they needed American help to implement the terms of the proposed surrender. These presurrender talks ended on a bittersweet note, however. As the Japanese filed down to their gig, "sorrow briefly brushed over their faces." The Americans, who had only reluctantly returned their salute when they came aboard the *Stack*, now vigorously saluted their departing, defeated foe.[30]

This successful presurrender encounter guaranteed that the formal capitulation ceremony on 2 September proceeded without a hitch. On that Sunday, Lieutenant General Mugikura Shinzaburō and Vice Admiral Hara Chūichi, who had commanded Japanese forces in the Battle of the Coral Sea back in May 1942, came aboard the heavy cruiser USS *Portland* (CA 33) to surrender the base at Truk and their respective forces to Vice Adm. George D. Murray, Commander Marianas. On that occasion, Lt. Aloysius M. Soden provided reinforcement to the American interpreter team; Soden was a Catholic brother who had taught high school in Japan before the war, suffered through internment and return on the exchange ship *Gripsholm*, and then graduated from the Boulder language school. In photographs of the event, he stands in the background, looking on as the flag officers solemnly signed the instruments of surrender. That posture captures perfectly the naval language officers' role as facilitators of the official surrender of the Caroline Islands.[31]

Actual surrender was quite another matter. Lt. (jg) Robert Falk discovered that two weeks later when he stepped ashore on Yap, still queasy after an 18-hour voyage in a tiny landing craft. The island, which lay 750 miles west northwest of Truk, had been an important transfer station in the transpacific cable that before the war linked the continental United States with Hawaii, the Philippines, and China. Naval postwar planners who looked forward to planting American bases in Micronesia wanted to put a communications facility on the island, and Vice Admiral Murray had hastened to get a handful of Americans to the island. Falk, who had trained for this moment at Columbia and CASA, was excited to be joining them and harbored great expectations about what he might be able to accomplish on Yap.[32]

Once there, however, Falk felt more like Daniel thrown into the lion's den than the "take-charge" officer he had trained to be. The thirty-one-year-old sometime professor of English at Michigan State University arrived alone rather than, as planned, with a fellow language officer. The harbor buzzed with small boats "full of grinning Japs," and once ashore he encountered hundreds of Japanese soldiers "dressed in nothing but a loincloth who were hauling huge shells and boxes of ammunition" and loading them into boats that shuttled out to American ships. Other "curious Jap soldiers" chattered questions at him "like a lot of monkeys." A few old tattooed native men, clad in nothing but colored paper loincloths, squatted nearby and rose to bow and exchange a few words of Japanese with him. The surrounding landscape was almost surreal—buildings turned into "concrete hulks with twisted iron frames" by American bombs, and a muddy campsite that would put Falk and others on the military government team cheek by jowl "with the Japs."[33]

When the officer Falk was to relieve escorted him into the Japanese officers' tent, he immediately discovered that they, rather than the Americans, were in control. They welcomed him with palm toddy and bananas. His fellow American started up a friendly conversation that very obviously violated the formal rule against fraternization with the enemy. Falk had no problem with that, for, as his companion put it, "When there are thirty or forty of our men unarmed on an island teeming with six thousand Japs, you damn well better fraternize!" He quickly came to realize just how anomalous and tenuous his position was, just as that of the nearly one hundred other Americans on the island or afloat on ships in its harbor. There was no American military force on Yap, and it would be 7 December before two dozen men from the 26th

Marine Regiment arrived. Formal military government authority rested with the Ulithi atoll commander nearly a hundred miles away. That left actual command authority in the hands of the SOPA—senior officer present afloat—in the harbor. That junior lieutenant commander had little appreciation for the linguists' skills and cared even less about what they might do. The shocking reality was that the Japanese remained in full control of their own forces and the Yap islanders.[34]

Thus Falk found his duties "pretty vague" during his first week on the island. He interpreted for marine officers who came to visit crash sites and interview Japanese about missing American flyers. He helped Japanese pilots bring patrol craft through the reef channel into the harbor. He looked on in amazement at enlisted Japanese soldiers, shoeless and wearing only a G-string, salute and bow before their better-clad officers and then move "like a procession of ants" up into the hills to haul down all kinds of ammunition and gun parts on poles over their shoulders. And he interpreted for an American naval doctor who went into the jungle to inspect wounded and sick Japanese soldiers scattered in huts where medicines and even dressings were "woefully lacking." At the end of that first week, he felt "as though I've been out here a year." And over the next two, when for a short time there were three other Boulder men and three army nisei interpreters on Yap, Falk had little or nothing to do, so he returned to Ulithi.[35]

At almost the same moment, lieutenants (jg) Oliver E. Benson and Clinton H. Gardiner arrived at Truk's South Pass aboard the USS *Columbia* (CL 56). They were assigned to assist Brig. Gen. Robert Blake, who would command the marine occupiers of Truk, with what turned out to be the first of several inspection tours of its lagoon islands. Like Falk, Benson and Gardiner were older than the average naval language officer, and both already had a Ph.D. degree. Gardiner had finished his while at Boulder, and Benson was already nearly seven years into what became more than four decades of teaching at the University of Oklahoma. But neither man had had any direct contact with the Japanese or experience in translating or negotiating with them.[36]

Nonetheless, their first encounter with the sometime enemy aboard the *Columbia* went well enough. The two men herded a larger-than-expected group of Japanese army and navy officers into General Blake's cabin and helped negotiate a change in the planned seating arrangements. Benson read a preprepared translation of General Blake's speech, and Gardiner handled questions and answers between the inspection party's doctor and his Japanese counterpart. The sometime enemy's own interpreters also helped. Before the session ended, Benson got the bulky, "fairly friendly" Admiral Hara to laugh and General Mugikura, whom he saw as "little old wizened, sour, bent little monkey" to light up a cigarette and relax a bit. The Americans ended the session by giving the Japanese general a detailed schedule of what they planned to do ashore.

Things got more complicated over the next two days, however. The Americans depended on the Japanese to pilot their LCVPs through the reef and safely past mines in the lagoon.[37] Once ashore on Dublon Island, General Blake became something of a problem for the two interpreters. He wanted to see things for himself, on his own terms; and occasionally he literally ran away from the rest of the inspection party to check out some Japanese military facility. The Japanese commander and their subordinates, by contrast, wanted to adhere rigidly to what they regarded as a prearranged inspection schedule. Lieutenant Benson found himself not just squished between generals Blake and Mugikura in vehicles but caught between their conflicting views of how and where the inspection should proceed. He and Gardiner thus had not only to field increasingly technical questions and answers but also to serve as negotiators between the two sides.

At first Benson was not particularly tolerant or understanding of the Japanese or their ways. He saw "rather superior smirks" and "feigned" elaborate concern on the faces of Japanese boatmen who had to be told to slow down for slower American craft crossing the lagoon. In his eyes, the "bright nasty red" of the keels of upside down sunken ships was "a beautiful sight." He delighted when "the Nips melted like flies" when trying to keep up with the Americans in climbing to inspect Japanese food depots. And he was disgusted by what he regarded as General Mugikura's effort to impugn General Blake's credibility when the American looked aside at enlisted Marines' picking up souvenirs in violation of general orders that were known to the Japanese. Indeed, Benson himself took great pleasure in appropriating a piece of metal from wrecked plane marked with Japanese insignia.

Gradually his attitudes toward the enemy softened, however. He pitied a bedraggled Japanese interpreter who was pressed into service clutching the very same Japanese-English dictionary that he himself used. He recognized that his superiors' repeated sudden demands to change schedules caused the

Japanese justifiable consternation. He calmed enlisted Marines accompanying him on a truck trip around one island when they protested the presence of an armed Japanese sergeant, explaining that the man was a *kempei*, or military policeman, who was allowed to retain his weapon during the interval between formal Japanese surrender and actual American occupation of islands. Indeed, by the time he left Truk, Benson had progressed from apprehension about and even some distaste for his duty there to satisfaction that "we got out of it with so little friction with the Nips, who seem[ed] to be thoroughly whipped in every way and to realize the same."[38]

Three weeks after Benson left Truk, George Nace, one of the most seasoned and skillful of all of the Boulder-trained linguists, arrived there as part of yet another, larger inspection party of nine senior officers. Nace was originally supposed to operate "under cover," searching for a Japanese doctor alleged to have performed medical experiments on American prisoners, and leave routine translation work to the Boulder men already there. But when he listened incognito to the exchanges between Japanese and Americans, he discovered to his dismay that neither their interpreters nor ours could do all that was asked of them. The American had a hard time getting the Japanese to understand that only Vice Admiral Hara and General Mugikura could come aboard the USS *Rhind* (DD 404), and the Japanese barely smoothed over the situation. Afterward, Nace learned that the American interpreter had not spoken a word of Japanese since leaving Boulder. He then got permission to shed his "cover" and serve as interpreter for the inspection party.

Nace had a very busy but enlightening sojourn at Truk. He had to sort out scheduling problems that arose because Americans and Japanese used different names for the docks on various islands where the inspecting party would arrive. He had to shepherd his seniors through what might have otherwise been several very embarrassing moments in their formal inspection of the Japanese troops who were disarming various islands in the Truk lagoon. Nace succeeded in his various tasks because he had a keen eye, as well as a sharp ear, for what the Japanese were saying, doing, and feeling. He saw the tough side of the Japanese military when Admiral Hara slapped a Japanese sailor for making a slight mistake in protocol as his boat came alongside the *Rhind*. He quickly recognized that General Mugikura, a "quiet, alert, and interesting" officer, commanded respect but could not hide his despondency over Japan's defeat. Later in the inspection tour, Nace saw even more than he had at

Yokosuka just how great the "disaster" of defeat was for the sometime enemy. The contrast between nearly naked Japanese enlisted men trudging around American-made bomb craters, cleaning up debris, and farming sweet potatoes to survive and their beribboned commanders "wearing long faces yet trying to be proud," [at] the ruins of what was once an important sea plane base" hammered home that truth to him.[39]

Nace felt a certain empathy toward the Japanese, but Robert Falk found it much harder to share such feelings when he returned to Yap early in November 1945. This time he got much closer to them—and the local people—because he was supposed to prepare a census of the native population, then find and translate pertinent Japanese civil administrative records. He brought decidedly mixed feelings toward that task because he had internalized many of his fellow Americans' negative stereotypes of the Japanese during the war. At first he enjoyed watching another Boulder man taunt Japanese officers who claimed to know English with sexually suggestive phrases they simply couldn't comprehend. But his attitude toward the former enemy softened, at least temporarily, when he read the compassionate words the Japanese had inscribed on gravestones for American flyers who had crashed on the island. He was grateful to the Japanese lieutenant and pilot who brought him safely back from an outlying island in a small boat during a storm. And as he traded language lessons and cigarettes for souvenirs with enemy staff officers, his negative feelings toward the sometime foe seemed to drop away.[40]

Upon closer and more sustained contact, the Japanese on Yap did not look good, however. Falk suspected, and native informants confirmed, that the Imperial Army officers who bowed, smiled, and plied him with tea and toddy were withholding information. The native who took him to a crash site said the Japanese had kept a dead American flier's watch—and then died suddenly himself under mysterious circumstances. Another native informant told tales of the Japanese beating natives who refused to work for them or sell them fish. When Falk himself spoke with Japanese officers and civilian officials, they sidestepped the truth on matters large and small. The officers refused to be drawn into discussions of the origins of the war, insisted that they would die rather than become prisoners of war, and showed little interest in the democracy American occupiers were imposing on their homeland. They even predicted that Russia and America would fight the next war over Japan. Falk disdained these Japanese because they were unable to relate to others in anything but a hierarchical manner—fawning on the Americans, "kick[ing] their own people in the teeth," and enslaving the natives. Falk came to regard even the civilian with whom he traded for souvenirs as utterly self-serving.[41]

The Japanese that Robert Falk met on Yap bore little resemblance to his teachers at Boulder or to the warm and gracious people depicted in the Naganuma texts he had studied there. Nonetheless, he retained respect for Japanese culture, voiced hopes of visiting Japan, and eventually came to feel sorry for the sometime enemy stuck on Yap. Surrounded by Americans who talked of nothing but getting home from the moment they set foot on the island, he could feel for the Japanese draftees who had been in the army for five years, overseas for three, and stranded without mail or supplies on Yap for a year. He shared in their joy when word came that two thousand of them would soon be repatriated. And when early in December 1945 the time for his own departure came, he graciously accepted their gift of an officer's sword in an inscribed wooden box.

Falk left Yap with a sense of accomplishment tempered by realism. He had at best made things a little bit better in a situation that, he predicted with some accuracy, would remain SNAFU—situation normal, all "fouled up." He had put the language he had studied so hard back at Boulder to work and at least marginally reduced frictions between the Japanese, the natives, and his fellow Americans. He saw Yap disarmed and the first repatriations of wounded Japanese and of natives taken from their home islands for forced labor on Yap. Falk, unlike language officers on other islands, had neither American armed force nor the presence of senior officers to back up what he said. Yet he took the initiative in dealing with undefeated Japanese military and civilian authorities and enjoyed some cross-cultural adventures in the process. Falk helped open the door to peace on Yap and began the process of transforming the island from a speck in Japan's maritime empire into an American naval protectorate.[42]

Falk left Yap before repatriation of the Japanese there began in earnest. But Clinton Gardiner and George Nace played more direct roles in that last step of the surrender process. Gardiner made two trips to the Mortlock [Nomoi] Islands aboard the USS *Booth* (DD 170). The first trip was an inspection followed by a picnic for the ship's crew, both of which were made possible only by borrowed small craft and navigational guidance from the Japanese. The Americans rewarded them for both with beer. The second was the formal raising of the Stars and Stripes followed by an unscarred Japanese destroyer's evacuation of more than six hundred "surviving Nips" from the islands. Gardiner left Mortlock happy to have helped transfer the islands from Japanese to American hands but wondering whether the new rulers would prove wiser and more benevolent than the old.[43]

George Nace took an even more active part in the repatriation of Japanese from Truk. Midway through December 1945, he boarded one of four LSTs (landing ship, tank) each carrying 3,000 former enemy soldiers homeward. Much as other Boulder men had for prisoners of war evacuated from the Marshalls and Marianas during the war, he served as their interpreter and go-between with the ship's captain and crew. On Christmas Eve 1945, he shared in their bittersweet return to Uraga, the tiny port near Yokosuka that had been designated as a processing center for repatriates. He watched their last humiliation at American hands: stripped naked and sprayed with DDT to prevent the introduction of disease into their homeland. But he shared their joy in coming home—home to the land of their birth and his youth. He knew that they were harbingers of a new life—for themselves, for more than 20,000 others who would follow them home from the Carolines, and for a Japan shorn of empire.[44]

WAR CRIMES INVESTIGATORS

Most of the language officers who facilitated surrenders in what had been Japan's maritime empire left with similarly positive feelings. Only a very few—those engaged in the apprehension, investigation and/or prosecution of war criminals—departed with impressions of the Japanese tinged by knowledge of their darkest deeds. The linguists' involvement in war crimes investigations began with a burst in August and September when Americans came to islands —Mille, Wake, Truk, and Chichijima—where they unknowingly accepted surrender from enemy commanders complicit in the torture and execution of their countrymen. That prompted their superiors to rush two of the most talented conversationalists, David Osborn and Otis Cary, into investigation of Admiral Sakaibara Shigematsu along with a dozen of his staff officers thought to be responsible for the murder of seventy civilians on Wake Island. Cary brought a prisoner from Pearl Harbor who had previously told him what had happened, but the man told a different story to investigators on Kwajalein. Osborn then isolated several of the Japanese staff officers on another island

and confronted them with a nisei who had been on Wake and was Cary's prisoner. They validated his account, which, when told to Admiral Sakaibara, prompted his confession. Although he repudiated it at his trial before a naval commission on Guam, he and nine others were convicted and sentenced to hang for what they had done.[45]

Four Japanese admirals who had served on Truk were charged with war crimes ranging from medical experimentation on prisoners to the beheading of nine Marines left behind in the disastrous August 1942 raid on Makin in the Gilbert Islands. Three Boulder men played a part in their eventual conviction in May 1946. Late in 1945 Omer Ostensoe was "borrowed" from his original duty on Truk for what became months of war crimes–related work. In March 1946 David Osborn was flown to Tokyo to translate at the interrogation of Vice Admiral Abe Koso. Until then, prosecutors had failed in attempts to convict the executioners of the Makin Marines on Kwajalein. But a Marshallese islander witness surfaced and said Abe had been present at their deaths. Even though Osborn translated eighty-six questions and answers in the ensuing interrogation, only a trick by the prosecutor elicited Abe's confession. Another Boulder man, Eugene Kerrick, assisted at the trial of Vice Admiral Kobayashi Masashi, who had toured the Makin Marines' graves with Abe. Like his counterpart on Wake, Abe was hung in June 1947.[46]

Two other Boulder linguists, Norton Williams and Robert Durden, were drawn into the investigation and prosecution of what was perhaps the most bizarre and horrific of Japanese war crimes. Durden was sent to Truk in September 1945 to search for evidence of war crimes that allegedly had been committed on Chichijima. Williams came to the island a month later thinking that his principal duty would be to facilitate the removal of the large Japanese garrison from the island. But his marine superior knew that many American fliers had been shot down over or, like future president George H. W. Bush, near Chichijima; he wanted to find out what had happened to those who had been held captive there. Williams, who arrived completely ignorant of allegations of war crimes, was plunged into interviews, translation work, and interrogations that stretched out over the next seven months. They took a dramatic turn in December 1945, when a returning civilian passed along rumors that members of Lieutenant General Tachibana Yoshio's staff had cut out and eaten the body parts of executed American fliers. That information was considered so grisly and likely to offend the victims' families that it was kept secret for months while a widening investigation continued.

When Tachibana and thirteen others were brought to trial on Guam in the summer of 1946, Robert Durden joined two others to interpret at the proceedings. They nearly foundered because the naval captain presiding demanded more evidence and sent a new team of investigators back to Chichijima. But the "cannibal case" burst into public view and quickly moved toward guilty verdicts once a Japanese American, caught in Japan during the war and drafted into service on Tachibana's staff, testified that he had witnessed the executions and directed investigators to the site where half-eaten body parts were found. That sealed the fate of the Chichijima cannibals, and in September 1947 General Tachibana and four of his staff were hanged.[47]

Death by hanging was also the verdict in what became the most controversial of all the trials of senior Japanese military and naval officers for war crimes. Harry Pratt served as chief interpreter for the Manila international war crimes tribunal that convicted generals Homma Masaharu and Yamashita Tomoyuki. Homma bore responsibility for the infamous Bataan "death march" of American and Filipino troops who had surrendered in May 1942. Yamashita was hung for his troops' murdering and destruction as they retreated from Manila early in 1945. Pratt claimed he got the job early in 1946 because he was the most senior regular marine language officer in Tokyo. In fact, his long experience—stretching back to the marines' Samoa language school through Guadalcanal and Tarawa, Boulder and Advanced ATIS in the Philippines—commended him for the job. In the summer of 1945 he, along with fellow Boulder graduate and future congressman Samuel Stratton Jr., had actually spent hours in Bilibid Prison in Manila talking with General Yamashita and his chief of staff, General Mutō Sanji.

Pratt functioned as supervisor of army linguists and interpreter of last resort at the trials. His combat experience and familiarity with polite modes of address enabled him to step in when his subordinates lacked the appropriate vocabulary to translate properly what was being said. That made it unnecessary to rely on General Yamashita's personal interpreter, who had studied at Harvard. More importantly, Pratt brought to his task a deep understanding of command responsibility in combat that led him to a mixed verdict on the results of the trials. He had "no sympathy" for General Homma. But he shared the view—one that eventually sent the case to review by the United States Supreme Court—that Yamashita was wrongly convicted for the sins of subordinates beyond his control. Thus, unlike most other Boulder linguists who dealt with war crimes in what had been Japan's maritime empire, he came away from such duty with a nuanced view of the deeds and fate of the accused.[48]

MAINLAND PEACEKEEPERS

The language officers who helped dismantle Japan's continental empire confronted the same tasks and challenges as those who went to islands scattered across the Pacific. They had helped to determine whether Japanese forces would offer armed resistance, effect the enemy's formal surrender, and facilitate the foe's repatriation to Japan. But the objects of the Americans' concern, the environment in which they worked, and the character of their larger mission differed dramatically from that of their Pacific island counterparts. Japanese forces on the Asian mainland were very large; the Imperial Japanese Army had nearly a million men in northern China plus three quarters as many soldiers in Korea.[49] Those troops were neither a broken battlefield foe nor half-starved wretches rotting on bypassed islands but were a highly disciplined force officered by proud, unbent, and highly patriotic leaders. They occupied China's cities, where tens of thousands of civilian Japanese—entrepreneurs and adventurers rather than the docile colonists found in the Pacific islands—also lived and worked. Chinese of all sorts detested these invaders, even as their country teetered on the brink of civil war between nationalists and communists. American forces plunged into this complex political and social environment determined to eject the Japanese, establish or renew their own permanent presence, and preserve order until stable and friendly local governments could assert control. In this very complicated environment the language officers came face to face with Japanese unlike those they had previously encountered. And they were very quickly transformed from mere instruments of surrender into peacekeepers.

Those who went to Japanese-occupied China and Korea differed from their classmates who served on Pacific islands. Most were attached to marine units in the III Amphibious Corps and knew the Japanese from combat experience as recent as Okinawa and Iwo Jima or, in some cases, as far back as Bougainville. A much smaller group of language officers already in "free" China also rushed to Japanese-occupied areas in August 1945. A handful got to Taiwan and Korea simply because they were attached to the staffs of admirals charged with extricating American and Allied prisoners of war or transporting Army occupation forces. A few had particular skills or personal backgrounds that demanded they be plucked from their current units and assigned to surrender duties in Japan's continental empire. Thus the sons of China missionaries such as Chuck Cross and David Anderson; men who had grown up in prewar Shanghai such as Dan S. Williams; particularly talented linguists who knew Chinese or Korean in addition to Japanese such as Donald Keene and William Linton; and a more senior, highly experienced marine interpreter, Capt. Donald Shively, were especially chosen to go to China to facilitate the surrender of Japanese forces there.[50]

At first the larger operation in which they participated looked very much like what had happened in Tokyo Bay and on Pacific islands. By August 26, their superiors had devised an overall operation plan for landing forces, evacuating prisoners, and securing surrenders from Korea in the north to Taiwan (Formosa) to the south to Shanghai on China's central coast. A week earlier the very first American naval operatives had rushed to that city hoping to rescue prisoners of war. On September 1 and 2 American ships showed themselves off Tsingtao, and U.S. Navy aircraft flew over Shanghai. Three days later a task group of two escort carriers and five destroyer escorts stood off Keelung, on Taiwan, ready to begin evacuating prisoners of war. A week later the USS *Minneapolis* (CA 36) threaded its way through the treacherous channel to Inchon, the port for Seoul, Korea's capital. On Sunday September 9, two glittering ceremonies marked the end of the war there. In the gilded throne room of his palace, the Japanese governor-general surrendered the 350,000 soldiers and sailors on the peninsula south of the 38th Parallel to an American admiral and general. And shortly thereafter, Archbishop Francis Spellman (soon-to-be cardinal) celebrated high mass in the city's Catholic cathedral.

Ten days later, American naval vessels were moored to the premier buoys outside the Shanghai bund. A day later the advanced party of what would become the U.S. Marine occupation force in North China landed at the mouth of the Peiho River and traveled to Tientsin, China's third-largest city, where it met with "exemplary" cooperation from Japanese military officials. Talks there and in Peking and Tsingtao guaranteed that the Marines and the Japanese-language officers accompanying them would not meet resistance when they stepped ashore in China. Indeed, barely one week later in Tientsin and two weeks later at Tsingtao the Marines presided over massive, resplendent formal Japanese surrender ceremonies.[51]

The smooth flow of these events belied the turmoil swirling all around them. The naval and marine linguists who went to Korea and Taiwan did not have to worry about what might happen there, for primary responsibility for Japanese capitulation and ensuing liaison there rested with the U.S. Army and the Office of Strategic Services, respectively. Wendell Furnas, who was dispatched to the Korean surrender ceremony in Seoul, received a memorable fitness report: "Lt. Furnas performed his duties satisfactorily. Unfortunately, there were no duties for him." Those who went to Japanese-occupied China, however, confronted great uncertainties in that war-torn and politically troubled land. The Japanese continued to guard the railway that ran from the sea through Tientsin to Peking, but they were surrounded by the Chinese Communist 8th Route Army and hostile Chinese Nationalist forces alike. Roger Hackett, who came with the 1st Marine Division, thought the situation was "just a mess." Lt. Col. Thomas E. Williams, the 6th Marine Division intelligence officer who had commanded language officers on Okinawa, described it as "nebulous and dangerous." Things were "definitely out of hand." He and his men faced the prospect of having to rescue more than a thousand Allied personnel in one camp and keep the peace between "Nips and Chinese Communists" who were fighting over Japanese weapons and equipment the latter wanted so as to be able to "tell Chiang [Kai-shek] to jump in the lake."[52]

The initial presurrender negotiations demanded Americans with Chinese- as well as Japanese-language skills. They revealed far more hostility from the Chinese than from the Japanese at the imminent arrival of Marines from the 1st and 6th divisions. In an ominous hint of what might follow elsewhere, Chou En Lai, future foreign minister of the Peoples Republic of China, told the leader of the American advance party that communists would fight to keep the Marines out of Peking. The communist leader in control of Chefoo, the port in Shantung that commanded the sea approaches to Tientsin and Peking, proved so hostile in preliminary talks that the 6th Division landing site had to be shifted to Tsingtao, which was less strategically located and occupied by ten thousand Japanese troops.[53]

First contacts with the Japanese in China had none of the suspense and latent hostility that language officers found on Pacific islands. Japanese commanders had long since gotten orders from Tokyo to cooperate fully. Their troops remained on bases surrounded by hostile peasants, many of whom sympathized with the communists. The Japanese destroyer captain whom Royal Wald and John Lacey apprehended at Shanghai trying to slip his ship out to sea before any substantial American forces arrived was the exception, rather than the norm. At Tientsin and Tsingtao, the 1st and 6th Marine divisions landed to the cheers of Chinese rather than the sullen silence that had greeted the American landing party at Yokosuka. Within hours of going ashore at Tsingtao, Donald Keene, no longer in marine battle dress but still carrying a revolver, toured the city. Japanese troops saluted him as his rickshaw passed by. Less than forty-eight hours after arriving in Tientsin, Chuck Cross found his eyes welling with tears as his train approached the very same railroad station he had used as a high school student in Peking. For him, the Marines coming to China to remove the Japanese was "a moment of supreme pride and joy." Don Shively had long since helped pave the way for Cross and his fellow Marines' peaceful arrival in China's traditional capital.[54]

Naval and marine language officers sent to the Asian mainland very quickly discovered that they were dealing with a different breed of Japanese than they had known during the war. In North China, the Japanese military remained intact, its officers very much in charge, and its men disciplined, obedient, and efficient. Donald Keene sensed that during his very first trip to Japanese army headquarters in Tsingtao. The corporal of the guard there left him "terrified speechless" when he bawled out "Saa-lute!" He grew angry and felt demeaned when told to wait for an English-speaking interpreter; when that hapless individual arrived, he quickly dismissed the man. Keene eventually spoke with a Japanese major, but he left the headquarters with "the strange feeling" that he had fallen into a place still locked in war even though peace had long since been declared.

Very quickly, Keene's anger and apprehension toward the Japanese gave way to something bordering on friendship. When he went to the Tsingtao Imperial Navy Headquarters the next day to interview two intelligence officers with whom he needed to work, he started "chatting with them as with old friends." One of them started talking with him about war literature, and as Keene started to leave even suggested that they might go have a drink together since the war was over. Before long the naval linguist was praising the captain of the Tsingtao Base Force Headquarters as an "officer and a gentlemen" who could not possibly be "a monster, or at best . . . will-less tool of his superiors" such as many other Japanese officers seemed to be.[55]

The same sort of thing happened to other language officers as they dealt with the Japanese military on a daily basis. In Peking, Chuck Cross discovered fairly quickly how shrewd Japanese military negotiators were in positioning themselves as "friends" of the Americans. In the tri-national staff officers' meetings at which he translated, the Chinese invariably raised objections to whatever the Japanese proposed for implementing the Americans' demands that they withdraw as quickly as possible. The Japanese negotiator would fall into silence and let the Americans and Chinese bicker during the meeting, then promise, as it ended, fresh proposals for the next day. Cross felt himself almost admiring the Japanese negotiator who after the meeting confided to him "Americans and Japanese have a hard time with the Chinese, don't we?"[56]

In Tsingtao, Howard Boorman worked as liaison to the Japanese military office that surveyed, controlled, and tried to keep out of Chinese hands onetime enemy equipment that ranged from guns to condoms. He came to admire and like his Japanese military and civilian coworkers for their efficiency and honesty. Even battle-hardened Hart Spiegel found his attitudes changed by the experience of working with a Japanese graduate of San Jose State University. Together they sought to control the nightly depredations of Chinese paramilitary forces against civilians in Tsingtao.[57]

Indeed, as agents of occupation charged with speeding the departure of their Japanese predecessors, the American language officers in China found themselves drawn much more to their onetime enemy than to their Chinese allies. In part, this was because they could communicate readily with the Japanese. This was also due to senior Japanese officers' professionalism and shrewd diplomacy. Major General Nagano Eiji saw to it that the surrender ceremony at Tsingtao went off without a hitch and cultivated good relations with Gen. Lemuel Shepherd, the Marines' commander. At the working level, the Americans also drew closer to the Japanese because they depended on the former enemy's knowledge and command of local entertainment resources, his generosity in sharing them, and his willingness to overlook their own sometimes boorish behavior. In Tsingtao, Hart Spiegel found himself actually enjoying geisha parties arranged by the Japanese. Leslie Fiedler was amazed by his hosts' handling of one that turned into a drunken brawl. When he offered a morning-after apology, the Japanese officer simply said the occasion at which the Americans had "honored us" by their presence was one "we will never forget."[58]

Their involvement in investigations of alleged war crimes might have poisoned the language officers' relations with the Japanese in North China, but for several reasons it did not. None were assigned to criminal investigation or interrogation as their primary duty. Their superiors were not so concerned with alleged Japanese war crimes because the victims (and eventual judges) were British and Chinese rather than American. And when the linguists were occasionally drawn into war crime–related work, what they found was often murky and sometimes inconclusive. Indeed, their involvement in war criminal investigations was important more for its impact on them than for bringing the guilty to justice. It planted the seeds of a more nuanced view of the Japanese armed forces and of the psychology of the Japanese people.

For some, war crimes investigation reversed the moral equation in China, shattering the simplistic notion that the Japanese were inhuman monsters and the Chinese their hapless victims. Glenn Nelson regretted having flown off to a distant city to collect an accused Japanese only to find out later that he was the wrong man. Leslie Fiedler felt "like a Gestapo man" when, in response to a Chinese request, he questioned a Japanese former factory owner who allegedly buried a fortune in his backyard and castrated a coolie. They found no treasure, but the Japanese was handed over to Chinese officers. When Fiedler subsequently went to question the man in prison, Chinese officials gave him the runaround and claimed the Japanese was not there. That left the American fearful that he had sent the man to his death, sympathetic to the plight of other Japanese in China, and anything but trusting of the Chinese.[59]

For others, delving into alleged war crimes complicated their understanding of the Japanese. Donald Keene harbored a residually positive image of them and repeatedly tried to disabuse ordinary Marines of the notion that Japanese were subhuman. But his investigation of allegations that the Korean head of the Tsingtao police had beaten foreigners turned into an eye-opening probe of bayoneting, beheading, and cannibalism by the Japanese. The Korean claimed that Japanese naval officers with whom Keene worked and whom he liked had sanctioned brutal executions in which the victim's liver was cut out of the body and eaten. In questioning the alleged perpetrators, Keene heard even more alarming tales of Japanese sailors being ordered to use living Chinese prisoners for bayonet practice. The more he delved into these allegations, the more troubling they became. He got corroboration of the executions; a maid at the officers' quarters told him she had made soup out of a liver-like substance that allegedly increased sexual potency. Keene arrested the alleged perpetrators. But then a Japanese captain whom the American admired seemingly excused his subordinates' behavior. He said he had heard tales of Chinese eating Japanese children's livers and claimed beheadings were necessary because firing squads were short of ammunition.[60]

Keene left Tsingtao in December 1945 before his Japanese coworkers' involvement in cannibalism was confirmed and before others accused in this matter were brought to trial. But his involvement in this case undoubtedly contributed to a hardening of his attitude toward the Japanese. Ironically, the future master translator and champion of Japanese literature in America left China with harsher views of the Japanese than most other language officers who served there. He was unconvinced that the mainland foe had truly accepted defeat and certain that a ten-year occupation of Japan was necessary.[61]

Had Keene stayed longer and helped repatriate Japanese, his attitude might have been very different. During the first nine months of their China duty, Marines presided over the return of more than 540,000 Japanese, both military and civilians, to their homeland. In that capacity they became protectors and escorts for a sometime enemy who now elicited their respect and understanding. The Japanese troops had laid down their arms but remained under their officers' discipline. They marched aboard LSTs, glad to see the American, rather than the Chinese, Russian, or British ensign flying from the jackstaff. But they, just like civilians, carried nothing more than a handbag of personal effects, a little cash, and five days' supply of food with them. The repatriates were completely dependent upon the Americans, and some managed to get to embarkation ports only after U.S. diplomats brokered a truce between contending nationalist and communist forces. Indeed, the Marines had to intervene to stop "mob violence" against the departing Japanese and "looting of their meager belongings" in port cities.[62]

The Japanese handled most of the processing of repatriates, so only relatively few language officers were directly involved in their departure and transfer to Japan. But those who were came away with surprisingly positive attitudes toward the former enemy. Linguists who themselves longed to go home as soon as possible could empathize with Japanese draftees who were doing just that. Hart Spiegel praised the Japanese for making good use of primitive stoves given to them and damned the Chinese for mishandling theirs. And language officers such as Richard K. Beardsley, who rode LSTs crammed with repatriates, recognized that escort duty was their ticket to seeing Japan on the way home to America.[63]

By late December 1945, when the first language officers who had come to North China with the Marines departed for home, they had undergone a remarkable transformation. Sent to be instruments of surrender and agents of occupation, they had become peacekeepers. They no longer saw the world in the black-and-white terms of the war years. They did not find their Chinese allies uniformly friendly, particularly trustworthy, or generally competent. Chuck Cross departed Peking fearing China would be more chaotic than democratic, and Hart Spiegel left convinced that the country "would never amount to a damn."[64] The Boulder men no longer regarded "the Japanese" as a singular enemy but encountered them collectively as collaborators in peacekeeping and aliens in need of repatriation to their homeland. Individually they were persons both good and bad, high in rank and low in station, with whom one had to work to get things done. Some among them might be unreconstructed militarists, others might be fawning or insincere collaborators, and still others presented themselves as genuine friends who shared the language officers' desire to get on with their lives in a new postwar world. In China, the onetime enemy became for the Boulder men a necessary partner in establishing peace in that world.

That perception of the enemy had developed amidst the chaos of defeat in scattered fragments of Japan's dying empire. From their experiences on remote Pacific islands and in war-torn North China, the Boulder men learned that there was no such thing as "the Japanese." Just as their counterparts had in the last bitter fighting on Okinawa, so now in the first days of peace they realized that there were a great variety of Japanese. The more sophisticated among them also sensed that contradictions lurked in their own feelings toward the sometime enemy. They knew that enemy better than ever before and recognized both good and bad in what they saw in him. But they also realized that only time and unknown future events would determine whether yesterday's foe became tomorrow's friend. The most important of those developments came about in the Japanese homeland, where Boulder-trained officer linguists became instruments of peace.

Chapter Seven

INSTRUMENTS OF PEACE

On Sunday evening 2 September 1945, Al Weissberg poured out his feelings about the day's historic events to his wife. Japan had formally surrendered, bringing to an end "the titanic battle of whole oceans and continents." That was one victory—but not the final one. The "victory of peace" was yet to be won. But how? The young language officer thought it would come only if Americans showed "the same resolution and perseverance that has brought us thus far."[1]

He was right—up to a point. Defeating an enemy and accepting his surrender is one thing. Occupying his homeland to ensure peace and friendship between former enemies in the future is quite another. Washington policymakers understood that truth and did all they could to make the occupation of Japan a success. They planned it well before Japan's defeat. They landed with overwhelming force, disarmed the Japanese, and kept a large force in the country for nearly seven years. They left intact a Japanese government possessed of sufficient power and authority, from the emperor in Tokyo down to local police, to preserve civil order. And they imbued the overwhelming majority of occupiers with the notion that they were agents for positive change who must act in ways that would prevent violence, minimize misunderstanding, and avoid planting seeds of future hatred.[2]

All of these things were necessary if Japan was to be changed from threatening foe to cooperative collaborator in a new and more peaceful postwar world. But no one—occupation planners, language officers, or the Japanese themselves—imagined how the quickly the most essential change of all came about. Attitudes shifted. Americans and Japanese stopped seeing one another as alien enemy "others" and recognized one another as individuals who shared a common humanity. That change was fundamental to all of the others—occupation-era reforms and postwar transpacific friendship alike—that followed.[3] The language officers stood at the forefront of those who helped bring that change about.

No one foresaw how rapidly that change would occur, and all were shocked at the ways in which it manifested itself. None was more striking than dancing. Dance halls staffed with pretty young girls to entertain GIs sprung up on Tokyo's Ginza. Geisha performed for the victors at parties large and small across the land. And most extraordinarily, victors and vanquished enjoyed dancing with one another. The language officers—Spencer Kimball in Sasebo, Dan Karasik in Kobe, Jim Durbin and Will Elsbree in Yokosuka, and Paul Boller and Phil Bridgham in Tokyo, to name but a few—all danced with the enemy.[4]

They did so figuratively as well as literally. They were the agents of occupation best equipped to promote a change in attitudes between Americans and Japanese. They knew the language. They had been exposed to Japanese culture and societal norms. They had encountered a wide variety of Japanese in combat, in captivity, and as refugees in a part of their homeland. Their wartime experiences had given them an empathy for the defeated that enhanced their curiosity about Japan and the Japanese that was born at Boulder. Beyond that, they carried with them the sense of responsibility not just for the immediate success of the occupation but also for the peace in the Pacific in the long term. As Jim Durbin told his parents, "The way we act . . . in the next few months will probably decide to a great extent the future of Japanese–American relations."[5] In short, the language officers came to Japan ready to experience themselves and to foster in others a change in attitudes that would transform yesterday's enemy into today's friend. They were poised to become actors of significance in the larger drama of transformation that was about to unfold.

During the first year of peace, these men—and a few Boulder-trained women—played a variety of roles in that drama. They reconnoitered key ports, paving the way for the rescue of American and Allied prisoners of war and the arrival of army occupation troops. They helped the Marines disarm and demilitarize the defeated in western Japan and softened the impact of their presence there. They became intelligence gatherers, traveling the length of the country and interviewing its former leaders to better understand and root out "militarism." Those who clustered around Tokyo Bay helped lay foundations for a permanent American naval presence at Yokosuka and restore ties to political and cultural elites in the capital. Only a few functioned as reformers, but all interacted with the Japanese in ways that began the shift of attitudes from enmity to friendship. What the language officers did in Japan thus demands closer attention.

HARBINGERS

Naval and marine forces landed quickly and easily at Yokosuka on 30 August 1945. That was the first of many such landings designed to pave the way for American and Allied forces' occupation of Japan. But before the victors could rescue prisoners of war there or put marine and army troops in significant numbers ashore, the Navy had to clear approaches to and secure necessary ports. Pioneering language officers played a key role in that endeavor as it repeated itself all over Japan. They helped turn what could have been hostile first encounters into halting steps toward Japanese acceptance of an alien enemy presence.

On 3 September 1945, barely twenty-four hours after the *Missouri* surrender ceremony, the USS *Adams* (DM 27), carrying Lt. Sam King, approached the entrance to Kagoshima Bay at the southern tip of Kyūshū. Ordered to the bridge, he passed his "reality test" with flying colors, bellowing orders to a waiting Imperial Japanese Navy minelayer, chatting with a pilot and Japanese interpreter, and translating the charts they brought aboard. Soon thereafter American minesweepers were clearing the channel so ships that would carry rescued prisoners of war away could proceed.[6]

Barely two weeks later, the USS *Appalachian* (AGC-1) appeared at the entrance to Ominato, near the northern tip of Honshū. Lt. (jg) Harold Wren disembarked, went ashore, and briskly told the admiral in charge of the Imperial Japanese Navy base there that "our orders . . . [must be] carried out efficiently and effectively." That allowed American ships to enter the harbor safely. Shortly thereafter, Lt. (jg) Arthur Kruckeberg was flown from the *Appalachian* to Sapporo, where he and his men entrained for Hakodate and Otaru, key ports on Hokkaido's southern shore. After wrapping up negotiations with local officials, they were treated to a "celebratory . . . and even . . . riotous evening" at a famous hot springs resort. Rather than talking tough to the defeated enemy, Kruckeberg found himself trying to prevent a potentially harmful incident. He restrained "naval 'bucks,'" who mistook pristine geisha for prostitutes.[7]

Lt. (jg) Dan Karasik had perhaps the most varied and rewarding experiences of all the naval language officers who served as harbingers of occupation during the first postwar weeks. He got there thanks to his Boulder roommate, Sam King, whose father commanded the squadron sent to clear central Honshū ports of mines. On 11 September, Karasik went ashore from the USCGS *Taney* at Shimizu, a tiny hamlet near Wakayama, the town that guarded the seaward approaches to Osaka, Kobe, and the Inland Sea. His mission was to get charts and piloting information so that American ships could safely enter local harbors and extricate prisoners of war. Karasik was thrilled to be "the absolute FIRST American to set foot there since the war began" but did not know quite what to expect. Neither did the local people who were "a little afraid at first" to approach or speak to him. He asked them to get the mayor, who sent Karasik and six men from the *Taney* on to a second, larger hamlet. A "crowd of kids" there took them "in quite a procession" to the town hall where Karasik conferred with a mayor dressed "in his very best suit." He apologized for not being more ready for the Americans whom the townspeople had not expected to see "quite so soon." After failing to persuade the linguist that he really ought to deal with the provincial governor, the mayor sent him to police headquarters. There the chief, "a nice little guy in a navy blue uniform [with] brass buttons, ceremonial sword, high black boots, and terrific gold braid shoulder boards" invited Karasik to his private quarters, where tea, beer, and peaches were served. The two men chatted pleasantly while the chief's minions readied a boat to take the Americans to a third hamlet.

Dejima clung, "like a little jeweled clasp," to mountains that plunged down to the sea. Karasik and his companions climbed its narrow streets until they came to an inn where maids met them, handed them slippers to replace their shoes, and ushered them into a suite of rooms. There Karasik met Americans who had come down from Yokohama to help arrange for the release of prisoners of war. He instantly mobilized two former captives and got a White Russian to telephone a demand for charts and documents to the prefectural governor's office and commandeer a huge Packard the Japanese had provided to the Australian for a drive around the town.

Karasik returned to the *Taney* that evening feeling that he had "really had the time of my life today." He would never forget his "fantastic" encounter with the police chief, which seemed "like a comic opera." "By God," he confided to his parents, "I was the man of the hour and riding on top of the world." Being the first American in those hamlets "was worth all those long hours at Boulder." He was very glad to have gotten to see ordinary Japanese people, living "as it really was during the war." But the linguist knew that what he had encountered was about to change dramatically. "When we land the army here a little later," he mused, "it will be very different."

Over the next three days, Karasik worked very hard to make arrangements for American ships to come to Wakayama and take aboard prisoners of war. He met his first Imperial Japanese Navy officials, more police, and even Adm. Raymond Spruance, who praised him for the work he was doing. He felt his job was almost "too interesting" and exclaimed that it "more than fulfills my wildest expectations." After a typhoon drove Americans in their ships out to sea for two days, Karasik returned to Wakayama as assistant port director. His most memorable task was arranging for the burial of five Americans who had perished in the storm. He persuaded a principal to inter them in his schoolyard, and the schoolmaster promised to plant flowers around the site. Karasik then handed over the personal effects of a Japanese woman who had been killed in the storm. His Japanese hosts took him to Wakayama where he saw a ruined hospital where fifteen hundred patients had died as a result of American bombs.

Two weeks after he had come ashore, Karasik looked on scornfully as seven thousand men of the U.S. Sixth Army stormed ashore at Wakayama in full battle gear, while sailors in their dress white uniforms were "watching and laughing at the whole show." He sensed that the troops' arrival marked the end of the fairy tale–like beginning of the occupation of Japan that he and other naval men had experienced. Once the Army took over, the easy informality they had enjoyed in dealing with the Japanese would vanish, and "non-fraternization" orders would keep most Americans from all but carefully controlled encounters with Japanese people. His own duties over the next week contributed to that result. Karasik worked with local police to put tea houses and brothels "off limits" to American personnel and helped commandeer the inn at Dejima and a rich man's garden as clubs for naval officers and enlisted men, respectively.[8]

What Dan Karasik and other Boulder pioneers did in their first encounters with Japanese in remote places was important for two reasons. First, they helped prevent misunderstandings that might have gotten the occupation off to a very unpleasant start. To be sure, the Japanese people followed their emperor's rescript to accept the occupiers' presence and suppress their anger and humiliation at having to do so. Tokyo also sent local police instructions on how to deal with the Americans that erased wartime images of them as barbarian "others."[9] But linguistically competent, culturally sensitive go-betweens such as Karasik were needed to buy American patience while Japanese hosts scrambled to meet the invaders' needs. Without the language officers, differences over procedures or small details might have exploded into real conflict.

Second, Karasik and other pioneers in small places provided the template for Japanese–American cooperation in larger and more significant urban locales. That became evident early in October when Henry May, now an interpreter for the naval force that covered the 25th Division's occupation of Nagoya, came ashore near Wakayama. He and the sailors had a "heartwarming experience" in its port where, by that time, Dan Karasik was managing the officers' club. The sailors met bowing and smiling Japanese townspeople, and exclaimed "Why these are *nice* people!" and "This is a *good* island," not at all like those that Americans had assaulted earlier. Boulder pioneers like Karasik helped make it possible for ordinary Americans and Japanese to interact in this way—barely a month after they had stopped killing one another.

Late in October 1945, as transports neared Nagoya, May was on the bridge of the command ship translating orders to and from the pilot. When the ship came into the harbor and the troops landed, two pioneer naval language officers were on hand to greet them. Sam King had interpreted for the minesweepers that had cleared the channel, and Dan Karasik had worked with the Japanese Navy Liaison Office to ensure the Americans' safe arrival in Nagoya. Together, May, King, and Karasik witnessed the end of the beginning of the occupation of central Japan.[10]

GENTLE OCCUPIERS

Eleven days after Dan Karasik first set foot in Japan, the USS *Shelby* (APA-105) glided past the five islands and wooded hills that guarded the approaches to Sasebo, the best deep-water port in western Japan, and dropped anchor. The ship came as part of an armada carrying some 53,000 Marines destined to occupy Kyūshū and western Honshū. The nearly 40 JICPOA linguists aboard the *Shelby*, much like the language officers attached to the 2nd and 5th Marine divisions, had mixed feelings about what lay ahead. They were thrilled at the prospect of finally seeing Japan but apprehensive about occupying an island that had been home for kamikaze and suicide boats and that reportedly still bristled with weapons and with soldiers and civilians ready and willing to use them. Yet their fears were tinged with romantic feelings, as if they were tourists rather than armed invaders.[11]

Once they came ashore, those mixed feelings vanished. There was no danger, for most Sasebo residents had fled to the surrounding hills in fear of the invaders. There were no surprises because a marine advance survey party carefully coordinated the landings with local police and naval officials. There was no romance, no beauty, but only stench and devastation in the abandoned city. Because night soil collectors had left, human excreta flowed down the sides of muddy streets. The city center was a mass of rubble, save for a huge concrete Catholic church that had withstood American bombing. Two wrecked aircraft carriers and large submarines littered its harbor. To Maj. Sherwood F. "Pappy" Moran, who had lived in the prewar Japan whose passing Dan Karasik mourned, Sasebo ranked first on the list of places he never wanted to revisit. The city was "about as desolate and unlovely as can be imagined," he wrote home. Lt. (jg) William Weil put it more bluntly: Sasebo was "the asshole of Japan."[12]

He and his fellow linguists spent a miserable first night ashore. They bedded down in filthy Japanese navy barracks where there was no water for drinking or showers. They supped on warm C rations but griped about having to squat over stinking Japanese-style toilets. Crammed thirty to a room that had been sprayed with DDT to kill fleas and mosquitoes, they battled through the night with "a desperate garrison of tough old three-inch cockroaches" and huge rats that ran above the ceiling. By morning fifty-two of the rodents had been dispatched. A wisecracking linguist quipped that they ought to catch three or four more and saddle them up for transportation around town. Theirs was not a happy introduction to the Land of the Gods.[13]

Unhappy though it was, the language officers' first twenty-four hours in Sasebo provided an appropriate introduction to their stay in western Japan. Those who came as the vanguard of the U.S. Naval Technical Mission (NavTechJapan) were supposed to work with other JICPOA intelligence men to probe Japan's wartime advances in naval and industrial technology. But their real duty was to make the best of a bad situation. They functioned as adjuncts to their brothers attached to the two marine divisions in facilitating the peaceful occupation of a sizeable portion of the enemy's homeland. They helped restore civil order in Sasebo, fanned out into the countryside to buffer combat-ready Marines' interaction with ordinary Japanese, and ferreted out men and weapons that might have resisted the American presence. But in performing these duties, the linguist-occupiers reaped an unexpected reward.

At first helping restore order in Sasebo seemed less demanding than they expected. Port officials were exceptionally cooperative, and officers on the Imperial navy base at the city's center spoke English so fluently that John Robinson felt his Japanese was hopelessly inferior and complained that he had little to do. Edgar Whan felt he spent too much time humoring souvenir-hunting admirals rather than doing meaningful work. And Verner Chaffin griped that NavTechJapan was "about the most overstaffed agency that I've seen yet!"[14]

Bringing the city back to life, however, posed considerable challenges for language officers and ordinary Marines alike. Griffith Way found himself struggling to master vocabulary—and social and political nuances—that he never dreamed of at Boulder. His first assignment was to accompany Marines sent to woo the "honey bucket" women down from the hills to take night soil from city cisterns to farmers in the fields. Then he had to deal with prostitutes from Sasebo's long-established pleasure quarter who had fled with the rest of the population in fear of the invaders. The general commanding the Kyūshū invasion force hated the Japanese soldiers he had fought in the war but regarded civilians as innocent victims of their former military masters. He knew his troops flush with testosterone had been "away from civilization," as he discreetly put it, for a long time and did not want them to cause any "unpleasant incidents" in Sasebo. So the 5th Division commander established a strict curfew at night but gave the go-ahead to reopen brothels. Their women would be regularly checked by naval doctors to prevent the spread of sexually transmitted diseases.[15]

That sent Way into the hills a second time to lure the women back into the pleasure quarter. Then he went on patrol with naval doctors. Despite considerable embarrassment on all sides, he quickly mastered, with the help of a cooperative Japanese nurse, the gynecologist's vocabulary. Ordinary Marines amused themselves by tossing candy to children and shouting comments to pretty young women passing by, and few, if any, rapes occurred. Many years later, long after Sasebo's pleasure quarter was demolished, the Japanese Ministry of Health and Welfare erected a handsome memorial to the women who had served their country by working there.[16]

Way soon found himself involved in far loftier matters. Police and firemen returned to the city to help Marines—and their huge bulldozers—clear away the rubble that American bombs had produced. But city officials were another matter. The mayor had cooperated with (if not having been handpicked by) the base's senior officers before and during the war. Now the admirals were gone, and citizens eager to embrace something new—democracy perhaps?—wanted the mayor ousted. The Americans created an advisory council that proposed holding an election. Before long three mayoral candidates emerged: the toadying president of the chamber of commerce, a milquetoast agronomist, and a nonentity. Way found himself explaining to his superiors why none would be good and fending off complaints from ordinary citizens clamoring for change. His commanding officer decided to postpone the election and leave the wartime mayor in place. Way came away from this episode with a rather sophisticated political vocabulary and greatly enhanced people management skills.[17]

Other language officers, some attached to marine regiments, others from NavTechJapan, traveled with the Marines as they established a presence in key locations throughout Kyūshū and western Honshū. The Americans did so cautiously, sending out small reconnaissance patrols, then road-building units with tanks and other heavy equipment, and finally battalion-sized occupation forces. They gradually took control of key places—airfields; railroad junctions; Fukuoka, Kyūshū's largest city, and Miyazaki on its east and Kagoshima on its south coast; Moji and Shimonoseki, guardians of the entrance to the Inland Sea and western Honshū's two largest cities. Then they set about "demilitarizing" the countryside and preparing for the day when army units would replace them.[18]

The language officers who accompanied the Marines on occupation patrols found plenty of challenging "demilitarization" work. Sometimes it was quite technical, such as assisting in the identification and destruction of coast fortifications and military and naval aircraft. That took Ed Seidensticker to remote and beautiful sites like the Goto archipelago, where Marines scooped up samurai swords by the armful, and to the island of Tsushima, where he and Ed Neville ended days of blowing up munitions with liberal doses of potato whiskey provided by their Japanese coworkers. Sometimes it was just sleuthing. Owen Zurhellen and Rich White stumbled upon a group of senior Japanese officers, all armed, in an inn; they called for police and reinforcements to disarm and arrest them. In the process, they confiscated a copy of Japanese plans for defending Kyūshū against American invaders.[19]

Other language officers plunged into a different sort of "demilitarization." Those who stayed in Sasebo helped process Japanese repatriates. They worked at nearby Hario, a few miles from the city center, where bedraggled soldiers and civilians from the Asian mainland and tough "comfort women" from Okinawa were identified, sprayed with DDT, given food, and put on trains to return to their hometowns. They had to deal with unrepentant Japanese army officers from China and Korea who claimed they had not been beaten because they never got a chance to fight the Americans. One arrogant major general so infuriated Spencer Kimball that he confided to his wife, "I think today was the first time in my life I really wanted to kill someone." Other language officers assisted repatriates of a different sort. Tom Ainsworth helped keep peace between communist and nationalist Chinese being returned to their homeland, and Ed Neville tried to pacify hordes of wartime Korean forced laborers who had to wait at Shimonoseki until the port was cleared of mines and ships bound for Korea arrived.[20]

The language officers also worked to soften the American presence and render it more humane. Sometimes they proved imperfect comforters, stunned themselves by the consequences of war. Roger Marshall and Allison "Jerry" Downs accompanied two naval doctors to a Nagasaki hospital full of atomic bomb victims. Downs still felt nuclear weapons had saved him from possible death in an invasion of Japan. But the sight of a badly burned child so seared itself into his memory that it took him fifty years to complete a poem that captured his mixed emotions on that day. When Sherwood F. Moran was pawing through the rubble of a burned house in Nagasaki, the owner came up to him, explained how his wife had died ten days after the bombing, and then took him to a hillside cave where his daughter and other children had been taken for safekeeping and had perished in the atomic attack. What could he say? Back in Sasebo, Japanese women came out of their houses brandishing photo albums. They insisted that Marines look through them, hoping against hope that they would be able to identify a still-missing son, brother, or spouse. Language officers could only mumble a few inadequate words in reply.[21]

In other instances, they functioned as police social workers. Ed Neville's first task in Miyazaki was to see that brothels had been marked "off limits," as his straitlaced regimental commander had ordered. Later he spent a lot of time dealing with the consequences of those who ignored that command. At one establishment kimono-clad women flitted out of his way like butterflies, and the offending men were pried sheepishly naked out of the closets in which they had hidden. At another, a Marine accidentally shot and killed the madam. Neville had to offer apologies and explanations as the Americans were hauled off for mild punishment and quick return to the United States.[22]

In virtually all of their official duties, Boulder linguists functioned as buffers between the occupiers and the occupied. But their most memorable experiences came off duty. Unlike most Marines, who had to resort to candy as "pogie bait" to attract Japanese children or their older sisters, or sailors who used gestures to buy souvenirs from starving merchants in the restricted zone where they were allowed liberty, the linguists could talk with Japanese of all sorts. They ignored curfews and marine and police "non-fraternization" rules, and they used the "wonderful passport" of language to get "every door" opened to them. Many made forays into country towns to see where the *kakiemon* pottery depicted in their Boulder textbook was made. John Robinson recalled playful give-and-take with boys and girls who tried on his gold-braid–trimmed cap and exchanged greetings in accented English and Japanese. Edgar Whan felt strange going to Mass in a tatami-floored church full of Japanese Catholics. But he left the service filled with a sense of awe over sometime enemies' worshipping together so soon after hostilities ceased.[23]

The most outgoing and lucky language officers got invitations into Japanese homes. On Sundays four of them piled into a jeep and drove out into the country, where they were "something of a sensation." At first the Japanese pointed and stared at them in an annoying way; then they tentatively engaged in conversation. Before long the locals were proffering gifts to the Boulder men—Arita porcelain, dolls for their children, and figurines for their parents. If they stayed for a meal, the menu, much like that of the Japanese that Robert Falk encountered on Yap, was heavy with sweet potatoes. Back in town, invitations came from local people who worked for the occupation force. Bob Hachenberg and Spencer Kimball particularly enjoyed an electrician's party. His beautifully clad daughter and sister-in-law performed traditional dances, his wife provided delicious "exotic" food, and the Americans taught them ballroom dancing. "We sang, they sang," and everyone felt happy. John Robinson left another such dinner feeling he had "come closer to the heart of the Japanese people than ever before."[24]

Encounters of this sort were of inestimable importance in guaranteeing that the Marines' occupation of western Japan was peaceful. They helped break down stereotypes and apprehensions built up during the war and in the very first days of peace. Japanese who had been taught to believe that a man had to kill another before he could wear the marine uniform met considerate young Americans. Yankees who destroyed suicide boats and torched would-be kamikaze aircraft came away amazed at the "kindly, generous" Japanese, mortal enemies barely two months earlier but now "perhaps . . . not so different from people in Iowa." The very same language officers who had complained about the stench and rubble of Sasebo upon their arrival left with entirely different feelings about the place and its people. No one captured their change of attitude and emotions better than Ed Seidensticker. Sasebo citizens represented "the first stirrings of the [Japanese] phoenix." Their comportment was "beautiful," as they "collected themselves from the shock of . . . defeat and [got] . . . to work." He was so impressed and enamored by what he saw in Sasebo that he decided to put Japan at the center of his postwar professional life, whenever it might begin.[25]

The language officers' superiors, however, harbored no such thoughts of a permanent Japan presence or connection. Sasebo became the U.S. Navy's second-most important Japanese port, but that was a result of the Korean War. Senior Marines planned to keep their troops in western Japan for as short a time as possible. The first marine occupiers left in late October 1945, and by June 1946 all had gone, their places filled by army and army air corpsmen. And barely a month after their arrival, senior NavTechJapan officers decided that Sasebo was too far from the seat of occupation power in Tokyo to be of real use. They determined to take all but a handful of their subordinates to the Japanese capital. Thus on 29 October 1945, most of language officers who had come to Sasebo on the *Shelby* embarked on the USS *Blackford* (APB-45), bound for Tokyo.[26]

INVESTIGATORS

They had quite a ride, for the *Blackford* was a converted LST that wallowed in the rough waves off Japan's eastern coast. But it came to a spectacular and happy ending. On 2 November they saw Mt. Fuji, "Japan's most famous scenic jewel," twice—"serene" in the morning, then "rising in solitary majesty against the faint red of the fading twilight, sky." The following day, the Sasebo language officers' ship tied up alongside Tokyo's Shibaura Ferry pier next to the USS *Ancon* (AGC-4). When they went aboard the amphibious command ship, "pure plush through and through, [with] a mass of chrome and streamlining and modernistic design" they felt as if they were stepping into a different world. The *Ancon* provided a home to linguists attached to the Pacific branch of the U.S. Strategic Bombing Survey [USSBS]. The two ships' proximity portended what was about to happen: fragmented American naval intelligence resources in occupied Japan were finally coming together.[27]

The very first naval intelligence agents, apart from the Yokosuka landing force, were communications intelligence experts rushed out from Washington to discover what their Japanese counterparts had been up to during the war. Boulder graduate Larry Myers had gone to Owada, the Imperial Japanese Navy's principal communications and code-breaking center, where he saw the pit in which the enemy had burned codebooks and other sensitive documents. But he managed to scoop up radio direction-finding and other equipment before U.S. Army men came to disarm the facility. The USSBS (Pacific) had sent a "spearhead group" to Tokyo in mid-September 1945 that included some of the most orally talented Boulder-trained men from Admiral Nimitz's advanced headquarters on Guam. And NavTechJapan had hurried Ted de Bary and Sherwood Moran to Tokyo to help lay foundations for its presence there.[28]

Although USSBS and NavTechJapan remained separate and quite different organizations, their language officers melded together from November 1945 onward. USSBS was definitely the more richly endowed of the two bodies. Its headquarters occupied a central Tokyo insurance company building, and its most senior officers lived at the Frank Lloyd Wright–designed Imperial Hotel. They had four destroyers plus vehicles ranging from jeeps to private planes to get USSBS men where they needed to go. The organization had fifteen divisions that focused on everything from military and naval analysis to civilian morale and medicine. These in turn were broken down into sections. Cdr. William P. Woodard, a longtime congregational missionary in prewar Japan and the father of a Boulder graduate, presided over the language section, which eventually grew to a pool of two hundred linguists—navy language officers, a few of their army counterparts, a substantial number of army nisei, and a few civilian Japanese speakers. By the time the NavTechJapan men arrived from Sasebo, USSBS was dispatching investigative teams of two to thirty men all over Japan. Every day FRUPAC veteran Lt. Frank L. Turner selected linguist fish from that pool to do whatever was needed.[29]

NavTechJapan, by comparison, was much more modestly endowed, even though its numbers swelled with time. A senior captain from JICPOA commanded it from the *Blackford*, where most of its language officers continued to live. It had barely half as many divisions as USSBS and suffered from constantly fluctuating personnel levels. Its linguists and the most junior USSBS officers had to be bused five miles to work in central Tokyo. Some of them got assignments such as interrogating senior civilian and naval leaders or interpreting for a special atomic bomb survey group that would have been impossible in Sasebo. Most contributed to the production of a mountain of translated Japanese documents and voluminous reports, and a few eventually did the same at ATIS, which had followed General MacArthur to Tokyo. NavTechJapan seized 3,500 documents and wrote 185 reports that totaled 10,000 pages. USSBS produced even more reports and eventually took dozens of language officers back to Washington, D.C., to help complete them.[30]

This finished intelligence was important for a time, but the process of producing it proved more significant over the long term. The language officers participated in investigations that brought them into contact with a much broader array of Japanese than their colleagues on Pacific islands or the Asian mainland encountered. Some assisted in interrogations of senior Japanese political, naval, and military officials conducted in the tiny rooms of USSBS and NavTechJapan's downtown Tokyo office. Orville Lefko found a vice admiral hiding in the countryside in farmer's clothes and brought him in for questioning. Robert Newell interviewed Genda Minoru, a master planner of, and lead pilot in, the Pearl Harbor attack. Griff Way spent two months visiting factories and aircraft facilities all over central and western Japan to probe their accounting techniques. Nick Vardac traveled for forty days with a "special Technicolor Team" that filmed the lives of ordinary Japanese. Spencer Kimball, son of one of the twelve apostles of The [Mormon] Church of Jesus Christ of Latter-day Saints, queried officials of the revived Japan Communist Party about their political program and attitudes toward the American occupation. Felix Gilbert and Robert M. Hendrickson helped naval doctors complete two wildly differing inquiries. One found that the Imperial Japanese Navy had never gone beyond testing a crude bomb to wage germ warfare. The other—buttressed by photographs of houses, inside and out; women; and smiling sailors departing the premises—showed that lower-class geisha houses were in fact brothels whose women threatened the health of the Navy.[31]

Participating in such investigations gave Boulder men an eye into the wartime sufferings of ordinary Japanese people that all but erased lingering wartime antagonism toward them. Larry Vincent's experience reveals how that change in feelings came about. Rather than returning home, the marine Iwo Jima veteran volunteered for duty in occupied Japan. He was assigned to interpret for a distinguished American social scientist who had designed a survey mission that would take a USSBS team on a month-long circuit through the west central region of the country. Before setting out late in November 1945 on what was meant to be a "scientific" inquiry into Japanese morale during and after the war, Vincent did some practice interviewing. Vincent had been coached on how to question people in a manner that would allay their natural hesitancy and establish his authorty as a representative of the Supreme Commander, Gen. Douglas MacArthur. But he came away from his first USSBS interview stunned by what an ordinary Tokyo housewife told him. When he asked her how she felt on the day the war ended, she simply replied "I'm not concerned with any of that. I have five children who need food. Please help me."[32]

A few days later he rode alongside his boss in a jeep heading into Hiroshima. Their GI driver confidently proclaimed "Hiroshima don't look no different from any other bombed town. . . . They been exaggerating about this place." As the Americans got closer to the city, they came upon more and more damaged houses and shops lining the road, like "a disorderly herd of animals with backs broken struggling to rise." Then suddenly, as if emerging from a forest onto a plain, all the buildings vanished, leaving only "crumbles of stone, bricks, read earth and rust." Black ribbons of road cut through the rubble, and people wearing clothing "as old and tattered as one would expect . . . the denizens of a dump" to wear trudged along them, some dragging heavily laden carts as if they were farm animals. The day's journey ended when they stepped through huge solid metal doors, "bent inward like cardboard" into a former bank building at the city center that had become police headquarters. The hands of its clock still pointed to 8:15—the moment when the first atomic bomb had struck.[33]

That was a grim introduction to what proved an emotionally grueling time in and around Hiroshima for Larry Vincent. His job was to find nearly a hundred civilian A-bomb survivors and persuade them to answer survey questions his boss had prepared. Once when he and his driver stopped to check their map, a group of boys came up and started chatting among themselves about what service Vincent belonged to. They were amazed when he explained in Japanese that he was a Marine. But he was "startled and disturbed" when he saw that the entire back of one boy's head was "a mass of red scar tissue." That was only the first of many emotional shocks he experienced. Later, he found a woman hanging clothes outside her home in a farm village about fifteen miles outside of Hiroshima. In the course of their conversation, she took off her cap to show him where how much of her hair had fallen out and exposed her shoulders where radiation burns had blackened her skin. The spirited Iwo Jima veteran and would-be thespian felt that "no one could adequately cope with the pain and suffering we saw." He and his boss left Hiroshima with an indelible image of its people, "smiling and waiting for the harvest of the wind that had been sown."[34]

Vincent's next stop, in a mountain village untouched by bombs but now dusted by snow, was more pleasant but bittersweet nonetheless. The townspeople were cooperative. After learning that he was interested in the arts, they invited him to the home of a talented koto player for a private concert. She and her family had taken refuge in this remote place far from American bombs falling on Tokyo. Then, after a banquet provided by the mayor, he and his party were invited to a superb Kabuki performance—with a twist. Normally men played all of the roles in this highly expressive traditional drama. Here, because war had taken all but a few away, women played every part with skill, grace, and great beauty. That night, Vincent plunged literally into the local lifestyle. He took his took his first Japanese-style bath in the inn where the mission was quartered. Emerging from a huge iron cauldron filled with water brought to near-scalding levels by a fire below, he returned to his room to sleep naked on a futon piled high with quilts to keep him warm.[35]

The rest of Vincent's journey proved uneventful. The information he obtained proved significant only for a time; but the human contacts he made remained etched in his memory for years to come. One of them helped restore friendly relations between America and Japan in a very personal way. A woman he had interviewed in Hiroshima asked him to deliver a letter to her sister, who was living in Los Angeles when the war broke out. Vincent somehow got it to the sister, who had been interned in Arizona and then moved to Salt Lake City. Deeply grateful, she wrote him describing how tears had welled up in her eyes when she read the first words received from her sister in Japan since the war began. They proved that she had survived its apocalyptic ending. Relief replaced anxiety for both women, and Vincent had the satisfaction of knowing that he had become a kind of courier for peace.[36]

Other USSBS and NavTechJapan officers contributed to a shift in Japanese attitudes toward the American conquerors in a similar way. They brought news of life to families who thought their prisoner-of-war sons, brothers, and husbands had long since perished. Not surprisingly, Otis Cary, who had sparked the JICPOA interrogation section, was among the most ardent in doing so. He carried letters from twenty-five prisoners he had interviewed at Pearl Harbor but paused after delivering the first three when he witnessed the mix of elation and shame that families who had already celebrated funerals for the supposedly deceased warriors experienced. Eventually he established a network of prisoner-of-war (POW) returnees to help them and their families adjust to postwar life. Paul Boller made similar visits to families of prisoners he had interrogated in the stockade on Guam but produced a different reaction. Whole neighborhoods came to greet those once bereaved and congratulate them on the news of their relative's survival.[37]

FOUNDATION LAYERS

The moments of mutual understanding that Vincent and other itinerant USSBS and NavTechJapan investigators experienced were memorable but transitory. Their fellow linguists who worked and lived in the Kantō (greater Tokyo) area had the opportunity to leave a more long-lasting impression upon vanquished and victor alike. They played only a small part in the official effort to reform Japan but a much larger one in creating a permanent American naval presence there. And their off-duty informal contacts with Japan's political and cultural elites helped vanquish trans-Pacific enmity.

Most of the linguists who worked in Tokyo were small cogs far down in the machinery of the burgeoning occupation bureaucracy known as SCAP, the acronym for General MacArthur's formal title of Supreme Commander, Allied Powers. Many of the men were thrown, for greater or lesser periods, into the civil censorship work. They monitored Japanese telephone and telegraphic communications and supervised Japanese who scanned articles for newspapers and magazines to purge them of anything deemed critical of the occupation. Many more worked in ATIS, alongside their army counterparts, enlisted nisei, and increasing numbers of local Japanese. The sixteen Boulder WAVES who eventually came to Tokyo during the first occupation year had had to leave the Navy to get army civil service positions in SCAP. They and the ATIS linguists translated mountains of documents with little or no apparent value. Their exasperation grew daily, tempered only by occasional reunions with fellow Boulder graduates and former sensei. It stoked a burning desire to see Japan but leave the country as soon as possible to rejoin family and friends back home. As Ardath Burks put it, "I'd even translate Japanese calendars if they told me to" as long as there was a prospect of going home soon.[38]

A lucky few landed more responsible and interesting positions. George Nace interpreted for Rear Adm. Richard E. Byrd who was sent by CNO Admiral King to cut through General MacArthur's lofty rhetoric and bring back the unvarnished truth about what was going on in Japan. Phil Bridgham served as interpreter for SCAP's chief engineer, Major Gen. "Pat" Casey, and scouted out a Japanese aristocrat's home as a possible residence for him. Fewer still worked directly on occupation-directed structural reforms. Walt Nichols, the bishop's son, helped Commander Woodard in an effort to democratize Shinto by depriving its shrines and priests of government financial support.[39]

Arthur Dornheim and John Ashmead worked under Lt. Cdr. Robert King Hall on one of the most radical proposed reforms: abolishing the use of Chinese characters and requiring Japanese to write with the same alphabet that Americans used. That change was premised on the notion that freeing the next generation of the burden of years of memorization to read and write would make them more individualistic and open to democratic ideas. But the linguistic revolutionaries achieved only limited success. In the end conservative Japanese educators' resistance and their own sobering recollection of how deeply ingrained kanji were in Japan's history and culture doomed the romanization project. Eventually the reformers settled for simplifying the way characters were written and limiting the number in common usage.[40]

The language officers who worked in Yokosuka left a more enduring mark on the Japanese landscape than their counterparts in Tokyo. They helped transform what began as a temporary incursion into a permanent American naval and cultural presence there. Several circumstances enlarged their possibilities for meaningful action. The city of Yokosuka, unlike Sasebo and Tokyo, had not suffered major damage from American bombs. Although many fled or locked themselves in their homes when the conquerors landed there, burning hostility toward Americans did not persist. Many residents who had labored on the Imperial Japanese Navy base and catered to its sailors' needs in town came back to work soon after the invaders landed. The Yankees' presence in increasing numbers, as the armada at the formal surrender ceremony paused for liberty and a taste of Japan before sailing for home, created a demand for support services on the base and souvenirs in town. Yokosuka was also far enough from Tokyo and was under navy, rather than army, governance. That gave local commanders greater freedom of action as well as more need for enlightened support and cross-cultural counsel from subordinates such as the language officers.[41]

The language officers lived in circumstances that raised their morale and enhanced their desire to promote greater understanding between Americans and Japanese. The most fortunate among them took over "House #9," a large Japanese-style residence on the base that came complete with garden and two servants to cook and clean. They did not experience the privations that their brethren in Sasebo did. Nor did they turn the place into a messy bachelors' den like the Bastille of their Boulder days. They kept a pet dog—and welcomed a self-styled British liaison officer and Boulder alumnus, Lt. W. G. "Bill" Beasley, into their midst. House #9 became a home away from home for other Boulder veterans at Thanksgiving and Christmas. And they celebrated New Year's with one of their houseboys who was both servant and friend. He went so far as to invite them to his humble home for traditional Japanese festivities.[42]

The Yokosuka language officers had good reason to feel that they lived and worked in "really an ideal spot." The city was close enough to Tokyo for them to take a train to the capital and enjoy its sights and attractions, but it was far enough away from the ruined metropolis and occupation bureaucracy to be free of "the accompanying rat race" there. Closer still lay Kamakura, a city of shrines and temples that centuries earlier had been the seat of a powerful shogunal government. Now it was a pleasant community of cultured and well-to-do residents, virtually unscathed by war. Yokosuka also became a kind of Grand Central Station through which old friends and fellow Boulder graduates passed on their way to or from America. Visiting with them enhanced the Yokosuka language officers' sense of camaraderie.[43]

The language officers performed two essential functions that helped bring about a permanent American naval presence in Yokosuka and softened Americans' and Japanese hostile attitudes toward one another. Lt. (jg) Harold J. "Jim"

Durbin's experience there demonstrates how they did so. On the one hand, he buffered the negative effects of the American presence in much the same way that his counterparts did in Sasebo. Working with the Marines for two months, Durbin "had a hell of a lot of fun" going out into the nearby countryside on demilitarization expeditions. They found guns, ammunition, and military supplies stored in caves but avoided confrontations with local people. Back in town, Durbin developed quite "a headache" negotiating ceiling prices for geisha house customers, but that headed off arguments over the women's services to the occupiers. When conflicts did occur, he intervened. Durbin investigated an allegation of rape that turned out to be false and served as defense counsel in a court-martial for a sailor who overstayed his leave and his welcome at a geisha house and for a Marine accused of stealing from a Japanese mechanic. He and his colleagues in the base provost marshal's office were so effective that local people came to see Marines as protectors rather enemy invaders.[44]

Durbin and his fellow officers also tried to mitigate as much as they could the overt hostility that the base commander showed toward the Japanese. Unable to put aside war hatreds, the sometime submarine skipper banned learning Japanese from the locals and posted obnoxious signs reminding everyone of past Japanese misdeeds. He noted "too bad it didn't kill him" on an accident report concerning a Japanese worker and even insisted that "Japanese" always be written with a lowercase *j*. Fortunately, the insensitive commander departed before 1945 ended.[45]

On the other hand, Durbin and his colleagues worked to give American sailors as positive impression of Japan as possible. Although he hated every minute of it, he vetted swords, rifles, and pistols for them to take home as souvenirs. He acted as impresario to bring 20 Japanese boxers and a classical dancer to perform for the troops. That, for him, was "a thrilling experience." He guided 150 officers and men on a day tour to Tokyo and Yokohama. Before long he found himself conducting a class in "survival Japanese" for ordinary sailors and Marines anxious to go out and see Yokosuka, Kamakura, or Tokyo on their own. Knowing even a few words of Japanese made their encounters with cute children, charming women, and shrewd shopkeepers all the more pleasant.[46]

The work that Durbin and other language officers did at Yokosuka in the first months of occupation laid the foundations for a permanent American naval presence there. When in April 1946 the third base commander, (later) Rear Adm. Benton W. "Benny" Decker arrived full of ambition to retain the base and reform the city, he had at his command language officers who were not only linguistically competent but also cross-culturally savvy in practical ways. Durbin and others had gotten to know the sort of people who made American and Japanese coexistence in the city possible—Yokosuka's mayor, the rich master of its biggest fish market, and the labor brokers who controlled the supply (and take-home pay) of base workers. They also attended meetings of those who would eventually challenge it—student protestors and communist labor organizers. At times they felt that "everyone in any position of importance . . . [here] is as crooked as possible," but they learned how to deal with them. Indeed, they cut through preexisting stereotypes and conflated press reports about the success of the occupation to see Japanese of many different sorts as they really were. That more sophisticated understanding of the local situation was essential for the survival of the American naval presence in Yokosuka.[47]

The language officers in the Tokyo area also had unique opportunities to repair relations with the elites who had shaped Japan's relations with America in the past and would do so again in the future. Their education, linguistic ability, and shared interests made it easier for them to relate to that segment of Japanese society. Sometimes those connections came about serendipitously. Sherwood R. "Sherry" Moran met a young man in Tokyo's bookstore district who introduced him to a leading pundit who expounded on the need for a revived Japanese merchant marine and good transpacific relations. Otis Cary's attempt to inform families of the fate of POWs presumed dead led to a connection that in turn brought about three meetings with the emperor's brother, Prince Takamatsu.[48]

Other times linguistic curiosity—what Paul Boller called "my quest for *kaiwa*" or conversation—led to encounters with members of the elite. He saw the first play presented at the Imperial Theater after war, met one of Japan's greatest actors, and eventually was invited to afternoon tea with the foremost translator of Shakespeare into Japanese. More striking still was his encounter with a group of broadcasters at NHK, the government radio station. There he got a taste of Tokyo University graduates' pride in their language, disdain toward country-dwellers, lingering resentment over American bombing, and concern over radicalism in Japan and nascent Cold War conflict between America and the Soviet Union.[49]

On many other occasions, shared cultural interests drew language officers into ongoing relationships with members of Japan's artistic elites. Jim Durbin's hiring of a classical dancer to perform for sailors at Yokosuka led to friendship with her family and introduction to her friends in Kamakura. Shared interest in the visual arts drew other linguists there, where repeated encounters with art dealers prompted purchases and impromptu invitations to dinner as well. Many Boulder graduates loved classical music, and that made them devoted concertgoers in Tokyo whenever the opportunity presented itself. On one occasion they heard fellow Boulder graduate John Wolaver, a talented pianist with a degree in music from the University of Michigan, perform with the Nippon Philharmonic Orchestra. And on Christmas Day 1945 a mixed chorus of American soldiers and Japanese performed Handel's *Messiah* with that orchestra.[50]

On still other occasions the accidents of wartime service and prewar experiences in Japan brought about connections and eventual friendship with members of the Japanese elite. Phil Bridgham had gotten to know Faubion Bowers during the conflict, one of General MacArthur's aides who had studied in Japan before the war. That netted him many an invitation to parties at the American Embassy in Tokyo. One was a birthday party for the daughter of a former ambassador to Germany who had befriended fellow Boulder graduate Paul Elicker during his 1940 visit to Tokyo. She had lost everything during the American firebombing of the city but managed to enjoy the evening with the conquerors. They also met Bowers' prewar Japanese teacher who, despite the fact that his ship had been sunk by American torpedoes and his home destroyed by firebombing, chatted amiably with the conquerors. Bridgham and Elicker left the party feeling that they had witnessed a "memorable . . . demonstration that intelligence and charm and understanding can overreach barriers of race [and] war hysteria."

That occasion was but the first of many that brought language officers into contact and eventual friendship with members of the Japanese elite. The relationship that the family of a shipping magnate manqué developed first with Phil Bridgham and then with John Robinson was perhaps the most extraordinary of these encounters. Despite fears that their mansion might be taken for senior American officers' use, they repeatedly invited language officers into their home. Bridgham enjoyed a lavish Christmas party with them and stayed overnight, awaking in the middle of the night "giddy . . . [with] the sensation of thinking in Japanese" after so much conversation. He returned for a New Year's celebration and was so impressed by one of the daughters who was "Christian educated" and entirely lacking "the bad characteristics of Japanese" that he asked his fiancée to write to her. That would be "a nice gesture [that] . . . might result in a lasting friendship." Bridgham's stays with the family continued through a wedding in late January and a Girls' Day festival in March. His friendship with the family survived even the forced appropriation of their home as a residence for senior occupation officers.[51]

REPORTERS

The intensity of their experiences as actors in the drama of occupying Japan made the language officers want to tell others about it. Many, if not most, of them wrote to fellow linguists outside the country and to family and friends back home about what they were seeing and doing. A few felt compelled to go beyond such private communications and explain to the public more generally how Japan was changing and what its transformation might portend for the future of Japanese–American relations. In their writing to and for others, the language officers helped launch "a remarkable reversal" of Americans' image of Japan from "hated racial enemy to [potentially] valuable ally."[52]

Their private letters reveal changes in their own attitudes and their struggle to come to grips with what would be called "the new Japan." Their language training and wartime experiences kept them from seeing the Japanese simply as "hated racial enemy," but most shared feelings of apprehension mixed with shock and distaste during their first days in Japan. Those who had lived in Japan before, such as the Morans, father and son, were appalled by what they saw in the ruins of Sasebo and Tokyo. Four days after his arrival in the capital, Sherry Moran wrote that he felt "like a tramp who has become used to sleeping in a graveyard." Months later when George Nace returned to the scenes of his childhood in northern Japan near Sendai, he came away with the same sort of feeling that newcomer Dan Karasik experienced as his first days near Wakanoura came to a close: prewar Japan had vanished in the fires of war. But what would arise from its ashes?[53]

The language officers wrestled with that question in their various interactions with Japanese previously described. Their sense of apprehension gave way when the initial fear and coldness with which they were greeted melted into cooperation, courtesy, and what seemed like friendship. Japanese behavior toward American occupiers posed troublesome questions: Was what they saw genuine change? Were the Japanese now something different from what Americans had been led to believe they were before and during the war? Who, indeed, were the Japanese? More difficult still was a second, related question: How should they, the language officers, respond to the individual Japanese they encountered?

All of the linguists in Japan wrestled with those questions to some degree in their letters home, but none did so more eloquently and with clearer result than Jim Durbin. His head told him that "all the fault for the agony and suffering that this war has brought [rested] directly on the shoulders of the Japanese people." They had, after all, supported and fought the war, and he was not ready to forget that. But his heart prompted him to behave toward his hosts as they did to him. "I have wined with 'em [the Japanese], dined with 'em, and shaken 'em by the hand . . . [even though] they have murdered prisoners by the thousands in cold blood . . . and caused us four long years of death and suffering." That left him wondering if he should "despise myself for returning their politeness with politeness, their kindness with kindness." Should he feel guilty because civility toward the Japanese he encountered amounted to "betraying the men who died on Iwo Jima and Bataan?" Durbin's answer to that question put him at loggerheads with his own parents: He saw no point in "hating, holding grudges, and fostering dreams of revenge." Indeed, it made no sense to speak of "the Japanese." Some he disliked; others he found to be "good and honorable people." The only thing to do was to "treat them [the Japanese] as individuals."[54]

That was, after all, what the language officers had learned to do in combat and what they did as instruments of surrender and as occupiers. Individualizing the onetime enemy destroyed the alien "other" of the war years and made it possible for the linguists to experience and share with others a wide range of feelings about Japanese people. Those emotions ranged from sympathy for the "staggering poverty and misery" of ordinary citizens in bombed-out Tokyo and Yokohama to a mix of fascination and disdain toward the elite individuals who had plunged Japan into war and seemed incapable of comprehending the meaning of defeat. Those feelings left the language officers simultaneously impressed and appalled by what they saw in occupied Japan and anxious to share their impressions of the country and its people with people back home. Verner Chaffin was so moved by his encounters and experiences in occupied

Japan that, in addition to daily letters to his wife, he wrote a richly detailed sixty-two-page missive to her about the country and its people.[55]

Their letters varied enormously in their particulars but expressed a common thought: there was reason for cautious optimism about change in Japan and hope for good relations with its people in the future. Phil Bridgham and Jim Durbin said as much when they described encounters with people who had lost homes, wealth, and status but seemed ready to cooperate with their conquerors. Otis Cary experienced it when he saw subtle shifts in attitudes toward men still held as prisoners of war. William Weil moved from abhorrence at the results of traditional Japanese male dominance to encouragement for Tokyo nurses who went on strike to protest food shortages and low wages. And Sherry Moran was encouraged by a conversation between two American soldiers he overheard as they left a joint Japanese-American singing of the "Hallelujah!" chorus of Handel's *Messiah* on Christmas Day 1945. One man expressed amazement at how quickly things had changed: "Those black Japanese heads! A year ago I was heaving mortar shells into formations like that!" The other drolly replied, "Yeah." As Verner Chaffin put it, "The East is now meeting the West and both sides are having their eyes opened to many things they hadn't known before. The result cannot help but be . . . one that bodes good for the future." Attitudes and behaviors were beginning to change, and that warranted hope for a peaceful future.[56]

Some of the Boulder-trained linguists felt compelled to play a more active part in that transformation by telling the public about their experiences in occupied Japan and sharing their thoughts on American policies there. They wrote for the elite and for the ordinary American, sending their words to publications ranging from *The Atlantic Monthly* and the *New Yorker*, aimed at the former, and *The Leatherneck*, meant for the latter. The tone and approach of their articles varied greatly. John Ashmead wrote about language reform in words that showed he had imbibed, and retained, some of the simplistic wartime notions about Japanese psychology. Yet he enthused over the people he met and prospects for positive change that language reform might bring. Dan Karasik filled a piece intended for the *New Yorker* with warmth and wry humor about his experiences in managing the inn-turned-officers' club at Wakanoura. It betrayed his genuine affection for the Japanese he encountered there. Hilary Conroy, who went on to become a distinguished historian of Japan, produced the draft of what might well have been a college text on contemporary Japanese politics and society. Henry May painted a cautiously optimistic portrait of defeated Japan struggling to find its way toward a better future and different relationship with America. Jack Craig and Larry Vincent tried, unfortunately without success, to convince *The Leatherneck*'s editors to publish an article about their encounters with a prisoner of war taken on Iwo Jima. It closed by predicting, "We shall be able to show the people of Japan that mutual understanding, still more sacrifice, and ceaseless effort can bring about a peaceful world." And Martin Bronfenbrenner wiled away his boredom in civil censorship work by penning wry portraits of interactions between Japanese and Americans high and low that revealed the foibles and follies of both. There were no foes in his stories, only human beings struggling fitfully toward what might be a better future.[57]

Not all of the language officers' screeds got into print. Those that did were simply drops in a wave of American writing about Japan in the first postwar year. But they were important for two reasons. First, they carried an authority missing in what so many others wrote. The language officers, after all, had come to know the language of the enemy, engage him in various ways during the war, and see the Japanese people firsthand in their defeated homeland. These authors knew the enemy and witnessed how he was changing in peace. Second, they demonstrated how war had changed the language officers themselves. No longer individuals caught up in events beyond their control, they had become individuals determined to help shape the future. Their attitudes had changed, and they came away from their experience as cross-cultural communicators convinced that they could help reshape ordinary Americans' image of the Japanese, thus promoting future peace.

The language officers in Japan turned out to be point men for peace. They played their assigned roles in the drama of occupation well. They helped get the occupation off to a good start and buffered its negative effects. They traveled throughout the country and occupied its capital region, laying the foundations for the establishment of a permanent American naval presence and the restoration of good relations with its elites and ordinary citizens alike. Dancing with the enemy made them realize that he was no more. And in telling Americans at home, privately and publicly, about their experiences, they began the process of convincing their countrymen that Japan, yesterday's enemy, might even become tomorrow's friend.

The linguists' wartime journey toward knowing the enemy was over. But their part in the dramatic transformation of postwar relations between America and Japan had only begun.

Chapter Eight

BRIDGE BUILDERS

Monday, 2 September 1946. A year after the surrender ceremonies aboard the USS *Missouri*, the war that had given birth to navy and marine language officers and sent them to fight and occupy Japan was truly over. In his report to mark the day, the Supreme Commander in Japan, Gen. Douglas MacArthur, looked ahead toward the Cold War struggle between communism and democracy, not back on past triumphs in war or occupation. The Navy proudly announced that the job of repatriating millions of Japanese combatants and civilians from all over Asia and the Pacific would be done in little more than ninety days. The very few language officers still in the fragments of the former Japanese empire looked forward to going home. And all but a handful of Boulder-trained men had completed their tours of duty in occupied Japan. Ironically, the single largest group of navy language trainees still in Japan—sixteen former WAVES turned translators within the occupation bureaucracy—came from the smallest group of students at the Boulder school. As one of its more literarily inclined graduates put it, the "big grey picnic"—the grand adventure of going off to learn a strange tongue, fight a war, and dismantle the enemy's empire—was over.[1]

A year after Japan surrendered, what had been a single, shared, and very public story for Navy Japanese Language School graduates was already splintering into individual, personal, and private stories that veered off in a thousand different directions. But despite that fragmentation, a common thread ran through those life accounts. Although they scattered all across and far beyond the United States, those who had served as navy and marine language officers became builders of a postwar bridge of friendship and understanding to Japan. Some were so busy with professional and family matters that they were scarcely cognizant of their role as bridge builders. Others made the betterment of relations between Japan and America the central focus of their lives and careers. Together, these men and women helped complete the shift from enmity and misunderstanding to peace and friendship that has defined the American–Japanese relationship to this day. How did the onetime Boulder students come to play such a role? What led them to help repair and strengthen existing ties, and create entirely new links, between America and Japan?

POSTWAR LIVES

A year after Japan surrendered, the Boulder school and its Stillwater satellite had closed, and those who had created, staffed, and studied there had scattered. Arthur McCollum, captain of the heavy cruiser USS *Helena* (CA-75), patrolled the seas off North China in support of U.S. Marines still deployed there. In Washington, Ellis Zacharias was finishing what became a best-selling account of his prewar and wartime exploits. Both men would achieve, upon retirement, their longed-for stars as rear admirals. Capt. Albert Hindmarsh, his wartime work recognized by receipt of the Legion of Merit and acceptance into the "regular" Navy, shuttled between Annapolis and Washington, D.C., organizing a postwar language training program that eventually morphed into the Defense Language Institute at Monterey, California.[2]

Florence Walne, who had returned to Berkeley two years earlier, had married and risen to the rank of associate professor. Death would claim her only a few weeks later. Susumu Nakamura, the head teacher at Boulder, had gone back to his old job at the University of California. Many of his devoted subordinates returned to the West Coast to try to pick up the pieces of their war-shattered lives. Takeo Okamoto was struggling in San Francisco to start what became a long and successful real estate career. Rayer Toki, having shepherded the last Navy Japanese class at Stillwater to its end, brought his bride and their infant daughter back to the Bay Area where he started a ceramics shop. Only a couple of Boulder sensei stayed on to open small businesses in Colorado. Another, Nobutaka Ike, was working on his doctorate at Johns Hopkins University in Baltimore, the first step toward a long and distinguished career as a Stanford professor of political science.[3]

A year after Japan surrendered, most Boulder students had put the Navy or Marine Corps behind them and were trying to shape their personal and professional identities. A minority who were somewhat older returned to careers that they had launched before the war. Lionel Casson, George Romani, and Ross Ingersoll went back to language teaching in various universities while Guy Riccio and Ken Lappin became professors of Romance languages at the U.S. Naval Academy. Verner Chaffin returned to civil service in the Department of Justice. Carl N. Jones went back to a government job that positioned him for later State Department and NASA careers. Most of the Boulder men returned to school, thanks to the GI Bill. The younger among them rushed to complete undergraduate degrees left half-finished when they went off to Boulder and war. Chuck Cross went back to Carlton College in Minnesota, despite his earlier insistence that he could never return there, and earned a degree in international relations. Dan Karasik returned to Yale and graduated as a Japanese studies major. Those who had finished college used government money to earn graduate and professional degrees. Arthur Kruckeberg fled a tyrannical father to study botany at Berkeley; and George Nace and Bill Amos earned doctorates in biology and zoology. Those who had left law school for war—Hart Spiegel, Frank Mallory, and Ted Chester—went back to New Haven and Palo Alto to finish coursework that enabled them to pass bar exams and go on to distinguished legal careers.

Boulder WAVES, by contrast, were less single-minded in their pursuit of the future. Some used their language skills to to live and work in Japan, which navy policies and public attitudes had previously denied them. Others took advantage of the GI Bill to complete interrupted undergraduate careers or test possibilities for earning graduate degrees. Most set out on what society then defined as the most appropriate path for a young woman—careers as wives and mothers. By September 1946, Pat O'Sullivan and Betty Billett had married fellow Boulder students Griffith Way and Sol Levine, respectively, and many other Boulder women were well on the way toward finding their life partners. In short, a year after the war most former language officers had discerned what they wanted to do in the future and were hard at work laying foundations for their postwar professional and personal lives.[4]

TOUCHED BY JAPAN

The vast majority of Boulder students went on to a future in which Japan was peripheral but never entirely absent. Especially in the first postwar decades, they provided the ground on which a bridge to friendship and understanding might be built. At a time when every American old enough to remember had neither forgiven nor forgotten Pearl Harbor, and when many still grieved for sons, spouses, or brothers killed in the war, these men and women—in various ways large and small—called their neighbors' attention to the positive aspects of Japanese life and character. They created and maintained human links that helped bridge the enormous physical and psychological distance between Japan and America. Some did so by bringing wives and children from Japan into their communities. Reed Irvine, who returned to Japan as a civilian occupation employee after leaving the Navy, fell in love with a beautiful young atomic bomb survivor from Nagasaki. Despite American official discouragement of "fraternization" in Japan and antimiscegenation laws in many states, he married her and brought her back to Washington, D.C. Ernest Wiles was another pioneer in cross-cultural marriage, choosing first a Hawaiian-Japanese bride, then after her death, marrying a Japanese woman who created a newsletter for other Japanese women living in or near the nation's capital. One very courageous married Boulder veteran who had fathered a son on Okinawa brought the lad to America, raised him alongside his six other children, and gave him the love and support needed to become a successful entrepreneur.[5]

Other Boulder men and women became activists in programs that brought Japanese to America and sent Americans to Japan. Dan S. Williams and his wife "adopted" two Japanese war orphans by providing monies for their care and education; later they visited one of them in Japan. Ex-marine Jack Craig and his WAVE wife, Ruth Halverson, reconnected with a Boulder sensei who became a New York City banker. She introduced them to visiting Japanese businessmen whom they welcomed to their home. Sam King helped establish the Japan-Hawaii Lawyers Association, and his wife, Boulder WAVE Anne Grilk, taught English to newly arrived Japanese in Honolulu. Dean Towner helped set up a student exchange program between his Austin, Texas, school and an Osaka school where he later taught for a year. John Ashmead put his Japanese to good use as a Fulbright professor of American literature and then told *Atlantic Monthly* readers about his adventures with Osaka students. Frank A. Bauman welcomed a young Japanese lawyer into his Portland, Oregon, firm. Elmer Stone and his wife "parented" fifteen Japanese exchange students in their Southern California home while Jim and Betty Brayshay hosted Japanese who came to San Diego on the State Department's Distinguished Visitors

Program. Houghton Freeman created a foundation that sent American leaders-to-be on study tours of Japan (and other Asian nations) so they might better understand ways of thinking, living, and doing business on the other side of the Pacific.[6]

Some Boulder veterans pioneered in creating and sustaining sister-city relationships between American and Japanese cities. Ex-marine Jack Pierce was perhaps the most diligent among them. A former hotelier and college instructor, he partnered with his best Japanese friend, a failed kamikaze pilot, to create one of the first and most enduring sister-city relationships. On four separate occasions over thirty-five years, he took mayors of Bellingham, Washington, to Tateyama City in Chiba Prefecture. He promoted "innumerable exchanges on every conceivable level" between these two small cities. Elmer Stone encouraged similar personal contacts between the citizens of giant Nagoya and the Los Angeles metropolis. Boulder veterans helped sister-city programs grow to the point that, fifty years after war's end, eighty-four American and Japanese cities were linked.[7]

Still other Boulder men and women strengthened trans-Pacific ties by reconnecting with Japanese they known during the war. Otis Cary pioneered such reunions by bringing former prisoners of war together in Japan in the late 1940s. Decades later Telfer Mook drew national television coverage in Japan and hometown newspaper reportage in Michigan when he returned to the site of the Tinian school for interned Japanese children that he had created. In 1990, ex-marine Japanese-language officers Glen Slaughter, Glenn Nelson, and Jim Jefferson went to Okinawa for a reunion with their guide, Tony Komesu. The story of their wartime exploits and postwar friendship appeared as a series of articles in Naha newspapers and reports in the *Washington Post* and *Baltimore Sun.*[8]

BEGUILED BY JAPAN

In all of these personal and public ways, former language officers whose life paths took them far from Japan laid foundations for building and sustaining postwar trans-Pacific peace and friendship. But a significant minority of former linguists found it impossible to push Japan away from the center of their lives once their wartime service came to an end. Who were they? Why did they choose the careers they did? And how did they become builders of a bridge of friendship and understanding to Japan?

Some had Japan in their blood, so to speak. Born or raised in East Asia, they could not imagine pursuing careers that did not focus on Japan and the Japanese. They followed in their parents' footsteps but resolved to go beyond them in restoring and sustaining trans-Pacific ties. Freed from conflicted wartime feelings and loyalties, they were infused with moral clarity, a sense of urgency, and genuine determination to be builders of a new and stronger bridge between America and Japan.

Without doubt, they succeeded. Jean Mayer, the daughter of a missionary educator, went back to Japan to work in SCAP, the occupation bureaucracy, then returned to Washington where she became a State Department, and later Defense Department, intelligence analyst. James V. Martin Jr., a missionary's son, built a long and distinguished Japan-centered State Department career. Daphne Shaw Stegmeier married a future consul general in Osaka, where her father Glenn had pioneered cross-cultural communication. She translated several books, including the major work on Japanese folk art. Otis Cary returned to Dōshisha University in Kyoto, where his grandparents had devoted their lives to preaching and teaching; he promoted American–Japanese friendship there and at Amherst College in Massachusetts. Walt Nichols, son of the Episcopal bishop of Kyoto, returned to Japan and helped spread understanding of America through the U.S. Information Agency. Charles A. "Sandy" Sims, who had entertained classmates at the American School in Japan before the war, built a musical career there that included broadcasting, singing, acting in Japanese films, and bringing Japanese performers to U. S. Air Force bases.[9]

The handful of young American-born language officers who had decided on Japan-centered careers before Pearl Harbor realized that the war that once seemed a terrible interruption to their studies was in fact an extraordinary gift. They had gained linguistic skills and cross-cultural understanding that they could never have gotten in college or graduate school. They emerged from the war all the more determined to pursue Japan-centered academic careers, and the GI Bill made it financially feasible to do so. Thus by 1946 Ted de Bary, Donald Keene, and John W. Hall were already uniquely positioned by their wartime naval experiences to become the intellectual leaders of Japanese studies in postwar America.[10]

The most interesting, and perhaps most significant among the postwar bridge builders, however, were those whose love affair with Japan began with their Navy or Marine Corps service. They went to war in 1941 knowing nothing about Japan. They learned a lot about it and its people between 1942 and 1945. They came out of the war in 1946 transformed, knowing how little they knew, determined to learn more, and passionate to share what they had discovered about Japan with others. James Morley spoke for these people when he confessed, many years later, that when he went to Boulder "I don't think I could have located accurately where Japan was on a map." He had never met a Japanese person. But when, after the war, he finally got to Japan, he was emotionally "overwhelmed." Seeing the "devastation of Tokyo . . . the night stalls and the rubble on the streets . . . [and] especially . . . Japanese veterans in their white hospital garb with limbs missing and standing there hanging out the hands begging" was unforgettable. That experience convinced him he must "devote my life to trying to have a better relationship between Japan and America."[11]

Translating that conviction into career choices came about in various ways. Some Boulder veterans decided on a Japan-centered professional life simply as a matter of rational calculation. They had invested four years of their lives into learning a difficult language. In surmounting the various challenges that the Navy put before them during the war, they developed the talents needed to listen to or speak with a wide variety of Japanese people. They had discovered that they enjoyed and profited from work for, or in proximity to, the government, which might lead to steady and larger incomes and more interesting careers than they might otherwise have expected to enjoy. The "sunk costs" of language learning and war pointed Frank Tucker and Hammond Rolph to naval intelligence work, just as it nudged Tom Ainsworth and Arthur Dornheim toward careers in the State Department and Robert Ward and Robert Scalapino to leadership in the study of Japanese politics and society.[12]

For others the decision to build careers around Japan came gradually and less directly. Robert Schwantes studied urban development at Boulder and American history at Harvard before drifting into a Japan-centered career that ended with the presidency of the Asia Foundation. Frank Ikle tried his hand at business before deciding to pursue a graduate degree in Asian history at Berkeley that led to a long and productive career at the University of New Mexico. Russell Stevens took his bride to what had been Japanese-occupied Yap for a year before returning to Boulder to finish a law degree. Then he recrossed the Pacific to become first an attorney general of Guam and later a chief justice of American-occupied Okinawa. Edward Seidensticker earned a master's degree at Columbia, studied Japanese at Harvard, and tried his hand as a junior diplomat in occupied Japan before realizing that his destiny was to become a great translator of Japanese literature.[13]

For many more former language officers—possibly even the majority of those who chose Japan-centered careers—the taproot of the decision was emotion. Its roots were in Boulder, where they learned a strange tongue under pressure but also befriended Japanese and Japanese-American teachers who previously had seemed alien. Their emotional involvement with Japan deepened as they empathized with the Japanese they captured, interrogated, and interned during and immediately after combat. When they arrived in Japan as occupiers, they reveled in discovering its people and culture firsthand; they could neither get enough of both nor imagine a future without either. For these young men, Japan became a beguiling mistress whose charms proved irresistible.

That sort of emotional engagement explains why Harry Packard left a wife and three children, first for the Marines and war, then for Japan and its arts for the rest of his life. It prompted John Rich to return to Tokyo as a journalist as soon as he could after taking off his marine uniform. It led Frank Gibney to seek his fortune, and perhaps escape from a troubled marriage as well, as a newsman in Japan. Similar feelings prompted Jim Jefferson to put his duties as assistant naval attaché in Tokyo above family obligations and spend as much time as he could in Japanese inns while on "inspection tours" of naval and military facilities far from the capital. And what, if not emotional engagement, could explain the decision of an ambitious and talented young attorney like Griffith Way to spend half of every year in Japan, away from his family, where he ran races, climbed mountains, and collected Japanese art? The one-time enemy's siren call simply stirred an inner passion that prompted many a Boulder veteran to keep Japan at the center of his life.[14]

This combination of knowledge, calculation, and emotional commitment combined to make former wartime language officers vigorous and skilled postwar trans-Pacific bridge builders. Some became new and better managers of government-to-government relations between America and Japan. Others revitalized traditional nongovernmental links between the two countries. And yet another, third group opened up entirely new channels of cross-cultural communication and understanding between Americans and Japanese. Just how they transformed postwar transpacific relations can be seen by considering the activities of each group in detail.

NEW AND BETTER "JAPAN HANDS"

Former language officers greatly enhanced the United States government's ability to do business with its Japanese counterpart. Collectively, they constituted a new element in Washington's postwar naval, intelligence, and diplomatic and financial agencies, one that was far more linguistically competent and culturally sensitive than its prewar counterparts. Postwar American officials in Japan could communicate directly with their Japanese opposites and, indeed, with the Japanese people at large. The cadre of former language officers in government reached more deeply into Japanese society, collected more useful information, and developed analytical capabilities far greater than their prewar counterparts. There were more of them, and they were better able to do their jobs because of their wartime experiences. Indeed, that shared past that reached back to Boulder and Bougainville, Saipan and Sasebo, helped some of them smooth working relationships in Washington and Tokyo that might otherwise have been much more friction-filled.

Barely a dozen Boulder graduates became career Navy or Marine Corps intelligence officers. But for the first decade after Japan regained full sovereignty in 1952, they monopolized naval attaché jobs in Tokyo doing things that would have been difficult or impossible for their prewar predecessors. Once he finished with the practical details of reestablishing an attaché's office, Lt. Hammond Rolph studied the nascent Japanese postwar maritime industry; cultivated ties with former Imperial Japanese Navy officers, including a prime minister-to-be, Nakasone Yasuhiro; and worked with Rosey Mason, who headed the naval advisory group to the nascent Japanese Maritime Self Defense Force. His successor, marine major Jim Jefferson, traveled extensively, "collecting hot spring resorts like some people do first editions of old books." Thanks to his language skills and friendships with former Japanese intelligence officers, Jefferson became the preferred aide and guide when, later in the 1950s as ranking Japanese Maritime Self Defense Force officers, they visited Marine Corps Headquarters in Washington, D.C. By 1960, Col. Harry Pratt, who had previously served as an assistant attaché alongside Rolph, became the naval attaché. He had the language skills and Japanese societal experience needed to help strengthen security relations in the wake of protests over the revision of the U.S.–Japan Security Treaty that had toppled the Japanese government. Collectively, these men laid foundations for what later blossomed into "maritime friendship" between the U.S. Navy and the Japanese Maritime Self Defense Force.[15]

A second somewhat larger group of Boulder veterans built upon linguistic and cryptological knowledge gained during the war to fashion careers in the postwar Office of Naval Intelligence (ONI) and the newly created National Security Agency (NSA). Their knowledge of Japanese and previous experience at Op-20-GZ or FRUPAC gave them the entrée into intelligence careers that took them to Japan and beyond. Lawrence S. Larry Myers is a case in point. He had rushed to Japan in the very first days of peace to investigate the former enemy's signals intelligence and cryptographic activities. After completing that task, he served with a cruiser/destroyer division charged with preventing illegal Korean immigration into Japan. Returning to Washington in 1947, he solved the cipher used by Japanese spies who reported on U.S. destroyer movements in and out of Sasebo. In 1950 he came back to Japan to work at what eventually became a major signals intelligence facility. In the midst of the Korean War, when his superiors were more interested in Chinese and Russian than Japanese language skills, Myers was shown a standard Chinese telegraph codebook. His knowledge of Japanese enabled him to solve its cipher. That success pointed him toward a career in China-related intelligence. But a decade later, when he became liaison officer to the commander of the Republic of Korea's Defense Security Agency, Myers used Japanese when his host's English faltered.[16]

Myers had more Japan-centered duty than his other peers who decided to stay in naval intelligence after the war. For them, Japanese became a bridge to mastery of other languages and the development of skills that enabled them to move up in the naval intelligence hierarchy. Some, such as Frank Tucker, were linguistic polymaths who went on to learn Chinese and Vietnamese. Others, such as Ernest Beath and A. W. Mike Foley, put their talents to work in cryptography and signals intelligence. A very few became innovative senior administrators. Wendell Furnas, who left the Navy for the newly created Defense Intelligence Agency (DIA) early in the 1960s, ended his career as a captain commanding the Defense Intelligence School. Robert I. Curts soared even higher, becoming a rear admiral, head of ONI's China desk, and later a special assistant to the deputy secretary of defense for intelligence during the Nixon and Ford administrations.[17]

At least twenty Boulder graduates joined the CIA and its predecessor organizations in the late 1940s. Most became linguists and analysts, and some moved into other non-Japanese Asia-related fields where their talents blossomed.

Only three, all former Marines, are known to have become agents in Japan. Two of them, John K. McLean and Glenn Nelson, got their starts during the later occupation years. The former worked in the Government and Civil Information and Education sections of SCAP, General MacArthur's occupation organization. The latter served alongside other Boulder graduates in the office of the general's State Department political advisor. The third, Tad VanBrunt, whom Okinawan internees liked so much, returned to Japan in 1953 after a stint as a movie actor and service with the Marines during the Korean War. He arrived just as the CIA was stepping up its efforts to broaden its contacts and the number of its collaborators in Japan.[18]

These men's linguistic talents and war-gained understanding of the Japanese enabled them to penetrate far more deeply into Japan's political, corporate, media, and intellectual circles than American diplomats and intelligence officers had in prewar days. Nelson, for example, progressed through a variety of assignments. He first worked with station chief Paul Blum, whose contacts with Japanese writers, artists, and intellectuals stretched back to prewar days. Then he moved on to liaison work with the Cabinet Research Council and the national and Tokyo metropolitan police. Eventually, his job became cultivating Japanese political leaders of all sorts. McLean's contacts with Japanese officials deepened to the point that he became the channel through which they warned President Dwight D. Eisenhower that protests against revision and extension of the U.S.–Japan Security Treaty made it unwise for him to visit Tokyo. The president took that advice, much to the chagrin of his ambassador there, canceling what was to have been, in June 1960, the first visit to Japan by a sitting American president. That episode demonstrated the skill and effectiveness of Boulder-trained CIA Japan hands.[19]

What relatively few of them did for intelligence agencies, many more did for the State Department, its ancillary diplomatic organizations, and other government agencies. At least fifty-eight Boulder graduates chose diplomatic careers. Six became ambassadors (alas, none to Japan) and two rose to become assistant secretaries of state. More than twenty had at least one tour of duty in Japan, and over time they became the backbone of the State Department's body of Japan experts. Many others put their linguistic skills gained and honed during the war to work as diplomats in other countries of the Asia/Pacific region. And a few—Ralph W. E. Reid for the Department of the Army and the Economic Cooperation Agency, and Reed Irvine at the Federal Reserve

Board—provided linguistic and cross-cultural communication skills to government agencies that previously had little or none.[20]

What this influx of fresh, young Japanese-speaking officials meant for American–Japanese relations can best be seen by considering their actions during the fifteen years following Japan's recovery of full sovereignty in 1952. In that period Washington wanted to dampen down antagonisms that lingered on after war and occupation; to promote cooperation under the terms of the 1951 peace and security treaties; and to check the spread of communist influence in Japan. Former language officers labored mightily on all three of these tasks in a variety of ways. As a junior diplomat in the occupation years, Richard Finn had drafted a reparations agreement for an American submarine's erroneous sinking of a Japanese ship traveling under a safe passage agreement. A decade later he forged an agreement that allocated Japanese repayment for America Occupation costs to cultural exchange purposes.[21]

As vice-consul in Fukuoka from 1951 to 1953, Tom Ainsworth dealt with more immediately human and personal issues left over from war and occupation. Aided by American court decisions, he assisted Japanese Americans and their Japanese relatives who had somehow been victimized by the war. He helped young Japanese-American men caught in Japan at the outbreak of war and forced to join the Japanese armed forces recover their American citizenship rights. He enabled onetime angry young Japanese-American men who had chosen repatriation to Japan over protracted incarceration in an internment camps to return to the United States. He also helped nisei in the United States bring to America aged or widowed parents who had remained in Japan during the war. Ainsworth and his staff also handled the legal technicalities for something virtually unthinkable before 1941: marriage (in ever-increasing numbers) between American servicemen and Japanese women and residence for these pioneering cross-cultural couples in the United States.[22]

Promoting cooperation between the two countries within the Cold War security system demanded cultivation of Japanese political and business leaders, old and new. Boulder graduates provided the skills and manpower for doing so with ever-increasing sophistication. Before the war, the American diplomatic establishment in Japan consisted of barely one hundred persons, and only one senior embassy official was truly fluent in Japanese. Fifteen years after the war ended, a thousand people, 40 percent of whom were Americans, staffed the American embassy in Tokyo. By the early 1960s, Navy-trained

Japanese-speakers performed key functions there. Two extraordinarily gifted linguists—first David Osborn, then J. Owen Zurhellen Jr.—served as counselor of embassy. JICPOA veteran Tom Ainsworth succeeded ex-marine John Farrior as first secretary. Further down in the hierarchy, marine colonel Harry D. Pratt was naval attaché, and Royal J. Wald, one of the few Boulder graduates sent to China during the war, took on the new job of assistant science attaché.[23]

Japanese-language officer veterans headed or staffed consulates where they reached out to local officials and entrepreneurs in ways simply unimaginable in prewar days. At Naha, James V. Martin Jr. gathered evidence that pointed to increasing Okinawan discontent with a continued large American military presence and American rule. Richard Petree, one of the last graduates of the Navy's wartime Japanese-language program, served as consul in Fukuoka. He traveled widely in southern and western Japan, liaising with American military and local community leaders to promote good understanding between the two. Daphne Shaw Stegmeier returned to the Kansai (Kobe-Osaka-Kyoto) region, accompanying her husband, the consul general, to many community and cultural occasions. Tom Murfin worked as consul general with city officials and traders in Yokohama, the port from which an ever-growing flow of exports was lifting Japan toward full economic recovery from the war and a favorable balance of trade with America.[24]

Navy Japanese Language School veterans also fought in the postwar culture war in Japan. Bryan Battey's activities show how deeply they reached into society in an effort to shape citizens' attitudes toward the United States and its archenemy, the Soviet Union. He came to Japan in 1952 as a foot soldier of American "soft power," armed with useful skills, connections, and experiences. He had worked briefly in naval intelligence in Washington, left the service for a brief and not particularly brilliant stint in advertising, and then joined a predecessor organization to the CIA. There he worked for his former naval supervisor, a graduate of the Berkeley Navy Japanese-language program. Putting his Russian, Chinese, and Georgian—not to mention Japanese—language skills to work, Battey eventually headed a CIA-funded private translation service in Washington.

Once in Tokyo, he engaged in various conventional—as well as highly unconventional—activities designed to stem communist influence and promote a favorable image of America. As cultural attaché, he helped transform occupation-era propaganda and programs into a comprehensive information system. Named head of the American Cultural Center in Tokyo, he made it a popular site for discussion groups, movies, art shows, and concerts. He helped manage visits by celebrities ranging from the poet Robert Frost and classical violinist Isaac Stern to the owner of Harrah's casino in Reno, Nevada, who brought along his collection of thirty classic automobiles. Battey helped translate scraps of Soviet newspapers that Japanese POW returnees from Siberia had been given to use as toilet paper. As book translation officer, he oversaw a program that translated and purchased large quantities of American-authored works to make them best-sellers that ordinary Japanese would want to buy and read. He advised a local CIA man on how best to support Japanese individuals or organizations. That led to funding a feature film about the skill and daring of American pilots that was meant to boost recruiting for Japan's Air Self Defense Force. As research officer, Battey presided over increasingly sophisticated public opinion surveys. Ever adventurous, he personally sampled Japanese opinion at sites ranging from resort hot spring pools to a Tokyo bar where he played the piano while salarymen popped the balloons that clothed dancing girls.

Battey left Tokyo in 1958 to become Japan desk officer in the U.S. Information Agency in Washington, D.C. In that capacity he eventually used his Japanese precisely as many a Boulder man had during the first days after the surrender: translating for pilots guiding ships into a harbor. But this time the vessels were heading into San Francisco's Golden Gate, the first flotilla of Japanese Maritime Self Defense Force vessels to visit the United States since the war.[25]

Bryan Battey's activities might seem naïve or inconsequential in hindsight. But 20 years after the war's end, another Boulder veteran, Robert Schwantes, in a report on American–Japanese cultural interactions commissioned by Ambassador Edwin O. Reischauer, found the growth of American cultural activities in Japan impressive. The embassy was better organized to direct them. The dozen American Cultural Centers bulged with 10,000 to 20,000 English-language books each, and 11 additional binational cultural centers were to be found between Hokkaido in the north and the Amami Islands far to the south. More than half of all foreign books translated into Japanese were by American authors. U.S. government subsidies helped double their numbers in a decade. The CIA-funded Asia Foundation spent between $500,000 and

$600,000 annually on "projects" in Japan that included funding research and travel for friendly Japanese scholars, promoting the use of American college textbooks, and distributing hundreds of thousands of books and magazines.[26]

All of these efforts to shape Japanese opinion could not prevent crises of confidence in the American–Japanese relationship. One exploded in 1954 when American H-bomb tests in the mid-Pacific irradiated Japanese fishermen. A second crisis came six years later, when protesters disrupted and delayed the Diet's ratification of a revised U.S.–Japan Security Treaty. But official "Japan hands," their numbers increased by linguistically talented and cross-culturally sensitive former naval and marine language officers, managed to smooth things over. By 1965, twenty years after the war ended, they helped Ambassador Edwin O. Reischauer succeed in an unprecedented effort to shape Japanese attitudes toward the United States. Together, they engaged the Japanese people in a wide-ranging dialogue on the issues of the day and assessed their thoughts about the United States. Their actions helped strengthen the bridge of peace and friendship between Japan and America.[27]

UNOFFICIAL AMBASSADORS

A vigorous group of nongovernmental former language officers helped American officials keep that bridge in good repair. Some of these unofficial "Japan hands" revitalized traditional trans-Pacific links as missionaries, businessmen, or journalists. Only a few veterans of the Navy Japanese Language School program chose careers in the ministry, but they swelled the ranks of a virtual army of missionaries active in postwar Japan. By the early 1960s some seventy-five Protestant mission boards were maintaining sixteen hundred missionaries in Japan at a cost of about $18 million annually. Roman Catholics added still more men and money to those numbers. Some were returnees. Paul Anspach and John H. Brady Jr. followed in their parents' footsteps, returning to the land of their birth to seek souls for Christ. Brother Aloysius Soden went back to a distinguished career as a Catholic educator in Yokohama. Others were newcomers who retraced traditional paths of missionary service. After completing his ministerial studies at Yale, Bob Bruns and his bride went to Japan and settled down in Ibaraki Prefecture. They spent twenty-one years teaching and preaching there, interrupted only by occasional furloughs during which they told believers back home about Japan. After retiring, Bruns returned to Boulder, where he taught Japanese in local high schools and at the University of Colorado.[28]

Other Boulder Japan missionaries took a more unconventional approach to their work. After working as lobbyist in Sacramento, California, for many years, Omer Ostensoe became business manager for the Lutheran mission in Japan and an ardent sponsor of transpacific student exchanges. Hal Shorrock earned a doctorate of divinity at Yale but plunged into postwar reconstruction work in Japan. Late in the 1940s he and his wife established a summer camp in which Japanese and American students labored side by side to repair the ravages of war. That very successful attempt to move the younger generation beyond enmity set Shorrock on course to a lifelong career in educational bridge-building between America and Japan. By 1960, not long before he became a vice president of the recently established International Christian University outside Tokyo, about nine hundred Japanese were studying in colleges and universities in the United States and twenty-four hundred Americans were learning in Japan. After retiring from his Japanese university post, Shorrock helped continue that transpacific educational flow by coordinating the University of California student exchange program in Japan for many years.[29]

Boulder veterans also helped restore and strengthen the economic links between America and Japan that war had shattered. None of those born or raised in Japan are known to have become industrial managers or import brokers like their fathers in prewar Japan. That may have been due to the parlous state of the Japanese economy during the early 1950s and Tokyo's subsequent resistance to direct foreign investment in the reviving Japanese economy. Consequently, relatively few Boulder veterans lived and worked in Japan as businessmen. Two of the most prominent built second careers there. Col. Harry Pratt became a very successful manager of Royal Crown Cola's operations in Japan, and journalist Frank Gibney returned to Tokyo to spark an extraordinary partnership between Encyclopedia Britannica and Tokyo Broadcasting System, which sold a translation of the popular reference work all over the country. Houghton "Buck" Freeman was probably the most financially successful former language officer residing in Japan. The communist revolution in China forced him to evacuate his family's AIG insurance business to Tokyo in 1949. Over the next twenty years he turned that franchise into one of the firm's most profitable, laying the foundation for his eventually becoming president and chief executive officer of the firm.[30]

Many more Boulder veterans strengthened transpacific economic links as legal facilitators for cooperation between Japanese and American firms.

Griffith Way was perhaps most prominent among them in Japan, where he became a partner in the prestigious and highly profitable Thomas Blakemore firm. His Seattle neighbor, ex-Marine Richard S. White used his linguistic and legal skills to smooth Japanese investment in the fishing, logging, and paper production industries of the Pacific Northwest, as did Frank Bauman in nearby Portland, Oregon. Further to the south, Elmer Stone helped engineer Japan Air Lines' purchases of planes from Santa Monica–based Douglas Aircraft. And on the East Coast, New York City lawyer Paul Sherman mixed legal, linguistic, and musical skills to broker deals for appearances and record sales by American performers in Japan, and vice versa.[31]

Boulder veterans also transformed transpacific journalism after the war. They formed the core of something new: a cadre of linguistically competent and culturally sensitive American journalists writing, broadcasting, and eventually televising from Japan. They differed fundamentally from their prewar counterparts. During the pre–Pearl Harbor decade, no American newsman read Japanese, only two tried to speak it, and all depended on government handouts and English speakers and journals for their information. The postwar Boulder journalist "Japan hands," by contrast, had the linguistic and cross-cultural skills needed to travel all over the country and develop lasting connections with important Japanese in all walks of life. Unlike prewar Japan reporters who suffered under "parsimonious and comparatively ignorant" editors, they rose in their profession to positions that enabled them to improve the quality and increase the volume of what Americans read and saw of Japan. The intersecting stories of four Boulder graduates show how journalists, too, built bridges for postwar peace and understanding between America and Japan.[32]

Wartime service as language officers prompted all of these men to pursue Japan-related careers in journalism. Of the four, only one, John Rich, had set his mind on becoming a newspaperman before Pearl Harbor, and he imagined that years of yeoman service at home would be necessary before he could become a foreign correspondent. Rich was first to take up journalistic duties in postwar Japan, arriving in 1946 not long after taking off his marine uniform. While working for William Randolph Hearst's International News Service, he led a freewheeling life with little interference from his war correspondent supervisor. Rich gained entrée to occupation authorities by wearing an old uniform without insignia. First he sat around in Tokyo's top business club and interviewed former senior officials with help from Japanese journalists. But once he got a jeep, he was on his own. Rich drove out into the country to interview Admiral Suzuki Kantarō, prime minister at the time of Japan's surrender, gave him and his wife a ride, and received homegrown vegetables in return.

Then he started meeting less exalted Japanese, whom he brought to the Press Club for a meals and interviews. After he rented a house at Kuganuma Beach on Sagami Bay, he got to know ordinary Japanese through conversations with fellow train commuters and neighbors. His spoken Japanese was so good that on one occasion he was pressed into service to interpret for General Tōjō Hideki, who was then being tried as a war criminal. Rich's athletic abilities also led to tennis matches with the emperor and other members of the imperial family. And his humanity and understanding of the complexities of Japanese Americans' wartime situation enabled Rich to befriend Iva Toguri—"Tokyo Rose"—when General MacArthur belatedly released her from prison. Rich clearly had access to Japanese, high and low, that prewar American journalists in Japan could only have dreamed of.[33]

Frank Gibney did not get back to Japan until the spring of 1949. By that time he was a *Time-Life* correspondent who had worked in New York, Paris, London, and Berlin. His Japanese came back quickly, and before long he reconnected with old occupation hands and Japanese friends from his naval days. Gibney's outgoing, fun-loving personality made it easy for him to plunge into life to the fullest in Japan. A chance meeting with the president of the Japan Mountain Climbing Association led to an early spring ascent of Mt. Fuji, followed by a stop at Prince Chichibu's villa on the way back to Tokyo. He went to Nagasaki to cover Spanish pilgrims' returning the arm of St. Francis Xavier to the Catholic cathedral there. And late in 1949, when he returned briefly to Okinawa, Gibney turned into a bylined *Time* magazine story an account of rapes, robberies, and murders committed by U.S. troops that a disgruntled local man had surreptitiously given him.[34]

Gibney and Rich had a hard time getting their Europe-oriented editors back in New York City to print their reports. The Russians, not the Japanese, commanded Americans' interest during the early Cold War years. When Rich proposed a story about Emperor Hirohito to his editors, they cabled back tersely: "No thanks on emperor." Gibney had to fight for every word he got into *Time* or *Life*. But once war broke out in Korea in June 1950, the Boulder-trained journalists' situation changed dramatically. They rushed to Japan's former colony, where their language skills proved immediately useful, and before long their reports appeared regularly. Not surprisingly, when Prime Minister Yoshida Shigeru came to San Francisco to sign peace and security treaties in September 1951, media executives turned to Rich and a third Boulder-trained journalist, Curt Prendergast, for in-depth reporting on that historic event. Gibney became a key consultant to *Time* and CBS reporters who covered the peace conference in the first live transcontinental television news broadcast. Thanks to his contacts with people in the prime minister's circle, he did a live interview, in Japanese, with Yoshida that became the basis for a major *Life* magazine article.[35]

By the mid-1950s, Curt Prendergast and Dan Karasik had become models of the new American journalist in Japan. Prendergast had first come to Japan a decade earlier, when he eavesdropped on Japanese cable and telegraph traffic for the Navy. He had gone on to cover the Korean War from Tokyo and was on his third and longest tour of duty as *Time*'s Japan correspondent. After leaving the Navy, Dan Karasik had returned to Yale, where he published an article about Okinawa. He returned to Japan as a midcareer graduate student in economics at Tokyo University, where he and his wife related easily to students and faculty. He used his language skills to explore aspects of Japanese life—the labor movement, the Crown Prince's love life, and communism—that prewar correspondents could never have touched. His writings on these subjects and such important postwar issues as Japan's resurgent trade, reparations, and burgeoning anti-Americanism in Okinawa appeared in Japanese and American publications.[36]

As time passed, these four Boulder veterans moved up into positions of greater responsibility that enabled them to shape even more directly what Americans saw and read about Japan. Frank Gibney told Americans more about Japanese politics and culture as *Newsweek*'s "back of the book" editor, a *Life* staff writer, and the author of a best-selling book about postwar Japan. He went on to head TBS-Britannica in Tokyo, write still more books, and eventually bring the *Pacific Century* documentary series to PBS television viewers. After the 1960 riots against renewal of the U.S.–Japan Security Treaty, Dan Karasik coproduced the first color documentary about Japan to be shown on network television. John Rich, as Tokyo as bureau chief for NBC, negotiated terms for television coverage of the Tokyo 1964 Olympics. Later he became vice president of the Far Eastern division of NBC's parent firm, RCA. Curt

Prendergast moved to New York City, where he became a *Time* editor. By 1970, Gibney and Rich were serving as vice president and president, respectively, of the Foreign Correspondents Club of Japan. They used the occasion of its twenty-fifth anniversary celebration to establish a scholarship program to train succeeding generations of Japan reporters. That guaranteed the continued flow of more informed reporting across the transpacific bridge that the journalists and other former language officers had helped build.[37]

CROSS-CULTURAL INNOVATORS

A third set of Boulder graduates widened and strengthened that bridge in two very different ways. One group turned the private avocation of collecting Japanese objects of art into a public good, presenting Japan to Americans visually as never before. The other professionalized the study of Japan, diffusing knowledge about the country and its people across America.

Tantalized by what they read in the Naganuma texts and saw in the homes of their sensei, Boulder-trained linguists were primed to become art collectors from the minute they set foot on Japanese soil. Virtually every one of the gentlemen—and lady—occupiers who went to Japan immediately after the war brought home artistic souvenirs: woodblock prints, hanging scrolls, kimonos, dolls, and ceramic pieces. The availability, cheapness, and attractiveness of Japanese works of art made them just too good to pass up. Most of what they brought back ended up in their homes, where it called attention to Japan for friends, family, and other visitors who might otherwise never have seen any Japanese artwork.[38]

A few Boulder men and women made significant contributions to the diffusion of Japanese art in the public sphere. Before the war, only Boston and Washington museums possessed Japanese art collections worthy of note. Despite the presence of Japanese Americans, virtually no Japanese art of the first order was to be seen on the West Coast or in Hawaii. Boulder veterans helped change that and foster American interest in Japanese art in various ways. In Japan in the immediate postwar years, Charles F. Gallagher helped protect Japanese art treasures from the ravages of defeat and social and economic turmoil. He served as Cultural Properties Adviser to SCAP from 1945 to 1948. Many years later, Daphne Shaw Stegmaier promoted appreciation for Japanese folk art by translating and publishing the major works on that subject. Boulder veterans made their greatest impact on Americans' awareness of and interest in Japanese art by building priceless collections that found their way into major museum collections from coast to coast.[39]

Some did so almost accidentally simply by accumulating works of art that burgeoned over time into significant collections. Bob Christy started his collection of woodblock prints while in Yokosuka late in 1945. By the time he retired from the Dartmouth physics faculty many years later, he had so many that they could be divided between museums in Hanover and Chicago.[40] Others pursued their passion for Japanese art in a more disciplined manner, maturing into major collectors—and marketers—of Japanese art. Griffith Way was perhaps the most successful and significant of these amateur collectors. He had been fascinated by Japanese calligraphy while a student at Boulder. When he came ashore at Sasebo in September 1945, he went to nearby Arita to see and purchase some of the *kakiemon* pottery he had read about in the Naganuma readers. His interest in Japanese art survived law school, and after he joined the Tokyo firm of Blakemore and Mitsuki in 1954, the chance to cultivate this interest opened up for him. Frequent travel to Japan and extended periods of residence there allowed him to visit galleries and read about Japanese art, first in English, then in Japanese. Back in Seattle, he befriended Glenn Webb, a professor of art history at the University of Washington, who further enriched his interest in and knowledge of Japanese art.

Eventually Way met a leading Kyoto art dealer and began seriously collecting Japanese art. Spurning conventional wisdom that virtually ignored more recent artists, he began buying the works of those who flourished in the in the late nineteenth and early twentieth centuries, "the golden age of modern Japanese painting." Then, with similar insight, he turned to woodblock print artists whose careers spanned the years of depression and war in the middle third of the last century. In time he amassed a collection of Japanese paintings so large and valuable as to merit display in Japan and at two separate exhibitions at the Japanese Pavilion of the Los Angeles County Museum of Art, the only building in America devoted exclusively to Japanese art. And the woodblock prints he donated or loaned to the Seattle Art Museum became a stellar attraction in its exhibitions of Asian art.[41]

Former marine Harry C. Packard played an even larger and more dramatic role in bringing Japanese art to the American public. As a child he had seen Asian art brought home by missionary relatives. When he went to New York City for intelligence training after completing the Boulder language course, the curator of what was then a very small collection of Asian art at the Metropolitan rekindled his curiosity about it. Little more than a year later, as a Marine in Tsingtao, he started buying drawings by the hated Japanese that poor Chinese were using to paper their walls. When he went to Tokyo to work as a civil engineer in 1946, Packard sold these works to get enough money to buy Japanese woodblock prints for next to nothing. Over the next three years he methodically collected and studied them, limiting the number he kept and trading the rest to acquire other still more valuable ones. By 1949, when he sold all to finance a return to graduate school, Packard provided much of the subject matter of the first major postwar books about Japanese woodblock prints.[42]

Packard was too old, too emotionally volatile, and too passionate about Japanese art to slog through a conventional art history doctoral program at Berkeley, so he returned to Japan to study at Waseda University. Although he learned from its scholars, his real education in Japanese art came experientially. The tiny, intense Packard left Tokyo every other month to roam the countryside in search of treasures hidden away in remote temples. Thanks to his Boulder training, his wartime experiences, and a love for the language that spurred him to practice writing kanji daily, he did what no prewar American collector or scholar had done. The former Marine communicated directly with experts and owners, bypassing the firms and individuals who had previously controlled the flow of art objects across the Pacific.

Creating a chart that outlined the history of Japanese art, Packard set out to acquire representative pieces from each major period. He returned to America with objects impoverished priests had been cajoled into selling—and then spent months studying them intensely to see how and where they fit into his grand scheme of Japanese art history. Just as he had with woodblock prints, he sold off some pieces to acquire others of greater value. In this way, even though he never finished his degree at Waseda, Packard became a recognized connoisseur and entrepreneur of the art world in Japan.

In the late 1950s, Packard began selling major works of Japanese art in the United States and Europe. Stashing them in his luggage, he traveled to places previously devoid of Japanese art—Denver and Dallas, Chicago and Cleveland, New Orleans and St. Louis—to sell what he had for the best price he could get. Using the proceeds of these sales, he flew to Europe, India, Indonesia, and Hong Kong, where he bought furniture and art objects he knew wealthy Japanese would snap up at significant profit to him. Peddler and pirate, this undocumented but increasingly shrewd and knowledgeable professional connoisseur used those monies to buy ever more rare and varied pieces of Japanese art. That raised some official and academic eyebrows in Japan but gave the onetime marine linguist ineffable pleasure.[43]

By the late 1960s, Harry Packard recognized that he could not continue his career as scholar-connoisseur-broker much longer. He began trying to find a home for his collection and himself at a major American art museum, preferably one on the West Coast. Nothing worked out until 1975, when New York's Metropolitan Museum of Art spent five years of its acquisitions budget to buy most of Packard's collection. He donated half of its estimated $11 million value, put half of the remaining funds into a charitable trust for the education of future scholars of Asian art, and kept only a quarter million dollars for himself. Packard used the money to build a magnificent retirement home near Kyoto that became a mecca for scholars, dealers, and enthusiasts of Japanese art over the years. Later he sold the rest of his collection to the San Francisco Museum of Art. When Harry Packard died forty years after Pearl Harbor, no one doubted that he had helped ensure an enduring and prominent place for Japanese art in America. Together with Robert Christy and Griffith Way, he helped Americans see Japan through its art as never before.[44]

GODFATHERS OF JAPANESE STUDIES

A second, larger group of former language officers became scholars who opened the eyes of their students, and of Americans more generally, to Japan. These men and women were among the best and the brightest of the naval and marine linguists. Many readily acknowledge that without exposure to Japan and its language, culture, and people during the war years, they would never have chosen the career paths they did. Collectively, they provided "the essential manpower and expertise for closer intellectual ties" between America and Japan during the quarter century after the Pacific War.[45]

Choosing a career in Japanese studies meant giving up higher incomes for long years of poorly paid graduate study. But doing so became possible because these veterans were eligible for the financial support provided by the GI Bill. Because there were so few places in the United States where one could hope to gain a decent understanding of Japan, they clustered around men and institutions who had figured in the Navy's first efforts to create a wartime

Japanese-language program. Studying at Harvard, Berkeley, and Columbia, they kept alive their sense of wartime camaraderie and built a network of professional acquaintances that served them well later in their careers.[46]

These men and women produced a veritable tidal wave of books and articles about Japan. Their range in subject matter, no less than their depth of scholarship, far exceeded that for Japan-related studies published in the United States during the two decades prior to Pearl Harbor. Many, not surprisingly, dealt with such war-related subjects as militarism, nationalism, and diplomacy in Japan. But an even greater number ranged far from such fields. Boulder graduates pioneered entirely new fields of Japan-related academic inquiry. Richard K. Beardsley, John W. Hall, and Robert Ward partnered in a unique sociological and historical study of an Inland Sea village. Ex-Marine Thomas Smith became the expert on premodern Japanese agriculture, and naval veteran Solomon Levine became the leader in the study of Japanese industrial relations. James Morley, Robert Ward, Ardath Burks, and Robert Scalapino became founding fathers of the study of Japanese politics in America. For decades former Marines Donald Shively and Edward Seidensticker and JICPOA veteran Donald Keene vied for preeminence as translators of Japanese literature while former Boulder WAVE Helen Craig McCullough quietly produced superb studies of medieval Japanese literature.[47]

The Boulder-trained academics also fanned out across America to become translators of Japan's literature, teachers of its history, explicators of its society, analysts of its polity, and guides to its arts for generations of students. The scholars who gathered at Cornell in the summer of 1941 to help start the Navy's Japanese-language program came from only seven colleges and universities. In 1950, there were six East Asian area studies programs in the United States and a Center for Japanese Studies at the University of Michigan. By 1970, 25 years after war's end, 17 such programs existed, and an estimated 500 Japan specialists were teaching in 135 colleges and universities scattered from Maine to California, Georgia to Washington. Onetime naval language officers armed with doctorates moved to places where previously there had been little or no knowledge of Japan. Sidney D. Brown at Oklahoma, John G. Oliver at Georgia Tech, Douglas Mendel at Wisconsin-Milwaukee, Frank Ikle at New Mexico, and Larry Olsen at Wesleyan exemplified this diaspora. They and others like them made it possible for students to study Japan in every state and at institutions as different as a small liberal arts school, Cornell College in Iowa, and the New York research university of the same name.[48]

Perhaps even more to the point, these new American Japan scholars strengthened transpacific ties by working hard to make the study of Japan and other Asian civilizations an integral part of the body of general knowledge encapsulated in the notion of "liberal education." Here naval veterans such as John W. Hall at Yale, William Theodore de Bary at Columbia, and Robert E. Ward at Michigan (and later Stanford) played indispensable roles within their own institutions and provided role models for others to follow elsewhere. Their endeavors bore fruit not just at the elite institutions where they taught but also in textbooks used at colleges and universities across the country.[49]

Boulder men and women as professional educators also changed the way in which their students related to Japan. They, unlike their prewar predecessors, had a depth of knowledge about their particular subjects that derived from their better command of the Japanese language. Their wealth of experiences when combined with their enthusiasm for their subjects, made Japan come alive for their students to a degree unimaginable before the war. Larry Thompson at USC, Jish Martin at San Jose State, and Norman Meller at Hawaii drew upon their personal war and early postwar experiences to make the study of Japanese religion, history, or sociology of compelling interest to their students. And they inspired some of the best among their charges to take up the study of Japan where they themselves left off.[50]

One particular group among the naval and marine language officers reached out to Americans far beyond college campuses by translating great works of classical and contemporary Japanese literature. Before the war, self-taught Glenn Shaw had put a handful of such works before English readers. After it, Donald Keene and Edward Seidensticker broadened enormously the range of works of Japanese poetry, drama, and fiction available to American audiences. Keene produced two anthologies of modern Japanese fiction and an edition of the great collection of classical Japanese poetry, the *Manyōshū*. Seidensticker made it possible for ordinary Americans to read both contemporary Japanese novels and the tenth-century masterpiece, *The Tale of Genji*. Both men reached out beyond the academy to offer ordinary readers evocative portraits of Japan and Japanese culture.[51]

These academic veterans of the Navy's wartime Japanese-language program dominated the organizational life of Japanese studies in America for decades. The oldest among them parented what became the preeminent professional organization for any Japan scholar: the Association for Asian Studies.

John W. Hall along with Earl Swisher and Hiram Bingham were among those present at its creation in 1948. For decades ex-Marine Roger Hackett served as its secretary-treasurer. During its first twenty-two years, two of the six Japan specialists who served as its president and nearly 60 percent of its Japan-related governing directors were former naval language officers. This organization sponsored a journal that published their works, held annual meetings that enabled them to share their findings with other scholars, and provided a launching pad for their graduate students seeking professional visibility and jobs. Little wonder, then, that young students in the late 1960s claimed that "the Establishment" dominated the Association for Asian Studies.[52] They might have asserted with greater accuracy that an interlocking group of former naval and marine language officers constituted the real godfathers of Japanese studies in America.

Their war and early postwar experiences bound these men tightly together, but they were not Mafioso godfathers. They became preeminent individual institutional and intellectual leaders who also cooperated to advance knowledge and understanding of Japan and its people. The six volumes of essays on Japan known as the "modernization series" that appeared between 1965 and 1971 attested to the significance of their collaboration. The books originated at an international scholarly conference that met in 1960 at Lake Hakone at the base of Mt. Fuji. The Association of Asian Studies' Conference on Modern Japan, chaired by John W. Hall, funded it. Seven of the dozen American scholars who participated were former naval or marine language officers, and Susumu Nakamura, once the head teacher at Boulder, served as a translator. The subject matter of these volumes ranged from economic development to political change to Japanese society, literature, and the arts. Three of the five American editors of these volumes and more than one out of four of their nearly sixty American essayists were naval or marine language school graduates. The depth and breadth of their contributions made these volumes "must read" items for successive generations of aspiring Japan scholars. All told, the Navy-trained "godfathers" left an impressive intellectual legacy that broadened their fellow Americans' understanding of Japan.[53]

PERMANENT BRIDGE BUILDERS

By 1970, twenty-five years after the war that taught them the Japanese language had ended, these Navy-trained Japan scholars sensed that their achievement was in danger. They glimpsed on the horizon a time when they would retire. And the foundation upon which they had built their careers—a solid knowledge of the Japanese language—showed signs of cracking. In particular, the ability to provide succeeding generations with the kind of intensive language training that they had received during the war was imperiled by insufficient foundation and government funding for what had become the Inter-University Center for Japanese Language Studies in Tokyo. Launched in 1961 by Stanford University with William McCullough and former WAVE Helen Craig McCullough as its first directors, the school had quickly grown into the preeminent language training center for graduate students from a consortium of ten American universities. But even as its graduates joined faculties all across the United States, the costs of the excellent training it provided spiraled to the point that the cooperating universities could not make up its deficits.[54]

Professor Robert E. Ward was among the first to recognize what this meant for the future of Japanese studies in America. Enlisting the support of his Navy-trained old friend and former colleague, he set out to repeat in a new and more formal way the success the John W. Hall had won a decade earlier. Under the aegis of then-ambassador to Japan Edwin O. Reischauer, Hall had helped create a permanent binational group of government officials and academics charged with overseeing and promoting the health of cultural exchange programs. Hall headed what became known as CULCON, the United States–Japan Conference on Cultural and Educational Exchange, which met annually and sponsored various conferences designed to advance Japanese studies in America and American studies in Japan. CULCON activities were funded by Japanese monies repaid to America for its occupation-era relief and rehabilitation endeavors in Japan. But Congress had never passed legislation authorizing the expenditure of the bulk of the funds.[55]

In the spring of 1970, Ward at Michigan, Hall at Yale, and James Morley at Columbia, began a campaign to get Congress to designate those monies, plus part of the more than $300 million Japan had agreed to pay Washington as compensation for American-built facilities on Okinawa when the island reverted to full Japanese control in 1972, to create a Japan-United States Friendship Commission. This body would fund CULCON, broaden student exchanges, and provide funds for the diffusion of knowledge about and understanding of Japan in America and America in Japan. Most importantly from the vantage point of these former naval language officers, the legislation would guarantee a steady flow of funds to improve communication between the two countries by supporting language teaching at the Inter-University Center in Tokyo and elsewhere.[56]

The broad trend of events in the early 1970s made the passage of such legislation seem increasingly urgent. Troublesome developments roiled the seemingly calm waters of U.S.–Japan relations. The two countries failed to shape a common approach to the Middle Eastern oil embargo. The Nixon administration shocked Japan by its secretive and high-handed "opening" to China and its unilateral modification of international monetary exchange mechanisms. Americans cast wary eyes across the Pacific as Japan's gross national product and exports to the United States soared. For a time early in 1973, even the security pact between the two countries came into question as Washington ham-handedly proposed and then withdrew a scheme for drastically reducing its naval presence in Japan. That same year in what struck John Hall as "a staggering blow," the Department of Health, Education and Welfare budget eliminated all spending for foreign language and area studies. Tokyo's creation of a Japan Foundation and a Japanese government gift of $1 million each to institutions it perceived as the "top ten" for Japanese studies in the United States were not enough to make up for that. Indeed, these gifts raised the specter of unhealthy dependence on uncertain foreign largesse.[57]

Despite these developments, it took far more time to turn a good idea into law than Ward and his former language officer collaborators could have imagined. Despite their shared past, senior academic and diplomatic "Japan hands" found it difficult to agree on terms for creating a Japan–United States Friendship Commission. The "giants" of political science in the field of Japanese studies—professors Ward, Hall, Morley, and Scalapino, later joined by Ardath Burks and Sol Levine—wanted the commission to have and control the disbursement of Government and Relief in Occupied Areas (GARIOA) and Okinawa reversion funds. Former ambassador Edwin Reischauer and State Department Japan desk director Richard Finn, who had authored the GARIOA spending-for-cultural-exchange proviso in the Japanese peace settlement, were skeptical about just how much largesse Congress might be willing to provide. They favored seeking only authorization to spend—with greater government supervision—remaining GARIOA funds for Japan-related cultural endeavors. Indeed, the State Department, backed by the White House and the Treasury Department, introduced its own bill to compete with the measure that the academics, with the help of Senator Jacob Javits of New York, had gotten the Senate to pass.[58]

The groups did not resolve their differences until the summer of 1975. By that time, the academics had pushed as hard as they could to get the necessary support for their version of a Japan–United States Friendship Act. Ward and Hall lobbied members of Congress and testified in hearings on their bill. They wrote President Gerald Ford, urging him to support it to take the "gift" of a commitment to friendship and understanding with him on the first presidential visit to Japan. When that did not happen, they renewed efforts to get the support of Rep. Wayne Hays of Ohio, the cosponsor of legislation that had funded the Fulbright exchange program and a powerful shaper of State Department appropriations. After he endorsed the proposal, senior diplomats who were also former naval language officers softened their objections, and a compromise proposal was agreed on. Ward and his associates then pressed Congress to approve it by the time the emperor and empress arrived in America on an unprecedented visit meant to symbolize an end to the enmity of the war. The legislators did not act that quickly, but within weeks of the imperial party's departure, Congress late in October 1975 created and generously funded the Japan–United States Friendship Commission.[59]

That act stood as a monument to the war-trained language officers and a commitment to the transpacific friendship that they had promoted in so many different ways over the preceding thirty years. The law effectively memorialized their achievements and guaranteed their legacy. Future Americans would be able to study the Japanese language as they had. It gave permanency to the government–academic link in the area of linguistic and cultural studies that the creation of the wartime naval language-training program had begun. It provided financial support for expanding into broad-based community organizations the Japan–American societies that they themselves had formed and joined in the postwar years. These revitalized groups would promote friendship by exposing a wide variety of Americans and Japanese to each other's cultures. In short, the legislation guaranteed that the bridge to the rising sun that the language officers had worked so hard and in so many different ways to build would remain strong.

Epilogue: The Power of Knowledge

Six years have passed since that golden evening in June 2002 at Boulder when I saw how time had transformed the naval and marine Japanese-language officers of the Pacific War. Then I grasped as never before their specific historical significance: Forced by war to change the course of their lives, they themselves were transformed by it from fledgling students into effective naval intelligence officers. They were the living embodiment of the change that world war had forced upon academia and government, turning them into partners in pursuit of the national interest rather than distant collaborators. They were the individuals who had helped salvage peace from the ruins of war and laid foundations for a bridge of permanent friendship and understanding between the United States and Japan. Those were great accomplishments that deserve to be remembered by succeeding generations.

What I did not fully realize then was the larger, more general significance of the language officers' story. Subsequent events have made it painfully clear. In June 2002 America teetered on the cusp of a war in Iraq that has lasted longer than the titanic struggle which the World War II language officers fought. Those within the George W. Bush administration who believed war with Iraq was necessary had already set America on course to the tragic conflict that has followed. That road was littered with ignorance, misunderstanding, and misjudgments. It led to swift military victory, but true peace has proven elusive in the disastrously mismanaged occupation that followed. American policymakers and those in our armed forces charged with carrying out their orders lacked knowledge of Iraq's history and culture and of the language of its people. That made it impossible for American forces to function effectively in the country and set it speedily on course toward becoming a democracy. Unfortunately, America has paid a heavy price in blood, treasure, and the good opinion of mankind as a result.

America's failures in war with Iraq make its successes in war with Japan stand out clearly. The America that fought Japan and destroyed its empire simultaneously laid foundations for peace with a democracy. It recognized its linguistic ignorance and created programs like the Boulder Navy Japanese Language School to remedy that deficiency. In the course of the fighting, the Navy and Marine Corps came to realize that linguistic and cultural knowledge could be a force multiplier. Such knowledge was essential if other kinds of power—the technology that made interception of enemy communications possible and the industrial might that produced the ships, planes, and weapons to defeat his forces—were to be used with full effect. The language officers were agents of that power. They themselves came to appreciate how linguistic and cultural understanding could be used to secure peace in the short term and ensure friendship and understanding in the long term.

Their story thus carries meaning beyond the specifics of their experience and the particulars of the war they fought. To win a war—and the peace—one must know the enemy. One must have a firm command of his language, knowledge of his culture, and an appreciation for the norms of his society and polity. Language is power. The cross-cultural understanding that comes with it is essential for true victory. Neither can be improvised, and both must be permanently embedded in America's armed forces if they are to meet the challenges that war presents.

Time inevitably takes its toll on each generation, and the surviving naval and marine language officers of World War II will pass from this world. But their story teaches enduring lessons that Americans of every generation would do well to remember.

Notes

Prologue: Chaff before the Wind

1. Rich, Dornheim, and Gorham interviews; Robert S. Schwantes, "*What Did You Do in the War, Daddy?" A Memoir* (San Mateo, CA: Robert Schwantes, 1998), 10; Hart H. Spiegel, "The War Years and Better Days 1942–1946," unpublished memoir in author's possession, 1; Donald Keene, *On Familiar Terms* (New York: Kodansha International, 1994), 13.
2. Cross and O'Sullivan Way interviews; Albert Weissberg to Megan H. Lillie, 21 January 2001, Albert O. Weissberg papers, Norlin Library, University of Colorado, Boulder. This archival site will hereinafter be cited as UCBL.
3. Suttles and Stone interviews.
4. Gordon W. Prange, *At Dawn We Slept: The Untold Story of Pearl Harbor* (New York: Penguin Books, 1982), 505, 539; Mark R. Peattie, *Sunburst: The Rise of Japanese Naval Air Power 1909–1941* (Annapolis, MD: Naval Institute Press, 2002), 161; "The Pearl Harbor Raid, 7 December 1941: Damaged Ships," Naval Historical Center, Washington, DC, at http://www.history.navy.mil/photos/events/wwii-pac/pearlhbr/ph-dmg.htm (August 2008).
5. O'Sullivan Way, Suttles, Newell, and Stone interviews; Eugene to Betty Gregg, 7 December 1943, G. Eugene Gregg papers, UCBL.
6. Brayshay, Kinsman, Dan S. Williams, and Stegmeier interviews; Charles T. Cross, *Born a Foreigner: A Memoir of the American Presence in Asia* (Boulder, CO: Rowman & Littlefield, 1999), 35.
7. Keene, *On Familiar Terms*, 13; Dornheim interview; Schwantes, "*What Did You Do*,"10.
8. Rich interview.
9. Ronald Spector, *Eagle against the Sun: The American War with Japan* (New York: Vintage Books, 1985), 7; Rich, Spiegel, Stegmeier, Stone, and O'Sullivan Way interviews; Spiegel, "War Years and Better Days," 37–41; Schwantes, "*What Did You Do*," 35.

10. Cross, *Born a Foreigner*, 50–51; Spiegel, "War Years and Better Days," 90–91, 99; Keene, *On Familiar Terms*, 47–48; Al Weissberg to Muriel Weissberg, 1 August 1945; interview 120, with Pfc. Iwasa Seijirō, 20 January 1944, RG 127, NA, Marine Corps Geographic File, U.S. National Archives, folder c-1: Interrogation Reports New Britain. Materials from this archival site will hereinafter be cited with RG for record group and NA to indicate the U.S. National Archives; Gorham, Newell, and Suttles interviews; Prange, *At Dawn We Slept*, 25–27.

Chapter 1: Partners

1. Harold D. Harris, midshipman and alumni records, U.S. Naval Academy archives (Annapolis, MD: Nimitz Library, U.S. Naval Academy); Brig. Gen. Harold D. Harris, officer biography file (Washington, DC: Marine Corps Historical Center, Washington Navy Yard). Florence Walne to Peter Boodberg, 2 November 1940, file 1940: 481, Oriental languages, CU-5 University of California archives, Bancroft Library, Berkeley, CA. Documents from this source will hereinafter be cited simply as CU-5, with appropriate date and file number.
2. Walne to Boodberg, 2 November 1940, file 1940: 481, CU-5.
3. Edwin O. Reischauer memorandum on the training of men for service as Japanese-language officers, folder 2/2 1940 Oriental language, CU-5.
4. Wyman H. Packard, *A Century of U.S. Naval Intelligence* (Washington, DC: Department of the Navy, 1996), 367; U.S. Naval Academy Alumni Association, Inc., *Register of Alumni 1845–1981* (Annapolis, MD: U.S. Naval Academy Alumni Association, 1981), 187. This source will hereinafter be cited as *USNARA*, with appropriate date and page indications. The other two pioneering naval Japanese-language students were Ens. George Ernest Lake, USN, a Naval Academy 1906 graduate who left the service in 1914 and died in 1935 (*USNARA*, 1981, 187), and Lt. William T. Hoadley, USMC; n.d. penciled account of 2-2-36 incident, folder 1; Transcript Record Service of Capt. Fred Fremont Rogers, USN (Ret.), 1 August 1945, official biography, Rogers papers. Rogers commanded the Naval Construction Training Center, Davisville, Rhode Island, from May 1942 to the end of World War II.
5. Packard, *Century of U.S. Naval Intelligence*, 367–68.
6. Ibid., 368–70. The six students in this group were Marines. John Prados, *Combined Fleet Decoded: The Secret History of American Intelligence and the Japanese Navy in World War II* (New York: Random House, 1995), 39.
7. Prados, *Combined Fleet Decoded*, 75–83. I have used the more common term "breaking" to encompass what technically was code recovery. Pedro Anthony Loureiro, "Intelligence Success: The Evolution of Navy and Marine Intelligence Operations in China, 1931–1941" (University of Southern California Ph.D. diss., 1995). Thomas G. Mahnken, offers a detailed and more critical

interpretation of navy and marine corps acquisition and use of intelligence about Japanese armed forces; Mahnken, *Uncovering Ways of War: U.S. Intelligence and Foreign Military Innovation, 1918–1941* (Ithaca, NY: Cornell University Press, 2002), 42–85. See also his earlier "U.S. Naval Intelligence and Japan," *Intelligence and National Security* 11 (July 1996), 437–38.

8. McCollum oral history, 56–58; Packard, *Century of U.S. Naval Intelligence*, 368.
9. McCollum oral history, 256–58; Packard, *Century of U.S. Naval Intelligence*, 367.
10. McCollum oral history, 259–60; C. W. Nimitz, Chief, Bureau of Navigation, to Lt. Albert E. Hindmarsh, USNR, May 27 1940, Albert E. Hindmarsh papers, in Alan Hindmarsh's possession, Livermore, CA.
11. Carol Hindmarsh Streiff and Margaret Hindmarsh Oberg to author, 31 May, 11 July 2000; Capt. Albert E. Hindmarsh 1955 biography, officer biography files, Classified Operational Archives (Washington, DC: Naval Historical Center, Washington Navy Yard). This archival site will hereinafter be cited as COA, NHC. Mrs. Merrill P. Hindmarsh to Roger Pineau, 20 May 1980, folder 22, box 13, Roger Pineau papers, UCBL. Hindmarsh lecture promotion flyer, 1934, Hindmarsh papers.
12. Albert E. Hindmarsh, "The Realistic Foreign Policy of Japan," *Foreign Affairs* 13 (January 1935), 3–11.
13. David F. Schmitz, *The First Wise Man: Henry L. Stimson* (Wilmington, DE: S. R. Books, 2001), 106–14; Albert E. Hindmarsh, *The Basis of Japanese Foreign Policy* (Cambridge, MA: Harvard University Press, 1936), especially v, 186, 193–99, 213–25, 234–38.
14. July 1936 course announcement, Academy of International Law at the Hague; Albert Hindmarsh, *Le Japon et la Paix en Asie* (Paris: Recueil Sirey, 1937); Chief of Bureau of Navigation to Lt. Albert E. Hindmarsh, I-V(S), USNR, 18 June 1936; Rear Adm. W. R. Gherardi, Commandant, First Naval District, to Capt. Ralston S. Holmes, Director of Naval Intelligence, 22 July 1937; Cdr. W. D. Kilduff to Hindmarsh, 23 July 1937, Hindmarsh papers. Hindmarsh, who became a naturalized citizen in 1928, first connected with the Navy as a lecturer at the Naval War College at Newport, Rhode Island, in 1935. Hindmarsh 1955 biography, Officer Biography files, COA, NHC.
15. Albert E. Hindmarsh confidential report, 1 March 1938; unidentified October 1937 Japanese newspaper clipping, Hindmarsh papers; First draft narrative, "United States Naval Administration in World War II Office of Naval Operations, School of Oriental Languages," 5, Type Command: Training, Schools, University of Colorado School of Oriental Studies folder, World War II Chronological File, COA, NHC. This source will hereinafter be cited as UCSOL. Copies are also in folder 6, box 1, Japanese Language School

papers, UCBL; Edgar L. Haff Jr. interview with Hindmarsh, 9 April 1970, Alexandria, Virginia, folder, 3, box 13, Pineau papers.

16. Hindmarsh 1 March 1938 report, Hindmarsh papers.
17. Waldo Heinrichs Jr., *American Ambassador: Joseph E. Grew and the United States Diplomatic Tradition* (Boston: Little, Brown, 1966), 181–84, 203, 212, 325, 341, 341–52, 355; Hindmarsh 1 March 1938 report, Hindmarsh papers.
18. William D. Leahy to Hindmarsh, 24 March 1938; Headquarters, First Naval District to Hindmarsh, 30 June, 3 November 1939, Hindmarsh papers.
19. McCollum oral history, 260.
20. Ibid.; Haff interview with Hindmarsh, Pineau papers; Chief of Bureau of Navigation to Lt. Albert E. Hindmarsh, 17 September 1940, with three endorsements through 10 October 1940, Hindmarsh papers.
21. McCollum oral history, 260–61.
22. "Biographic Register of the Department of State," April 1, 1950 (Washington, DC: Department of State, 1950), 458. Shaw, born in Los Angeles, earned his bachelor's degree from Colorado College in 1910. After working his way to and from Europe on a cattle boat, he returned home and took a ship for Honolulu, where he taught English to nonnative speakers at the Mills School for two years. He then did the same in Japan for a year, came home to marry, and returned with his bride to Japan for the next twenty-four years; autobiographical fragment, n.d., *Trends for the Record, Class of 1910, Colorado College; Colorado Springs Gazette,* 10 May 1958; Ueda Keisuke, "Inu memoriamu: Gurenu Shou fusai, [In Memorium: Mr. and Mrs. Glenn Shaw]" and Hara Eachrow, "In Memoriam: Professor Glenn W. Shaw," in *Mangekyo: Osaka Gaikokugo daigaku Eigo gakka kinenbunshu* [*Collected Essays Commemorating the English Department at the Osaka University of Foreign Languages*] 2 (Winter 1998), 12–14, 66. Besides two collections of essays about life in contemporary Japan—*Osaka Sketches* (Tokyo: Hokuseido Press, 1929) and *Living in Japan* (Tokyo: Hokuseido Press, 1936)—Shaw published five translations of the works of major Japanese novelists and dramatists between 1922 and 1938. Shaw was accorded that recognition by Nori Chihan, "Nihon bungaku no Oyakusha," [Western Translators of Japanese Literature] in *Asahi Picture News* (March 1955), 10. I am grateful to Mrs. Daphne Shaw Stegmaier for making the foregoing materials pertinent to her father's career available to me. Hackett interview.
23. UCSOL, 1.
24. Ibid.; James William Morley, ed., *Japan's Road to the Pacific War: The Final Confrontation: Japan's Negotiations with the United States, 1941* (New York: Columbia University Press, 1994), 19.
25. Monroe Deutsch to Robert Gordon Sproul, 12 March1941, folder 1941: 481: Oriental Languages, CU-5; Eugene Powers Boardman oral history, done by Edward Coffman, 2 February 1982 (Washington, DC: History and Muse-

ums Divisions, Headquarters, U.S. Marine Corps, 1982), 1; Dan S. Williams and John R. Shively interviews; John Shively to Florence Walne, 24 February 1941, file 1941: 487, CU-5, series 2.

26. John Shively interview; Boardman oral history, 1; McCollum oral history, 73.
27. U.S. War Department, General Staff, Military Intelligence Division, *MISLS: The Training History of the Military Intelligence Service Language School, Annex 10: Personnel Procurement Office* (Washington, DC: U.S. War Department, 1949), 1–2, cited by Allison B. Gilmore, "ATIS at War: The Recruitment, Training, and Accomplishments of U.S. Army Japanese Language Officers," paper presented at the Society for Military History annual meeting, 7 April 2002, Madison, WI; James C. McNaughton, *Nisei Linguists: Japanese Americans in the Military Intelligence Service during World War II* (Washington, DC: Department of the Army, 2006), 20–28. The Army's initial canvass for Japanese linguists found only forty-six regular army officers with some Japanese capability. See List R. A. Officers with Knowledge of Language, Japanese, 27 March 1941, file 350.03 Japanese (9-16-42), Army Intelligence decimal file 1941–48, box 707, Records of the Army Intelligence Command, 1917–73, RG 319, NA.
28. Walne to Monroe E. Deutsch, and Walne to Peter Boodberg, 2 November 1940, Oriental Language folder, file 1940: 409, CU-5, series 2.
29. Monroe E. Deutsch to Robert Underhill, 7 November, Deutsch to Walne, 20 November, Deutsch to Peter Boodberg, 28 November 1940, file 1940: 480: Oriental Languages, CU-5.
30. Walne to Robert Gordon Sproul, 17 February 1941, file 1941: 487: Oriental languages, CU-5. The other two alternatives were for Walne to teach at the Harvard-directed institute in Cambridge, or for Berkeley to decline cooperation with the Navy by insisting on teaching Japanese solely for historical and cultural purposes.
31. Deutsch to Sproul, 4, 12 March; Walne to Deutsch, 10 March; J. B. Rakestraw to Sproul, 25 March, 3 April; Sproul to Maj. H. D. Harris et al., 11 April 1941, file 1941: 487 Oriental Languages, CU-5.
32. Brig. E. A. Ostermann, UMSC, rejected Sproul's proposal (Ostermann to Sproul, 17 April), noting that the Corps had already arranged to send officers to the University of Hawaii. J. Edgar Hoover declined to back any conference between Berkeley and U.S. government officials (Hoover to Sproul, 21 April); the War Department received Sproul's letter but lost it in between bureaucratic subunits without ever replying; McCollum to Sproul 2 May, Pomeroy to Sproul, 14 May, Woodbridge Bingham to Sproul, 20 June, Walne to Sproul, 10 July 1941, file 1941: 487: Oriental languages, CU-5.
33. Hindmarsh to Sproul, 17 June 1941, file 1941: 487: Oriental languages, CU-5; UCSOL, 1–2; Hugh Borton, Chair, Committee on Japanese Studies, American Council of Learned Societies, to William R. Acker, Serge Elisseef,

Charles B. Fahs, Mortimer Graves, H. G. Henderson, E. O. Reischauer, Henry S. Tatsumi, Florence Walne, and Joseph Yamagiwa, 17 June 1941, file 1941: file 731; list of those in attendance at Japanese Language Teachers' Conference, Ithaca, New York, July 25–26, 1941, file 1941: 487: Oriental languages, CU-5. In addition to those noted above, R. M. J. Fellner of the Department of Justice; Col. William F. Friedman, U.S. Army Signal Corps; R. D. Jones, Federal Communications Commission; George A. Kennedy, Yale University; and David H. Stevens, Rockefeller Foundation participated in the meeting. Spector, *Eagle against the Sun*, 68.

34. UCSOL, 2.
35. Hindmarsh to Sproul, 17 June; Walne to Sproul, 12 August 1941, file 1941: 487: Oriental Languages, CU-5.
36. Enclosure A in Chief of Naval Operations (by R. M. Brainerd) to Chief of Bureau of Navigation, n.d., enclosed with Hindmarsh to Sproul, 27 August 1941, file 1941: 487: Oriental languages, CU-5.
37. CNO (by R. M. Brainerd) to Chief of Bureau of Navigation, 1941, file 1941: 487: Oriental languages, CU-5; McCollum oral history, 282.
38. Enclosure B to CNO to Bureau of Navigation, August 1941, file 1941: 487: Oriental languages; UCSOL, 3–4.
39. UCSOL, appendix 2; R. E. Ingersoll, for CNO, to Rear Adm. Chester W. Nimitz, Chief of the Bureau of Navigation; Nimitz to Dean George H. Chase, 19 November 1941, folder 29, box 18, Pineau papers.
40. Edwin O. Reischauer, *My Life between Japan and America* (New York: Harper and Row, 1986), 83–84; Andrew Roth to Pineau, 6 March 1982, folder 27, box 22, Pineau papers.
41. Hindmarsh to Chase, 19 November 1941, appendix 6, UCSOS. The original Harvard group included David F. Anthony, William R. Black, Lawrence M. Bucans, Schuyler V. Cammann, Raymond Conley, Wesley R. Fishel, John W. Hall, James Donald Hare, James J. Hitchcock, David S. Huggins, Albert E. Kane, Ernest Kroll, James V. Martin Jr., Gantt William Miller Jr., Seymour Millstein, Walter Nichols, Donald P. Ray, Ralph W. E. Reid, Bernard T. Ring, Jay Robinson, Andrew Roth, Edward H. Schafer Jr., Ralph W. Sell, Carleton A. Siemer, Edward Van Der Rhoer, and William T. Wheat. Black, at forty-three, was the oldest in the group, and Huggins, at eighteen was the youngest. "Harvardites" list, file 10, box 2; David and Frank Huggins, file 13, box 34, Pineau papers; appendix 4, UCSOL; James Victor Martin Jr. unpublished memoir, "Recollections of the Navy Japanese Language School at Harvard University, 1941–1942," in his possession, Washington, D. C. ; James V. Martin Jr. interview.
42. Eliseef to Nimitz, Chief of the Bureau of Navigation, 28 November 1941, folder 29, box 18, Pineau papers.
43. UCSOL, 13. The problems included Harvard's charging more per student

than Berkeley charged, paying instructors less, and blaming the Navy for their penury. The Harvard Navy ROTC unit commander also refused to have anything to do with administering the language program. Edwin O. Reischauer to Pineau, 5 September 1980, folder 10, box 2, Pineau papers; Col. Felix J. de Rohan memorandum for executive officer, Military Intelligence Service, enclosing Edwin O. Reischauer memorandum, 14 April 1942, 350.03 Japanese (9-16-42), box 707, Army Intelligence decimal file, 1941–48, RG 319, NA.

44. UCSOL, 12; "Harvardites" list, folder 10, box 2, Roth to Pineau, 6 March 1982, file 27, box 22, Pineau papers.

45. Walne to Deutsch, 2 November 1940, file 1940: 400 Oriental Languages; Deutsch to Sproul, 4 March 1941, file 1941: 487, CU-5. Reischauer (43–75) describes the five-year course of study that Serge Eliseef prescribed for him, with supporting fellowships that took him to Tokyo and Kyoto, Korea and China, and Paris. One of Walne's Berkeley students who later became a distinguished scholar of Chinese remembered her as a "horrible" teacher whose "beautiful" spoken Japanese could not make up for her "pitiful" attempts to write the language. Richard Rudolph oral history interview with Kenneth D. Klein, 4 March 1983, Oral History 300/237, 33, UCLA Special Collections and Archives, University of California at Los Angeles.

46. Preliminary Proposal for a School of Practical Instruction in the Language and Civilization of Japan in California, file 1941: 487 Oriental Languages, CU-5.

47. Susumu Winston Nakamura, 18 March 1946 personnel report, University of California personnel files, Archives of the University of California, Bancroft Library, Berkeley, California. Nakamura had studied at Keio University in Tokyo before taking his undergraduate degree at Berkeley. Nakamura obituary, *San Francisco Chronicle*, 17 June 1989, file 3, box 6, Pineau papers; Nakamura and Ellengale Toki Oakley interviews; R. Stuart Hummel diary, 30 October 1941, 24 February, 9 June 1942, R. Stuart Hummel papers, UCBL. This source will hereinafter be cited as Hummel diary, with appropriate date citations. Willard F. Topping biographical data, and *Boulder Daily Camera*, 18 July 1958. I am grateful to John Ferree of Boulder for providing information on the Topping family. They, like the parents of Arthur McCollum and Florence Walne, were missionaries for the American Baptist Foreign Mission Society. James McAlpine, a Presbyterian missionary, was asked, first informally on 9 September 1941, then formally on 13 October, to teach in the naval school. See Pauline McAlpine, *Diary of a Missionary: Pauline S. McAlpine*, (Decatur, GA: Quill Publications, 1986), 82. I am indebted to sensei Daniel Date, whose late wife Kathleen collected such materials, for making this source available to me. Commandant, 12th Naval District to Commanding General, 4th Army, 21 March 1942, Daniel and Kathleen Date papers, Oakland, CA; Chitoshi Yanaga, *Japan since Perry* (New York: McGraw Hill,

1949); *Japanese People and Politics* (New York: John Wiley, 1956); and *Big Business in Japanese Politics* (New Haven: Yale University Press, 1968). Imai, Ariake "Larry" Inouye, and Ida Inouye interviews.

48. UCSOL, 5; "Original Berkeleyites" list, folder 2, box 2, Pineau papers. The first Berkeley students were Gerald J. Bagnall, Ernest B. Beath, W. A. T. Bielefeldt, G. N. Brayley, William W. Burd, D. A. Corlett, Louis Hennessy, William Himel, John H. Holtom, Harned P. Hoose, Frank B. Huggins, R. Stuart Hummel, George W. McClure, Robert Patton, William Quinn, Edward N. Robinson, Charles Alexander "Sandy" Sims, Wayne P. Suttles, Wilvan G. Van Campen, R. M. Van Patten, J. T. Wood, and William W. Woodworth. Wilvan Van Campen to author, 3 October 2005; Suttles interview; Hummel diary, 20, 22 October 1941. The Navy modified its position to say that nongraduates would simply be honorably discharged. William W. Burd to William J. Hudson Jr., 30 November 1993, William W. Burd papers, Berkeley, CA. The more worldly naval commander simply told the student, who later married his girlfriend, that he simply didn't want to hear any more about his amorous doings.
49. Hummel diary, 5–7 November, 18 December 1941. Imai interview; Ariake and Ida Inouye interviews; "Original Berkeleyites" list. William Himel, one of those who departed, later became an Army Military Intelligence Service officer.
50. UCSOL, 12–13.
51. Fujimoto interview; Sandra C. Taylor, *Jewel of the Desert: Japanese American Internment at Topaz* (Berkeley: University of California Press, 1993), 45.
52. Taylor, *Jewel of the Desert*, 46–54. Greg Robinson details the president's decision for, and implementation of, forced relocation; Robinson, *By Order of the President: FDR and the Internment of Japanese Americans* (Cambridge, MA: Harvard University Press, 2001), 73–176.
53. McAlpine, *Diary of a Missionary*, 84–85.
54. OpNav to Commandant, 12th Naval District, 4 April 1942, Deutsch to Sproul dictated telegram text, pre–4 April 1942, box 35, 12th Naval District records, accession number 181-58-3223/3224, made available to H. R. Montgomery via Freedom of Information Act Request. These records are held by the Pacific Region National Archives and Records Center, San Bruno, California. I am grateful to Ariake Larry Inouye for making copies of these documents available. Hindmarsh to Walne, 1 April 1942, file 1942: 487, CU-5.
55. Commandant, 12th Naval District to Commanding General, Fourth Army, 21 March, 5 May; Assistant Adjutant General, Headquarters Western Defense Command and Fourth Army to "To Whom It May Concern," 27 March; Lt. Cdr. J. E. Brenner, USN (Ret.) to Chief of Staff, Commandant, 12th Naval District, 7 April, 12th Naval District Intelligence Officer R. P.

McCullough to Director of Naval Intelligence, 28 March 1942, 12th Naval District Records.

56. District Intelligence Officer, 12th Naval District, to Commandant, 12th Naval District, 11 April 1942, 12th Naval District records.
57. McCollum oral history, 287. For weeks thereafter the Navy tried to delay movement of the Berkeley program out of California, going so far as to propose shifting it on an interim basis to military zone two, in the San Joaquin Valley. But the Army resisted even that temporary accommodation. See Capt. F. J. Horne, Office of Chief of Naval Operations, to Deputy Chief of Staff, U.S. Army, 23 May 1942, file 350.03 Japanese (9-16-42), Army Intelligence decimal file, 1941–48, box 707, RG 319, NA.
58. Deutsch to Sproul, 11 May 1942, file 1942: 481 file, CU-5; Commandant, 12th Naval District to Commanding General, Western Defense Command and Fourth Army, 16 May 1942, 12th Naval District records.
59. McCollum oral history, 288; UCSOL, 14; the contract and its ratification can be found in University of Colorado Regents' minutes, June 6, 1942, box 1, Japanese Language School papers, UCBL. The Navy proposed revisions to this contract, but the regents on 21 August 1942 instructed the university president to stand firm on the original agreement.
60. H. E. Kays, Professor of Naval Science, University of California, Berkeley, to Commanding General, Fourth Army, 12 June 1942, 12th Naval District records; "Original Berkeleyites" list; Ariake and Ida Inouye interviews. The original nine Japanese and Japanese American teachers were reduced to eight after the 12th Naval District's intelligence officer insisted that one be released from his teaching duties "due to personal activities which have caused him to be a suspect." District Intelligence Officer to Commandant, 12th Naval District, 14 April 1942, 12th Naval District records.

Chapter 2: Students on an Island of Understanding

1. Student class lists, 1941–July 1943, file 5, box 2, Pineau papers; July 1943 University of Colorado faculty salary list, Edwin S. Nakamura papers, Berkeley, CA.
2. Hart Spiegel to family, 24 August 1942, in Spiegel, "War Years and Better Days," 124.
3. Data on members of the July 1943 graduating class in this and preceding paragraph compiled from individual biographical information in Pineau papers, 1992 and 2002 Boulder Navy Japanese/Oriental Language School reunion pamphlets, and from interviews. Spiegel, "War Years and Better Days," 9.
4. UCSOL, 14; Marshall and Mallory interviews.
5. Newell interview.
6. Cross, *Born a Foreigner*, 42; Hackett and Hussey interviews; Roger Pineau, Far East Luncheon remarks, file 3, box 21, Pineau papers.

7. Edward Seidensticker, *Tokyo Central: A Memoir* (Seattle: University of Washington Press, 2002), 20; Rich interview.
8. Lawrence Vincent, "Semper Fi: Memoirs of a Japanese Language Officer with the United States Marine Corps in World War II," unpublished memoir, 6.
9. McCollum oral history, 195.
10. Roegge interview; Hart Spiegel to mother, 1942; Spiegel, "War Years and Better Days," 119.
11. Hummel diary, 25 June, 2 July 1942; James Durbin to parents, 20 June, 7 September 1943, James Durbin papers, UCBL. Durbin's papers were collected, edited, and presented to the University of Colorado by his friend and classmate, Ross Ingersoll.
12. Hummel diary, 2 July 1942; McAlpine, *Diary of a Missionary*, 87. Arase, Nobutaka, and Hoshino interviews; Henry S. Tatsumi, *American Students of the Japanese Language in World War II*, n.p. reprint from *The Northwest Times*, 1 January 1951, copy in Donald S. Willis papers, Boulder, CO; Tatsumi 1991 obituary, file 6, box 3, Pineau papers.
13. Casson, Luthy, and Rich interviews.
14. Arase and Okamoto interviews.
15. Pineau, Far East Luncheon remarks, Pineau papers; Willis interview; Spiegel to family, 18 July 1942, in Spiegel, "War Years and Better Days," 120.
16. Spiegel to family, 24 August 1942, in Spiegel, "War Years and Better Days," 122; Ball interview; Morley conference remarks; Roegge interview; Naganuma Naoe, *Hyōjun Nippongo Tokuhon Dai Ikkan* [*Standard Japanese Reader, Volume One*], rev. ed., 1, copy in Neal Jensen papers, UCBL. The University of California Press reprinted the Naganuma volumes in various editions between 1942 and 1944. UCSOL, 5.
17. Hummel diary, 17 July 1942; Spiegel to family, 24 August 1942, in Spiegel, "War Years and Better Days," 123.
18. Spiegel to family, 24 August 1942, in Spiegel, "War Years and Better Days," 123.
19. This description of the complexities of Japanese is based on the author's experience in learning the language, first conversationally while a junior naval officer stationed in Japan, then more formally in intensive courses at Harvard and the Inter-University Center for Japanese Studies in Tokyo. Explanations of the writing system are drawn from Andrew Nathaniel Nelson, *The Modern Reader's Japanese-English Character Dictionary* 1st ed. (Tokyo and Rutland, VT: Charles E. Tuttle, 1962), 1001–16. The examples of pronunciation–meaning linkages appear in Katsumata Senkichiro, ed., *Kenkyusha's New Japanese-English Dictionary* (Tokyo: Kenkyusha, 1954), 347, 612.
20. Tatsumi eventually formalized his methods in *Spoken Japanese: A Self-Interpreter* (Seattle: privately printed, 1959). I am indebted to Henry Hoshino for providing a copy of this work.

21. Nelson, *Modern Reader's Japanese-English*, 1014.
22. UCSOL, 6–7; Spiegel to family, 24 August 1942, in Spiegel, "War Years and Better Days," 122.
23. Spiegel to family, 18 July 1942, in Spiegel, "War Years and Better Days."
24. UCSOL, 6–7; Paul F. Boller to parents, 9, 23 October 1942, box 1, Paul F. Boller papers, UCBL.
25. Dornheim, Foley, Mallory, and Dan S. Williams interviews.
26. Spiegel, "War Years and Better Days," 12–13, 17; Spiegel, 24 August 1942 to parents, 123; Boller, 1942 letter to parents, Boller papers.
27. Casson interview; Spiegel to parents, 18 July 1942, in Spiegel, "War Years and Better Days," 119.
28. Hoshino interview; Rayer Toki to Akiko Nishioka, 30 June 1943, Rayer Toki papers in possession of Ellengale Toki Oakley, Alamo, CA; Cross to parents, October 1942, Charles T. Cross papers, UCBL.
29. Pineau, Far East luncheon remarks, Pineau papers; UCSOL, 19; Spiegel to family, 24 August 1942, in Spiegel, "War Years and Better Days," 11, 123.
30. Thompson interview; Boller to parents, 9, 14 October 1942, Boller papers.
31. Naval Training School (Japanese Language) Graduation Exercises program, 10 July 1943, folder 1, box 4, Japanese Language School papers, UCBL; Japanese text of school song, Donald Willis papers; *Sono hi no uwasa* [*News of the Day*], 10 September, 1 October 1942, folder 6, box 6, Pineau papers. This source will hereinafter be cited as *Uwasa*, with appropriate date indicated.
32. *Uwasa*, 2, 17 September; 1, 29 October 1942.
33. Hummel diary, 23 July, 15 August 1942; "The Naval Language School, Boulder, Colorado" pamphlet, Willis papers.
34. Hummel diary, 15 August, 3 October; *Uwasa*, 1 October 1942; Paul Boller to his sister, 9 December 1942, Boller papers.
35. Spiegel, "War Years and Better Days," 16; Mallory interview.
36. Willis Fiftieth Reunion Conference [1992] remarks, Willis papers.
37. *Uwasa*, 24 September, 1 October, 20 November 1942; Thompson interview.
38. Spiegel, "War Years and Better Days," 16; Dornheim and Slaughter interviews; *Uwasa*, 17 September 1942; Boller to parents, 13, 24 November 1942, Boller papers.
39. *Uwasa*, 10, 24 September, 29 October; Dornheim, Hackett, and Slaughter interviews.
40. Cross to parents, 22 July, 19 September, 6 and (n.d.) October 1942, Cross papers.
41. Rear Adm. H. C. Train to Professor of Naval Science and Tactics University of Colorado, 12 November 1942, file 6, box 5, Pineau papers; *Uwasa,* 20 November 1942; Ball interview.
42. UCSOL, 15; Gilmore "ATIS at War," 8; McNaughton, *Nisei Linguists*, 102–5.

43. UCSOL, 15–20; *Boulder Daily Camera*, December 1942, copy in Date papers.
44. 7 June 1944 Revised [University of Colorado] List of Instructors on the Faculty of the Navy School of Oriental Languages, Nakamura papers; Imai, and Ida Inouye interviews; Hummel diary, 11 September 1942. The regular faculty numbered twenty-four in July 1942.
45. Jessica Natsuko Arnston, "Journey to Boulder: The Japanese American Instructors of the Navy Japanese Language School, 1942–1946," unpublished M.A. thesis (University of Colorado, 2003), 44, 168. The three teachers acquired by these means were Daniel Date, Kay Kawaii, and Dr. Lee Watanabe. Sensei Ari Inouye's wife, Ida, was Dr. Watanabe's niece. M. R. Montgomery, *Saying Goodbye: A Memoir for Two Fathers* (New York: Knopf, 1989), 127.
46. 5 August 1942 *Manzanar Free Press*, cited by Arnston, 44; Walne to James G. Lindley, 19 November 1942, file 3, box 6, Pineau papers; Japanese Language School Payroll, 13 July 1943, Nakamura papers make it clear that only three of the Tule Lake selectees actually taught at Boulder.
47. Robert Harvey, *Amache: The Story of Japanese Internment in Colorado during World War II* (Lanham, MD: Taylor Trade Publishing, 2004), 38, 49, 62–70, 75–79, 117, 156; Walne to Lindley, 19 November 1942, file 1942, 487, CU-5; 4 June 1944 Revised List of Instructors; 13 July 1943 Japanese Language School Payroll, Nakamura papers.
48. 13 July 1943 Japanese Language School Payroll. Generalizations in the preceding and following paragraphs about the eighty-eight instructors are drawn from analysis of the Japanese American National Museum's War Relocation Authority WRA-26 digital files for those who were sent to assembly centers; previously cited interviews; sensei correspondence and lists, file 3, box 6, Pineau papers; and interviews with sensei and surviving family members in Arnston, "Journey to Boulder." Montgomery, *Saying Goodbye*, 117; Fujimoto interview; Takewo Takekoshi, *Reminiscences of My Sixty Years in the United States* (Los Angeles: Takewo Takekoshi, 1990), 146, 154; Brian Masaru Hayashi, *"For the Sake of Our Japanese Brethren": Assimilation, Nationalism, and Protestantism among the Japanese of Los Angeles, 1895–1942* (Stanford, CA: Stanford University Press, 1995), 3; Brian Masaru Hayashi, *Democratizing the Enemy: The Japanese American Internment* (Princeton: Princeton University Press, 2004), 48–49, 52–54; Minoru Kiyota, *Beyond Loyalty: The Story of a Kibei.* Linda Klepinger Keenan, trans. (Honolulu: University of Hawaii Press, 1997), ix.
49. NJLS Boulder sensei list, file 3, box 6, Pineau papers; Grace Minto to Frank Minton, 16 January 1984, enclosing list of Henry Tatsumi's former students, copy made available by Mrs. Catherine Oberg, his daughter; Montgomery, *Saying Goodbye*, 127; Arnston, "Journey to Boulder," 138–39; Dr. Watanabe was also Ari Inouye's brother-in-law. James Gorō Otagiri to A. Asano, 22 March 1943, James Gorō Otagiri papers, UCBL; Ota interview.

50. Takekoshi, *Reminiscences*, 91, 140–43, 162, 171. Drafted later into the U.S. Army, Takekoshi became an American citizen after the war. Arnston, "Journey to Boulder," 154–55; Hayashi, *Democratizing the Enemy*, 16–19.
51. Rayer Toki to Akiko Nishioka, 10, 28 October, n.d. December 1942, Toki family papers; Ellegale Toki Oakley interview. I am grateful to Mrs. Oakley for making her parents' correspondence available to me. Taylor, *Jewel of the Desert*, provides a graphic account of conditions at the Utah relocation center.
52. Rayer Toki to Akiko Nishioka, 10, 22 April, 1 September 1943; Terry T. Toki WRA-26 digital files, Japanese American National Museum, Los Angeles, CA; Oakley interview.
53. *USNARA*, 187; n.d. August 1942 *Christian Science Monitor* clipping, Date papers, Oakland, CA; Boller to parents, 9 October, 14 November 1942, 20 January 1943, Boller papers; Cross to parents, 15 November 1942, Cross papers; Durbin to parents, 23 April 1943, Durbin papers; Vincent, "Semper Fi," 10; UCSOL, 7, 20.
54. Boller to parents, 14 November 1942; 20, 23, 25 January 26 October 1943, Boller papers; 17 January 1943 Boulder *Daily Camera* clipping, Date papers, Oakland, CA; Slaughter, Luthy, and Moss joint interview; Slaughter, Luthy, and Cross interviews.
55. UCSOL, 21; Boller to parents, 8, 21 December 1942; 20 January 1943; Boller to Vickie, 8 January 1943, Boller papers. Students mocked Lieutenant Conover with a song that ran: "Twas in the town of Boulder in the spring of 43/A man by the name of Conover came from across the sea/Said, my ship is made of concrete my crew I think the same/The way they keep their portholes indeed a bloody shame. The crew forsook their kanji for the dustpan and the mop/The captain soon decided all paddling he would stop/But when he cut out smoking as bad for the cardiac/Twas the final regulation that broke the camel's back." Text enclosed in David Stocking to Ed Hart, 22 July 1943, Edward S. Hart papers, UCBL; Cross, *Born a Foreigner*, 42.
56. Jason Brockman biographical sketch of Ralph L. Carr in "Guide to the Governor," Ralph L. Carr Collection at the Colorado State Archives, Denver, at http://www.colorado.gov/dpa/doit/archives/govs/carr/html (June 2005); Arnston, "Journey to Boulder," 57; Boulder City Council Minutes, 21 July, 4 August 1942, Inouye papers, Roseville, CA; Harvey, *Amache*, 42.
57. Boulder City Council minutes, 20 October 1942; 5, 19 January 1943; Harvey, *Amache*, 57, 172; *Christian Science Monitor*, August 1942; *Boulder Daily Camera*, 14 November 1942 in file 3 box 45, President Henry Bennett papers, Oklahoma A&M University, Stillwater, OK; *Boulder Daily Camera*, 17 January 1943, Date papers, Oakland, CA.
58. Boller to parents, 24, 28 November 1942, 3 May 1943, Boller papers; Harvey, *Amache*, 118–20; Donald Paul Irish, "Reactions of Residents of Boulder,

Colorado, to the Introduction of Japanese into the Community," unpublished M.A. thesis (University of Colorado 1950), 126; McAlpine, *Diary of a Missionary*, 88.

59. Boller to parents, 18 January 1943, Boller papers; McAlpine, *Diary of a Missionary*, 89; Fujimoto and Ota interviews; Arnston, "Journey to Boulder," 60–64, 119, 127; Irish, "Reactions of Residents," 69–72.
60. Roster of Navy Language School instructors at University of Colorado, Boulder, Nakamura papers; Stone and Luthy interviews; Spiegel to family, November 1942, Spiegel, "War Years and Better Days," 128; Muriel Weissberg, "Contact with Dr. R. G. Gustafson," *The Interpreter*, no. 41 (15 March 2002): 1; Muriel Weissberg to Megan H. Lillie, 21 December 2001, Weissberg papers.
61. Spiegel to family, 24 August 1942, in Spiegel, "War Years and Better Days," 123; Dornheim and Marshall interviews.
62. UCSOL, 15.
63. McAlpine, *Diary of a Missionary*, 89; UCSOL, 9–10; Toki to Nishioka, 15, 18 April; 5, 10, and 30 June 1943, Toki papers; Oakley interview; Boller to parents, 3 May 1943, Boller papers.
64. Boller to parents, 8, 21 December 1942; 20 January, 3 May 1943; Boller to Vickie, 8 January 1943, Boller papers; Spiegel to family, 13 February 1943, in Spiegel, "War Years and Better Days," 130; Arthur Dornheim to parents, 13 February 1943, Dornheim papers, Bethesda, MD; Spiegel to family, 30 May 1943, in Spiegel, "War Years and Better Days," 133–34.
65. Toki to Nishioka, 26 April, 8 May 1943, Toki papers; Boller to sister, 8 May; Boller to parents, 23 May 1943, Boller papers.
66. Boller to Anne, 13 April 1943, Boller papers; McAlpine, *Diary of a Missionary*, 89; *The Mikado* performance song, file 6, box 1, Japanese Language School papers, UCBL.
67. Ota interview; Toki to Nishioka, 16 April, 2, 4, 11 May 1943, Toki papers; Boller to parents, 23 May 1943, Boller papers; Dornheim interview.
68. Casson interview; Boller to parents, 30 October 1943, Boller papers describes this switch in reading material at this point in the course.
69. Cross to mother, 5 April 1943, Cross papers; Cross interview; Spiegel, "War Years and Better Days," 9, 11.
70. Toki to Nishioka, June 1943, Toki papers; song words in Willis Fiftieth Reunion remarks, Willis papers.
71. Hummel diary, 1 October 1942; McAlpine, *Diary of a Missionary*, 90.
72. Pineau, Far East Luncheon remarks, Pineau papers.
73. Ibid.
74. Naganuma Naoe, *Hyōjun Nihongo Tokuhon Dai Gokan* [Berkeley: University of California Press, 1943], 255. Copy in Hilary Conroy papers, UCBL.

75. Naval Training School (Japanese Language) University of Colorado, Boulder, Graduation Exercises program, 10 July 1943, Toki papers; Casson, Luthy, and Thompson interviews; Roger Pineau, *Japanese Language Officers, USN 1910–1928* file 3, box 21, Pineau papers; Betty Gregg, 2002 memoir, box 1, Gregg papers.
76. Faculty Recognition Certificate, 10 July 1943, Date papers; Henry S. Tatsumi et al. to Robert L. Stearns, 6 July 1943, University of Colorado Regents Minutes, 16 January 1942–17 December 1943, Inouye papers.
77. Naval Training School (Japanese Language) University of Colorado, Boulder, Colorado Graduation Exercises Program, 10 July 1943, Toki papers.
78. Pineau to Lebra, 9 November 1988, Pineau papers; appendix 41, UCSOL; Boulder WAVE alumni roster, Irene Slaninka Thiel papers, Bellingham, WA.
79. UCSOL, 22; appendix 41, 4; Susan H. Godson, *Serving Proudly: A History of Women in the U.S. Navy* (Annapolis, MD: Naval Institute Press, 2001), 109–13; Billet Levine, Mayer, Webb Sigerson, and Stegmeier interviews; Phi Beta Kappa *Key Reporter*, Summer 1943, file 8, box 5; 1991 Hammond and Julia Hilts Rolph to Pineau, 23 October 1992, Julia Hilts Rolph to Pineau, file 24, box 22, Pineau papers.
80. University of Colorado *Silver and Gold* article, 1943, Thiel papers; *Uwasa*, August 1943.
81. *Silver and Gold* article, August 1943; Evelyn "Betty" Knecht Hansson letters to parents, in 1993 WAVEs reunion biography, file 1, box 5, Pineau papers; Anne Grilk King conference presentation, 7 April 2000; Stegmeier and Mayer interviews.
82. Toki to Nishioka, 6 March 1944; Mary Jane Konnold Carroll 1993 biography, WAVES 1993 reunion biography, file 1, box 5, Pineau papers.
83. Irene Slaninka Thiel interview; Evelyn "Betty" Knecht Hannson to parents, n.d. 1943–44, in 1993 WAVEs reunion biography, file 1, box 5, Pineau papers.
84. Thiel, O'Sullivan Way, and Billett Levine interviews; Evelyn "Betty" Knecht Hansson to parents, n.d. 1943–44 letters, Anne Grilk King biography, both in WAVE 1993 reunion biography, file 1, box 5, Pineau papers.
85. Ruth Webb Sigerson, Jean Mayer, and Julia Hilts Rolph interviews; Ruth Halverson Craig, Barbara McVay Hitchcock, Clarene Suter Saarni, and Mary Lou Siegfried Williams biographies, 1993 WAVE reunion biography, file 1, box 5, Pineau papers.
86. List of Japanese-language officers from Great Britain, 21 April 1982, Donald Menzies to Pineau, folder 4, box 3, Pineau papers; Beasley interview. Two other groups of five British officers each arrived in April 1944 and early 1945.
87. Beasley interview; Julia Hilts Rolph to Pineau, 1991, folder 22, box 24, Pineau papers.
88. Rolph and Beasley interviews; unidentified 1944 RNVR officer letter, quoted in appendix 56, UCSOL.

89. UCSOL, 24; Durbin to parents 28 April, 5 May, 29 September 1943; Toki to Nishioka, fall 1943, Toki papers.
90. Boller to parents, 23 September 1943, Boller papers; Toki to Nishioka, December 1943, Alamo, CA; Kramer and Muheim interviews.
91. UCSOL, 22–23; Walne to Yūji Imai, 8 May 1944, Yūji Imai papers, San Mateo, CA; Toki to Nishioka, 25 May 1944, Toki papers.
92. UCSOL, 23; "Florence Walne MacFarquhar, 1895–1946: In Memoriam," 3–4, Ross Ingersoll papers, UCBL.
93. *Boulder Daily Camera*, 16 September 1944, clipping courtesy of A. W. "Mike" Foley.
94. UCSOL, 26, 34–35.
95. UCSOL, 36; McAlpine, *Diary of a Missionary*, 92, 95.
96. Oakley and Smith interviews; Barbara Dean and Sidney DeVere Brown, "From Pearl Harbor to Theta Pond: The Navy Japanese Language School at Oklahoma A&M College, 1945–1945," unpublished 1995 manuscript provided by Professor Brown to Pedro Loureiro, 12; James McAlpine, Memorandum on the Nature and Scope of the Japanese Language Curriculum [at Oklahoma A&M College], 1 July 1946, list of 232 Stillwater students, Bennett papers; Leonard Weiss to Pineau, 28 October 1981, box 2, file 12 Pineau papers; Shorrock interview.
97. Barbara McVay Hitchcock biography, 1993 WAVE reunion biography, file 1, box 5, Pineau papers; Toki to Nishioka, n.d. March 1943, Toki papers.

Chapter 3: Marine Combat Interpreters

An earlier version of this chapter appeared as "Language at War: U.S. Marine Corps Japanese Language Officers in the Pacific War," *Journal of Military History* 68 (July 2004), 853–83.

1. Naval Training School (Japanese Language) University of Colorado graduation exercises program, 10 July 1943, Toki papers; Commandant, U.S. Marine Corps to Below-named Officers, Marine Corps Reserve, Naval Training School (Japanese Language), 11 June 1943, Lawrence C. Vincent papers, UCBL; Boulder graduates class lists, 1942–45, file 4, box 4, Pineau papers.
2. Eugene to Betty Gregg, 20 September 1943, Gregg papers; Vincent, "Semper Fi,"10; Thompson and White interviews.
3. Spiegel to family, 24 August 1942, in Spiegel, "War Years and Better Days," 10, 20, 122; Hackett, Gibney, and Karr interviews. Karr, who spent his naval career at Pearl Harbor, coined the "LMD" designation.
4. Spiegel, "War Years and Better Days," 13, 23; Spiegel to parents, 13 February, May 1943 in ibid., 130, 132; Slaughter, Luthy, and Moss joint interview; Cross, Luthy, and Slaughter interviews.
5. Edward M. Coffman interview with Eugene Boardman, Madison, WI, 2 February 1982 (U.S. Marine Corps Oral History Program) 1; Lt. Col. John

E. Merrill, oral history; Brig. Gen. Bankson T. Holcomb oral history, 13; Dan S. Williams and John Shively interviews.

6. Roger Pineau notes, U.S. Marine Corps School, file 11, box 2, Pineau papers; Donald Shively to Florence Walne, 24 February 1941, file 1941: 487, box CU-5, series, 2; Merrill oral history, 20–21; Eugene Boardman oral history, 2–3; Gard interview.
7. Gerald Holtom to Tom and Olive Holtom, 14 February, Holtom to parents, 6 July 1942, Gerald Holtom papers, UCBL; John Shively interview; Merrill oral history, 23–24; Boardman oral history, 2–3.
8. James S. Santelli, *A Brief History of the 8th Marines* (Washington, DC: History and Museum Division, Headquarters, U.S. Marine Corps, 1976), 11, 99; Stone interview; Harry D. Pratt, conference presentation and interview.
9. Merrill oral history, 26; Course syllabi, Division Japanese Language School, July 1942, Paul S. Dull papers, Research Archives, Marine Corps University, Quantico, VA. This site will hereinafter be cited as MCU; Slesnick and Slesnick, *Kanji and Codes: Learning Japanese for World War II* (Bellingham, WA: Carol Slesnick and Irwin Slesnick, 2006), 178–84 notes that a third instructor, Donald Nugent, a student in the Hawaii class, was reassigned almost immediately after reaching Camp Elliott.
10. Merrill oral history, 26–28; Dull to Edwards Brothers photolithography company, 10 October 1942; Dull to McGraw Hill Book Company, 13 April 1943; Dull to Colonel Clark, 14, 18 January 1944; J. C. Pelzel and E. P. Boardman, Proposals Regarding the Employment of Japanese Personnel within the Marine Division, 28 March 1943, Dull papers, MCU.
11. Kinsman and Stone interviews; Pelzel and Boardman memorandum, 28 March 1943, Dull papers, MCU.
12. Cross, *Born a Foreigner*, 44; Rich, Hackett, and Kinsman interviews; Spiegel to family, 6 August 1943, in Spiegel, "War Years and Better Days," 140–43; Vincent, "Semper Fi," 12–13.
13. Spiegel to family, 6, 13 August 1943 in Spiegel, "War Years and Better Days," 141–42; Vincent, "Semper Fi," 13.
14. Kinsman and Rich interviews; Cross, *Born a Foreigner*, 44–45.
15. Luthy, Thompson, and Kinsman interviews; Cross, *Born a Foreigner*, 44; Spiegel to family, 23 September 1943, in Spiegel, "War Years and Better Days," 149.
16. List of USN and USMC Language Students in Japan, file 3, box 11, Pineau papers; Boardman oral history, 2.
17. Sherwood F. Moran autobiographical fragment, Sherwood F. Moran papers, MCU; Sherwood F. Moran to Ursul Moran, 31 October 1942, Sherwood F. Moran letters, in possession of Sherwood R. Moran, Madison, WI. Materials from this source will hereinafter be cited as Moran family papers, Madison, WI.

18. Cory had served in the U.S. Army in World War I. "Register of the Department of State October 1, 1938" (Washington, DC: Government Printing Office, 1938), 75; Richard Tregaskis, *Guadalcanal Diary*, 2nd ed. (New York: Modern Library, 2000), 85–86; Prados, *Combined Fleet Decoded*, 367; Richard Frank, *Guadalcanal* (New York: Random House, 1990), 129–31. Five days later, on 17 August 1942, the second death of a marine language officer occurred during the Second Raider Battalion's surprise attack on Makin, far to the north in the Gilbert Islands. Capt. Gerald P. Holtom rushed ashore in search of prisoners and enemy documents only to be felled by a sniper's bullet even before he had a chance to speak a word of Japanese. Cruel though it was, his fate was kinder than what befell nine of his fellow Marines who were left behind when this operation was aborted. The Japanese beheaded them. John C. Erskine, "Language Officers Recall Combat Roles in the Pacific," *Fortitudine*, 12 (Spring 1986), 23–24; Tripp Wiles, *Forgotten Raiders of '42: The Fate of the Marines Left behind on Makin* (Washington, DC: Potomac Books, 2007) is the most recent and most accurate account of this unfortunate episode.
19. Boardman oral history, 6; the young man deemed "incompetent" was Frederick Wolf. Harry D. Pratt conference presentation; Sherwood F. Moran to Ursul Moran, 22 September, 7 October 1942, Moran family papers, Madison, WI; Stone interview; Rex Alan Smith and Gerald Meehl, *Pacific Legacy* (New York: Abbeville Press, 2002), 96.
20. Sherwood F. Moran to Ursul Moran, 12 August, 22 September, 31 October 1942, Moran family papers, Madison, WI.
21. Boardman oral history, 6. Harry Pratt to George Barr, 16 November 1942, Harry D. Pratt papers, UCBL; Moran to unknown, 1943, Moran family papers, Madison, WI.
22. Eugene Boardman and John C. Pelzel memorandum, 28 March 1943, Dull papers, MCU; Boardman was willing to consign army-trained Japanese Americans to document translating because he felt they "weren't much good" as interpreters. The Second Division language officers and enlisted interpreters at this time were Eugene Boardman, John C. Pelzel, Elmer Stone, and Harry D. Pratt.
23. Eugene to Betty Gregg, 15 June, 15 July, 1943, Gregg papers; Stone interview. For details of the prisoner uprising at the Featherston camp, see Ian McGibbon, ed., *The Oxford Companion to New Zealand Military History* (Auckland: Oxford University Press, 2000), 164; and Hata Ikuhiko, *Nihonjin horyo* [Japanese Prisoners of War], vol. 1 (Tokyo: Hara shobo, 1998), 222–41. Boardman oral history, 12.
24. Sherwood F. Moran Report on the Activities and Organization of the Japanese Interpreters Sub-Section (1 January 1943–1 February 1944), Moran papers, MCU; Gregg biographical sketch, Eugene to Betty Gregg, 15 February 1944, Gregg papers.

25. John B Hasbrouck to Pineau, 12 December 1992, 25 April 1993, file 13, box 12, Pineau papers; Gregg to Betty Gregg, 4 December 1943, Gregg papers; Sherwood F. Moran to Ursul Moran, 10 December 1943, Moran family papers, Madison, WI.
26. Gordon L. Rottman, *World War II Pacific Island Guide: A Geo-Military Study* (Westport, CT: Greenwood Press, 2002), 184–86, 188; Bernard C. Nalty, *Cape Gloucester: The Green Inferno* (Washington, DC: Marine Corps Historical Center, 1994), 2, 4, 13–24; Sherwood F. Moran to Ursul Moran, 4, 6 January 1944, Moran family papers, Madison, WI; Eugene to Betty Gregg, 27 November 1943, 4 February 1944, Gregg papers.
27. Hackett interview; Moran, Interrogation of Prisoners of War segment of Intelligence Annex to General Report on the Cape Gloucester Operation, 26 December 1943 to 18 February 1944, Moran papers, MCU.
28. Interrogation reports, New Britain, especially #109, 7 January; #116–17, 15 January; #122, 7 February; and #179, 27 February 1944, New Britain (Cape Gloucester), Marine Corps Geographic file, Box 239, RG 127, NA.
29. Moran Report; Interrogation of Prisoners of War, Cape Gloucester Intelligence Annex; Gregg to Betty Gregg, 15 January, 16, 21 February, 18 March 1944, Gregg papers. These officers also honed their skills by interviewing nearly three hundred Japanese prisoners after the fighting stopped. Interrogation report, New Britain, folders 1-2, box 239, RG 127, NA.
30. Rottman, *World War II Pacific Island Guide*, 135–40; Jon T. Hofman, *From Makin to Bougainville* (Washington, DC: Marine Corps Historical Center, 1993), 36–37.
31. Capt. Harold J. Noble, the senior Third Division interpreter, was a veteran of the Camp Elliott language school rather than combat. Capt. John Merrill, who might have played a role analogous to Gene Gregg's, was twice detached from the Third Division to serve alongside New Zealand forces taking the Treasury Islands and Green [Nissan] Island. Merrill oral history, 28, 46–54; Vincent and Slaughter interviews; Moran Personal Notation to foregoing Report on Interrogation of POW, Intelligence Annex to General Report on the Cape Gloucester Operation, 26 December 1943 to 18 February 1944, Moran papers, MCU.
32. Rottman, *World War II Pacific Island Guide*, 1: 140–41; Kinsman, Thompson, Slaughter and Spiegel interviews; Spiegel to family, 26 February 1944, in Spiegel, "War Years and Better Days," 41, 152; Slaughter interview.
33. Spiegel interview. The "souvenir mania" term appears in Smith and Meehl, *Pacific Legacy*, 96.
34. Spiegel, "War Years and Better Days," 39.
35. Thompson interview.
36. Glen Slaughter conference presentation; Spiegel to family 29 December

1943, in Spiegel, "War Years and Better Days," 151; Thompson interview; Vincent, "Semper Fi," 26.

37. Cross and Luthy interviews; Cross, *Born a Foreigner*, 47–48.
38. Rich, Luthy, and Cross interviews. Four men—Gerald Hoeck, Donald Redlin, Thomas C. Smith, and Dan S. Williams—were assigned to division headquarters. Charles T. Cross and David L. Anderson went to the 23rd regiment; William Brown and Charles Bennett Johnson to the 24th; and John Rich and Walter Rockler to the 25th.
39. Rottman, *World War II Pacific Island Guide*, 355, 361–62; Luthy interview.
40. Dan S. Williams, Luthy, and Rich interviews.
41. Luthy, Dan S. Williams, and Cross interviews; Cross, *Born a Foreigner*, 47; Dan S. Williams, "Recollections of the Navy's WWII Japanese Language School and Duty as Translator with Marines," *The SASA [Shanghai American School Association] News* (Spring 2001), 5; Prados, *Combined Fleet Decoded*, 531–32; JICPOA item 7265, Japanese atrocities folder, file Japan 1939–46, POW Camps and Atrocities, box 121, ONI Monograph files, RG 38, NA.
42. Rottman, reports ninety-one prisoners taken on Kwajalein, but that number appears to have been conflated by the number of captives taken in the Eniwetok operation; Rottman, *World War II Pacific Island Guide*, 362, 368–69. Rich, Luthy interviews; n.d., D-2 Section, 4th Marine Division Summary of POW interrogation information gathered during Flintlock operation, 1944, box 213; Commanding Officer, 25th Marines to Commanding General, 4th Marine, 12 March 1944, forwarding Report of Interrogation of Japanese Prisoners of War as of 1–8 March 1944, aboard the USS *Electra* at sea, folder C4-1, Commanding Officer, 3rd Battalion, 25th Marines to Commanding Officer, 25th Marines, March 1944, Reports of interrogation of prisoners, file C5-1, box 224, RG 127, NA.
43. Cross, *Born a Foreigner*, 46; Cross, Rich, and Luthy interviews; Dan S. Williams, "Recollections," 5, 8.
44. Rottman, *World War II Pacific Island Guide*, 108–17, 188, 192, 336–40, 359, 362.
45. Ibid., 108–17, 138–43, 376–78, 380–82, 385–87, 390.
46. Smith and Meehl, *Pacific Legacy*, 148; Rottman, *World War II Pacific Island Guide*, 378, 382, 389; Boardman oral history, 18.
47. Rottman, *World War II Pacific Island Guide*, 378, 384; Robert F. Rogers, *Destiny's Landfall: A History of Guam* (Honolulu: University of Hawaii Press, 1995), 189–90.
48. Reed Irvine to parents, 6 September 1945, Reed Irvine papers, UCBL; Irvine interview; Irvine biographical statement, Japanese Language School 50-Year Reunion pamphlet, August 1992, folder 1, box 3, Japanese Language School Collection, UCBL.
49. Stone and Sheeks interviews; Boardman oral history, 16–17; Joseph H.

Alexander, *Utmost Savagery: The Three Days of Tarawa* (Annapolis, MD: Naval Institute Press, 1995), 237–38; Alexander, *Across the Reef: The Marine Assault of Tarawa* (Washington, DC: Marine Corps Historical Center, 1993), 50; 2nd Marine Division, D-2 periodic report Tarawa 2000, 23 November 1943; 2nd Marine Division Special Action Report, Intelligence Annex, 4 January 1944, file a7-6.2, box 27; Commanding General, 2nd Marine Division to Commandant, U.S. Marine Corps, List of POWS captured by 2nd Marine Division Tarawa from 20 November to 3 December 1943, enclosure A, 15 December 1943, file c8-1, box 36, RG 127; Harry Pratt to George Barr King, 22 January 1944, box 1, Pratt papers.

50. Cross, Sheeks, Stone, and Dan S. Williams interviews; Williams to J. Owen Zurhellen Jr., 23 April 1944, folder 4, box 2, J. Owen Zurhellen Jr. papers, UCBL.
51. Sheeks interview.
52. Rich interview; Boardman oral history, 18; Vincent, "Semper Fi," 28; Rogers, *Destiny's Landfall*, 185.
53. Glen Slaughter conference presentation; Cross and Griffith Way interviews; John A. Lorelli, *U.S. Amphibious Operations in World War II* (Annapolis, MD: Naval Institute Press, 1995), 251–52.
54. Rogers, *Destiny's Landfall*, 194.
55. Rottman, *World War II Pacific Island Guide*, 379, 384, 392; Lorelli, *U.S. Amphibious Operations*, 247.
56. Rich, Luthy, and Martin interviews; Rottman, *World War II Pacific Island Guide*, 384; Smith and Meehl, *Pacific Legacy*, 156.
57. Spiegel, "War Years and Better Days," 58, 60–61, 66; Wayne MacGregor, *Through These Portals: A Pacific War Saga* (Pullman: Washington State University Press, 2002), 73–74; Lorelli, *Amphibious Operations*, 248–50; Rogers, *Destiny's Landfall*, 192.
58. Spiegel, "War Years and Better Days," 65.
59. Lorelli, *U.S. Amphibious Operations*, 239, 241–43; Smith and Meehl, *Pacific Legacy*, 145.
60. Cross, Rich, and Sheeks interviews; Cross, *Born a Foreigner*, 41, 43.
61. Rich, Sheeks, and Dan S. Williams interviews; Annex E: Special comments, 4th Marine Division Operations Report 15 June–9 July 1944, file a 14-1, box 329, RG 127, NA; Reed Irvine to parents, 6 September 1945, Irvine papers.
62. Reed Irvine to parents, 6 September 1945, Irvine papers; Cross, *Born a Foreigner*, 50–51; Cross interview; 23rd Marine Regiment unit reports, 3–30 July 1944, box 335, RG 127.
63. Cross to parents, 21 August 1944, cited in Cross, *Born a Foreigner*, 52–53; Smith and Meehl, *Pacific Legacy*, 150; Rottman, *World War II Pacific Island Guide*, 379; Harold J. Goldberg, *D-Day in the Pacific: The Battle for Saipan* (Bloomington: University of Indiana Press, 2007), 200–202.

64. Cross, Sheeks, and Thompson interviews; 4th Marine Division Operations Reports, 24 July–1 August 1944, Annex H to Commanding General to all holders, Commanding Officer, 23rd Marine Regiment, folder A14-3, box 330, RG 127; War Diary of LCI (G) 466, 2 September 1944, cited in Lorelli, *U.S. Amphibious Operations*, 250.
65. Cross, Luthy, Rich, and Sheeks interviews; Annex E, Special comments, 4th Marine Division Operations Report 15 June–9 July 1944; Annex I: Commanding Officer, 24th Marine Regiment to Commanding General, 4th Mar-ine Division, Final Report on Saipan, 28 August 1944, Commanding Officer; 24th Marine Regiment to Commanding General, 4th Marine Division, Final Report on Tinian Operation 30 August 1944, Regimental Combat Team 23 Special Action Report Forager Phase 1 Saipan, 6 September 1944, file a14-1, box 329; Special Action Report, 19 August 1944, folder A18-1.5, box 57, RG 127, NA.
66. Sheeks interview; Sheeks, "Civilians on Saipan," *Far Eastern Survey* (9 May 1945), 112; Smith and Meehl, *Pacific Legacy*, 150.
67. Rottman, *World War II Pacific Island Guide*, 379.
68. Ibid., 426; Robert S. Burrell, "Breaking the Cycle of Iwo Jima Mythology: A Strategic Study of Operation Detachment," *Journal of Military History* 68 (October 2004): 1162; Robert S. Burrell, *The Ghosts of Iwo Jima* (College Station: Texas A&M University Press, 2006), 83.
69. Brayshay interview; Seidensticker, *Tokyo Central*, 25–28.
70. Merrill oral history, 48, 55–56; Tom Bartlett, "Two Linguists," *Leatherneck* (February 1986): 28; Halsey Wilbur memoir, chap. 12, p. 2, 5, Halsey F. Wilbur papers, UCBL; White interview.
71. July 1945 Headquarters 5th Marine Division to Commanding General V Amphibious Corps, 14 July 1945, folder 9, box 25, RG 127; Zurhellen memorandum for Lieutenant Colonel Roll, 13 July 1944, Zurhellen papers.
72. John B. Hasbrouck to William Hudson, 12 December 1992, file 12, box 13, Pineau papers; 1st Marine Division Special Action Report Palau Operation, Annex B, included in CGFMF Pac to Commandant, USMC, 20 April 1945, folder AS-1, box 298, RG 127, NA.
73. Seidensticker, *Tokyo Central*, 31–32; Bertraim A. Yaffe, *Fragments of War: A Marine's Personal Journey* (Annapolis, MD: Naval Institute Press, 1999), 95; Cross, *Born a Foreigner*, 56–57; Cross and Luthy interviews.
74. Cross, White, and Dan S. Williams interviews; Vincent, "Semper Fi," 37.
75. Cross interview; U.S. Marine Corps Camerman's report, Photo Section, 5th Marine Division, 8 March 1945, folder 9, box 25, RG 127, NA; John J. Craig and Lawrence C. Vincent draft article, "Our Japanese 'Ally'," box 1, Vincent papers.
76. Smith and Meehl, *Pacific Legacy*, 226, 228; Seidensticker, *Tokyo Central*, 33.

Chapter 4: Navy Distant Listeners

1. Weekly reports, Navy Unit, Tracy, California to Special Activities Branch, ONI, 28 July, 18, 25 August 1943, Records of the Special Activities Branch, ONI, (Op-16-Z) Office of Chief of Naval Operations, box 13, RG 38, NA; Lionel Casson to Roger Pineau, 28 September 1992, Willis papers; Willis interview.
2. Casson to Pineau, 28 September 1992, Willis papers; Willis interview. George Nace, the first to arrive, stayed on in New Caledonia for another year after the others left. Nace to Pineau, 3 March 1980, file 1, box 19, Pineau papers.
3. Hummel diary, 8, 10 June, 11 September 1942.
4. McCollum oral history, 375.
5. Ellis M. Zacharias, with Ladislas Farago, *Secret Missions: The Story of an Intelligence Officer* (Annapolis, MD: Naval Institute Press, 2003), 282. First published 1946 by G. P. Putnam.
6. David Brinkley, *Washington Goes to War* (New York: Ballantine Books, 1988), vii; poet Ernest Kroll, quoted in Frank Tucker to Roger Pineau, 2 June 1987, folder 6, box 28, Pineau papers. A later graduate, Ross Ingersoll, may have echoed these men's feelings when he described his assignment to Washington rather than Pearl Harbor or sea duty as "a bitter blow." Ross Ingersoll and Ball interviews.
7. Martin and Newell interviews.
8. Op-20-GZ stands for the Office of Chief of Naval Operations, 20th Division of the Office of Naval Communications, GZ Section. Within p-20-G, separate sections dealt with different phases of the "breaking" process. Op-20-GX was responsible for interception; Op-20-GY, for cryptanalysis and code recovery; and Op-20-GZ, for translation; Edward Van Der Rhoer, *Deadly Magic: A Personal Account of Communications Intelligence in World War II in the Pacific* (New York: Scribner's, 1978), 49.
9. Technically, the task of the Japanese-language officers was to "recover," not "break," codes. The difference between the two processes is explained later. I have retained the "breaker" terminology because it is that most commonly used those who are not specialists in cryptography.
10. "Interview with Walter Nichols," 10 October 1989, Foreign Affairs Oral History Collection of the Association for Diplomatic Studies and Training, accessible at http://memory.loc.gov/ammem/collections/diplomacy/index.html; Martin interview; Rear Adm. Earl E. Stone oral history interview, 9 February 1983, NSA OH03-83, National Cryptological Museum, Fort Meade, MD; Van Der Rhoer, *Deadly Magic*, 83.
11. Wyman H. Packard, *A Century of U.S. Naval Intelligence* (Washington, DC: Department of the Navy, 1994), 369; *USNARA*, 1997 edition, 162; Prados, *Combined Fleet Decoded*, 267. Kramer had little to do with Op-20-GZ because he was preoccupied with the subunit that focused on the Japanese diplomatic

code and still brooding over allegations that he had mishandled the final "winds" message that indicated the direction of the Japanese navy's attack on Pearl Harbor. Robert Louis Benson, *A History of U.S. Communications Intelligence during World War II: Policy and Administration* (Fort Meade, MD: NSA Center for Cryptological History, 1997), 45.

12. Capt. Prescott Currier, USN (Ret.) National Security Agency interview, February 1972, NSA OH 02-72, 68, 104, National Cryptological Museum Library, Fort Meade, MD; Van Der Rhoer, *Deadly Magic*, 50–51, 73–79.
13. Mallory, Newell interviews; Frank H. Tucker to Pineau, 2 June 1987, Frank H. Tucker papers, Colorado Springs, CO.
14. David F. Anthony to Roger Pineau, 16 September 1993, David F. Anthony papers, UCBL; Currier oral history, 89–90; Van Der Rhoer, *Deadly Magic*, 53–54.
15. McCollum oral history, 275–77; Prados, *Combined Fleet Decoded*, 80; Roland H. Worth Jr., *Secret Allies in the Pacific: Covert Intelligence and Code-Breaking Prior to the Attack on Pearl Harbor* (Jefferson, NC: McFarland, 2001), 28–29; Benson, *History of U.S. Communications Intelligence*, 46.
16. Michael Smith, *The Emperor's Codes: The Breaking of Japan's Secret Ciphers* (New York: Arcade Publishing, 2001), 59–60; Sherwood R. Moran conference presentation, Bridge to the Rising Sun Conference April 2000, Claremont, CA.
17. Mallory, Myers, and Newell interviews.
18. Anthony to Pineau, 16 September 1993, Anthony papers; Myers interview; Van Der Rhoer, *Deadly Magic*, 81, 156–58.
19. Ball, Mallory, and Newell interviews.
20. Ball and Mallory interviews; Currier NSA oral history, 102. UCSOL, 30–32. James V. Martin Jr. details the shift of one group of Boulder men from Washington to Pearl Harbor; June 1945 journal, in Betty Martin to David Anthony 14 July 1945, Anthony papers.
21. McCollum oral history, 330, 358; "Report of Intelligence Activities in the Pacific Ocean Areas," Pearl Harbor, T.H.: 15 October 1945, 3; folder 645 JICPOA, Box 1 (formerly box 5876) Records of Naval Operating Forces, RG 313, NA. This source will hereinafter be cited as JICPOA History.
22. McCollum oral history, 359–72; Edwin T. Layton, *"And I Was There": Pearl Harbor and Midway—Breaking the Secrets* (New York: Morrow, 1985), 465; W. Jasper Holmes, *Double-Edged Secrets: U.S. Naval Intelligence Operations in the Pacific during World War II* (Annapolis, MD: Naval Institute, 1979), 89–90.
23. JICPOA History, 3; Prados, *Combined Fleet Decoded*, 408; author's calculation of distribution of Berkeley and February 1943 Boulder graduating class; Suttles interview; "Translation Section of the Joint Intelligence Center Pacific Ocean Area," 1945, file 26, box 3, Pineau papers. This source will hereinafter be cited as TSH; Frank L. Turner to Roger and Maxine Pineau, 28 February 1943, file 7, box 28, Pineau papers.

24. Prados, *Combined Fleet Decoded*, 411; Chester S. Chard to Roger Pineau, 20 November 1987, file 13, box 9; John Harrison to Pineau, 4 April 1984, file 13, box 10; Frank Roegge to Roger Pineau, file 22, box 19, Pineau papers. Admiral Nimitz's assistant chief of staff for intelligence shared the Japanese-language officers low estimate of Kramer. Layton, "*And I Was There*," 478.
25. TSH, 2; Harrison to Pineau, 4 April 1984, Pineau papers; Keene, *On Familiar Terms*. 34.
26. John S. Robinson to parents, September 1945, box 33, John S. Robinson Jr. papers, Special Collections, University of Washington Library (UWL), Seattle; Wilvan van Campen to author, 1 August, 10 September 2005; Burd interview; John A. Harrison to Roger Pineau, 29 January 1981, file 13, box 10; Frank Roegge to Roger Pineau, 31 March 1980, file 22, box 19, Otis Cary to Roger Pineau, 24 September 1984, file 9, box 8; Frank L. Turner to Roger Pineau, 3 May 1976, file 7, box 26, Pineau papers. William Amos and Lawrence A. Olson also shifted to FRUPAC. John Ashmead and Richard A. "Dick" Miller joined DeBary. Keene, *On Familiar Terms*, 29–30.
27. UCSOL, 15; JICPOA History, 5, 8, 40; Benson, *History of U.S. Communications Intelligence*, 82–83; TSH, 5; Muheim, Riccio, and Hammond Rolph interviews; Henry F. May, *Coming to Terms: A Study in Memory and History* (Berkeley: University of California Press, 1987), 277–78; Boller to parents 20 September, 12, 22 November 1943, Boller papers; James Durbin to parents, 2 March 1944, Durbin papers; William Michael Weil, 1 May 1946 Record of Separation from U.S. Naval Service, Weil papers, Jewish Historical Society of Denver, Denver, CO.
28. JICPOA History, 5; UCSOL, 27; Jeffrey M. Moore, *Spies for Nimitz: Joint Military Intelligence in the Pacific War* (Annapolis, MD: Naval Institute Press, 2004), 14–15; Mark Royden Winchell, "*Too Good to Be True*": *The Life and Work of Leslie Fiedler* (Columbia: University of Missouri Press, 2002), 39.
29. *USNARA, 1845–1981*, 239; Robinson to parents, September 1945, UWL; Robert Thornton, May 2004 memoir, Thornton papers; Howard, Boorman, "Pirandello Revisited: Eight Decades in Search of a Scenario: Part 3: The Great Escape (1943–1946)," unpublished memoir, 54 (I am grateful to Mary Lou and D. Norton Williams for making a copy of Boorman's memoir available); Wendell Furnas, 31 July 1999 interview; Chester, Karr, and Muheim interviews.
30. JICPOA History, 40–41; Suttles and Muheim interviews; Z Section Routing Slip A, 15 September 1944, William C. Sigerson papers, UCBL; Boorman, "Pirandello Revisited," 54; Harold G. Wren, "Memoir of a Japanese Language Office," *Naval Intelligence Professional*, 8, Harold G. Wren papers, UCBL.
31. Dornheim memoir, Arthur R. Dornheim papers, UCBL; Boorman, "Pirandello Revisited," 54–55; Karr interview.

32. Ainsworth interview; Keene, *On Familiar Terms*, 32–33; Charles Hamilton to David Hays, n.d., e-mail, Charles Hamilton papers, UCBL.
33. Wilvan Van Campen to author, 1 August 2005; Beth Bailey and David Farber, *The First Strange Place: The Alchemy of Race and Sex in World War II Hawaii* (New York: Free Press, 1992); Amos to Roegge, 20 June 2000,William H. Amos papers, UCBL; Dornheim memoir, Dornheim papers; Roegge interview.
34. Bailey and Farber, *The First Strange Place*, 116–20, 126-28; Muheim interview; Kimball memoir, in Spencer L. Kimball papers, UCBL.
35. Boller and Furnas joint interview, 27 December 2005; Amos to Roegge, 20 June 2000, Amos papers; Arthur R. Kruckeberg 2002 memoir, Arthur R. Kruckeberg papers, UCLB; Keene, *Chronicles of My Life: An American in the Heart of Japan* (New York: Columbia University Press, 2008), 42; Kimball memoir, in Kimball papers; Orville K. Lefko to David Hays, 10 March 2001, box 1, Orville K. Lefko papers, UCBL; McLendon obituary, *Los Angeles Times*, 16 September 1968.
36. Furnas interview, with Mori Futoshi, 15 July 2005; Thornton, *Snafu!*, 10, Thornton papers; John Ashmead, *The Mountain and the Feather* (New York: Popular Library, 1962); Robinson to parents, 26 January 1944, Robinson papers.
37. *Aloha JICPOA*, songbook compiled February 1945, 13, 16, box 1, Lawrence A. Seymour papers, UCBL.
38. Wilvan Van Campen to author, 10 September 2005; John S. Robinson to parents, 2 May 1944, Robinson papers; Chester interview.
39. Otis Cary to Pineau, 24 September 1981, file 9, box 8, Pineau papers; Cary interview by Loureiro and Gibney; Keene, *On Familiar Terms*, 25. The additional language officers were William Theodore "Ted" de Bary, John Harrison, Richard "Dick" Miller, John Ashmead, and Wilvan Van Campen. Harrison to Pineau, 4 April 1984, file 13, box 10, Pineau papers; Van Campen to author, 10 September 2005.
40. Keene to mother, 9 May 1943, box 1, Donald Keene papers, UCBL.
41. Keene, *On Familiar Terms*, 26–29; Cary to Pineau, 24 September 1981, file 9, box 8, Pineau papers; Fern Chandonnet, ed., *Alaska at War, 1941–1945: The Forgotten War Remembered* (Anchorage: The Alaska at War Committee, 1995), 85; Rottman, *World War II Pacific Island Guide*, 457–58.
42. Cary to Pineau, 24 September 1981, file 9, box 8, Pineau papers.
43. H. P. Willmott, *The War with Japan: The Period of Balance May 1942–October 1943* (Wilmington, DE: Scholarly Resources, 2002), 164; Brian Garfield, *The Thousand-Mile War: World War II in Alaska and the Aleutians* (Fairbanks: University of Alaska Press, 1995), 369–72; Karl Kaoru Kasukabe, "The Escape of The Japanese Garrison from Kiska," in Chandonnet, 121–23; Van Campen to author, 10 September 2005; Cary interview by Loureiro and Gibney; Harrison to Pineau, 4 April 1984, Pineau papers; Keene, *On Familiar Terms*, 32.

44. Commander Task Force (CTF) 51 to Ens. Donald L. Keene, n.d., Commendation for performance of duty in occupation of Attu, Keene papers; Keene, *On Familiar Terms*, 32; Keene, *Chronicles of My Life*, 39–41; Cary to Pineau, 24 September 1981, file 9, box 8, Pineau papers; Ashmead provides a thinly veiled fictional account of his Aleutian experiences in *The Mountain and the Feather*, 103–21.
45. TSH, 6; Frank L. Turner to Roger Pineau, 3 May 1976, file 7, box 26, Pineau papers; Rottman, *World War II Pacific Island Guide*, 338–41; Holmes, *Double-Edged Secrets*, 147–51.
46. Suttles interview; Wayne Suttles, Harry L. McMasters, and Donald M. Allen constituted the JICPOA language officer team for the Kwajalein operation.
47. Holmes, *Double-Edged Secrets*, 155, 163; Suttles interview.
48. JICPOA History, 41; TSH, 3; Van Campen to author, 10 September 2005; Cary, Dornheim, Martin, and Riccio interviews.
49. Furnas presentation, Bridge to the Rising Sun Conference, 7 April 2000; Martin and Dornheim interviews; Dornheim to parents, 5 August 1944. Dornheim papers, Bethesda, MD. Martin got the nickname "Jish" which was short for the Japanese word *jisshin*, meaning earthquake, because he was born in Japan the day after the great Kantō temblor of 1923.
50. Van Campen to author, 10 September 2005; Furnas presentation, Bridge to the Rising Sun Conference, 7 April 2000.
51. Furnas to Pineau, 6 September 1991, file 23, box 12, Pineau papers; JICPOA History, 41–44.
52. Griffith Way interview; Rottman outlines the debate between Admiral Turner and Lt. Gen. Howland "Howlin' Mad" Smith over the landing site on Tinian, *World War II Pacific Island Guide*, 382–84. Way's was one of a dozen such discoveries of Japanese documents that, together with information derived from POWs on Saipan, provided superb preinvasion intelligence on Tinian. Moore, *Spies for Nimitz*, 138–39. In June 2006 I visited Tinian and was astounded to find that I could easily walk the width of one of the landing beaches in less than three minutes.
53. JICPOA History, 45; Cary to Pineau, 24 September 1981, file 9, box 8, Pineau papers; Casson interview; Kenneth Lamott, "Memoirs of a Brainwasher," *Harpers* 212 (June 1956), 73–74; Christine Nasso, ed., *Contemporary Authors*, vol. 25–28 (Detroit: Gale Research, 1977), 409.
54. The number of prisoners taken in the Marianas operations remains imprecise because counting on Tinian mixed combatants and civilians. I have also excluded from the count nearly 950 Koreans taken prisoner. Rottman, *World War II Pacific Island Guide*, 329, 384, 392; Dornheim to parents, 3 September 1944, Dornheim papers, Bethesda, MD; Dornheim interview.
55. Underwood interview with Gibney; Dornheim interview.

56. Kawakami Tei, "*Enjeru no tora*" [Tiger Angel] *Sekai no ugoki* [World Events] (December 1950), 28–29, in Otis Cary papers, Oakland, CA; Dornheim interview.
57. Cary to Pineau, file 9, box 8, Pineau papers; Griffith Way interview; Dornheim broadened his critique by drawing on conversations with C. Alexander "Sasha" Sims and Wilvan VanCampen; Dornheim, *Recommendations for the Future Use of Japanese Language Personnel*, Dornheim papers, Bethesda, MD.
58. Van Campen to author, 10 September 2005; Cary to Pineau, 24 September 1981, file 9, box 8, Pineau papers; *JICLOG* (JICPOA in-house newspaper) [February 1945], Dornheim papers, Bethesda, MD; Rottman, *World War II Pacific Island Guide*, 407–8; Muheim, Willis, and Underwood interviews; Gibney autobiographical fragment, Frank B. Gibney papers, Santa Barbara, CA.
59. Sheridan Sims to author, 22 August 2004; William W. Burd to Pineau, 12 May 1980, Burd papers; Burd interview. Burd, for example, served on five different carriers and took part in nine raids or operations.
60. The three longest-serving and most experienced RIU officers were Ernest Beath, William W. Burd, and C. A. "Sandy" Sims. Charles Alexander Sims Naval Record, and Table of RIU Activities, Charles A Sims file 1, box 26, Pineau papers.
61. Pineau to Burd, 1 July 1987, Burd papers; Wright oral history; Forrest R. Biard memoir in *Cryptolog* 3 (n.d.), the newsletter of the Navy Cryptological Veterans Association; Holmes, *Double-Edged Secrets*, 57; Ernest B. Beath, "Radio Intelligence in Combat," *Naval Security Group Bulletin* (August 1978), 16–19; Sheridan Sims to author, 22 August 2004.
62. Burd to Pineau, 12 May 1980, 13 July 1987, Burd papers. Those awarded the Bronze Star included Beath and Sims. Burd was nominated for that award, as Beath was for a Silver Star, but neither received such. The number of RIU linguists remains imprecise. Roger Pineau found fourteen; Slesnick and Slesnick, *Kanji and Codes*, 136, reported that there were twenty-one. Captain Hindmarsh included them in the approximately sixty naval Japanese-language officers assigned to sea duty with the fleet in his 1949 *Words at War* report, folder 5, box 2, Seymour papers.
63. List of Officer and Enlisted Personnel Who Have Served with U.S. Naval Group China, NARA printouts, box 47, Records of U.S. Naval Group China and Vice Adm. Milton E. Miles 1942–57, RG 38, NA, Chief of Naval Operations Papers, NHC; Harned Hoose materials, file 19, box 13, Pineau papers; Houghton B. Freeman to Pineau, 19 March 1984, file 21, box 12, Pineau papers; Nancy Smith, "The Freeman Orientation," Mansfield Freeman Center for East Asian Studies, Wesleyan University, at http://www.wesleyan.edu/east/mansfieldf/history/freeman5_buck.html (May 2008); T. Howell Breece

memoir, T. Howell Breece papers, UCBL; Wald interview. The exact number of war-trained naval Japanese linguists who served in China remains unclear.

64. Breece memoir, Breece papers.
65. Curts interview.
66. ATIS Progress Report, 14 September 1944, box 38, Assistant Chief of Staff, G-2 Intelligence, Historical Studies 1918–50, RG 319, NA.
67. Curts, Ikle, Kramer, and Ward interviews; Ward to John W. Hall, 5 April 1983, box 21, Robert E. Ward papers, Hoover Institution, Stanford, CA.
68. Slesnick and Slesnick, *Kanji and Codes*, 140; Fabian oral history; Curts interview; McCollum oral history, 377, 547–49; Alan Harris Bath, *Tracking the Axis Enemy: The Triumph of Anglo-American Naval Intelligence* (Lawrence: University Press of Kansas, 1998), 197–98.
69. Philip Low Bridgham to fiancée, 23 September, 8 October 1944, 10 January, 8 March 1945, box 1, Phillip Low Bridgham papers, UCBL; Robert G. Shedd to Pineau, 20 February 1980, box 25, file 17, Maurice Hellner to Pineau, 7 May 1976, file 17, box 13, Pineau papers.
70. McCollum oral history, 552–53; Ashmead to Marion Levy, 4, 8 November, file 5, box 7, Marion Levy papers, UCBL; Robert Wade's duties with the Army's X Corps paralleled Ashmead's service with the XXIV Division. Robert H. B. Wade to David Hays, 20 July 1980, Robert H. B. Wade papers, UCBL; Curts interview.
71. McCollum oral history 552–53; Walter F. Snyder to Pineau, 21 July 1980, file 10, box 26; Gordon Wattles to Pineau, 11 June 1980, file 23, box 28; Richard B. Finn 1943–46 naval career summary, file 9, box 12, Pineau papers; Mary Ryder to Cynthia, n.d., Frank G. Ryder papers, UCBL.
72. GHQ (General Headquarters), FEC (Far East Command), MIS (Military Intelligence Service), General Staff, Operations of the Allied Translator and Interpreter Section GHQ, SWPA(Southwest Pacific Area), Volume V Intelligence Series (Tokyo: 12 July 1948), 14, Section 2, box 686. RG 94, NA; Prados, *Combined Fleet Decoded*, 698–99; Hammond Rolph 26 April 2000 interview; Curts interview.
73. Packard, *Century of U.S. Naval Intelligence*, 137–38; chart of Boulder WAVE graduates, prepared for 1993 Boulder WAVE reunion, in possession of Irene Slaninka Thiel; Tucker and Ross Ingersoll interviews.
74. Susan H. Godson, *Serving Proudly: A History of Women in the U.S. Navy* (Annapolis, MD: Naval Institute Press, 2001), 109–12, 117–18; Patricia O'Sullivan Way, Ruth Webb Sigerson, Daphne Shaw Stegmeier, Betty Billett Levine, and Irene Slaninka Thiel interviews; Anne Grilk King conference remarks.
75. Billett Levine, Mayer, and Tucker interviews; Blanche Belitz, Kathryn Hoeriger Clauset, and Nancy Pearce Heimbold WAVE 1993 reunion statements, file 1, box 5, Pineau papers.

76. Thiel and Mayer interviews. Anne Grilk King and Sam King, the one married couple among the translators working in the same unit in Washington were advised not to spend too much time together during coffee breaks lest they arouse the jealousy of their single coworkers. Samuel King conference remarks.
77. Billett Levine and Stegmeier interviews.
78. UCSOL, 24–30.

Chapter 5: Warriors Transformed

1. Roger Fleming Hackett biography, *Who's Who in America, 2000* (Detroit: Gale Publishing, 2000), 1333; *New York Times* 7 October 1993, file 5, box 13, Pineau papers.
2. George Feifer, *Tennozan: The Battle of Okinawa and the Atomic Bomb* (New York: Ticknor and Fields, 1992), 76–77; Benis M. Frank and Henry I. Shaw Jr., *Victory and Occupation: History of U.S. Marine Corps Operations in World War II* (Washington, DC: Historical Branch, G-3 Division, Headquarters, U.S. Marine Corps, 1968), 72; Smith and Meehl, *Pacific Legacy*, 260. The term "L-Day" was used for Okinawa to avoid confusion with D-day on Iwo Jima because the invasion of the former island was expected to occur less than a month after that of the latter.
3. Arnold G. Fisch Jr., *Military Government in the Ryukyu Islands 1945–1950* (Washington, DC: Center of Military History, United States Army, 1988), 35–38; Feiffer, *Tennozan*, 88–93; Yahara Hiromichi, *The Battle for Okinawa.* Roger Pineau and Uehara Masatoshi, trans. (New York: Wiley, 1995), xi–xxi; Translation 145, 9 June 1945 of 1 April Proclamation, file 312 correspondence, Headquarters 10th Army, G-2 section, box 56, RG 338 NA.
4. Spector, *Eagle against the Sun*, 532–33; Rottman, *World War II Pacific Island Guide*, 433; Moore, *Spies for Nimitz*, 202–3; Suttles interview.
5. Burd and Suttles interviews; Otis Cary, *War-Wasted Asia: Letters: Letters, 1945–1946* (Tokyo and New York: Kodansha, 1975), 13–14; James M. Jefferson memoir, in the possession of Brad Jefferson, Fruita, CO.
6. Prados, *Combined Fleet Decoded*, 620–23; 707–8; *Fighting Facts 1: Why Japan Struck* (2 October 1944), Gibney papers.
7. Keene, *On Familiar Terms,* 39, 42–43.
8. Daniel D. Karasik to parents, 4 April 1945, Daniel D. Karasik papers, Bethesda, MD; Keene, *On Familiar Terms*, 43; Rottman, *World War II Pacific Island Guide*, 436–38; Thomas W. Zeiler, *Unconditional Defeat: Japan, America, and the End of World War II* (Wilmington, DE: Scholarly Resources, 2004), 163–64; Keene, *On Familiar Terms*, 43.
9. Moore, *Spies for Nimitz*, 205–7; Frank and Shaw, *Victory and Occupation*, 172–73; Nelson interview.
10. Brayshay and Spiegel interviews; Spiegel, "War Years and Better Days," 79.

11. Spiegel, "War Years and Better Days," 83–84; Jefferson memoir, Jefferson papers, Fruita, CO; Jefferson interview.
12. Smith and Meehl, *Pacific Legacy*, 255–56; Zeiler, *Unconditional Defeat*, 169–70; Spiegel, "War Years and Better Days," 92–97; Eugene Sledge, *With the Old Breed at Peleliu and Okinawa* (New York: Oxford University Press, 1981), 205–80.
13. Brayshay, Jefferson, and Nelson interviews; Karasik to parents, 6, 15 April 1945, Karasik papers.
14. Karasik to parents, 4, 12, April 1945, Karasik papers.
15. Jefferson interview; Jefferson memoir, Jefferson papers. Jefferson believed that his run-in with the regiment's intelligence officer explained his "banishment" to Guam to teach enlisted Marines Japanese after the Okinawa fighting stopped.
16. Feiffer, *Tennozan*, 424, 448, 452.
17. U.S. Army XXIV Corps, G-2 periodic reports, 16 April–7 May 1945, Gibney papers; G-2 periodic report, U.S. Army XXIV Corps, 1 May, copy provided by Allen Meyer, Chicago, IL; Okinawa taimuzu sha, ed., *Shomin ga tsuzuru: Okinawa sengo seikatsu shi* [*The Common People Write: A History of Postwar Okinawan Life*] (Naha: Okinawa taimuzu sha, 1998), 13–22.
18. 6th Marine Division Special Action Report, Phase III Okinawa Operation, 30 June 1945, files 7–8, box 24, RG 127, NA; Glen Slaughter to Uehara Masatoshi, 12 May 1989, Glen K. Slaughter papers, Santa Fe, NM.
19. Slaughter to Uehara, 12 May 1989, Slaughter papers; Nelson to author, 8 August 2004; Glenn Nelson translation of Uehara 1 July 1989 *Okinawa taimuzu* article, Slaughter papers; Slaughter conference remarks, 7 April 2000; Slaughter interview.
20. Frank and Shaw, *Victory and Occupation*, 323; Slaughter memoir, 98, Slaughter papers.
21. Slaughter to Uehara, 12 March 1989, Slaughter papers; Nelson translation of Uehara *Okinawa taimuzu* article, 4 July 1989; Slaughter to author, 27 June 2004.
22. Frank and Shaw, 121–22; "Searching Caves: A Summary of Techniques Developed at Okinawa, CINCPAC-CINCPOA Bulletin No. 189-45, "15 August 1945, folder 189-45, box 137, Japanese Sources Collection, COA, NHC; Feiffer, *Tennozan*, 415–18.
23. Keene, *On Familiar Terms*, 46; Spiegel interview; Spiegel, "War Years and Better Days," 90–92, 100–101; Feiffer, *Tennozan*, 443.
24. Lt. (jg) William H. Allman report to Captain Larsen on search of Okinawa Area Naval Base Force Headquarters, 18 June 1945, 312 correspondence folder, box 56, Headquarters 10th Army G-2 Section G-2 Section, RG 338, NA; Spiegel, "War Years and Better Days," 92; Feiffer, *Tennozan*, 437.

25. Slaughter to Uehara, 12 March 1989, Slaughter papers; Uehara, *Okinawa taimuzu* articles, 6–7 July 1989.
26. Smith and Meehl, *Pacific Legacy*, 259–60; Zeiler, *Unconditional Defeat*, 171; Belote, *Typhoon of Steel*, 314–15.
27. Edgar to Shirley Whan, 12 August 1945, Edgar W. Whan papers, UCBL; Al Weissberg to Muriel Weissberg, 1 August 1945, Weissberg papers, UCBL; Frank and Shaw, *Victory and Occupation*, 368; June 1945 Morgan notes, in file: Morgan manuscripts, box 4, James T. Watkins IV papers, Hoover Institution, Stanford, CA.
28. Feiffer, *Tennozan*, 484–85, 488.
29. Brayshay interview; Solomon Levine, "The Battle of Okinawa: A Personal Memoir," *The Ryukyuanist* [*Newsletter for the International Society for Ryukyuan Studies*], no. 28 (Spring 1995), 6; Online Scope and Content Note, David Lawrence Osborn papers, Dwight D. Eisenhower Presidential Library, Abilene, KS.
30. Robert D. Thornton, *Snafu!* memoir manuscript, VII-38, box 1, Thornton papers.
31. Al Weissberg to Muriel Weissberg, 1 August 1945, box 2, Weissberg papers.
32. Gibney interview, 23 September 2000; Frank Gibney introduction to Yahara, *The Battle for Okinawa*, xx; Solomon B. Levine interview; Levine, "The Battle of Okinawa," 2–4.
33. Lt. Col. George J. Clark memorandum: "Handling and Disposition of Prisoners of War," 10 July 1945, 10th Army G-2 section file, box 56, RG 338, NA; Gibney interview, 23 September 2000; 10th Army Prisoner of War Interrogation Report # 28, 6 August; Gibney to Lt. George J Clark, 11 July; 32nd Army Operations report, 5 August 1945, Gibney papers.
34. Thornton, *Snafu!*, VII-30-33, Thornton papers; Kenneth Lamott, "Memoirs of a Brainwasher," *Harpers* 212 (June 1956), 73; Kenneth Lamott, *The Stockade* (Boston: Little Brown, 1952).
35. Thornton, *Snafu!*, VII-31-33, Thornton papers; *So What!*, May 2004 addition to *Snafu*, folder 2, box 1, Thornton papers.
36. Stillwell 2 July 1945 diary entry, in Nicholas Sarantakes, ed., *Seven Stars: The Okinawa Battle Diaries of Simon Bolivar Buckner, Jr., and Joseph Stillwell* (College Station: Texas A&M University Press, 2004), 91; Karasik interview; Karasik to Frank Gibney, 28 March 2000, in author's possession; Karasik to parents, 2 July, 15 August, 2 September 1945, Karasik papers.
37. May, *Coming to Terms*, 287–90; May interview.
38. Whan interview; USS *Winged Arrow* (AP 170) deck log, 7–22 July 1945, RG 24, NA.
39. Frank and Shaw, *Victory and Occupation*, 379; Richard B. Frank, *Downfall: The End of the Japanese Empire* (New York: Random House, 1999), 72.
40. Dorothy E. Richard, *United States Naval Administration of the Trust Territory*

of the Pacific Islands (Washington, DC: Office of the Chief of Naval Operations, Department of the Navy, 1957) 1:429; Rottman, *World War II Pacific Island Guide,* 378, 382.

41. Richard, *U.S. Naval Administration*, 1:455–59, 547–50. Martin and Stevens interviews; Warren R. Johnston biographical summary, box 1, Warren R. Johnston papers, UCBL. Other Boulder graduates on the Saipan civil affairs team included Lt. H. M. Cary and Lt. (jg) Lance LaBianca. Ensigns W. K. Etter, Euan G. Davis, and Charles Frankel, joined later by lieutenants junior grade J. D. Congleton and Bernard A. Gerow, who rounded out the Tinian team.
42. Richard, *U.S. Naval Administration*, 1:435–51, 481, 490; Norman Meller, "Saipan's Camp Susupe," Occasional Paper 42 (Honolulu: Center for Pacific Islands Studies, University of Hawaii, 1999), 2–4, 15.
43. Martin and Stevens interviews; Richard, *U.S. Naval Administration*, 1:486.
44. Martin interview; Meller, "Saipan's Camp Susupe," 43–45, 66–68, 100–101; Richard, *U.S. Naval Administration*, 1:501–27.
45. Meller, "Saipan's Camp Susupe," 18, 89; Richard, *U.S. Naval Administration*, 1:491–92; H. I. Martin, "Naval Civil Affairs Unit," in *Saipan: Oral Histories of the Pacific War*, ed. Bruce M. Petty (Jefferson, NC: McFarland and Company, 2002), 159–60.
46. Meller, "Saipan's Camp Susupe," 75; Martin, "The Navy," 159; Stevens interview.
47. Richard, *U.S. Naval Administration*, 1:533, 538, 547; Warren R. to Bobby Johnston, 15 November 1944, Johnston papers.
48. Warren R. Johnston to D. P. Cottrell, Johnston to C. E. "Bud" Barbier, both 19 April 1945, Johnston papers; *Christian Science Monitor*, 7 March 1945; *Honolulu Star-Bulletin*, 4 April 1945; H. T. Mook, *English for You and Me* (Tinian: July 1945); Mary Jean Kempner, "Protective Custody, U.S. Style: In the Pacific, Camp Churo," *Vogue*, n.d., [mid-1945], n.p.; *Brunswick, Maine Times Record*, 26 September 1985, Johnston papers; *Benzie County Record-Patriot*, Frankfort, Michigan, 4 December 1991, in possession of H. T. Mook; "Our World: Keeping School in the Marianas," *International House Quarterly* (1945), n.p., folder 4, box 7, Japanese Language School papers, UCBL; Mook interview.
49. Fisch, *Military Government in the Ryukyu Islands*, 12–14, 21–26; E. Eastman Irvine, ed., *The World Almanac 1942* (New York: New York World-Telegram, 1942), 600.
50. Hussey and Suttles interviews; Fisch, *Military Government in the Ryukyu Islands*, 14; Hanna memoir, "Planning Period," MG Government Planning folder, box 6, Watkins papers.
51. Hanna memoir, "Planning Period," Watkins papers; Fisch, *Military Government in the Ryukyu Islands*, 62; Hussey interview; Watkins diary, 24, 27 June

1945, box 22, Watkins papers; minutes of meeting of General Crist and staff officers, 15 May 1945, staff meeting minutes folder, box 4, Watkins papers.

52. Watkins to wife, 1 May 1945, letter for Okinawa II file, box 24, Watkins papers; Report on military government operations in northern Okinawa, 21 April–28 May 1945, folder 2-I-L, box 24; Lt. C. S. Ford to Commanding General, Military Government, Headquarters, Island Command, June 1945, folder 2-I-1, box 4; Watkins diary, 25, 27 June 1945, box 22, Watkins papers.
53. Deputy Commanding Officer for Military Government to Commandant Naval Operating Base, Okinawa and Chief Military Government Officer, Ryukyus, *Report of Military Government Activities for Period from 1 April 1945 to 1 July 1946,* MG monthly reports March–May 1946 folder, box 3, Watkins papers; note on Captain [Edward Lender] Woodyard 17 July 1945 remark, folder 2-I-L, box 4, Watkins papers; Fisch, *Military Government in the Ryukyu Islands*, 47–57, 72–73.
54. 1945 newspaper clipping, Brayshay scrapbook, in possession of James W. Brayshay, El Cajon, California; Scalapino interview.
55. May 1945 war diary entry, Okinawa Military Government Detachment B-5, box 1600, World War II drawer, RG 38, NA; Hussey and Suttles interviews.
56. Deputy Commanding Officer for Military Government to Commandant Naval Operating Base, Okinawa and Chief Military Government Officer, Ryukyus, *Report of Military Government Activities for Period from 1 April 1945 to 1 July 1946*, MG monthly reports March–May 1946 folder, box 3, Watkins papers; Col. C. I. Murray to all hands, 1 April 1946, first anniversary review green folder, box 6, Watkins papers; June 1945 Morgan notes, in file: Morgan manuscripts, box 4, Watkins papers; John T. Caldwell March 1993 memoir for family, box 1, John T. Caldwell papers, Hoover Institution, Stanford, CA; Hussey interview; Lt. (jg) N. G. Thorlaksson made the "we did it" comment. See Watkins diary, 29 June 1945, box 22, Watkins papers.
57. Al Weissberg to Muriel Weissberg, 21 May 1945, Weissberg papers; Edgar Whan to Shirley Whan, 22 April, 24 July 1945, Whan papers.
58. Al Weissberg to Muriel Weissberg, 26 June 1945, Weissberg papers.
59. Thornton, *Snafu!*, VII-34-35, Thornton papers; Al Weissberg to Muriel Weissberg, 1 September 1945, Weissberg papers.
60. Jefferson interview; Levine, "The Battle of Okinawa," 4–5.
61. Edgar Whan to Shirley Whan, April 1945, Whan papers.
62. Ibid.; Spiegel, "War Years and Better Days," 92–93; Thornton, *Snafu!*, VII-29, Thornton papers.

Chapter 6: Instruments of Surrender

1. Vincent, "Semper Fi," 41–42.
2. Seidensticker, *Tokyo Central*, 34; Al Weissberg to Muriel Weissberg, 10 August 1945, Weissberg papers.

3. Paul J. Sherman to Walter Wager, 30 August 1945, Paul J. Sherman papers, UCBL.
4. Siegfried Williams, Stegmeier, Mayer, Thiel interviews.
5. Newell and Hackett interviews; Burks interview; T. Howell Breece memoir, 11, Breece papers; Paul F. Boller Jr., *Memoirs of an Obscure Professor and Other Essays* (Fort Worth: Texas Christian University Press, 1992), 51; Boorman, "Pirandello Revisited," 67.
6. Al Weissberg to Muriel Weissberg, 13–14 August 1945, Weissberg papers; Rich interview; Cross, *Born a Foreigner*, 59–60; Ulrich Strauss, *The Anguish of Surrender: Japanese POWs in World War II* (Seattle: University of Washington Press, 2003), 221.
7. Ronald Spector, "After Hiroshima: Allied Military Occupations and the Fate of Japan's Empire, 1945–1947," *Journal of Military History* 69 (October 2005), 1123; Spiegel, "War Years and Better Days," 164–65; Al Weissberg to Muriel Weissberg, 14 August 1945, Weissberg papers; S. P. Kramer to Wager, 30 August 1945.
8. Sherman to Wager, 30 August 1945, Sherman papers; James Durbin to parents, 12 August 1945, Durbin papers.
9. Dorris Clayton James, *Years of MacArthur*, vol. II, *1941–1945* (Boston: Houghton Mifflin, 1975), 771–78; Michael Schaller, *Douglas MacArthur: The Far Eastern General* (New York: Oxford University Press, 1989), 117; Charles R. Smith, *Securing the Surrender: Marines in the Occupation of Japan* (Washington, DC: Marine Corps Historical Center, 1997), 1–3; Ronald H. Spector, *In the Ruins of Empire: The Japanese Surrender and the Battle for Postwar Asia* (New York: Random House, 2007), 26.
10. Spiegel, "War Years and Better Days," 104; Martin interview; Smith, *Securing the Surrender*, 8; Sherman to Wager, 30 August 45. Boulder graduates who participated in the Yokosuka landing and surrender included William Burd, Harry M. Cary, Lionel Casson, Robert W. Christy, James Durbin, Willard H. Elsbree, Richard J. Hyman, James M. Jefferson, Harris I. Jish Martin, George Nace, George Romani, Paul J. Sherman, Glen Slaughter, Hart Spiegel, and James M. Wells.
11. Martin interview; Durbin to parents, 27 August 1945, in Durbin memoir, Durbin papers; Spiegel to family 29 August 1945, in Spiegel, "War Years and Better Days," 166–67.
12. Smith, *Securing the Surrender*, 10–11; Sherman to Wager, 30 August 1945. The Yokosuka landing force was officially designated Task Force Able (Task Group 31.3) and consisted, in addition to battalions from the 4th Marine Regiment, of a marine and naval landing force made up of men in the Third Amphibious Force and a small battalion–sized British landing force of about five hundred sailors and Marines. Gordon L. Rottman, *U.S. Marine Corps World War II Order of Battle: Ground and Air Units in the Pacific War, 1939–*

1945 (Westport, CT: Greenwood Press, 2002), 155; the most comprehensive visual record of the landings and occupation of Yokosuka is found in Yokosuka shi shi hensan shitsu, ed., *Senryōka no Yokosuka: Rengōkoku gun no jōriku to sono jidai* [*Yokosuka—Under Occupation: The Landing of Allied Forces and That Era*] (Yokosuka: Yokosuka shi, Heisei 17, 2005). This book combines Japanese and U.S. Navy and Marine Corps official photographs.

13. Sherman to Wager, 30 August 1945, Sherman papers; Durbin to parents, 30 August 1945, Durbin papers; Jefferson 14 March 2000 interview; Takemiya interview; *Asahi shimbun* 2–4 July 2003; Smith, *Securing the Surrender*, 11.
14. Smith, *Securing the Surrender*, 11; Sherman to Wager, 30 August 1945, Sherman papers.
15. Burd to Pineau, 12 May 1980, Burd papers; Burd and Slaughter interviews; Sherman to Wager, 30 August 1945, Sherman papers; E. B. Potter, *Bull Halsey* (Annapolis, MD: Naval Institute Press, 1985), 353.
16. Casson interview. The five potential USS *Missouri* interpreters included Harry M. Cary, Lionel Casson, George Nace, and James M. Wells. Paul Stillwell, *Battleship Missouri: An Illustrated History* (Annapolis: Naval Institute Press, 1996), 57.
17. Stillwell, *Battleship Missouri*, 57, 67; James, *Years of MacArthur*, 2:788; Thomas T. Sakamoto, "The MIS Aboard the Battleship USS *Missouri*," in *Unsung Heroes: Military Intelligence Service Past Present Future* (Seattle: MIS-Northwest Association, 1996), 32–35; Wilvan Van Campen to author, 8 June 2005.
18. Rottman, *World War II Pacific Island Guide*, 352, 370–71; Naval Japanese Language Officers, file 4, box 4, Pineau papers; U.S. Navy Japanese/Oriental Language School Graduation List, David M. Hays and Scott E. Shaver, comp, Japanese Language School papers, UCBL; E. Richard Harris materials, file 10, box 13, Japanese Language School papers, UCBL; Navy photograph 80-G-490369, reproduced at http://www.history.navy.mil/photos/events/wwii-pac/japansur/js-10b.htm (November 2006); "First Japanese Surrender on Board USS *Levy* DE 162," at http://www.desausa.org/Stories/uss_levy_japanese_surrender.htm. (November 2006).
19. Richard, *U.S. Naval Administration*, 2:7–8; Everett Greenbaum, *The Goldenberg Who Couldn't Dance* (New York: Harcourt Brace Jovanovich, 1973), 48–50. Greenbaum was the evicted junior officer who discovered Shiga's suicide.
20. Richard, *U.S. Naval Administration*, 2:26–27; Frank and Shaw, *Victory and Occupation*, 607.
21. Kathryn Martin O'Neil et al., *Rand McNally Millennium World Atlas* (Chicago: Rand McNally, 1999), 46; Frank and Shaw, *Victory and Occupation*, 452; *USNARA*, 1981, 206; William Sigerson interview; *Honolulu Advertiser*, 21 July 2000; Meller, "Saipan's Camp Susupe," 113; Sigerson to Ruth Webb, letter, August–2 September 1945, Sigerson papers; *USNARA*, 1981, 198, 206.

22. Sigerson to Webb, letter, August–2 September 1945, Sigerson papers; *US-NARA*, 1981, 198.
23. Sigerson to Webb, letter, August–2 September 1945, Sigerson papers. Rear Admiral Whiting confiscated the Japanese sword at the Marcus surrender ceremony meant for Sergeant Furuiye, saying it was inappropriate for an enlisted man to possess such a thing. Nobuo Furuiye, "Winning the Purple Heart with the Marines on Iwo," in *MIS in the War against Japan: Personal Experiences Related at the 1993 MIS Capital Reunion*, "The Nisei Veteran: An American Patriot," Stanley L. Falk and Warren M. Tsuneishi, eds. (Washington, DC: Japanese American Veterans Association of Washington, DC, 1995), 59–60.
24. Sigerson to Webb, letter, August–2 September 1945; Frank and Shaw, *Victory and Occupation*, 453; Meller, "Saipan's Camp Susupe," 117, 120.
25. Frank and Shaw, *Victory and Occupation*, 452, 456; Meller, "Saipan's Camp Susupe," 122–25.
26. John G. Oliver biography, 1992 Boulder reunion biography, Japanese Language School papers, UCBL; Calvin W. Dunbar, "The Surrender of Rota, Marianas Islands, August 1945," unpublished memoirs, West Yellowstone, Montana: Corporal Dunbar served as interpreter in the presurrender negotiations for Rota; USS *Currier* (DE-700) in *Dictionary of American Naval Fighting Ships* entry at http://www.ibiblio.org/hyperwar/USN/ships/DE/DE-700_Currier.html (May 2008); Boller, *Memoirs of an Obscure Professor*, 45, 54–58. Boller earned his nickname on Guam where he spent many an hour in the officers' club bar. "M is-X" (unofficial history of CINCPAC Advanced Headquarters, Guam), 17, 1945 miscellaneous folder, box 3, Ardath Burks papers, Rutgers University Library, New Brunswick, NJ; Richard, *U.S. Naval Administration*, 2:29.
27. Gardiner to Pineau, 12 June 1980, file 27, box 12, Pineau papers; Richard, *U.S. Naval Administration*, 2:198; Ostensoe interview; Benson biographical sketch; 19 September 8th Section Law of Military Government Exam, folder 29; 22 November memo for 8th Section—Military Government Group Problem, folder 32, Oliver Earl Benson papers, Western Historical Collection, University of Oklahoma Library, Norman; Robert P. Falk to Jane Falk, 11, 22 January, 9 February 1945, file 2, box 12, Robert P. Falk papers, UCBL.
28. Benson field notes, 30 September 1945, Benson papers.
29. Rottman, *World War II Pacific Island Guide*, 411–14; Willard Price, *Japan's Islands of Mystery* (New York: John Day, 1944), 172; Benson field notes, 3 October 1945, Benson papers.
30. Charles Stuart Blackton, "The Surrender of the Fortress of Truk," *Pacific Historical Review* 15 (December 1946), 400–408; Dunbar, "The Surrender of Truk, Caroline Islands, August 1945," unpublished memoir. The identity of the third language officer at the presurrender negotiations remains unknown.

31. Soden photograph, 2 September 1945, http://www.ussportland.org/truk.html (May 2008); William Thomas Generous Jr., *Sweet Pea at War: History of USS* Portland *(CA-33)* (Lexington: University Press of Kentucky, 2003), 200–202; Soden 1966 obituary, necrology file, box 2, Pineau papers.
32. Rottman, *World War II Pacific Island Guide,* 411; Hal M. Friedman, *Governing the American Lake: The U.S. Defense and Administration of the Pacific, 1945–1947* (East Lansing: Michigan State University Press, 2007), 83–85; Price, *Japan's Islands of Mystery*, 101–3; Robert Falk to Jane Falk, 17 September 1945, Falk papers.
33. Robert Falk to Jane Falk, 17 September 1945; Falk to Pineau, 21 August 1992, Falk papers.
34. Richard, *U.S. Naval Administration*, 2:19, 213; Robert Falk to Jane Falk, 3 October, 7 November 1945, Falk papers.
35. Robert Falk to Jane Falk, 21–22 September, 8 October 1945, Falk papers.
36. Benson biographical sketch, Benson papers; Gardiner to Pineau, 9 June 1980, file 12, box 27, Pineau papers.
37. An LCVP is a landing craft, vehicle and personnel.
38. Benson field notes, 3–6 October 1945, Benson papers; Frank and Shaw, *Victory and Occupation*, 916.
39. Biographical note, and Nace to family and friends, 26 November 1945, George Nace papers, UCBL. Nace to Pineau, 3 March 1980, folder 1, box 19, Pineau papers. Nace was one of the original ten Boulder graduates sent to interpret and interrogate prisoners of war in New Caledonia in 1943, and had interpreted for the sole survivor of the *Awa maru*, a cargo-passenger ship promised safe passage but sunk in error by an American submarine commander. See Record of Proceedings of a General Court-Martial Convened at Headquarters, Commander Forward Area, Central Pacific by order of Commander in Chief, U.S. Pacific Fleet and Pacific Ocean Areas: Case of Charles E. Loughlin, U.S. Navy. Transcript of proceedings, 19 April 1945, microfilm copy, NRS 1970-36, Navy Department Library.
40. Robert Falk to Jane Falk, 22, 27 September, 9, 31 October 1945, Falk papers.
41. Ibid., 10, 23, 27–28 November, 3 December 1945.
42. Ibid., 9, 13, 17, 28 November 1945; Richard, *U.S. Naval Administration*, 2:19.
43. Clinton H. Gardiner, "Two Days at Mortlock," n.d. memoir, file 27, box 12, Pineau papers.
44. Nace to family and friends, 26 November 1945, Nace papers; Richard, *U.S. Naval Administration*, 2:30; Frank and Shaw, *Victory and Occupation*, 456.
45. Tim Maga, *Judgment at Tokyo: The Japanese War Crimes Trials* (Lexington: University Press of Kentucky, 2001), 112–13; Bill Sloan, *Given Up for Dead: America's Heroic Stand at Wake Island* (New York: Bantam Books, 2003), 337–38, 354–55; Rottman, *World War II Pacific Island Guide,* 39.

46. Omer Ostensoe biography, 1992 Boulder reunion biography, UCBL; Wiles, *Forgotten Raiders '42*, 62–66, 94.
47. Norton Williams and Mary Lou Siegfried Williams interviews; Durden, n.d. document in Robert F. Durden papers, UCBL; Maga, *Judgment at Tokyo*, 98–104; James Bradley, *Flyboys: A True Story of Courage* (New York: Little, Brown, 2004), 308–21.
48. Pratt conference presentation; Pratt interview.
49. Frank and Shaw, *Victory and Occupation*, 542; Daniel E. Barbey, *MacArthur's Amphibious Navy: Seventh Amphibious Force Operations, 1943–1945* (Annapolis, MD: Naval Institute Press, 1969), 328; Spector, *In the Ruins of Empire*, 26.
50. Boulder graduates known to have taken part in this phase of the surrender process included Royal Wald and T. Howell Breece from Naval Group China at Shanghai; David Anderson and Charles Cross at Peking; Howard Boorman, Jack Bronston, Samuel Weisbard, and Dan S. Williams at Tientsin; and Richard K. Beardsley, Tony DiGrassi, Frank A. Ecker, Leslie Fiedler, Norton Ginsburg, Donald Keene, William Linton, Glenn W. Nelson, Spencer Silverthorne, Glen Slaughter, Hart Spiegel, and Robert Stillman at Tsingtao.
51. Gerald E. Wheeler, *Kinkaid of the Seventh Fleet* (Washington, DC: Naval Historical Center, 1995), 432–34; Milton E. Miles, *A Different Kind of War* (Garden City, NY: Doubleday, 1967), 528, 539; Barbey, *MacArthur's Amphibious Navy*, 327–28, 332–36; Frank and Shaw, *Victory and Occupation*, 551–65.
52. For details of the Americans' arrival on Taiwan, see George H. Kerr, *Formosa Betrayed*, reprint ed. (New York: Da Capo Press, 1976), 67–78. Furnas 15 July 2005 interview; Frank and Shaw, *Victory and Occupation*, 542; Hackett interview; Lt. Col. Thomas E. Williams to wife, 2 October 1945, Thomas E. Williams papers, UCBL.
53. Frank and Shaw, *Victory and Occupation*, 540–47, 559; Barbey, *MacArthur's Amphibious Navy*, 333–36; Spector, *In the Ruins of Empire*, 54–55.
54. Wald interview; Barbey, *MacArthur's Amphibious Navy*, 332–36; Spector, *In the Ruins of Empire*, 51–52; Keene to Cary, 13 October 1945, in Cary, *War-Wasted Asia*, 87; Cross, *Born a Foreigner*, 61; Keene, *Chronicles*, 50–51; Charles T. Cross 19 November 1997 interview with Charles Stuart Kennedy, accessible at http://memory.loc.gov/ammem/collections/diplomacy/index.html (January 2009); Donald Shively interview; Glenn Nelson letter to editor, *Scuttlebut* [*Journal of the Marines China Association*], 1998, copy provided by Glenn Nelson.
55. Keene to Cary, 13 October; Keene to DeBary, 30 October 1945, in Cary, *War-Wasted Asia*, 94–95, 137.
56. Cross, *Born a Foreigner*, 63–64.
57. Boorman, "Pirandello Revisited," 79–80; Spiegel, "War Years and Better Days," 108.
58. Spiegel, "War Years and Better Days," 109; Winchell, "*Too Good to Be True*,"

47. Fiedler fictionalized his North China occupation experiences in his novel, *Back to China* (New York: Stein and Day, 1965).
59. Nelson interview; Winchell, "*Too Good to Be True*," 47.
60. Keene to DeBary, 25 November 1945, in Cary, *War-Wasted Asia*, 196–214.
61. Ibid., 20 December 1945, 265–70.
62. Frank and Shaw, *Victory and Occupation*, 580–608, passim.
63. Slaughter interview; Frank and Shaw, *Victory and Occupation*, 580; Spiegel, "War Years and Better Days," 109.
64. Boorman, "Pirandello Revisited," 88; Cross, *Born a Foreigner*, 74; Spiegel, "War Years and Better Days," 109.

Chapter 7: Instruments of Peace

1. Al Weissberg to Muriel Weissberg, 2 September 1945, Weissberg papers.
2. Among the many works that stress these points, former language officer Richard B. Finn's *Winners in Peace: MacArthur, Yoshida, and Postwar Japan* (Berkeley: University of California Press, 1992) stands out.
3. Naoko Shibusawa, *America's Geisha Ally: Reimagining the Japanese Enemy* (Cambridge: Harvard University Press, 2006), 4.
4. Phil Bridgham to Betty, 12 December 1945, 2 January 1946, Bridgham papers; Edgar to Shirley Whan, 7 November 1945, Whan papers; Durbin to parents, 16 December 1945, Durbin papers; Kimball memoir, Kimball papers 119, Dan Karasik to parents, 22 November 1945, 20 February 1946, Karasik papers.
5. James Durbin to parents, 5 September 1945, Durbin papers.
6. USS *Adams* (DD739/DM-27) entry at http://www.destroyersonline.com/usndd/dd739/ (January 2009); Samuel King Jr. conference presentation.
7. USS *Appalachian* [AGC-1] entry at http://www.ibiblio.org/hyperwar/USN/ships/dafs/AGC/agc1.html (January 2009); Harold G. Wren, "Memoir of a Japanese Language Officer," *Naval Intelligence Professional*, n.d., copy in Wren papers; Arthur Kruckeberg, "Reminiscences," Kruckeberg papers.
8. Karasik to parents, 12, 15, 22, 27 September 1945, Karasik papers; Karasik to Frank Gibney, 28 March 2000, in author's possession; Karasik interview.
9. John W. Dower, *Embracing Defeat: Japan in the Wake of World War II* (New York: Norton, 1999) provides a brilliant analysis of the Japanese response to the American invaders; Barak Kushner, *The Thought War: Japanese Imperial Propaganda* (Honolulu: University of Hawaii Press, 2006), 172–73.
10. May, *Coming to Terms*, 292–93; Karasik to parents, 26 October 1945, Karasik papers; Karasik to Gibney, 28 March 2000, in author's possession. Dean Towner reprised May's role when the Navy occupied Kure, near Hiroshima early in October, and Harry Muheim and Robert Schwantes did the same at Maizuru in December. Dean Towner to Mr. and Mrs. H. Ford Towner, 8 October 1945, Dean Towner papers, UCBL; Raymond A. Higgins, *From*

Hiroshima with Love: The Allied Military Governor's Remarkable Story of the Rebuilding of Japan's Business and Industry after World War II (Central Point, OR: Hellgate Press, 1997), 43–44; Schwantes and Muheim interviews.

11. Smith, *Securing the Surrender*, 26; Capt. Clifton G. Grimes, "History of U.S. Naval Technical Mission to Japan," 1 November 1946 report to Chief of Naval Operations, Office of Naval Intelligence, 1, folder 11, box 1, Pineau papers. This source will hereinafter be cited as NTJ History; U.S. Naval Technical Mission to Japan: Roster of Naval Personnel Attached, Office of Naval Intelligence, Naval Technical Mission to Japan 1945–1946 Reports, box 9, RG 38, NA; USS *Shelby* (APA-105) entry at Naval Historical Center Web site, http://www.history.navy.mil/danfs/s11/shelby.htm (May 2008); Gibney and Griffith Way interviews; Francis L. Bitney, *4 B's in Sasebo, 1945*, a 1997 memoir. I am grateful to Thomas Ragan, Public Affairs officer at U.S. Fleet Activities, Sasebo for providing a copy of this document; Corp. William A. Corpe, USMCR, *Peace Comes Our Way: Occupation Duty in Kyushu Japan* unpublished memoir, Roger L. Marshall papers, Hillsborough, NC.
12. Smith, *Securing the Surrender*, 25–26; Etō Jun, *Senryō shiroku 4: Nihon hondo shinchū* [*The Occupation of the Japanese Mainland: Occupation Documents, Volume 4*] (Tokyo: Kodansha, 1989), 261, 350; Sherwood F. Moran to Ursul Moran, 27 September, 24 October 1945, Moran family papers, Madison, WI; William Weil to parents, 2 November 1945, Weil papers; Iida Jirō , *Senryōgun ga shashita sensō chokugo no Sasebo* [*Sasebo Immediately after the War as Photographed by the Occupation Force*] (Sasebo: Geibundo, 1986), 6–33.
13. John S. Robinson to Dinnie, 30 September 1945, box 33, Robinson papers; Griffith Way interview.
14. Smith, *Securing the Surrender*, 32; Sherwood F. Moran to Ursul Moran, 27 September 1945, Moran family papers, Madison, WI; John S. Robinson to family, September; Robinson to Ginnie, 30 September 1945, Robinson papers; Verner Chaffin to Ethel Chaffin, box 2, Verner F. Chaffin papers, UCBL; Whan to Shirley, 29 September, 13, 26 October 1945, Whan papers.
15. Smith, *Securing the Surrender*, 27; Sherwood F. Moran to Ursul Moran, 24 October 1945, Moran family papers, Madison, WI; Griffith Way interview.
16. Author's observation, Sasebo, Japan, June 1999; Griffith Way interview.
17. Ted de Bary to Donald Keene, 15 October 1945, in Cary, *War-Wasted Asia,* 98–99; Griffith Way interview.
18. Smith, *Securing the Surrender*, 32–37; James S. Santelli, *A Brief History of the 8th Marines* (Washington, DC: History and Museums Division, Headquarters, U.S. Marine Corps, 1976), 52; Robert E. V. Johnson, ed., *The Spearhead, III* (Los Angeles: Pictorial California, 1946), n.p., copy in Zurhellen papers.
19. *The Spearhead, III*, Zurhellen papers; Edward Seidensticker, "Remembrances," *International House of Japan Bulletin* 21 (Autumn 2001): 40; White interview; Edwin Neville Jr., "Japanese and G.I. Rapport," in *The Occupation of Japan:*

The Grass Roots, ed. William F. Nimmo (Norfolk, VA: The General Douglas MacArthur Foundation, 1991), 137–38.

20. Smith, *Securing the Surrender*, 33, 38; Iida, *Senryōgun ga shashita*, 114–27; Kimball memoir, 113, Kimball papers; Corpe unpublished memoir, copy provided by Roger L. Marshall; Seidensticker, "Remembrances," 38; Paul R. Schratz, *Submarine Commander: A Story of World War II and Korea* (Lexington: University Press of Kentucky, 1988), 199; Neville recalled querying civilian returnees from Manchuria about what the Soviet Army was doing there, "Japanese and G.I. Rapport,"140; Ainsworth conference presentation.
21. Marshall and Downs interviews; Sherwood F. Moran to Ursul Moran, 12 November 1945, Moran family papers, Madison, WI; Bitney, "Four B's in Sasebo," memoir.
22. Neville, "Japanese and G.I. Rapport,"138.
23. Kimball memoir, 118, Kimball papers; Bitney, "Four B's in Sasebo," memoir; Rear Adm. George Van Deurs 1969 Naval Institute oral history, 574–75; Sherwood F. Moran to Ursul Moran, 24 October 1945, Moran family papers, Madison, WI; Whan to mother, 24 September 1945, Whan papers; Robinson to Ginnie, 30 September 1945, Robinson papers.
24. Griffith Way interview; Wilbur memoir, Wilbur papers; Kimball memoir, 115, 118, Kimball papers; Robinson to parents, 27 November 1945, Robinson papers.
25. Kimball memoir, 118, Kimball papers; Bitney, "Four B's in Sasebo," memoir; Seidensticker, "Remembrances," 36–37.
26. Smith, *Securing the Surrender*, 38, 43–44; *NTJ History*, 3; USS *Blackford* (APB-45) entry at the Naval Historical Center Web site, http://www.history.navy.mil/danfs/b6/blackford-i.htm (May 2008).
27. Al Weissberg to Muriel Weissberg, 1, 2, 4 November 1945, Weissberg papers; USS *Ancon* (AP-66) entry at the Naval Historical Center Web site, http://www.history.navy.mil/danfs/a8/ancon-ii.htm (May 2008). Another five naval linguists traveled by train from Sasebo to Tokyo. See Chief, Naval Technical Mission to Japan to Lt. (jg) T. A. Chester, 20 October 1945, Theodore A. Chester papers, Pasadena, CA.
28. Myers interview; Prados, *Combined Fleet Decoded*, 592–93; Cary, *War-Wasted Asia*, 13–15, 45, 53; Maj. James Beveridge, U.S. Army, "History of the United States Strategic Bombing Survey (Pacific) 1945–1946" (Washington, DC: War Department, 1946), 1:10–13.
29. Beveridge, "History of USSBS," 1–4, 10–14, 18–19, 31–40, 68ff; Pineau memoir, Pineau papers; Rolph to Pineau, 19 March 1991, folder 24, box 22, Pineau papers; Riccio interview.
30. *NTJ History*, 13; Al Weissberg to Muriel Weissberg, 16 and 17 November 1945.
31. Orville Lefko to David Hays, 10 March 2001, Lefko papers; Newell and Way

interviews; Kimball memoir, 120, Kimball papers; Richard B. Finn interview in Etō Jun, *Senryō shiroku*, 14–15; USSBS Operation Order 16, 23 October 1945, in Chester papers detailed assignments for half a dozen other Boulder men on similar inspection tours around the country. "Medical Targets: Japanese Bacteriological Warfare, Report M-05," 18 November 1945; "Medical Targets: Information Relative to Venereal Disease Control in Japan, Report M-04, Naval Technical Mission to Japan Report M-04," CNO, ONI, Naval Technical Mission to Japan 1945–1946 Reports, box 2, RG 38, NA.

32. Commanding General 3rd Marine Division orders to Capt. Earl Swisher and first lieutenants James W. Johnson, Lawrence Vincent, and Walter B. Williams, 12 November; USSBS orders to Vincent, 24 November 1945, Vincent papers; Vincent, "Semper Fi," 45–46.
33. Cdr. Alexander H. Leighton, MC, USNR, *The Sown Wind*, unpublished memoir, 1–6, in Vincent papers; Vincent, "Semper Fi," 48.
34. Vincent, "Semper Fi," 48–50; Leighton, *Sown Wind*, 27–28, in Vincent papers.
35. Vincent, "Semper Fi," 51–53.
36. Kiyoto Hashimoto to Vincent, 4 March 1946, Vincent papers.
37. Cary to Donald Keene, 25 November 1945, in Cary, *War-Wasted Asia*, 217–27; Boller, *Memoirs of an Obscure Professor*, 63–64.
38. Prendergast to Pedro Loureiro, 13 March 2000, in author's possession; Grant Goodman, *America's Japan: The First Year 1945–1946* (New York: Fordham University Press, 2005), 38–47, 52; Thiel and Mayer interviews; Al Weissberg to Muriel Weissberg, 8, 12, 16, 17 November 1945; Arthur Dornheim to John Robinson, 24 April 1946, Robinson papers; Boulder graduates' 1946 reunion dinner in Tokyo photograph, folder 8, box 6, Pineau papers.
39. Nace to Pineau, 30 March 1980, file 1, box 19, Pineau papers; Phil Bridgham to Betty, 25 September, 10 October 1945, Bridgham papers; Nichols oral history, 26–32, http://memory.loc.gov/ammem/collections/diplomacy/index.html. Nichols had left the Navy and returned to Japan as a civilian SCAP worker by this time.
40. Dornheim, "Reflections," 5–7, enclosed in Dornheim to author and Pedro Loureiro, 14 March 2000; Dornheim to parents, 7, 20 May 1946, copy provided to author by Arthur Dornheim; John Ashmead Jr., "A Modern Language for Japan," *Atlantic Monthly* 179 (January 1947), 68–72.
41. Yokosuka shi shi hensan shitsu, ed., *Senryōka no Yokosuka: Rengōkokugun no jōriku to sono jidai* [*Yokosuka under Occupation: The Landing of Allied Forces and that Era*] (Yokosuka: Yokosuka shi, 2005), 12–13, 21–24; Robert W. Christy to parents, 8, 12, 20 September 1945, Robert W. Christy papers, UCBL; Benton Weaver Decker and Edwina Decker, *Return of the Black Ships* (New York: Vantage Press, 1978), 2, 7.
42. Christy to parents 30 September 1945, Christy papers; Durbin to parents, 4 November, 4 and 26 December 1945, 2 January, 12 March 1946, Durbin

papers; Dean Towner to Mr. and Mrs. H. Ford Towner, 21, 27 December 1945, Towner papers; Holland Gary to Betty Gary, 22 November 1945, Holland Gary papers, UCBL; Christy and Beasley interviews. Residents of House #9 included John Ashmead, W. G. "Bill" Beasley, Lionel Casson, Robert W. Christy, Frank Dawson, Jim Durbin, George Nace, and James M. Wells.

43. Durbin to parents, 13, 26 November, 2, 23, 29 December 1945, 10 January 1946, Durbin papers; Christy to parents, 20, 30 September 1945, Christy papers; Holland Gary to Betty Gary, 22 November 1945, Gary papers.
44. Durbin to parents, 1, 5, 7 September 1945, Durbin papers; Willard H. Elsbree, 2002 Boulder reunion biography.
45. Christy to parents, 10 November, 4, 10 December 1945, Christy papers; Decker and Decker, *Return of the Black Ships*, vi.
46. Durbin to parents, 13, 18, 23, 25 September, 2, 4 October, 6 December 1945, Durbin papers.
47. Durbin to parents, 16 December 1945, 26 February, 10 April 1946, Durbin papers; Christy to parents, 4 December 1945, 13 January, 23 February 1946, Christy papers; Julian Burke interview.
48. Sherwood R. Moran to Donald Keene, 14 November, and Otis Cary to Keene, 25 November, 21 December 1945, 6 January 1946, in Cary, *War-Wasted Asia,* 151–56, 217–28, 273–88.
49. Boller, *Memoirs of an Obscure Professor*, 62–69.
50. Durbin to parents 12 October, 4, 13, 18, 21 November 1945, 10, 14 April 1946, Durbin papers; Holland Gary to Betty Gary, 4–6 November, Gary papers; Al Weissberg to Muriel Weissberg, 3–6, 10–11, 18–19 November 1945, Weissberg papers; Robinson to family, post-October 1945, Robinson papers; Sherwood R. Moran to Ted Debary, 3 January 1946, in Cary, *War-Wasted Asia,* 302–5.
51. Robinson to family, post-October 1945, Robinson papers; Bridgham to Betty, 14, 25 September, 10 October, 10 November, 18, 25 December 1945, 2 January, 2, 27 March 1946, Bridgham papers.
52. Shibusawa, *America's Geisha Ally*, 4.
53. Sherwood R. Moran to Keene, 30 September 1945 in Cary, *War-Wasted Asia,* 61; Nace to family, 15 April 1946, Nace papers; Karasik to parents, 12 September 1945, Karasik papers.
54. Durbin to parents, 5, 29 September, 4 October 1945, Durbin papers.
55. Cary to Keene, 6 January, Cary to DeBary, 24 January 1946, in Cary, *War-Wasted Asia,* 305–22; Verner Chaffin to Ethel Chaffin, December 1945–January 1946, box 2, Chaffin papers.
56. Bridgham to Betty, 2, 28 January, 2, 27 March 1946, Bridgham papers; Durbin to parents, 13 November 1945, 13 March, 14 April 1946, Durbin papers; Cary to Keene, 25 November 1945; Sherwood R. Moran to DeBary, 3 January 1946, in Cary, *War-Wasted Asia,* 303–5; William Weil to parents, 25

November 1945, Weil papers; Verner Chaffin to Ethel Chaffin, December–January 1946, Chaffin papers.

57. John Ashmead, "The Japs Look at the Yanks," *Atlantic Monthly* 177 (April 1946), 86–91; and "A Modern Language for Japan," *Atlantic Monthly* 179 (January 1947), 68–72; Karasik, "Farewell to Happy Bottom," enclosed in Karasik to author, 29 June 2000; Hilary Conroy, "Japan Changes Faces: A Memoir of Occupied Japan," unpublished draft, 1946, Conroy papers; Henry F. May, "MacArthur Era, Year One," *Harpers* 192 (March 1946): 267–73; John J. Craig and Lawrence C. Vincent, "Our Japanese 'Ally'," unpublished draft, Vincent papers; Vincent interview; Martin Bronfenbrenner began this work in 1946, saw some of it published in Tokyo in 1952, and finished this collection of tales in 1973, *Tomioka Stories from the Japanese Occupation: Comedies and Tragedies of Japan under the American Forces after World War II* (Hicksville, NY: Exposition Press, 1975), 7.

Chapter 8: Bridge Builders

1. *New York Times*, 1–2 September 1946; Boulder WAVES at work in Japan included Blanche Belitz, Abbie White, Jean Mayer, Nancy Pearce, Evelyn Knecht, Sara Dilley, Pat Shannon, Barbara Shuey, Odette Jensen, Orrel Riffe, Irene Slaninka, Helen Craig, Marie Estes, Marion Walker, Avis Pick, and Jacqueline Reifsnider. Boulder WAVES 1993 Reunion data, file 5, box 30, Pineau papers; Muheim interview.
2. Biography and career highlights prefacing McCollum oral history; Zacharias with Farago, *Secret Missions*; Secretary of the Navy to Hindmarsh, 1946; Chief of Naval Personnel to Hindmarsh, 10 January 1946; Hindmarsh career summary, 1971, Hindmarsh papers.
3. "University of California: In Memoriam 1946: Florence Walne MacFarqahar," Ingersoll papers; Appraisal of Achievement and Promise [for] Susumu W. Nakamura, 13 June 1956 personnel files, University Archives, Bancroft Library, Berkeley, CA; Okamoto, Oakley, John Toki, Hoshino, and Nobutaka interviews.
4. Casson to Pineau, 23 September 1992, Willis papers; Riccio interview; Ann Arbor Michigan *News Court*, 27 March 1987, box 2, Pineau papers; Verner F. Chaffin biographical sketch, Navy School of Japanese [and Oriental] Language 60th anniversary reunion pamphlet, June 2002, UCBL; Jones interview; Cross career summary, box 9, Japanese Language School papers, UCBL; Arthur R. Kruckeberg 2002 memoir, Kruckeberg papers; William H. Amos to Frank Roegge, 20 June 2000, Amos papers; O'Sullivan Way and Billett Levine interviews.
5. Leonard Spigelman's *A Majority of One*, the 1959 Broadway hit and 1961 movie, explores Americans' conflicted postwar feelings toward Japan. http://

www.imdb.com/title/tt0055124 (February 2008); Yukiko Koshiro, *Trans-Pacific Racisms and the U.S. Occupation of Japan* (New York: Columbia University Press, 1999), 160, 199–200; Reed Irvine conference remarks; Reed Irvine autobiography in *Japanese Language School 50-Year Reunion 1992*; and Reed Irvine *Los Angeles Times* obituary, 19 November 2004; *Who's Who in America, 1999* 1:2163; Wiles and Suttles interviews.

6. Dan S. Williams, Craig, Stone, Towner, and Brayshay interviews; Sam King and Anne Grilk King conference remarks; Ashmead, "These Were My Japanese Students," 56–59; Frank A. Bauman career summary in *Japanese Language School 50-Year Reunion* pamphlet, box 1, Japanese Language School papers, UCBL; Houghton "Buck" Freeman letter to Frank Gibney, 9 March 2000, Bridge to the Rising Sun Conference papers, Pacific Basin Institute, Pomona College, Claremont, CA.
7. John Hadley Pierce letter to Frank Gibney, March 2000, Bridge to the Rising Sun Conference papers; Pierce obituary in Bellingham, Washington, *Herald*, January 2002, provided by Patricia Pierce; Stone, Siegfried, and D. Norton Williams interviews; http://en.wikipedia.org/wiki/List_of_twin_towns_and_ister_cities_in_Japan (January 2009).
8. Cary unpublished memoir, 272–78, Cary papers; Nippon Television documentary, December 1991, copy provided by Telfer Mook; *Benzie County Record-Patriot,* Frankfort, MI, 4 December 1991, file 1, box 9, Japanese Language School papers, UCBL; *Ryūkyū Taimuzu* clippings, September–October 1990; *Washington Post,* 31 May 1991; *Baltimore Sun,* 30 May 1991, Slaughter papers.
9. Mayer, James V. Martin, and Stegmeier interviews; Cary, *War-Wasted Asia*, 13; *Biographical Register of the Department of State*, 1960: 415; and 1966: 344, 393; Sheridan Sims to author, 24 August 2004.
10. John W. Hall obituary, 31 October 1997, http://www.hartford-hwp.com/archives/55/107.html (January 2007); De Bary interview; Thomas J. Rimer, ed., *The Blue-Eyed Tarokaja: A Donald Keene Anthology* (New York: Columbia University Press, 1996), 9; Keene, *Chronicles*, 65.
11. Morley conference remarks.
12. Tucker, Hammond and Julia Rolph, Ainsworth, Dornheim, Ward, and Scalapino interviews.
13. Schwantes, Ikle, and Stevens interviews; Seidensticker, *Tokyo Central*, 40–57.
14. Packard, Rich, Gibney, Jefferson, and Griffith Way interviews.
15. Hammond Rolph 26 April 2000 interview; Jefferson 14 March 2000 interview; Jefferson memoir, in Brad Jefferson's possession, Fruita, CO; Pratt conference presentation; Pratt interview, 15 July 2001; *Maritime Friendship* is the title of Agawa Naoyuki's study of the postwar U.S.–Japan naval relationship, *Umi no yūjō* (Tokyo: Shinchosha, 2001).

16. The facility, then known as COMMUNIT 35, eventually became Naval Security Group Facility, Kamiseya, Japan. See Jay R. Browne, "Kamiseya Update P-2," *Cryptolog* 16 (Spring 1995), 1–2; Myers interview.
17. Foley and Tucker conference presentations; Curts, Foley, and Tucker interviews; Furnas to Pineau, 27 May 1976, file 23, box 12, Pineau papers.
18. McLean, Nelson, and Brayshay interviews; John K. McLean biography, Navy Japanese Language/Oriental Language School Boulder 60th anniversary reunion program, June 2002, UCBL; H. B. Van Brunt to Pineau, 22 June 1980, folder 28, box 11, Pineau papers; Bina Cady Kiyonaga, *My Spy: Memoir of a CIA Wife* (New York: Avon Books, 2000), 115, 124–25, 136.
19. Nelson and McLean interviews; Keene, *Chronicles*, 26–27; Michael Schaller, *Altered States: The United States and Japan since the Occupation* (New York: Oxford University Press, 1997) 153–58.
20. These statistics are based on a 1993 list of Boulder veterans prepared by Roger Pineau, file 15, box 3, Pineau papers, and entries for additional men and women in *Biographical Register*, 1950–1965. For details of Ralph W. E. Reid's career, see Howard B. Schonberger, *Aftermath of War: Americans and the Remaking of Japan, 1945–1952* (Kent, OH: Kent State University Press, 1989), 180–81; *Who's Who in America, 1999* (Chicago: Marquis Who's Who, 1999) 1:2163–64; Reed Irvine conference presentation.
21. Roger Dingman, *Ghost of War: The Sinking of the* Awa maru *and Japanese-American Relations, 1945–1995* (Annapolis, MD: Naval Institute Press, 1997), 124–25, 134; Robert E. Ward to John W. Hall, 8 May 1970, box 21, Ward papers.
22. Ainsworth conference presentation; Ainsworth interview; Elfrieda Berthiaume Shuker and Barbara Smith Scibetta, *War Brides of World War II* (New York: Penguin Books, 1989), 209–18.
23. John K. Emmerson, *The Japanese Thread: A Life in the U.S. Foreign Service* (New York: Holt, Rinehart, and Winston, 1978), 96, 386. Robert A. Fearey points out that by 8 December 1941 the embassy staff had shrunk to sixty-five people; Fearey, "Was Pearl Harbor Inevitable? 1941," in Curtis Prendergast, ed., *Tokyo Memoirs 1941–1955* (Washington, DC: Byron S. Adams, 2005), 6; Ainsworth, Pratt, and Wald interviews; *Biographical Register*, 1966: 164, 388, 409, 561, 602.
24. Martin interview; Richard W. Petree Narrative Career Description, Richard W. Petree papers, UCBL; Shaw Stegmeier interview; Reischauer, *My Life between Japan and America*, 226; *Biographical Register*, 1966: 388; Emmerson, *The Japanese Thread*, 375.
25. *Biographical Register*, 1966: 30; Bryan Battey, "Creating Japanese Best Sellers," in *Tokyo Memoirs 1941–1955*, 181–86; Battey to author, 25, 31 August, 20–21, 28 September, 11–13, 22 October 2005.

26. Nakaya Kenichi and Robert S. Schwantes, "Ten Years of Cultural and Education Interchange between Japan and America 1952–1961: A Report Submitted to the Joint United States–Japan Conference on Cultural and Education Interchange." Unpublished manuscript circulated by the U.S. Embassy Tokyo, Introduction, 4–6, 10; chapter 3, 6–12, box 1, Robert S. Schwantes papers, Hoover Institution, Stanford, CA; Schwantes interview.
27. Reischauer, *My Life between Japan and America*, 226–32, 295; Roger Dingman, "Alliance in Crisis: The Lucky Dragon Incident and Japanese-American Relations," in *The Great Powers in East Asia, 1953–1960,* eds. Warren Cohen and Akira Iriye, (New York: Columbia University Press, 1990); 187–214 Schaller, *Altered States*, 143–62. For a different, more negative view of both the agents of America's postwar cultural offensive in Japan and its longer-term effects, see Matsuda Takeshi, *Soft Power and Its Perils: U.S. Cultural Policy in Early Postwar Japan and Permanent Dependency* (Stanford: The Wilson Center and Stanford University Press, 2007), xv–xvi.
28. Bruns conference remarks; Bruns autobiographical statement, *Japanese Language School 60-Year Reunion* pamphlet (June 2002), UCBL; Paul P. Anspach obituary, reprinted in *The Interpreter* 101A (15 July 2006); *Black Mountain* [North Carolina] *Focus,* 8 January 1998, in John H. Brady Jr., papers, UCBL. Brady was a Presbyterian minister in Kobe; death announcement for Brother Aloysius M. Soden, file 1, box 27, Pineau papers; Nakaya and Schwantes, "Ten Years," chapter 1, 12, Schwantes papers.
29. Ostensoe and Shorrock interviews; Nakaya and Schwantes, "Ten Years," chapter 2, 11–14, Schwantes papers.
30. Neither Bill nor Don Gorham chose to follow their father as technical advisers to Japanese firms, and Jim Brayshay preferred first the Marines and then insurance to his parent's cotton brokerage work. Tad VanBrunt tried but never achieved the sort of success his father had in prewar Japan. Gorham, Brayshay, and Pratt interviews; Schaller, *Altered States*, 108–12; Aaron Forsberg, *America and the Japanese Miracle: The Cold War Context of Japan's Postwar Economic Revival, 1950–1960* (Chapel Hill: University of North Carolina Press, 2000), 169–97; Doreen Freeman, "*Language Lessons*," in *Tokyo Memoirs, 1941–1955*, ed. Curtis W. Prendergast, (Washington, DC: Byron S. Adams, 2005), 147–49.
31. Griffith Way, White, and Stone interviews; Frank A. Bauman letter and Sherman autobiographical statement in *Japanese Language School 50-Year Reunion* pamphlet (Boulder, CO, 1992), UCBL.
32. Ernest R. May, "U.S. Press Coverage of Japan 1931–1941" in *Pearl Harbor as History: Japanese–American Relations 1931–1941*, eds. Dorothy Borg and Shumpei Okamoto (New York: Columbia University Press, 1973), 515, 519–25, 531.
33. Gibney, 2001 autobiographical fragment, Gibney papers; Karasik to Pedro

Loureiro and author, 28 March 2000; Karasik, Prendergast, and Rich interviews; Prendergast to Loureiro 13 September 2000. A fifth Boulder graduate, Kermit Lanser, never served in Japan, but as editor of *Newsweek*, he greatly expanded cultural coverage, including that on Japan. "Obituaries," *Art in America* (July 2000) at BNET Business Network, http://www.findarticles.com/cf_dls/m1248/7_88/63365677/p2/article.html (January 2007); Rich conference presentation; John Rich, "Unexpected Encounters," in *Tokyo Memoirs 1941–1955*, ed. Curtis Prendergast, 95–101.

34. Gibney 23 September 2000 interview. Frank Gibney, "Missionary's Return," *Time* 53 (13 June 1949), 59; Gibney, "Arm of St. Francis," *Life* 26 (27 June 1949), 49–52; Gibney, "Forgotten Island," *Time* 54 (28 November 1949), 24.
35. Gibney 23 September 2000 interview; Gibney, "Birth of a New Japan," *Life* 31 (10 September 1951), 134–38; Rich interview.
36. Karasik interview; Karasik to author and Pedro Loureiro, 28 March 2000; Dan Karasik, "Okinawa: A Problem in Administration and Reconstruction," *Far Eastern Quarterly* 7 (May 1948), 254–67; Karasik articles in *Sangyō keizai*, 17 January, 4 February 1954; [*Tokyo*] *Mainichi*, 12 December 1953, 3 March 1954; *New Haven Journal-Courier*, 22 February; *Milwaukee Journal*, 27 February; *Louisville Courier-Journal*, 14 March 1954; Karasik papers. Although he had commissioned it, the editor of *The Reporter* thought it unwise to publish Karasik's October 1953 expose of American military administration errors in Okinawa. Curtis W. Prendergast, "Bujika hen matsu okane," in *Tokyo Memoirs, 1941–1955*, 49–52.
37. *Who's Who in America 1999*, 1:1595; Gibney 23 September 2000 interview; Frank Gibney, *Five Gentlemen of Japan* (New York: Farrar, Strauss, and Young, 1953). Gibney repeated this success nearly twenty years later with *Japan: The Fragile Superpower* (New York: Norton, 1975), which went through three subsequent editions. Gibney may have gotten a boost from another former language officer, Kermit Lansner, who joined *Newsweek* in 1954 and served as its editor from 1969 to 1972. Lansner obituary, *Los Angeles Times*, 24 May 2000; Stephanie Cash, "Kermit Lansner Obituary," July 2000, at http://www.findarticles.com/p/articles/mi_m1248/is_7_88/ai_63365677/pg_2 (August 2006); Karasik to author and Pedro Loureiro, 28 March 2000; Karasik, Prendergast, and Rich interviews; Charles Pomeroy, ed., *Foreign Correspondents in Japan* (Tokyo: Tuttle, 1998), 186–91.
38. I saw particularly noteworthy displays of Japanese art in the homes of Richard Gard, Dan Karasik, Frank Ikle, Jean Mayer, Glen Slaughter, and Irene Slaninka Thiel.
39. Michael Shapiro, "The American Who May Be the Canniest Collector of Japanese Art of All Time," *The Connoisseur* (March 1987), 107; Warren I. Cohen, *East Asian Art and American Culture* (New York: Columbia University Press, 1992), 105; Charles F. Gallagher, "Charles F. Gallagher American,

Scholar," in Ronald Bell, ed., *The Japan Experience* (Tokyo: Weatherhill, 1973), 172; Stegmaier and Mayer interviews. Daphne Shaw Stegmaier translated, among other books, Murata Kageo and Okamura Kichiemon, *Folk Arts and Crafts of Japan, Heibonsha Survey of Japanese Art*, vol. 26 (New York: Weatherhill, 1973).

40. Christy interview.
41. Griffith Way, "A Collector's View," in Michiko Morioka and Paul Berry, *Modern Masters of Kyoto: The Transformation of Japanese Painting Traditions* (Seattle: University of Washington Press, 1999), 12–14; Griffith Way interview.
42. *New York Times*, 2 November 1991. Packard also saved some Japanese businessmen from execution at the hands of the Chinese, and years later, when the engineering firm they founded had prospered, they made him a well-paid partner in it. Brotherton interview; Shapiro, "American Who May Be the Canniest Collector," 107. Packard's original prints appeared in Edwin E. Grabhorn, *Figure Prints of Old Japan: A Pictorial Pageant of Actors and Courtesans of the Eighteenth Century Reproduced from the Prints in the Collection of Marjorie and Edwin Grabhorn, with an introduction by Harold P. Stern* (1959), and Edwin E. Grabhorn, *Ukiyo-e: "The Floating World"* (1962) cited by Yoko Woodson and Richard L. Mellott, *Exquisite Pursuits: Japanese Art in the Harry G. C. Packard Collection* (Seattle: University of Washington Press, 1994), 16.
43. Shapiro, "American Who May Be the Canniest Collector," 108–9; Kenneth Baker, "Harry Packard's Japanese Treasures," *Architectural Digest* 49 [August 1992], 56. Cohen, *East Asian Art and American Culture*, 37–39, passim; Brotherton interview; Brotherton, *The Immortality Game: A Book About Art Collectors and Some Rules for Collecting*, unpublished manuscript in author's possession, 61. Packard eventually published *Nihon Bijutsu Shūshūki* [*A Record of Collecting Japanese Art*] (Tokyo: Shinchosha, 1993); Joe Brotherton, "Packardo-San: Harry G. C. Packard (1914–1991)," *Orientations* (February 1992), 76–77. On one occasion, Packard shrewdly agreed to donate a Sung dynasty painting to the Ueno National Museum in Tokyo in return for receiving a license to sell Japanese art objects abroad.
44. Woodson and Mellott, *Exquisite Pursuits*, 14–15; Baker, "Harry Packard's Japanese Treasures," 58; Brotherton, "Packardo-San," 77; Shapiro, "American Who May Be the Canniest Collector," 109–10; Brotherton and Packard interviews.
45. Burks, Morley, Scalapino, Ward interviews; Akira Iriye, *U.S.-Japan Cultural Exchange: An Overview*, paper prepared for October 1982 symposium on U.S.–Japan Cultural Exchange, box 2, John W. Hall papers, Sterling Memorial Library, Yale University, New Haven, CT.
46. Robert Ward pointed out that among senior American Japan experts who were still teaching in the late 1940s, only Edwin Reischauer and Hugh Borton had a real command of the Japanese language; Ward to John W. Hall,

5 April 1983. The Berkeley faculty included three wartime naval language officers: Woodbridge Bingham, Delmer M. Brown, and Denzel Carr, as well as former Harvard and Boulder sensei Betty McKinnon Carr, Delmer Brown oral history, 94.

47. Richard K. Beardsley, John W. Hall, and Robert E. Ward, *Village Japan* (Chicago: University of Chicago Press, 1959); Thomas C. Smith, *The Agrarian Origins of Modern Japan* (Stanford, CA: Stanford University Press, 1960); Solomon Levine, *Industrial Relations in Postwar Japan* (Champagne-Urbana: University of Illinois Press, 1958); Morley, Burks, and Scalapino interviews. Representative samples of these translations include Chikamatsu Monzaemon, *The Love Suicide at Amijima*, 2nd ed., trans. Donald Shively (Ann Arbor: University of Michigan Press, 1991); Murasaki Shikibu, *The Tale of Genji*, trans. Edward Seidensticker (New York: Knopf, 1976); and Mishima Yukio, *Five Modern Nō Plays*, trans. Donald Keene (New York: Knopf, 1957); Helen Craig McCullough and William H. McCullough, *Eiga monogatari: A Tale of Flowering Fortunes: Annals of Japanese Aristocratic Life in the Heian Period* (Stanford, CA: Stanford University Press, 1980). Helen Craig McCullough autobiography, *WAVES 1993 Reunion biography* pamphlet, file 5, box 1, Pineau papers.

48. Walne to Robert Gordon Sproul, 12 August 1941, enclosing list of Cornell Conference attendees, file 1941:487, CU-5, series 2; *Japanese Studies 1970*, 17; John W. Hall, *Japan in the Mind of America: A Half Century of Change* (Kyoto: Doshisha University Press, 1990), 13–14, box 1, Hall papers; Sidney DeVere Brown autobiographical statement, *Japanese Language School 60-Year Reunion*; Ikle interview; Mendel: *Contemporary Authors Online 2001*; Susan M. Trosky and Donna Olendorf, eds., *Contemporary Authors*, vol. 137 (Detroit: Gale Research, 1992), 335.

49. Texts by wartime language officers included John W. Hall, *Japan: From Prehistory to Modern Times* (New York: Delacorte Press, 1970); Woodbridge Bingham, Hilary Conroy, and Frank W. Ikle, *A History of Asia*, 2nd ed. (Boston: Allyn and Bacon, 1964–65); Ryūsaku Tsunoda, William Theodore de Bary, and Donald Keene, eds., *Sources of Japanese Tradition* (New York: Oxford University Press, 1958); Ardath Burks, *The Government of Japan* (Philadelphia: Crowell, 1962); Lawrence A. Olsen, *Japan in Postwar Asia* (Boulder, CO: Praeger, 1970). Robert E. Ward, *Japan's Political System* (Englewood Cliffs, NJ: Prentice-Hall, 1967); Francis Hilary Conroy, *Contemporary Authors*, vol. 115 (Detroit: Gale Publications, 1985), 102–3.

50. Thompson and Martin interviews; *Honolulu Advertiser*, 21 July 2000.

51. Keene and Seidensticker entries, *Contemporary Authors Online*. See, for example, Donald Keene, *Living Japan* (Garden City, NY: Doubleday, 1959); Keene, ed., *Anthology of Japanese Literature* (New York: Grove Press, 1955), and Keene, ed., *Anthology of Modern Japanese Literature* (New York: Grove

Press, 1956); Keene, *The Manyōshū* (New York: Columbia University Press, 1965); Edward Seidensticker, *This Country Japan* (Tokyo and New York: Kodansha, 1977); Seidensticker, *Kafu the Scribbler: The Life and Writings of Nagai Kafu, 1879–1959* (Stanford, CA: Stanford University Press, 1965), Murasaki Shikibu, *The Tale of Genji*, trans. Edward Seidensticker (New York: Knopf, 1976).

52. Charles O. Hucker, *The Association for Asian Studies: An Interpretive History* (Seattle: University of Washington Press, 1973), 9–10, 25, 93–95; David Hays et al., List of Navy School of Japanese [later Oriental] Language Graduates, Japanese Language School papers, UCBL. Former Berkeley sensei Chitoshi Yanaga, later a professor of history at Yale, also served as an AAS director.
53. Although Army-trained wartime Japanese-language officers made major contributions to the growth of postwar Japanese studies in the United States, they were overshadowed in this series by former naval and marine linguists. The linguists and former sensei Nobutaka Ike contributed nearly twice as many essays as Army-trained writers. Five of the seven multiple contributors were former navy language officers. The books, all published by Princeton University Press, were Marius B. Jansen, ed., *Changing Japanese Attitudes toward Modernization* (1965); William W. Lockwood, ed., *The State and Economic Enterprise in Japan* (1965); Ronald P. Dore, ed., *Aspects of Social Change in Modern Japan* (1967); Robert E. Ward, ed., *Political Development in Modern Japan* (1968); Donald H. Shively, ed., *Tradition and Modernization in Japanese Culture* (1971); and James William Morley, ed., *Dilemmas of Growth in Prewar Japan* (1971).
54. John W. Hall Neesima lecture, 18, Hall papers. I attended the opening ceremonies for the Center in 1961; SSRC-ACLS Joint Committee on Japanese Studies in the United States, "Japanese Studies in the United States: A Report on the State of the Field, Current Resources and Future Needs" [1970] 56, box 17, Peter Duus to Ward, 20 January 1975, box 21, Ward papers.
55. John W. Hall and Yoshinori Maeda, "CULCON: The US-Japan Conference on Cultural and Educational Interchange: A Brief History," paper prepared for 1980 Washington meeting of CULCON, 25–31, Hall papers. Reischauer indicated that Congress had appropriated only a small portion of the Government and Relief in Occupied Areas (GARIOA) funds, in effect raiding them for current expenses rather than devoting them, as originally intended, to new cross-cultural endeavors; Reischauer to Hall, 17 July 1970, box 2, Hall papers.
56. Ward 1976 memorandum, "The Japan-United States Friendship Commission," box 21, Ward papers; Ward to John W. Hall, James Morley, and Edwin O. Reischauer, 17 July 1970, box 2, Hall papers.
57. Schaller, *Altered States*, 210–44; Walter La Feber, *The Clash* (New York:

Norton, 1997), 352–58; Julian Burke interview. For the most detailed account of naval policy turbulence in the early 1970s, see Nagao Hidemi, *Nihon yōsaika no shinario* [*A Scenario for Japan's Fortification*] (Tokyo: Kantō sha, 2003), 50–239. John W. Hall to Senator Jacob Javits, 21 February 1973, Hall papers; Ward et al. to President Gerald Ford, 29 August 1974, box 2, Hall papers. Six of the eight cosigners of this letter were students or instructors in the wartime naval Japanese-language program.

58. Reischauer to Ward, 17 July 1970, box 2, Hall papers; Ward to Joint Committee on Japanese Studies, et al., 20 December 1971; Ward to George Akita et al., 21 May 1973; Ward to George Beckmann et al., 29 August 1974, box 21, Ward papers.
59. Ward memorandum to files, 19 March 1975; Ward to Hays, 28 April, 30 July 1975, box 21, Ward papers; *Interaction* (October 1975), n.p., box 2, Hall papers; *Congressional Record*, 94 Cong, 2 session, U.S. House of Representatives, H9480-9483.

Bibliography

UNPUBLISHED SOURCES

Archives

Japanese American National Museum, Los Angeles, CA
War Relocation Authority-26 digital database
Marine Corps Historical Center, Washington, DC (MCHC)
Marine Corps Oral History Collection
Officer Biography File
Naval Historical Center, Washington, DC
Classified Operational Archives (COA, NHC)
Command File, World War II
Japanese Sources Collection
Officer Biography File
Records of the Japanese Navy and Related Items, 1940–60
Type Command, Training, Schools, University of Colorado School of Oriental Studies (UCSOL)
Navy Department Library
Record of Proceedings of a General Court-Martial Convened at Headquarters, Commander Forward Area, Central Pacific by order of Commander-in-Chief U.S. Pacific Fleet and Pacific Ocean Areas: Case of Charles E. Loughlin, U.S. Navy Transcript of Proceedings 19 April 1945, microfilm NRS 1970-36
Pacific Region National Archives and Records Center, San Bruno, CA
Records of the Commandant 12th Naval District, Accession Number 181-58-3223/3224
United States National Archives and Records Administration, College Park, MD
Record Group 24, United States Navy Ship Deck Logs (RG 24, NA)

USS *Ormsby* (APA-49)
USS *Winged Arrow* (APA-170)
Record Group 38, Records of the Office of the Chief of Naval Operations (RG 38, NA)
Naval Technical Mission to Japan, 1945–46 Reports
Office of Naval Intelligence Far East Section Op 16FE/Op23-F 141 Translations 1944–48
Office of Naval Intelligence Monograph Files
Records of the Special Activities Branch, Office of Naval Intelligence (Op 16-Z)
Records of U.S. Naval Group China and Vice Adm. Milton E. Miles 1942–57
Record Group 80W, U.S. Navy Photographs, World War II (RG 80W, NA)
Record Group 94, Supreme Commander Allied Powers, General Headquarters Library File
World War II Operations Reports, 1940–48, Pacific Theater GHQ, SCAP, Vol. V: Operations of the Allied Translator and Interpreters Service Assistant Chief of Staff, G2 Intelligence Historical Studies, 1918–50 (RG 94, NA)
Record Group 127, GW U.S. Marine Corps Photographs, World War II (RG 127, NA)
Record Group 127, Marine Corps Geographic File, 1940–1946; Marine Corps Geographic File, 1940–1946; General Subjects, 1940–1953 (RG 127, NA)
Record Group 313, Records of Naval Operating Forces
Folder 645: Joint Intelligence Center Pacific Ocean Area (JICPOA)
World War II Diaries, War Diary, Okinawa Military Government Detachment B-5.
Record Group 319, Records of the U.S. Army Intelligence Command, 1917–73 (RG 319, NA)
Army Intelligence Decimal File, 1941–48
Assistant Chief of Staff, G-2, Intelligence, Historical Studies, 1918–50
Record Group 338, Records of Allied and Occupation Headquarters, World War II, Records of General Headquarters, Far East Command, Supreme Commander Allied Powers Headquarters, Tenth Army Headquarters, G-2 Section File 312, Correspondence

Institutional Papers

Bancroft Library, University of California, Berkeley University Archives, Files 1941: 487; 1940–1943: 400 series 2, CU-5, Faculty Personnel Files (CU-5); Pacific Basin Institute, Pomona College, Claremont, CA; Bridge to the Rising Sun Conference, April 2000 Records

United States Naval Academy, Annapolis, MD, Midshipmen and Alumni Records (USNA)

Personal Papers

Bennett, Henry G., Edmond Low Library, Oklahoma State University

Benson, Oliver Earl, Western Historical Collection, University of Oklahoma Library, Norman, OK.

Boorman, Howard L., Nashville, TN.

Brayshay, James W., El Cajon, CA.

Burd, William W., Berkeley, CA.

Burks, Ardath, Rutgers University Library, New Brunswick, NJ.

Caldwell, John T., Hoover Institution, Stanford, CA.

Cary, Otis, Oakland, CA.

Chester, Theodore A., Pasadena, CA.

Date, Daniel, and Kathleen S., Oakland, CA.

Dornheim, Arthur R., Bethesda, MD.

Downs, Allison J., Baltimore, MD.

Dull, Paul S., Research Archives, Marine Corps University (MCU), Quantico, VA.

Dunbar, Calvin W., West Yellowstone, MT.

Gibney, Frank B., Santa Barbara, CA.

Hall, John W., Sterling Memorial Library, Yale University, New Haven, CT.

Hindmarsh, Albert E., in the possession of Alan Hindmarsh, Livermore, CA.

Hummel, R. Stuart, Hoover Institution, Stanford, CA.

Imai, Yūji, San Mateo, CA.

Inouye, Ariake "Larry," and Ida, Roseville, CA.

Jefferson, James M., Fruita, CO.

Karasik, Daniel D., Bethesda, MD.

Marshall, Roger L., Hillsborough, NC.

Moran, Sherwood F., Research Archives, Marine Corps University (MCU), Quantico, VA.

———, Madison, WI.

Nakamura, Edwin S., Berkeley, CA.

Navy Japanese Language School Collection, Norlin Library, University of Colorado, Boulder (UCBL)

Amos, William H.

Anthony, David F.

Boller, Paul F.

Brady, John H., Jr.

Brandson, Robert E.

Breece, T. Howell.

Bridgham, Phillip Low.

Bronfenbrenner, Martin B.

Chaffin, Verner R.

Christy, Robert W.

Conroy, F. Hilary
Cross, Charles T.
Dornheim, Arthur R.
Durbin, James
Durden, Robert F.
Ebling, William F.
Edwards, Marie
Falk, Robert P.
Foley, A. W. "Mike"
Gardiner, Clinton H.
Gary, Holland
Gregg, G. Eugene
Hamilton, Charles E.
Hart, Edward L.
Hasbrouck, John B.
Holtom, Gerald
Hummel, R. Stuart
Ingersoll, Ross H.
Irvine, Reed J.
Jensen, Neal
Johnston, Warren R.
Keene, Donald J.
Kimball, Spencer L.
Kruckeberg, Arthur R.
LaBianca, Lance
Lefko, Orville K.
Levy, Marion J.
Luthy, Raymond V.
McCubbin, John B.
Nace, George W.
Otagiri, James Gorō
Petree, Richard W.
Pineau, Roger
Pratt, Harry D.
Ryder, Frank G.
Seymour, Lawrence A.
Sherman, Paul J.
Sigerson, William C.
Snyder, Walter F.
Thornton, Robert D.
Towner, Dean
Vincent, Lawrence C.
Wade, Robert H. B.
Weissberg, Albert O.
Whan, Edgar W.
Wilbur, Halsey F.
Williams, Thomas E.
Wren, Harold G.
Yumoto, John M.
Zurhellen, J. Owen, Jr.

Osborn, David Lawrence, Dwight D. Eisenhower Presidential Library, Abilene, KS.
Robinson, John S. Jr., Special Collections, University of Washington Library (UWL), Seattle, WA.
Rogers, Fred Fremont, U.S. Naval War College Library, Newport, RI.
Schwantes, Robert S., Hoover Institution, Stanford, CA.
Slaughter, Glen K., Santa Fe, NM.
Spiegel, Hart, San Francisco, CA.
Tatsumi, Henry, Special Collections, University of Washington Library, Seattle, WA.
Thiel, Irene Slaninka, Bellingham, WA.
Toki, Rayer, and Akiko Nishioka, Alamo, CA.
Tucker, Frank H., Colorado Springs, CO.
Ward, Robert E., Hoover Institution, Stanford, CA.
Watkins, James T., IV, Hoover Institution, Stanford, CA.
Weil, William, Jewish Historical Society of Denver, Denver, CO.
Willis, Donald S., Boulder, CO.

Interviews

Note: [PL] indicates interview conducted jointly by author and Pedro Loureiro.

Ainsworth, Thomas W., 26 June 2003. Bethesda, MD.

Arase, Nobuo, 11 May 2000. Claremont, CA. [by Pedro Loureiro]

Ashikaga, Toshi, 4 May 2000. Venice, California. [PL]

Ball, Leo S., 29 September 2004. Grand Junction, CO.

Beasley, William G., 15 July 2001. Twickenham, England.

Boller, Paul F., Jr., with Wendell Furnas, 27 December 2005. Santa Monica, CA.

Brayshay, James W., 28 April 2000. El Cajon, CA. [PL]

Brotherton, Joseph, 10 November 2000. San Francisco, CA. [PL]

Burd, William W., 9 December 2000. Berkeley, CA. [PL]

Burke, Rear Adm. Julian T., Jr., 5 March 1999. Alexandria, VA.

Burks, Ardath, 12 October 2004. New Brunswick, NJ. (telephone)

Cary, Otis, 8 December 1999. Oakland, CA. [by Frank Gibney and Pedro Loureiro]

Casson, Lionel, 22 May 2000. New York, NY. [by Pedro Loureiro]

Chester, Theodore, 23 December 2001. Pasadena, CA. [PL]

Christy, Robert W., 26 May 2005. Hanover, NH. (telephone)

Craig, Jack J., 8 June 2002. Boulder, CO.

Cross, Charles T., 8 June 2002. Boulder, CO.

Curts, Robert I., 8 December 2004. Larkspur, CO.

de Bary, William Theodore, 23 May 2000. Tappan, NY. [by Pedro Loureiro]

Dornheim, Arthur F., 1 July 2002. Bethesda, MD.

Downs, Allison J., 8 April 2001. Baltimore, MD.

Foley, A. W. Michael, 6 April 2000. Pomona, CA; and 6 June 2002. Boulder, CO.

Fujimoto, Dorothy, 8 May 2000. San Francisco, CA. [PL]

Furnas, Wendell J., 31 July 1999. Santa Monica, CA. [by Pedro Loureiro and Suzanne Borghei]

——— with Mori Futoshi, 15 July 2005. Santa Monica, CA.

——— with Paul Boller, 27 December 2005. Santa Monica, CA.

Gard, Richard A., 11 October 2004. Old Field, NY.

Gibney, Frank B., 4 June 1999. Claremont, CA. [PL]

———, 8 May and 23 September 2000. Santa Barbara, CA. [PL]

Gorham, William H., 10 May 2000. Los Gatos, CA. [PL]

Hackett, Roger F., 11 April 2000. Los Angeles, CA.

Hester, James M., 22 May 2000. New York, NY. [by Frank B. Gibney and Pedro Loureiro]

Hoshino, Henry, 10 May 2000. Sunnyvale, CA. [PL]

Hussey, Ward M., 5 December 2003. Alexandria, VA. [by Pedro Loureiro]

Ike, Nobutaka, 28 March 2000. Stanford, CA. [PL]

Ikle, Frank W., 12 September 2003. Albuquerque, NM. [PL]

Imai, Martha, 29 May 2000. San Mateo, CA. [PL]
Ingerson, Ross H. 28 April 2000. San Diego, CA. [PL]
Inouye, Ariake "Larry," 16 October 2000. Roseville, CA. [PL]
Inouye, Ida, 16 October 2000. Roseville, CA. [PL]
Irvine, Reed J., 29 February 2000. Washington, DC. (telephone)
Jefferson, James M., 14 and 16 March 2000. Fruita, CO.
Jensen, Neal F., 14 September 2003. Albuquerque, NM. [PL]
Jones, Carl N., 13 June 2002. Washington, DC.
Karasik, Daniel D., 20 June 2000. Bethesda, MD.
Karr, Albert S., 6 July 2000. Huntington Beach, CA. [PL]
Kinsman, Robert S., 8 October 2001. Los Angeles, CA. [PL]
Kramer, S. Paul, 6 December 2003. Washington, DC. [by Pedro Loureiro]
Levine, Betty Billett, 8 April 2002. Madison, WI.
Levine, Solomon B., 8 April 2002. Madison, WI.
Luthy, Raymond V., 8 November 2003. Concord, CA. [PL]
———, 7 June 2002. Boulder, CO.
Mallory, Frank L., 11 January 2002. Newport Beach, CA. [PL]
Marshall, Roger L., 8 and 10 July 2004. Hillsborough, NC. (telephone)
Martin, Harris I. "Jish," 10 December 2000. San Jose, CA. [PL]
———. 15 June 2002. Palo Alto, CA.
Martin, James V., Jr., 26 June 2003, Washington, DC.
May, Henry F., 23 February 2001. Kensington, CA. (telephone)
Mayer, Jean E., 19 June 2000. Bethesda, MD.
McLean, John K., 7 June 2002. Boulder, CO.
Mook, H. Telfer, 28 June 2000. Beulah, MI. (telephone)
Moran, Frances, 6 April 2002. Madison, WI.
Moran, Sherwood R., 6 April 2002. Madison, WI.
Morley, James W., 15 October 2004. South Natick, MA.
Moss, Richard H., 7 June 2002. Boulder, CO.
Muheim, Harry M., 10 November 2000. San Francisco, CA. [PL]
Myers, Lawrence S., 20 July 2000. Knoxville, TN. [by Pedro Loureiro]
Nakamura, Edwin S., 8 December 2000. Berkeley, CA. [by Frank B. Gibney]
Nelson, Glenn W., 19 June 2000. Vienna, VA.
Newell, Robert, 26 March 2001. Newport Beach, CA. [PL]
Oakley, Ellengale Toki, 9 December 2000. Alamo, CA. [PL]
Oka, Seizō, 20 January 2003. San Francisco, CA.
Okamoto, Takeo, 29 March 2000. San Francisco, CA. [PL]
Ostensoe, Omer, 8 July 2002. McLean, VA.
Ota, Kay, 18 September 2000. Hermosa Beach, CA. [PL]
Packard, Katherine, 11 November 2000. Concord, CA. [PL]
Pratt, Col. Harry D., USMC (Ret.), 15 July 2001, 9 October 2004. Los Angeles, CA. [PL]

Prendergast, Curtis W., 29 June 2005. Bethesda, MD.
Riccio, Guy J., 12 June 2003. Annapolis, MD.
Rich, John H., 12 July 2002. Cape Elizabeth, ME.
Roegge, Frank, 13 October 2004. Madison, CT.
Rolph, Hammond M., 24 February 1999 and 26 April 2000. San Gabriel, CA. [PL]
Rolph, Julia Hilts, 24 February 1999 and 26 April 2000. San Gabriel, CA. [PL]
Scalapino, Robert A., 6 November 2002. Los Angeles, CA.
Schwantes, Robert S., 8 November 2003. Burlingame, CA. [PL]
Sheeks, Robert B., 8 May and 23 September 2000. Santa Rosa, CA. [PL]
Shively, Donald H., 9 May 2000. Berkeley, CA. [PL]
Shively, John R., 9 May 2000. Berkeley, CA. [PL]
Shorrock, Hallam C., Jr., 24 October 2000. Claremont, CA. [PL]
Sigerson, Ruth Webb, 13 September 1003. Albuquerque, NM. [PL]
Sigerson, William C., 13 September 1003. Albuquerque, NM. [PL]
Slaughter, Glen K., 13 September 2003. Santa Fe, NM. [PL]
———. 7 June 2002. Boulder, CO.
Smith, Warren W., Jr., 9 December 2000. Alamo, CA. [PL]
Spiegel, Hart H., 22 September 2000. San Francisco, CA. [PL]
Stegmeier, Daphne Shaw, 19 June 2000. Bethesda, MD.
Stevens, Russell D., 27 October 2003. Fallbrook, CA. [PL]
Stone, Elmer J., 19 September 2001. Palm Desert, CA. [PL]
Suttles, Wayne P., 22 January 2002. Friday Harbor, WA.
Takekoshi, Elaine, 29 September 2000. Pasadena, CA. (telephone)
Takemiya Takeji, 7 July 1999. Yokohama, Japan.
Thiel, Irene Slaninka, 23 January 2002. Bellingham, WA.
Thompson, Lawrence G., 21 April 2000. Los Angeles, CA. [PL]
Toki, John, 4 December 2000. (telephone)
Towner, Dean, H. 7 October. Austin, TX.
Tucker, Frank H., 6 June 2002. Colorado Springs, CO.
Underwood, Horace G., 15 August 1999. Seoul, Korea. [with Frank Gibney]
Vincent, Lawrence C., 12 October 2004. Englewood, NJ.
Wald, Royal J., 7 November 2003. Clayton, CA. [PL]
Ward, Robert E., 11 November 2000. Portola Valley, CA. [PL]
Way, Griffith, 19 January 2002. Seattle, WA.
Way, Patricia O'Sullivan, 19 January 2002. Seattle, WA.
Whan, Edgar, 2 April 2003, Athens, OH (telephone)
White, Richard S., 23 January 2002. Seattle, WA.
Wiles, Edward E., 14 June 2003. Potomac, MD.
Williams, D. Norton, 13 October 2004. Wallingford, CT.

Williams, Dan S., 8 May 2000. San Rafael, CA. [PL]
Williams, Mary Lou Siegfried, 13 October 2004. Wallingford, CT.
Willis, Donald S., 6 June 2002. Boulder, CO.

Other Sources

Arnston, Jessica Natsuko. "Journey to Boulder: The Japanese American Instructors of the Navy Japanese Language School, 1942–1946." Unpublished M.A. thesis, University of Colorado, 2003.

Bitney, Francis L. "Four B's in Sasebo." Unpublished memoir, 1997.

Boorman, Howard. "Pirandello Revisited: Eight Decades in Search of a Scenario." Part 3: "The Great Escape (1943–1946)." Unpublished memoir.

Dean, Barbara, and Sidney DeVere Brown. "From Pearl Harbor to Theta Pond: The Navy Japanese Language School at Oklahoma A&M College, 1945–1945." Unpublished manuscript, 1995, provided by Professor Brown to Pedro Loureiro.

Dunbar, Calvin W. "The Surrender of Rota, Marianas Islands, August 1945." Unpublished memoir, West Yellowstone, Montana.

Irish, Donald Paul. "Reactions of Residents of Boulder, Colorado, to the Introduction of Japanese into the Community." Unpublished M.A. thesis, University of Colorado, 1950.

Loureiro, Pedro Anthony. "Intelligence Success: U.S. Navy and Marine Intelligence Operations in China, 1931–1941." Unpublished Ph.D. diss., University of Southern California, 1995.

Schwantes, Robert S. 1998. *"What Did You Do in the War, Daddy?" A Memoir*. San Mateo, CA: Robert Schwantes.

Spiegel, Hart. "The War Years and Better Days 1942–1946." Unpublished memoir in author's possession.

Vincent, Lawrence. "Semper Fi: Memoirs of a Japanese Language Officer with the United States Marine Corps in World War II." Unpublished memoir, 6.

Oral Histories

Boardman, Eugene. 2 February 1982. Marine Corps Historical Center, Washington, DC.

Brown, Delmer M. 1995. Regional Oral History Office, Bancroft Library, University of California, Berkeley.

Cross, Charles T. 19 November 1997. interview with Charles Stuart Kennedy. Foreign Affairs Oral History Collection of the Association for Diplomatic Studies and Training. Accessible at http://memory.loc.gov/ammem/collections/diplomacy/index.html.

Currier, Capt. Prescott, USN (Ret.). February 1972. NSA OH02-72, National Cryptological Museum, Fort Meade, MD.

Fabian, Capt. Rudolph T. NSA OH09-83, n.d. 1983, National Cryptological Museum, Fort Meade, MD.

Holcomb, Brig. Gen. Bankson T. 14 September 1970. Marine Corps Historical Center, Washington, DC.

Lasswell, Colonel Alva B. 1968. By Benis M. Frank. Marine Corps Historical Center, Washington, DC.

McCollum, Rear Adm. Arthur, USN. 8 December 1970. By John T. Mason. Naval Institute Oral History, Annapolis, MD: U.S. Naval Academy Library.

Merrill, Lt. Col. John E., USMCR. February–March 1979. Marine Corps Historical Center, Washington, DC.

Nichols, Walter. 10 October 1989. Foreign Affairs Oral History Collection of the Association for Diplomatic Studies and Training. Accessible at http://memory.loc.gov/ammem/collections/diplomacy/index.html.

Rudolph, Richard. 4 March 1983. OH 300/237. By Kenneth Klein. Special Collections/Archives, University of California Los Angeles.

Stone, Adm. Earl E. 9 February 1983. NSA OH03-83. National Cryptological Museum, Fort Meade, MD.

Van Deurs, Rear Adm. George. 1969. Naval Institute Oral History, U.S. Naval Academy Library, Annapolis, MD.

Wright, Capt. Wesley A. "Ham." 24 May 1982. NSA OH11-82. National Cryptological Museum, Fort Meade, MD.

Conference Presentations

Bridge to the Rising Sun Conference, Pacific Basin Institute, Pomona College, Claremont, CA, 7–8 April 2000.

Ainsworth, Thomas W.
Bruns, Robert
Cary, Otis
Conroy, F. Hilary
de Bary, William Theodore
Foley, Arthur W. "Mike"
Furnas, Wendell J.
Gibney, Frank B.
Irvine, Reed J.
Keene, Donald J.
King, Anne Grilk
King, Samuel P.
Moran, Sherwood R.
Morley, James W.
Pratt, Harry D.
Rich, John
Rolph, Hammond M.
Rolph, Julia Hilts
Scalapino, Robert A.
Seidensticker, Edward
Slaughter, Glen K.
Swanson, Eleanor Wells
Tucker, Frank H.

Society for Military History Meeting, Madison, WI. 7 April 2002.

Gilmore, Allison B. "ATIS at War: The Recruitment, Training, and Accomplishments of U.S. Army Japanese Language Officers."

PUBLISHED SOURCES

Agawa Naoyuki. *Umi no yūjō* [*Maritime Friendship*]. Tokyo: Shinchosha, 2001.

Alexander, Joseph H. *Across the Reef: The Marine Assault of Tarawa*. Washington, DC: Marine Corps Historical Center, 1993.

———. *Utmost Savagery: The Three Days of Tarawa*. Annapolis, MD: Naval Institute Press, 1995.

Ashmead, John, Jr. "The Japs Look at the Yanks," *Atlantic Monthly* 177 (April 1946): 86–91.

———. "A Modern Language for Japan," *Atlantic Monthly* 179 (January 1947): 68–72.

———. *The Mountain and the Feather*. 2nd ed. New York: Ballantine Books Popular Library, 1962.

———. "These Were My Japanese Students," *Atlantic Monthly* 204 (September 1959): 56–59.

Bailey, Beth, and David Farber. *The First Strange Place: The Alchemy of Race and Sex in World War II Hawaii*. New York: Free Press, 1992.

Baker, Kenneth. "Harry Packard's Japanese Treasures," *Architectural Digest* 49 (August 1992), 56–62.

Barbey, Daniel E. *MacArthur's Amphibious Navy: Seventh Amphibious Force Operations, 1943–1945*. Annapolis, MD: Naval Institute Press, 1969.

Bartlett, Tom. "Two Linguists," *Leatherneck* (February 1986): 28–30.

Bath, Alan Harris. *Tracking the Axis Enemy: The Triumph of Anglo-American Naval Intelligence*. Lawrence: University Press of Kansas, 1988.

Battey, Bryan. "Creating Best Sellers," in *Tokyo Memoirs 1941–1955*, ed. Curtis Prendergast, 181–86. Washington, DC: Byron S. Adams, 2005.

Beardsley, Richard K., John W. Hall, and Robert E. Ward. *Village Japan*. Chicago: University of Chicago Press, 1959.

Beath, Ernest B. "Radio Intelligence in Combat," *Naval Security Group Bulletin* (August 1978): 16–19.

Belote, James H. *Typhoon of Steel*. New York: Harper and Row, 1970.

Benson, Robert Louis. *A History of U.S. Communications Intelligence during World War II: Policy and Administration*. Fort Meade, MD: NSA Center for Cryptological History, 1997.

Beveridge, Maj. James, U.S. Army. "History of the United States Strategic Bombing Survey (Pacific) 1945–1946." Washington, DC: War Department, 1946.

Biard, Forrest R. "Memoir," *Cryptolog* 3, n.p., n.d., in author's possession.

Bingham, Woodbridge, Hilary Conroy, and Frank W. Ikle. *A History of Asia*, 2nd ed. Boston: Allyn and Bacon, 1964–65.

Biographic Register of the Department of State, Washington, DC: Government Printing Office, 1950–53, 1954–66.

Blackton, Charles Stuart. "The Surrender of the Fortress of Truk," *Pacific Historical Review* 15 (December 1946): 400–408.

Boller, Paul F., Jr. *Memoirs of an Obscure Professor and Other Essays.* Fort Worth: Texas Christian University Press, 1992.

Borg, Dorothy, and Shumpei Okamoto, eds. *Pearl Harbor as History: Japanese-American Relations 1931–1941.* New York: Columbia University Press, 1973.

Bradley, James. *Flyboys: A True Story of Courage.* New York: Ballantine Books, 2004.

Brinkley, David, *Washington Goes to War.* New York: Ballantine Books, 1988.

Bronfenbrenner, Martin, *Tomioka Stories from the Japanese Occupation: Comedies and Tragedies of Japan under the American Forces after World War II.* Hicksville, NY: Exposition Press, 1975.

Brotherton, Joe. "Packardo-San: Harry G. C. Packard (1914–1991)," *Orientations* 22 (February 1992), 76–77.

Browne, Jay R. "Kamiseya Update P-2," *Cryptolog* 16 (Spring 1995), 1–2.

Burks, Ardath. *The Government of Japan.* Philadelphia: Crowell, 1962.

Burrell, Robert S. "Breaking the Cycle of Iwo Jima Mythology: A Strategic Study of Operation Detachment," *Journal of Military History* 68 (October 2004): 1143–86.

———. *The Ghosts of Iwo Jima.* College Station: Texas A&M University Press, 2006.

Cameron, Craig M. *American Samurai: Myth, Imagination, and the Conduct of Battle in the First Marine Division, 1941–1951.* New York: Cambridge University Press, 1994.

Cary, Otis, ed. *War-Wasted Asia: Letters, 1945–1946.* Tokyo and New York: Kodansha, 1975.

Chandonnet, Fern, ed. *Alaska at War 1941–1945: The Forgotten War Remembered.* Anchorage: The Alaska at War Committee, 1995.

Chikamatsu Monzaemon. *The Love Suicide at Amijima,* 2nd ed., trans. Donald Shively. Ann Arbor: University of Michigan Press, 1991.

Cohen, Warren I. *East Asian Art and American Culture.* New York: Columbia University Press, 1992.

Congressional Record, 94 Cong., 2 Session, House. Washington, DC: Government Printing Office, 1974.

"Conroy, Francis Hilary." *Contemporary Authors,* 115: 102–3. Detroit: Gale Publications, 1985.

Cross, Charles T. *Born a Foreigner: A Memoir of the American Presence in Asia.* Boulder, CO: Rowman & Littlefield, 1999.

Decker, Benton Weaver, and Edwina Decker. *Return of the Black Ships.* New York: Vantage Press, 1978.

Dingman, Roger. "Alliance in Crisis: The Lucky Dragon Incident and Japanese-

American Relations," in *The Great Powers in East Asia 1953–1960*, eds. Warren Cohen and Akira Iriye, 187–214. New York: Columbia University Press, 1990.

———. *Ghost of War: The Sinking of the* Awa maru *and Japanese-American Relations, 1945–1995*. Annapolis, MD: Naval Institute Press, 1997.

———. "Language at War: U.S. Marine Corps Japanese Language Officers in the Pacific War," *Journal of Military History* 68 (July 2004): 853–83.

Dore, Ronald P., ed. *Aspects of Social Change in Modern Japan* Princeton, NJ: Princeton University Press, 1967.

Dower, John W. *Embracing Defeat: Japan in the Wake of World War II.* New York: Norton, 1999.

Emmerson, John K. *The Japanese Thread: A Life in the U.S. Foreign Service.* New York: Holt, Rinehart, and Winston, 1978.

Erskine, John C. "Language Officers Recall Combat Roles in the Pacific," *Fortitudine* 12 (Spring 1986), 23–24.

Etō Jun. *Senryō shiroku 4: Nihon hondo shinchū* [*Records of the Occupation, Volume 4: The Entry of Forces into Japan Proper*] Tokyo: Kodansha, 1989.

Falk, Stanley L., and Warren M. Tsuneishi, eds. *MIS in the War against Japan: Personal Experiences Related at the 1993 MIS Capital Reunion*, "The Nisei Veteran: An American Patriot." Japanese American Veterans Association of Washington, DC, 1995.

Fearey, Robert, "Was Pearl Harbor Inevitable? 1941," in *Tokyo Memoirs 1941–1955*, ed. Curtis Prendergast, 3–18. Washington, DC: Byron S. Adams, 2005.

Feifer, George. *Tennozan: The Battle of Okinawa and the Atomic Bomb.* New York: Ticknor and Fields, 1992.

Fiedler, Leslie. *Back to China.* New York: Stein and Day, 1965.

Finn, Richard B. *Winners in Peace: MacArthur, Yoshida, and Postwar Japan.* Berkeley: University of California Press, 1992.

Fisch, Arnold G., Jr. *Military Government in the Ryukyu Islands 1945–1950.* Washington, DC: Center of Military History, United States Army, 1988.

Forsberg, Aaron. *America and the Japanese Miracle: The Cold War Context of Japan's Postwar Economic Revival, 1950–1960.* Chapel Hill: University of North Carolina Press, 2000.

Frank, Benis M., and Henry I. Shaw Jr. *Victory and Occupation: History of U.S. Marine Operations in World War II*, Vol. 5. Washington, DC: Historical Branch, G-3 Division, Headquarters, U.S. Marine Corps, 1968.

Frank, Richard. *Downfall: The End of the Imperial Japanese Empire.* New York: Random House, 1999.

———. *Guadalcanal.* New York: Random House, 1990.

Freeman, Doreen. "*Language Lessons*," in *Tokyo Memoirs, 1941–1955*, ed. Curtis W. Prendergast, 147–49. Washington, DC: Byron S. Adams, 2005.

Friedman, Hal M. "The Beast in Paradise: The United States in Micronesia, 1943–1947," *Pacific Historical Review* 62 (May 1993), 173–95.

———. *Governing the American Lake: The U.S. Defense and Administration of the Pacific, 1945–1947.* East Lansing: Michigan State University Press, 2007.

Furuiye, Nobuo. "Winning the Purple Heart with the Marines on Iwo," in *MIS in the War against Japan: Personal Experiences Related at the 1993 MIS Capital Reunion*, "The Nisei Veteran: An American Patriot," eds. Stanley L. Falk and Warren M. Tsuneishi. Japanese American Veterans Association of Washington, DC, 1995.

Gailey, Harry A. *Bougainville: The Forgotten Campaign, 1943–1945.* Lexington: The University Press of Kentucky, 1991.

Gallagher, Charles F. "Charles F. Gallagher, American Scholar," in *The Japan Experience*, ed. Ronald Bell. Tokyo: Weatherhill, 1973.

Garfield, Brian. *The Thousand-Mile War: World War II in Alaska and the Aleutians.* Fairbanks: University of Alaska Press, 1995.

Generous, William Thomas Jr. *Sweet Pea at War: A History of USS* Portland *(CA-33).* Lexington: University Press of Kentucky, 2003.

Gibney, Frank. "Arm of St. Francis," *Life* 26 (27 June 1949), 49–52.

———. "Birth of a New Japan," *Life* 31 (10 September 1951), 134–38 ff.

———. *Five Gentlemen of Japan.* New York: Farrar, Strauss, and Young, 1953.

———. "Forgotten Island," *Time* 54 (28 November 1949) 24.

———. *Japan: The Fragile Superpower.* New York: Norton, 1975.

———. "Missionary's Return," *Time* 53 (13 June 1949), 59.

Godson, Susan. *Serving Proudly: A History of Women in the U.S. Navy.* Annapolis, MD: Naval Institute Press, 2001.

Goldberg, Harold J. *D-Day in the Pacific: The Battle of Saipan.* Bloomington: University of Indiana Press, 2007.

Goodman, Grant. *America's Japan: The First Year 1945–1946.* New York: Fordham University Press, 2005.

Greenbaum, Everett. *The Goldenberg Who Couldn't Dance.* New York: Harcourt Brace Jovanovich, 1973.

Hall, John W. *Japan: From Prehistory to Modern Times.* New York: Delacorte Press, 1970.

———. *Japan in the Mind of America: A Half Century of Change.* Kyoto: Doshisha University Press, 1990.

Harvey, Robert. *Amache: The Story of Japanese Internment in Colorado during World War II.* Lanham, MD: Taylor Trade Publishing, 2004.

Hata Ikuhiko. *Nihonjin Horyo* [*Japanese Prisoners of War*], 2 vols. Tokyo: Hara shobo, 1998.

Hayashi, Brian Masaru. *Democratizing the Enemy: The Japanese American Internment.* Princeton, NJ: Princeton University Press, 2004.

———. *"For the Sake of Our Japanese Brethren": Assimilation, Nationalism, and Protestantism among the Japanese of Los Angeles, 1895–1942.* Stanford, CA: Stanford University Press, 1995.

Heinrichs, Waldo H., Jr. *American Ambassador: Joseph C. Grew and the Development of the United States Diplomatic Tradition.* Boston: Little, Brown, 1966.

Higgins, Raymond A. *From Hiroshima with Love: The Allied Military Governor's Remarkable Story of the Rebuilding of Japan's Business and Industry after World War II.* Central Point, OR: Hellgate Press, 1997.

Hindmarsh, Albert E. *The Basis of Japanese Foreign Policy.* Cambridge, MA: Harvard University Press, 1936.

———. *Le Japon et la Paix en Asie.* Paris: Recueil Sirey, 1937.

———. "The Realistic Foreign Policy of Japan," *Foreign Affairs* 13 (January 1935): 3–11.

Hofman, Jon T. *From Makin to Bougainville.* Washington, DC: Marine Corps Historical Center, 1993.

Holmes, Wilfred Jasper. *Double-Edged Secrets: U.S. Naval Intelligence Operations in the Pacific during World War II.* Annapolis, MD: Naval Institute Press, 1979.

Hucker, Charles O. *The Association for Asian Studies: An Interpretive History.* Seattle: University of Washington Press, 1999.

Iida Jirō. *Senryōgun ga shashita sensō chokugo no Sasebo* [*Immediate Postwar Sasebo as Photographed by the Occupation Force*]. Sasebo: Geibundo, 1986.

Irvine, E. Eastman, ed. *The World Almanac 1942.* New York: New York World-Telegram, 1942.

James, Dorris Clayton. *Years of MacArthur*, vol. II, *1941–1945.* Boston: Houghton Mifflin, 1975.

Jansen, Marius B., ed. *Changing Attitudes toward Modernization.* Princeton, NJ: Princeton University Press, 1965.

Karasik, Dan."Okinawa: A Problem in Administration and Reconstruction," *Far Eastern Quarterly* 7 (May 1948), 254–67.

Kasukabe, Karl Kaoru. "The Escape of the Japanese Garrison from Kiska," in *Alaska at War 1941–1945: The Forgotten War Remembered*, ed. Fern Chandonnet, 121–24. Anchorage: The Alaska at War Committee, 1995.

Katsumata Senkichiro, ed. *Kenkyusha's New Japanese-English Dictionary.* Tokyo: Kenkyusha, 1954.

Keene, Donald. *Anthology of Japanese Literature.* New York: Grove Press, 1956.

———. *Anthology of Modern Japanese Literature.* New York: Grove Press, 1955.

———. *The Blue-Eyed Tarokaja: A Donald Keene Anthology*, ed. Thomas J. Rimer. New York: Columbia University Press, 1996.

———. *Chronicles of My Life: An American in the Heart of Japan.* New York: Columbia University Press, 2008.

———. *Living Japan.* Garden City, NY: Doubleday, 1959.

———. *The Manyōshū*. New York: Columbia University Press, 1965.
———. *On Familiar Terms*. New York: Kodansha International, 1994.
Kerr, George H. *Formosa Betrayed*. New York: Da Capo Press, 1976. First published 1965 by Houghton Mifflin.
Kiyonaga, Bina Cady. *My Spy: Memoir of a CIA Wife* New York: Avon Books, 2000.
Kiyota, Minoru. *Beyond Loyalty: The Story of a Kibei*, trans. Linda Klepinger Keenan. Honolulu: University of Hawaii Press, 1997.
Koshiro, Yukiko. *Trans-Pacific Racisms and the U.S. Occupation of Japan*. New York: Columbia University Press, 1999.
Kushner, Barak. *The Thought War: Imperial Japanese Propaganda*. Honolulu: University of Hawaii Press, 2006.
Lamott, Kenneth. "Memoirs of a Brainwasher," *Harpers* 212 (June 1956), 73–74.
———. *The Stockade*. Boston: Little, Brown, 1952.
Layton, Edwin T., with Roger Pineau and John Costello. *"And I Was There": Pearl Harbor and Midway—Breaking the Secrets*. New York: William Morrow and Company, 1985.
La Feber, Walter. *The Clash*. New York: Norton, 1997.
Levine, Solomon. "The Battle of Okinawa: A Personal Memoir," *The Ryukyuanist* [*Newsletter for the International Society for Ryukyuan Studies*] no. 28 (Spring 1995), 1–6.
———. *Industrial Relations in Postwar Japan* (Champagne-Urbana: University of Illinois Press, 1958.
Lockwood, William W., ed. *The State and Economic Enterprise in Japan*. Princeton, NJ: Princeton University Press, 1965.
Lorelli, John A. *U.S. Amphibious Operations in World War II*. Annapolis, MD: Naval Institute Press, 1995.
MacGregor, Wayne. *Through These Portals: A Pacific War Saga*. Pullman: Washington State University Press, 2002.
Maga, Tim. *Judgment at Tokyo: The Japanese War Crimes Trials*. Lexington: University Press of Kentucky, 2001.
Mahnken, Thomas G. *Uncovering Ways of War: U.S. Intelligence and Foreign Military Innovation, 1918–1941*. Ithaca, NY: Cornell University Press, 2002.
———. "U.S. Naval Intelligence and Japan," *Intelligence and National Security* 11 (July 1996), 437–38.
Martin, H. I. "Naval Civil Affairs Unit," in *Saipan: Oral Histories of the Pacific War*, ed. Bruce M. Petty, 156–59. Jefferson, NC: McFarland and Company, 2002.
Matsuda Takeshi. *Soft Power and Its Perils: U.S. Cultural Policy in Early Postwar Japan and Permanent Dependency*. Stanford, CA: The Wilson Center and Stanford University Press, 2007.
May, Ernest R. "U.S. Press Coverage of Japan 1931–1941" in *Pearl Harbor as*

History: Japanese-American Relations 1931–1941, eds. Dorothy Borg and Shumpei Okamoto, 515–46. New York: Columbia University Press, 1973.

May, Henry F. *Coming to Terms: A Study in Memory and History*. Berkeley: University of California Press, 1987.

———. "MacArthur Era, Year One," *Harpers* 192 (March 1946): 267–73.

McAlpine, Pauline S. *Diary of a Missionary: Pauline S. McAlpine*. Columbus, GA: Quill Publications, 1986.

McCullough, Helen Craig, and William H. McCullough. *Eiga monogatari: A Tale of Flowering Fortunes: Annals of Japanese Aristocratic Life in the Heian Period*. Stanford, CA: Stanford University Press, 1980.

McGibbon, Ian. *The Oxford Companion to New Zealand Military History*. Auckland: Oxford University Press, 2000.

McNaughton, James C. *Nisei Linguists: Japanese Americans in the Military Intelligence Service during World War II*. Washington, DC: Department of the Army, 2006.

Meller, Norman. "Saipan's Camp Susupe," Occasional Paper 42. Honolulu: Center for Pacific Island Studies, University of Hawaii, 1999.

Miles, Milton E. *A Different Kind of War*. Garden City, NY: Doubleday, 1967.

Mishima Yukio, *Five Modern Nō Plays*. Donald Keene, trans. New York: Knopf, 1957.

Montgomery, M. R. *Saying Goodbye: A Memoir for Two Fathers*. New York: Knopf, 1989.

Moore, Brenda L. *Serving Our Country: Japanese American Women in the Military during World War II*. New Brunswick, N.J.: Rutgers University Press, 2003.

Moore, Jeffrey M. *Spies for Nimitz: Joint Military Intelligence in the Pacific War* Annapolis: Naval Institute Press, 2004.

Morioka, Michio, and Paul Berry. *Modern Masters of Kyoto: The Transformation of Japanese Painting Traditions*. Seattle: University of Washington Press, 1999.

Morley, James William, ed. *Dilemmas of Growth in Prewar Japan*. Princeton, NJ: Princeton University Press, 1971.

———, ed. *Japan's Road to the Pacific War: The Final Confrontation: Japan's Negotiations with the United States, 1941*. New York: Columbia University Press, 1994.

Murasaki Shikibu. *The Tale of Genji*. Edward Seidensticker, trans. New York: Knopf, 1976.

Naganuma Naoe. *Hyōjun Nippongo Tokuhon*. Berkeley: University of California Press, 1943.

Nagao Hidemi. *Nihon yōsaika no shinario* [*A Scenario for Japan's Fortification*]. Tokyo: Kantōsha, 2003.

Nalty, Bernard C. *Cape Gloucester: The Green Inferno*. Washington, DC: Marine Corps Historical Center, 1994.

Nasso, Christine, ed. *Contemporary Authors*, vol. 25–28. Detroit: Gale Research, 1977.

Nelson, Andrew Nathaniel. *The Modern Reader's Japanese-English Character Dictionary*, 1st ed. Tokyo and Rutland, VT: Charles E. Tuttle, 1962.

Neville, Edwin, Jr. "Japanese and G.I. Rapport," in *The Occupation of Japan: The Grass Roots*, ed. William F. Nimmo, 135–41. Norfolk, VA: The General Douglas MacArthur Foundation, 1991.

Okinawa Taimuzu, ed. *Shomin ga tsuzuru: Okinawa sengo seikatsu shi* [*The Common People Write: A History of Postwar Okinawan Life*]. Naha: Okinawa taimuzu sha, 1998.

Olsen, Lawrence A. *Japan in Postwar Asia*. Boulder, CO: Praeger, 1970.

O'Neil, Kathyrn Martin, et al. *Rand McNally Millennium World Atlas*. Chicago: Rand McNally, 1999.

Packard, Harry G. C. *Nihon Bijutsu Shūshuki* [*A Record of Collecting Japanese Art*]. Tokyo: Shinchosha, 1993.

Packard, Wyman H. *A Century of U.S. Naval Intelligence*. Washington, DC: Department of the Navy, 1996.

Peattie, Mark R. *Sunburst: The Rise of Japanese Naval Air Power 1909–1941*. Annapolis, MD: Naval Institute Press, 2002.

Pomeroy, Charles, ed. *Foreign Correspondents in Japan*. Tokyo: Tuttle, 1998.

Potter, E. B. *Bull Halsey*. Annapolis, MD: Naval Institute Press, 1985.

Prados, John. *Combined Fleet Decoded: The Secret History of American Intelligence and the Japanese Navy in World War II*. New York: Random House, 1995.

Prange, Gordon W. *At Dawn We Slept: The Untold Story of Pearl Harbor*. New York: Penguin Books, 1982.

Prendergast, Curtis W. "Bujika hen matsu okane," in *Tokyo Memoirs, 1941–1955*, ed. Curtis W. Prendergast, 49–52. Washington, DC: Byron S. Adams, 2005.

———, ed. *Tokyo Memoirs, 1941–1955*. Washington, DC: Byron S. Adams, 2005.

Price, Willard, *Japan's Islands of Mystery*. New York: John Day, 1944.

Register of the Department of State October 1, 1938. Washington, DC: Government Printing Office, 1938.

Reischauer, Edwin O. *My Life between Japan and America*. New York: Harper and Row, 1986.

Rich, John. "Unexpected Encounters," in *Tokyo Memoirs 1941–1955*, ed. Curtis Prendergast, 95–101. Washington, DC: Byron S. Adams, 2005.

Richard, Dorothy E. *United States Naval Administration of the Trust Territory of the Pacific Islands*. 3 vols. Washington, DC: Office of Chief of Naval Operations, Department of the Navy, 1957.

Rimer, Thomas ed. *The Blue-Eyed Tarakoja: A Donald Keene Anthology*. New York: Columbia University Press, 1996.

Robinson, Greg. *By Order of the President: FDR and the Internment of Japanese Americans.* Cambridge, MA: Harvard University Press, 2001.

Rogers, Robert F. *Destiny's Landfall: A History of Guam.* Honolulu: University of Hawaii Press, 1995.

Rottman, Gordon L. *U.S. Marine Corps World War II Order of Battle: Ground and Air Units in the Pacific War, 1939–1945.* Westport, CT: Greenwood Press, 2002.

———. *World War II Pacific Island Guide: A Geo-Military Study.* Westport, CT: Greenwood Press, 2002.

Ryūsaku Tsunoda, William Theodore de Bary, and Donald Keene, eds. *Sources of Japanese Tradition.* New York: Oxford University Press, 1958.

Sakamoto, Thomas T. "The MIS Aboard the Battleship USS Missouri," in *Unsung Heroes: Military Intelligence Service Past present Future*, eds. Roy Inui, George Koshi, Mitzi Matsui, Takashi Matsui, and Ken Sato, 31–36. Seattle: MIS-Northwest Association, 1996.

Santelli, James S. *A Brief History of the 8th Marines.* Washington, DC: History and Museum Division, Headquarters, U.S. Marine Corps, 1976.

Sarantakes, Nicholas E., ed. *Keystone: The American Occupation of Okinawa and U.S.-Japanese Relations.* College Station: Texas A&M University Press, 2000.

———. *Seven Stars: The Okinawa Battle Diaries of Simon Bolivar Buckner, Jr., and Joseph Stilwell.* College Station: Texas A&M University Press, 2004.

Schaller, Michael. *Altered States: The United States and Japan since the Occupation.* New York: Oxford University Press, 1997.

———. *MacArthur: The Far Eastern General.* New York: Oxford University Press, 1989.

Schmitz, David F. *The First Wise Man: Henry L. Stimson.* Wilmington, DE: S. R. Books, 2000.

Schonberger, Howard B. *Aftermath of War: Americans and the Remaking of Japan 1945–1952.* Kent, OH: Kent State University Press, 1989.

Schratz, Paul R. *Submarine Commander: A Story of World War II and Korea.* Lexington: University Press of Kentucky, 1988.

Sebald, William Joseph. *With MacArthur in Japan: A Personal Memoir of the Occupation* New York: Norton, 1965.

Seidensticker, Edward. *Kafu the Scribbler: The Life and Writings of Nagai Kafu, 1879–1959.* Stanford, CA: Stanford University Press, 1965.

———. "Remembrances," *International House of Japan Bulletin* 21 (Autumn 2001): 36–46.

———. *This Country Japan.* Tokyo and New York: Kodansha, 1977.

———. *Tokyo Central: A Memoir.* Seattle: University of Washington Press, 2002.

Shapiro, Michael. "The American Who May Be the Canniest Collector of Japanese Art of All Time," *The Connoisseur* (March 1987), 87–92, 107.

Sheeks, Robert B. "Civilians on Saipan," *Far Eastern Survey* (9 May 1945): 112–16.

Shibusawa, Naoko. *America's Geisha Ally: Re-imagining the Japanese Enemy*. Cambridge: Harvard University Press, 2006.

Shively, Donald H., ed. *Tradition and Modernization in Japanese Culture*. Princeton, NJ: Princeton University Press, 1971.

Shuker, Elfrieda Berthiaume, and Barbara Scibetta Smith. *War Brides of World War II*. New York: Penguin Books, 1989.

Sledge, Eugene. *With the Old Breed at Peleliu and Okinawa*. New York: Oxford University Press, 1981.

Slesnick, Irwin L., and Carole E Slesnick. *Kanji and Codes: Learning Japanese for World War II*. Bellingham, WA: Carole Slesnick and Irwin Slesnick, 2006.

Sloan, Bill. *Given Up for Dead: America's Heroic Stand at Wake Island*. New York: Bantam Books, 2003.

Smith, Charles R. *Securing the Surrender: Marines in the Occupation of Japan*. Washington, DC: Marine Corps Historical Center, 1997.

Smith, Michael. *The Emperor's Codes: The Breaking of Japan's Secret Ciphers*. New York: Arcade Publishing, 2001.

Smith, Rex Allen, and Gerald Meehl. *Pacific Legacy*. New York: Abbeville Press, 2002.

Smith, Thomas C. *The Agrarian Origins of Modern Japan*. Stanford, CA: Stanford University Press, 1960.

Spector, Ronald. "After Hiroshima: Allied Military Occupations and the Fate of Japan's Empire, 1945–1947," *Journal of Military History* 69 (October 2005), 1121–36.

———. *Eagle against the Sun: The American War with Japan*. New York: Vintage Books, 1985.

———. *In the Ruins of Empire: The Japanese Surrender and the Battle for Postwar Asia*. New York: Random House, 2007.

Stillwell, Paul. *Battleship Missouri: An Illustrated History*. Annapolis, MD: Naval Institute Press, 1996.

Strauss, Ulrich. *The Anguish of Surrender: Japanese POWs in World War II*. Seattle: University of Washington Press, 2003.

Takekoshi Takewo. *Reminiscences of My Sixty Years in the United States*. Los Angeles: Takekoshi Takewo, 1990.

Tatsumi, Henry. *Spoken Japanese: A Self-Interpreter*. Seattle: Henry Tatsumi, 1959.

Taylor, Sandra C. *Jewel of the Desert: Japanese American Internment at Topaz*. Berkeley: University of California Press, 1993.

Tregaskis, Richard. *Guadalcanal Diary*. 2nd ed. New York: Modern Library, 2000.

Trosky, Susan M., and Donna Olendorf, eds. *Contemporary Authors*, vol. 137. Detroit: Gale Research, 1992.

U.S. Naval Academy Alumni Association. *Register of Alumni 1845–1981*. Annapolis, MD: U.S. Naval Academy Alumni Association, 1981.

Van Der Rhoer, Edward. *Deadly Magic: A Personal Account of Communications Intelligence in World War II in the Pacific.* New York: Scribner's, 1978.

Ward, Robert E. *Japan's Political System.* Englewood Cliffs, NJ: Prentice-Hall, 1967.

———, ed. *Political Development in Modern Japan*. Princeton, NJ: Princeton University Press, 1968.

Way, Griffith. "A Collector's View," in *Modern Masters of Kyoto: The Transformation of Japanese Painting Traditions*, eds. Michiko Morioka and Paul Berry, 12–14. Seattle: University of Washington Press, 1999.

Wheeler, Gerald E. *Kinkaid of the Seventh Fleet.* Washington, DC: Naval Historical Center, Department of the Navy, 1995.

Who's Who in America, 2000. Detroit: Gale Publishing, 2000.

Wiles, Tripp. *Forgotten Raiders '42: The Fate of the Marines Left Behind on Makin.* Washington, DC: Potomac Books, 2007.

Williams, Dan S. "Recollections of the Navy's World War II Japanese Language School and Duty as Translator with Marines," *The SASA* [*Shanghai American School Association*] *News* (Spring 2001), 4–5, 8.

Willmott, H. P. *The War with Japan: The Period of Balance May 1942–October 1943.* Wilmington, DE: Scholarly Resources, 2002.

Winchell, Mark Royden. "*Too Good to Be True*": *The Life and Work of Leslie Fiedler.* Columbia: University of Missouri Press, 2002.

Woodson, Yoko, and Richard L. Mellott. *Exquisite Pursuits: Japanese Art in the Harry G. C. Packard Collection.* Seattle: University of Washington Press, 1994.

Worth, Roland H., Jr. *Secret Allies in the Pacific: Covert Intelligence and Code-Breaking Prior to the Attack on Pearl Harbor.* Jefferson, NC: McFarland, 2001.

Yaffe, Bertraim A. *Fragments of War: A Marine's Personal Journey.* Annapolis, MD: Naval Institute Press, 1999.

Yahara, Hiromichi. *The Battle for Okinawa.* Roger Pineau and Uehara Masatoshi, trans. New York: Wiley, 1995.

Yanaga, Chitoshi. *Big Business in Japanese Politics.* New Haven: Yale University Press, 1968.

———. *Japan since Perry.* New York: McGraw Hill, 1949.

———. *Japanese People and Politics.* New York: John Wiley, 1956.

Yokosuka shi shi hensan shitsu, ed. *Senryōka no Yokosuka: Rengōkokugun no jōriku to sono jidai* [*Yokosuka under Occupation: The Landing of Allied Forces and That Era*]. Yokosuka: Yokosuka shi, 2005.

Zacharias, Ellis M., with Ladislas Farago. *Secret Missions: The Story of an Intelligence Officer.* Annapolis, MD: Naval Institute Press, 2003. First published 1946 by G. P. Putnam.

Zeiler, Thomas W. *Unconditional Defeat: Japan, America, and the End of World War II.* Wilmington, DE: Scholarly Resources, 2004.

WEB SITES

Carr, Ralph L. Papers, Colorado State Archives, Denver, at http:www.colorado.gov/dpa/doit/archives/govs/carr.html.

Cash, Stephanie. "Kermit Lansner Obituary," *Art in America* (July 2000), at http://www.findarticles.com/p/articles/mi_m1248/is_7_88/ai_63365677/pg_2 (August 2006).

Department of the Navy, Navy Historical Center, Online Library of Selected Images U.S. Navy Ships. "USS *Levy* (DE-162), 1943–74," at http://www.history.navy.mil/photos/sh-usn/usnsh-l/de162.htm (January 2009).

———. "The Pearl Harbor Raid, 7 December 1941: Damaged Ships," at http://www.history.navy.mil/photos/events/wwii-pac/pearlhbr/ph-dmg.htm (January 2009).

Destroyer Escorts Sailors Association. "First Japanese Surrender On Board USS *Levy* DE 162," at http://www.desausa.org/Stories/uss_levy_japanese_surrender.htm (January 2009).

Destroyers Online, USS *Adams* (DD739), at http://www.destroyersonline.com/usndd/dd739/ (January 2009).

Dictionary of American Naval Fighting Ships, Office of the Chief of Naval Operations. "USS *Appalachian* (AGC-1)," at http://www.ibiblio.org/hyperwar/USN/ships/dafs/AGC/agc1.html (January 2009).

———. "USS *Currier* (DE 700)," at http://www.ibiblio.org/hyperwar/USN/ships/DE/DE-700_Currier.html (November 2006).

Internet Movie Database. *A Majority of One*, at http://www.imdb.com/title/tt0055124 (February 2008).

Library of Congress, American Memory, The Foreign Affairs Oral History Collection of the Association for Diplomatic Studies and Training, http://memory.loc.gov/ammem/collections/diplomacy/index.html.

Naval Historical Center. Dictionary of American Naval Fighting Ships. "USS *Ancon*," at http://www.history.navy.mil/danfs/a8/ancon-ii.htm (May 2008).

———. "USS *Blackford*," at http://www.history.navy.mil/danfs/b6/blackford-i.htm (May 2008).

———. "USS *Shelby*," at http://www.history.navy.mil/danfs/s11/shelby.htm (May 2008).

USS *Portland*. "Surrender of Truk Atoll, 2 September 1945," at http://www.ussportland.org/truk.html (May 2008).

Wesleyan University, Mansfield Freeman Center for East Asian Studies. "The Freeman Orientation," part 5, by Nancy Smith at http://www.wesleyan.edu/east/mansfieldf/history/freeman5_buck.html (May 2008).

Wikipedia, List of Twin Towns and Sister Cities in Japan, at http://en.wikipedia.org/wiki/List_of_twin_towns_and_sister_cities_in_Japan (January 2009).

Index

About the Author

Born and raised in Los Angeles, Roger Dingman was educated at Stanford and Harvard universities. He was a professor of history at the University of Southern California for thirty-six years. Naval service in Japan sparked his interest in the Asia-Pacific region, in which he has traveled and taught extensively. His previous publications include *Power in the Pacific: The Origins of Naval Arms Limitation, 1914–1922,* and *Ghost of War: The Sinking of the* Awa maru *and Japanese-American Relations, 1945–1995.* He and his wife divide their time between Harbor City, California, and Glade Park, Colorado.

The Naval Institute Press is the book-publishing arm of the U.S. Naval Institute, a private, nonprofit, membership society for sea service professionals and others who share an interest in naval and maritime affairs. Established in 1873 at the U.S. Naval Academy in Annapolis, Maryland, where its offices remain today, the Naval Institute has members worldwide.

Members of the Naval Institute support the education programs of the society and receive the influential monthly magazine *Proceedings* or the colorful bimonthly magazine *Naval History* and discounts on fine nautical prints and on ship and aircraft photos. They also have access to the transcripts of the Institute's Oral History Program and get discounted admission to any of the Institute-sponsored seminars offered around the country.

The Naval Institute's book-publishing program, begun in 1898 with basic guides to naval practices, has broadened its scope to include books of more general interest. Now the Naval Institute Press publishes about seventy titles each year, ranging from how-to books on boating and navigation to battle histories, biographies, ship and aircraft guides, and novels. Institute members receive significant discounts on the more than eight hundred Press books in print.

Full-time students are eligible for special half-price membership rates. Life memberships are also available.

For a free catalog describing Naval Institute Press books currently available, and for further information about joining the U.S. Naval Institute, please write to: